CAPITAL AND GROWTH

CAPITAL AND GROWTH

BY

JOHN HICKS

1965
OXFORD UNIVERSITY PRESS
NEW YORK AND OXFORD

Oxford University Press 1965
Library of Congress Card Catalogue Number: 65-25577
Printed in the United States of America

PREFACE

No attempt is made in this book to present a Theory of Economic Growth, or of Economic Dynamics, which is to be defended as *the* theory, superior in every respect, or even in every important respect, to any other. I do not think that there is such a theory; I much doubt if there can be. The phenomena that are presented by a developing (changing) economy are immensely complex; any theory about them is bound to simplify, and at least in some way to over-simplify. In order to deal with those aspects with which it can deal, it must neglect others; there is no known approach which is not based upon omissions, omissions that can easily prove to be of critical importance. Each of the main approaches (or Methods, as I shall call them) that I shall here be considering is able to cast some light upon some aspect of the phenomena; each can be misapplied, and is dangerous when misapplied. Thus it is perfectly proper to change one's method, when one's interest changes, or when there is a change in the facts to which it is to refer; it would indeed be improper not to do so. Yet though the change is necessary, it is also confusing; confusing to the student, confusing indeed to the writer (or teacher) who makes the change. To sort out some of the main methods (regarded as alternative tools that we should keep in our tool-box) ought thus to be a useful undertaking. It should make it easier for some of the cross-purposes (only too apparent in the relevant economic literature) to be resolved.

I may add a personal reason which has led me to this inquiry; I have a good deal of experience of such changes myself. In my *Theory of Wages* (1932) I used what I would now regard as one of these methods; in the dynamic parts of *Value and Capital* (1939) I used another; in the main part of my book on the *Trade Cycle* (1950) I used a third. Though there are qualifications I would now want to make about all these former works, none of them seems to me even now to be wholly wrong; there is some sense in which (with most reservations about the *Theory of Wages*)[1] I still want to stand by them all. But I have naturally been asked—and I have asked myself—how I can do so. One of my objects in writing Part I of this

---

[1] The qualifications which I would now want to make about it are set out in some detail in the Commentary that is attached to the Second Edition (1963).

book (I have tried to keep it a very subsidiary object) has been to explain my own former work, even to myself.

There is, however, another method, which is perhaps entitled to be regarded as being, in a special sense, *the* method of Growth Theory, on which in my books I have hitherto had little to say. This is the method which uses as its central concept the *equilibrium* of an expanding economy—an equilibrium towards which (as towards the static equilibrium of economic statics) there is supposed to be some sort of (strong or weak) tendency. There is a sense in which this concept (in its original form, derived from Harrod and Domar) does appear in my *Trade Cycle*; but its appearance there is mainly for illustrative purposes—I did not myself attach much importance to it. This, I suspect, was a principal reason why the earlier stages of the new developments (at the hands of Joan Robinson and Kaldor at the English Cambridge, of Samuelson and Solow at the American) rather passed me by. Looking at the matter in terms of cycle theory (the main way in which I had hitherto regarded it) theirs was a direction I did not want to follow.

I still retain a little of that earlier scepticism; the version of 'Growth Equilibrium' theory, which is given in Parts II and III below, will (I expect) be found by enthusiasts to be rather cool. But I am not as cool as I was;[1] I am ready to recognize that (especially on the mathematical side) the new approach has major achievements to its credit. There are some fundamental issues (such as the perennial question of the working of factor substitution) that it can go a long way towards clearing up. On this level the new growth theory is important; but if its importance is to be assessed— neither over- nor under-assessed—it has to be set out systematically. That is not a thing that can be done in an article; yet since Joan Robinson's *Accumulation of Capital* (1956) there has been no full-scale treatment. Much has happened since then of which it is necessary to take account.

The theory, as I understand it, is in essentials a mathematical theory; but I have been anxious that in my statement of it I should keep myself writing economics. I have tried to keep a firm eye on the economic meaning; and to be on the look-out for devices (there are several such that are available if one looks for them) by which the purely mathematical points can be by-passed. Though I have

---

[1] As when I wrote my 'Thoughts on the Theory of Capital' (*Oxford Economic Papers*, 1960).

allowed myself a freer use of algebra in the text of this book than would have been appropriate in the old days (such as those of *Value and Capital*) it is only in a few places that the algebra does more than express, a shade more sharply, what can be (and generally is) also expressed in words. I do not think that interested readers, even those who reckon themselves to be non-mathematicians, will usually find much difficulty with it. There is nevertheless a danger that by adopting this method of exposition, one should lose touch with the mathematical work. In the Appendixes (especially B and C) something is done towards building a bridge.

Though I have been influenced, in many ways, by the 'growth models' that swarm in economic literature, I have allowed myself to make less reference to the work of contemporaries than the reader may well feel that he would have preferred. The field is vast; and I am well aware that my knowledge of it is only a sample. Now, as I write this preface, but after the body of the book has gone to the printer, there comes into my hands the 'Survey' by Hahn and Matthews (*Economic Journal*, December 1964). If I had had this earlier (but it would have to have been much earlier) I might have made an attempt to give further references. As it is, I must leave the reader—with their help—to fill the gap for himself.

I have one major acknowledgement to make. It was when I was working with Morishima at Osaka in 1960 that I first began to get to grips with mathematical growth theory; it has been an immense help to have had him with me in All Souls from the summer of 1963 to that of 1964, a period during which a large part of this book was written. There are few chapters in it which have not benefited from his criticisms; though there are some, written or rewritten after he left Oxford, which he will not have seen before they went into print. It is naturally in the chapters on the Turnpike (XVIII and XIX), his special subject, where his influence is at its maximum. I could not have written those chapters without his help; though the central diagram (Fig. 9, p. 229) was my idea, it is only through his buttressing that it has been made to stand up. The corresponding Appendix (C) is, as there stated, in effect a joint work by us both.

J. R. H.

February 1965

CONTENTS

PART III

OPTIMUM GROWTH

PART I

METHODS OF DYNAMIC ECONOMICS

I

GROWTH, DYNAMICS—AND STATICS

1. WHAT is Growth Theory? What, that is, do economic theorists mean when they say that they are constructing growth models, or that they are working in a department of economics which they call the Theory of Economic Growth? My original purpose in writing this book was to clear my own mind on this question—a question of scope and method, or of methodology. But before I had done I found that it was necessary for me to write out my own version of Growth Theory (which is what will be found in Parts II–III of this book). Perhaps it is only in terms of that version (which nevertheless includes a great deal of what is found in other versions) that the question of method will prove to have been cleared up. I have, however, thought it important to set my version against a more general background. For there are quite a number of things which Growth Theory may be doing (or attempting). We shall be at endless cross-purposes (as much of the discussion in the journals has, I think, been at cross-purposes) unless we keep these objectives distinct—and understand the relations which one bears to another. That is why I propose to begin by inflicting upon the reader quite a dose of methodology.

2. I begin with one meaning that I shall set, quite firmly, on one side. 'Growth Economics' is often taken to be particularly associated with the problem of 'developing the underdeveloped'. The appearance of a branch of theory called Growth Theory, at a time when the economics of underdevelopment has been a major preoccupation of economists, has made it look as if there must be a real connexion.[1] I much doubt if there is. Underdevelopment economics is a vastly important subject, but it is not a formal or theoretical subject. It is a practical subject which must expect to call upon any branch of theory (including non-economic, for instance sociological, theory) which has any relevance to it. If there is

---

[1] *The Theory of Economic Growth*, by Sir Arthur Lewis, is an admirable work on underdevelopment economics, but it is not much concerned with Growth Theory in the sense that I mean here.

any branch of economic theory which is especially relevant to it, it is the Theory of International Trade.[1] Growth Theory (as we shall understand it) has no such special relation. It has no particular bearing on underdevelopment economics, nor has the underdevelopment interest played any essential part in its development. It is concerned with economic growth in general, not in any particular way with the relative growth of 'advanced' and 'backward' countries.

3. A natural (but perhaps a little unsophisticated) definition of Growth Theory would be to make it that part of economic theory which is specially concerned with long-term trends, long-term trends of the economy as a whole. Any time-series can of course be analysed, by well-known statistical methods, into trend and fluctuations about the trend. We have a Theory of Fluctuations to deal with the fluctuations; let us match it with a Theory of Growth, to deal with the trend. That, I am sure, is the way in which the matter has often been taken; but one of the troubles is that when it is taken in that way it does not come out quite right. And this, perhaps, is hardly surprising. The distinction between trend and fluctuation is a statistical distinction; it is an unquestionably useful device for statistical summarizing. Since economic theory is to be applied to statistics, which are arranged in this manner, a corresponding arrangement of theory will (no doubt) often be convenient. But this gives us no reason to suppose that there is anything corresponding to it on the economic side which is at all fundamental. We have no right to conclude, from the mere existence of the statistical device, that the economic forces making for trend and for fluctuation are any different, so that they have to be analysed in different ways. It is inadvisable to start our economics from the statistical distinction, though it will have to come in at an appropriate point, as an instrument of application.

  I believe that Growth Theory is a part of that department of economic theory which deals with both trend and fluctuation; but what separates it from the rest of that department is an economic, not a statistical distinction. For the department as a whole, we may

[1] I have myself made some attempts to discuss the underdevelopment problem in terms of International Trade theory in the essay on 'National Economic Development in an International Setting' in my *Essays on World Economics* (1959); and in the lectures on International Trade and Development that I gave in Cairo, published by the Central Bank of Egypt (1964).

(I think) continue to use the old term—Economic Dynamics. Growth Theory is a branch of Economic Dynamics; or better, it is one of the *methods* of Economic Dynamics.

It is in that light that I shall be considering it in this book. But in order to deal with it properly in that manner, we shall have to wander (at times) quite a way from it. For we shall have to distinguish it from other methods; and there is a good deal to be said about some of the other methods before their nature can be clearly understood. In order to get Growth Theory into its place we shall have to conduct some sort of a survey of the methods of Economic Dynamics as a whole. But this is itself a task which needs to be undertaken. What is Economic Dynamics? What are the main methods by which economists have sought to cope with dynamic problems?

4. The definition of Economic Dynamics has itself been a controversial question; but we need not be much troubled by that controversy here. It is easy enough, at this time of day, to see why there should be various definitions. It is very natural that an author, approaching what (until lately) has been largely uncharted territory, should distinguish as *his* dynamics that stretch of it which lay immediately ahead of him on his own selected approach. (Then, when that strip had been colonized, the name would shift to the next strip that lay ahead.) Special definitions of that sort are abundant; they have been helpful, in their own places, as marks for the stages of some particular argument; but the meanings of dynamics which they give are not general meanings. The general meaning, which concerns us here, must be something more inclusive.

When we look for a general meaning it is not hard to see what it must be. There is a simple line of thought which impels us directly to it.

If there is one thing which dynamics must mean, which it cannot help meaning, it is 'not statics'. The definition of Economic Dynamics must follow from the definition of Economic Statics; when we have defined one we have defined the other.

The distinction between statics and dynamics is (of course) not originally an economic distinction. It is an echo of a far older distinction in mathematical mechanics; a reference to that older meaning will always be at the back of one's mind. It is a fault to allow oneself to become the victim of such analogies; but it is desirable, if we are to avoid confusion, to pay some attention to them.

It is undoubtedly true, in this case, that there cannot be a perfect fit. In mechanics, statics is concerned with rest, dynamics with motion; but no economic system is ever at rest in anything like the mechanical sense. Production is itself a process; by its very nature it is a process of change. All we can do is to define a static condition as one in which certain key variables (the quantities of commodities that are produced and consumed, and the prices at which they are exchanged) are unchanging. A dynamic condition is then, by inevitable opposition, one in which they are changing; and dynamic theory is the analysis of the processes by which they change.

This is in fact the definition of the scope of Economic Dynamics which I shall be using in the following chapters. It is obvious that it is a wide definition, which does not merely abstain from drawing a line between trend and fluctuation. It includes the study of change in particular markets as well as in the whole economy. It should deal with specialization and diversification as well as with 'growth'. It is indeed so wide that it may be suspected of being too wide. Will not dynamics, defined in this way, swallow up the whole of economics? Is any place left for Economic Statics?

I believe that there is a place for Economic Statics, quite an important place, though what it is requires some clearing up. Because our books start with statics, they take it much too much for granted. There is a good deal to be said about the scope (and method) of Economic Statics; and some of this I must inflict on the reader (in this chapter and in that which follows). We shall not be in a proper position to discuss dynamics until we are really clear about statics. If dynamics is 'not statics', then by deepening our conception of statics, we are (by implication) deepening our conception of dynamics also.

5. The static–dynamic distinction looks rather different according to the kind of economic theory where it is used. It is rather different in Welfare Economics from what it is in Positive Economics, and (as we shall see) in different kinds of Positive Economics. It will be useful to look at it, as it appears in these various fields; and perhaps to clear our ideas about the relations between these fields, just a little, as we go along.

I begin with Welfare Economics. It is only too obvious that most traditional Welfare Economics—whether of the 'old' (Pigouvian) or of the 'new' variety—has in fact been static. It has assumed that wants are constant, and resources are constant; it has then inquired into the characteristics of 'optimum' organization, of the organization which, according to some conception of 'best', will satisfy these wants in the 'best' way. It was no doubt necessary to begin in that manner, since the problems that arise, even at that stage, are difficult enough. The static assumption is a simplification, which makes the problem more tractable, so that some progress can be made with it, as could hardly be made if the full complexities of a changing economy were faced at the start. Concentration upon static Welfare Economics has, however, proved to be quite dangerous. Though many of the static welfare problems are real problems, and many of the static 'solutions' give a guide to real solutions, which will persist however the welfare problem is dynamized, that is not always true. It is important (and it is increasingly realized to be important) to rethink the welfare problem in terms of a changing economy, in which resources (at least) are varying, either 'autonomously' or as a consequence of present behaviour. I shall have a good deal to say about Dynamic Welfare Economics in Part III of this book.

In principle, then, in the welfare field, statics is just a preliminary to dynamics, a preliminary which it was no doubt necessary to explore before proceeding to dynamic complications, but whose ultimate destination looks like being for a role which will be mainly pedagogic. That, however, may be going too far. For the dynamic complications are great, and are very hard to handle; thus, whenever it can be shown that, in relation to some particular problem, they are unimportant, it may be justifiable to neglect them. But often (one fears) one will not be able to show, only to guess, that they are unimportant; different people will guess in different ways.

6. Let us, however, on the way to our next topic, that of Positive Economics, consider a case in which Static Welfare Economics has at least thrown up interesting subjects for discussion. This is in the analysis of industrial structure (monopoly and competition). Here we have both a welfare problem and a positive-economic problem; we are contrasting the welfare optimum (or a welfare optimum) with the (possibly or probably) non-optimum position thrown up by some 'actual' organization. The welfare term in this comparison is relatively clear (or at least we may say that its ambiguities are by now well understood); but on the 'actual' side there is a distinction, which cries out to be made, but which is in fact too often overlooked.

What we may be doing is to compare the optimum position (that which *would* be achieved if wants were satisfied 'best' on some criterion) with the position which *would* be realized if the economy were organized on some given principle: such as profit maximization without collusion, profit maximization with a certain kind of collusion, normal cost pricing, discriminatory pricing, and so on. To what extent, we may ask, will the distribution of resources that is established under one of these systems, or market forms, approximate to, or depart from, the welfare optimum as above defined? (This includes, of course, the question whether organization, on the principle that is under examination, is possible at all.) All these questions, it should be noticed, are theoretical questions, like the welfare questions. They cannot be answered by an appeal to facts. The most that facts can do is to throw some indirect light upon them.

Contrasted with these is the much more empirical problem, in which we are concerned with actual behaviour, trying to make sense of actual data, coming (as actual data have to come) from some particular time and place. We can then test out upon them, as hypotheses, the maximum profit hypothesis, the full cost hypothesis, or any other that one can think up; we must, however, be prepared to find that the principles (if they can be called such) on which the actual economy which we are examining is run are very mixed. The most that we can expect is that there will be an approximation to one or other of the standard types of organization. If so, we can use the results that we have derived from a study of these types to judge (in terms of departure from the welfare optimum) the actual organization, at the particular time, of the particular economy. If not, we may only be able to judge it when we have invented a new type, and constructed the new theory (simple or complicated) which belongs to it.

7. It seems to be suggested by this example (it is only an example) that Positive Economics has a 'pure' branch as well as an 'applied' branch, and that it is important to distinguish them. Welfare Economics is pure economics, but it is not the only part of pure

economics. A considerable part of economic theory is not Welfare Economics; but, like Welfare Economics, it is pure theory, not *Ref.*
tied down to particular time and place.

In setting against this pure branch an applied branch, I do not
mean to imply that the applied branch is non-theoretical. For one of
the major constituents of the applied branch is econometrics.
Econometric hypotheses (or models) are meant to be checked
against facts, so that they belong to the applied branch; but they
appear, at least on the surface, to be quite as theoretical in character
as the models of 'pure' theory. The one kind can indeed quite easily
be mistaken for the other. It may indeed be true that in the beginning they were hardly differentiated. It was then not evident that
Pure Positive Economics offered any choice of model; the task of
the econometrist could then be thought to be confined to the
'fitting' of a model, given to him by the theorist, to the facts—
indeed to any facts. But as time has gone on (and perhaps also as
econometricians have become more ambitious) it has become apparent that this is not, at all precisely, what they have to do. The
econometric model is to be fitted to *particular* facts—to U.S. data
over a certain period, or something like that. Its object is to explain
the working of that economy (or of some aspect of that economy)
in the simplest possible terms. The wise econometrist will accordingly use his general knowledge of that economy to select
'strategic factors' which seem likely to be important, so that they
must be incorporated into his model; and to reject things which, on
general knowledge, seem unlikely to be important in that case. (He
does, of course, have methods by which he can test the desirability
of including such factors as, on general knowledge, seem to be on
the margin of doubt.) But he can hardly proceed at all without some
hunch about the kinds of things he is going to include.

Econometric models of this sort are very important; I have no
desire to depreciate them. But I would insist that they are not the
only sort of positive model that we need.

For there is another kind of question which we may properly
ask, which is not a normative, or 'welfare' question, and not an
econometric question. Instead of asking, like the econometrists,
how *did* such and such an economy work, over such and such
a past period, we may ask—what would be the working of an
economy, which was constructed on given lines, whether an economy
of that sort has actually existed or not. This is a purely theoretical

question, like the welfare question; it cannot be answered by an appeal to facts. Nor can the answer be tested by an appeal to facts, save in special cases, where we may be able to find an economy that looks as if its working should be interpretable in terms of the prescribed rules. We can then perhaps test the hypothesis that this is so. Some of the answers to questions that are of this sort may be testable to that extent, but certainly not all. Yet, among those that are untestable, there are some to which we should much like to have some kind of an answer.[1]

That Pure Positive Theory of this sort is necessary, is (I think) made apparent by the 'monopoly-competition' example given above. When the economist has got his 'welfare' rules and has established (if he can) that existing organization does not satisfy them, he has still not finished his job. For he has no right to criticize the existing organization simply on account of what he has so far shown. For anything that is yet apparent, it may be that there is no *practicable* organization which will satisfy wants any 'better', which will approach the optimum any more nearly. In order to have a basis for criticism it has to be shown that there is a practicable alternative organization which can be expected to do this. But that alternative organization (by definition) does not yet exist; its properties cannot be established, at least in general, by econometric methods. They can only be perceived, however dimly, by theoretical inquiry—by what I am calling Pure Positive Economics.[2]

8. I return to statics—and dynamics. The status of statics in Pure Positive Theory is not very different from what it is in Welfare Economics—as is not surprising, in view of the strictly theoretical character of both branches. Here, as in Welfare Economics, if we begin with statics, we do so because it is easier. Again, as in Welfare Economics, there may be some cases where static analysis gives us

[1] Thus, when what we are doing is Pure Positive Economics, we should not allow ourselves to be bullied by those who insist that all our concepts must be 'operationally meaningful'. That demand is fair enough, if we are doing econometrics, or preparing theory for the econometrist; but it is not fair if we have a different intention.

[2] It may be observed, in passing, that the characteristic of econometrics which we have been discussing—that its theory is applied theory, not pure theory—explains why it is that it can only lead up to 'projections' or prognostications: forecasts of what will happen, if the same forces as have been operating continue to operate in the future, not what will happen if a new form of organization (in the widest sense) is introduced. Once 'policy' is introduced as a variable, we have to go beyond econometrics.

all that we require, so that we can rest without going further. But there are others—as we learn more they become increasingly frequent—where we cannot get all that we need by the use of static methods, or where the use of static method is seriously misleading. It then becomes necessary to push on into dynamic territory; the sorting out of the problems that then arise—in Pure Positive Economics—will be the main subject of Chapters VI–XVI, below.

But before we come to that let us look at the position on the applied side, which we shall find to be appreciably different. Statics, here, is not a mere preliminary to dynamics; it has an independent status of its own. There exist applied problems which, by their nature, are purely static. For the study of such problems static analysis requires to be elaborated much more fully than it would have to be if its role were no more than that of a preliminary.

Take, as a simple example, the question: why are Englishmen, on the average, richer than (say) Greeks? This is quite a normal question of applied economics, and as such it must of course have a time reference; it refers (obviously) to Englishmen and Greeks in the twentieth century A.D. and not to any earlier period of history. The particular date of reference is not, however, of much importance; one would not mind too much if the figures on which one was commenting were 1955 figures for one country and 1960 figures for the other. The question is one about the *states* of the economies in question, not about any process of change. Questions such as this (and there are very many such questions which concern economists) are static questions; it ought to be possible to deal with them without going outside static theory.

Accordingly, in applied economics, there is nothing unrealistic about statics; the line between statics and dynamics is not a line between abstraction and realism. It may indeed be noticed (as a confirmation) that a similar distinction appears in the wholly realistic field of economic history. One of the standard ways of writing economic history (much practised by political historians in their economic chapters) is to survey the state of the economy under consideration, as it was in various historical periods, comparing one state with another. This is comparative statics. It is when the economic historian tries to throw his work into the form of a narrative that it becomes, in our sense, dynamic. And any examination of the work of economic historians will show what a difficult threshold has to be crossed at that point.

9. Static problems, then, are real problems, but static theory is a matter of static method, and that is rather a different matter. By the *state* of a given economy, one would appear to mean its average performance over a fairly long period, short-run fluctuations being cancelled out. Since one was not interested in short-run fluctuations it would seem to be adequate to represent the economy by a model which was in this average condition throughout the whole of the period; so that it was in a static condition, as we have been using the term. This is the way in which static models are used, and I think must be used, for appropriate purposes in applied economics. The model exhibits an unchanging economy, although it is to be applied to the study of an economy which is in fact in a condition of change.

So far as that one must go; but the ground on which one is treading is already beginning to be treacherous. Suppose, to take a simple but (as it turns out) most important case, that the actual economy being studied is in fact a progressive economy, in the sense that it is accumulating real capital, having (in some sense) more real equipment at the end of the period under consideration than it had at the beginning. We have then to do considerable violence to it if we are to fit it into a static model. We must replace its actual (changing) stock of capital by a constant stock of capital, not (in strictness) the capital that it had at the beginning of the period, but its average capital over the period. But if we do that, what do we do about investment? There is no difficulty about the part of investment which makes good the wastage of capital; such replacement investment is entirely consistent with a static model. But the net investment, which increases the capital stock, cannot be shown as increasing the capital stock. It is, of course, a part of production, and will have to be shown as part of the social product. The point is that it cannot be distinguished, as investment, from other parts of the social product. In statics, consumption goods and investment goods are just things that are produced; there is no economic difference between them, save the ordinary imperfect substitutability by which any sort of good differs from another.

Consider, as an illustration of this principle, the question of distribution among factors. There is no obvious reason why this should not be treated as a static problem; it is certainly capable of being formulated in static terms. Suppose we take the particular question: why is the share of (say) rent in the British National

Income lower in the twentieth century than in the eighteenth? (I take a case where the fact is pretty indubitable.) We are clearly then asking a question about states, not about processes, so that it seems to call for treatment on static lines. It then follows at once from the general characteristic of static analysis, just elucidated, that we must not expect to find an explanation of the change in question in any of the things that are excluded from static analysis —as for instance anything to do with saving and investment (as such). All that could possibly be relevant in this direction (I do not say that it would be important in this particular case) is a change in the characteristics of the particular sorts of consumption and investment goods being produced in the periods under consideration; a change in the proportion of much-land-using goods, for instance, in the whole national product (consumption goods and investment goods together). It is only in this sense (so long as we consider the problem statically) that anything to do with saving and investment can possibly be relevant.

Nevertheless, once it is realized that we have to do this kind of violence to the facts in fitting them to a static model, so that we are compelled by our method to leave out things which may well be relevant, the question emerges: cannot we find a way of doing better? If the economy with which we are dealing (or even one only of the economies which we are comparing) is in fact a progressive economy, it may be claimed that its progressiveness is one of its characteristics: that it is in a *state* of progress, or growth. Even though we are only concerned with its average performance over the period, its average growth rate over the period is a part of that average performance.

It was, I believe, first shown by Cassel[1] that a model of steady growth can be constructed which can be handled in much the same way as the static model. Through the work of Harrod, Domar, Mrs. Robinson, Kaldor, and many others, the use of such a 'growth model' has in our day become familiar. What I mean by Growth Theory (now at last to be revealed) is the particular kind of Dynamic Economics which uses a model of this kind as an analytical tool. As we shall find, it is a tool that may be used in several ways—so that to define Growth Theory in this way is not to give it a narrow definition. No doubt it is a definition which will not suit

[1] *Theory of Social Economy*, ch. i, sect. 6. It may be that Cassel was developing a suggestion of Marshall's (see below, p. 49).

everyone; but that it is a convenient definition I shall hope to show as we go on.

Growth Theory (in this sense) is no more than a particular method of Dynamic Economics. It is not claimed (it ought not to be claimed) that it is *the* method—that there do not remain many dynamic problems to which some other approach would be much more relevant. It may indeed be questioned whether it is 'dynamic' enough; there are too many ways (they may be significant ways) in which it remains 'semi-static'.[1] In order that we should be able to handle it (to use it in the way that static models have long been used), we must assume that all elements in the economy (or rather, all elements in which we are interested) are growing at the same rate. Such uniformity of growth is of course quite unrealistic; it is quite as unrealistic as the stationariness of the static model. Thus we do not greatly diminish the violence that we do to the facts when we fit them to a steady growth model, instead of a static model. We are doing much the same thing in each case; in each case we need to offer justification for what we are doing.

[1] For though some of the 'variables in which we are interested' (outputs, for instance) are changing, there are others (including the growth rate itself) which are constant.

II

THE CONCEPT OF EQUILIBRIUM

1. THERE is one further matter, not specially belonging to dynamic theory, on which something must be said before we start on dynamics. What is the meaning which we are to give to the concept of 'equilibrium'? In statics, equilibrium is fundamental; in dynamics, as we shall find, we cannot do without it; but even in statics it is treacherous, and in dynamics, unless we are very careful, it will trip us up completely. It is inevitable that we should build our concept of dynamic equilibrium on the more familiar conception of equilibrium in statics. It will be wise to begin by getting the static foundation as firm as we can.

Like 'statics' and 'dynamics' themselves, 'equilibrium' is a borrowing from mathematical mechanics; but it is a question whether the mechanical and economic concepts of 'equilibrium' have much more than a name in common. The static equilibrium of mechanics is a balance of forces; but though economists began by thinking of their static equilibrium as a balance of forces—as, for instance, the 'forces' of supply and demand—that is a very poor account of what the static equilibrium of economics means. Attempts have been made (most notably by Samuelson, in his *Foundations of Economic Analysis*)[1] to find a closer association at a deeper level; but I have myself come to doubt whether they give us much help. It is safer, in this case, to define the static equilibrium of economics as an independent concept in its own right.

The static economy (in which wants are unchanging, and resources unchanging) is in a state of equilibrium when all the 'individuals' in it are choosing those quantities, which, out of the alternatives available to them, they prefer to produce and to consume. (*Individuals* is to be taken in a wide sense, to include any units, as for instance firms, to which we attribute some freedom of independent choice. *Preference* is interpreted to mean maximizing something—whether objective (profit) or subjective (utility) does not here matter.) The alternatives that are open are set in part by

---

[1] Especially ch. 9.

external constraints (which may be differently defined, according as we select the data of a particular problem, but must generally include the supplies of land and of physical capital, and the state of technology); these, in a static economy, must be taken to be constant. But they are also set in large part by the choices made by other 'individuals'; and the way in which the choices made by 'individuals' set constraints on the choices made by other 'individuals' will differ from one market form (or more generally from one type of economic organization) to another.[1]

The crucial assumption of static theory (without which it could not have been developed as it has been developed) is that a static economy (static, because tastes and resources are unchanging) can be treated as if it were in equilibrium: the quantities produced and consumed will be (near enough) the equilibrium quantities that have just been described. Economists are so used to this equilibrium assumption that they are inclined to take it for granted; for present purposes, however, we must not let it slip by without noticing it.

Even if we do not make the equilibrium assumption, there are some properties of the static economy which can be established. Even without it, we can write down certain relations ('social accounting identities'), of which equality between demand and supply in any market (in the sense of actual quantitity bought and actual quantity sold) may be regarded as typical. It is not to be denied that these relations, in themselves, give us a certain insight into the structure of the economy; but they are of little use for comparative purposes. For such purposes (to take the simplest illustration) the demand and supply, which are necessarily equal as an identity, have to be reinterpreted as a point of intersection on demand and supply schedules; and for the construction of such schedules (as for the construction of the more complicated functions which play the same role in the study of interrelated markets) we require the equilibrium assumption. It is essential for *comparative* statics that the quantities chosen can be taken to be equilibrium quantities.

But because we need the equilibrium assumption, it does not follow that we have a right to it. And indeed, as soon as we allow ourselves to question it, it becomes obvious that it needs much

[1] That we do have some freedom on what constraints shall be treated as external constraints is made evident by the case of the national economy. When we are considering it by itself, we treat the trading opportunities open to it as external constraints; but when we treat it as part of the international economy, these must be taken as consequences of the choices of other 'individuals'.

justification. There is much to be said about it, even on the static level; but to go into it at all fully would draw us aside from our main task. There are just a few things (which, as we shall see, have dynamic counterparts) that must be said.

2. It has first to be noticed that the equilibrium assumption looks distinctly different, according as it is used in one or another of the three branches of economic theory (even confining attention to the static departments of those three branches) that were distinguished in Chapter I.

In Welfare Economics there is no problem; the equilibrium assumption is included in the way the theory is set up. This is certainly so if we define our social optimum by some sort of 'social welfare function'; for if we do that we are treating the economy *as if* it consisted of a single 'individual'; it is the equilibrium choice of that single chooser which *is* the optimum choice. And the position does not seem to be radically different if we insist on pluralism, as for instance when we 'reconcile' the maximization of utility by distinct 'individuals' by compensation devices, so long as the maximization of utility by each individual is kept as *one* of the conditions of optimization. A static welfare optimum has to be an equilibrium.

It is in Positive Economics that there is a problem; but it is a different problem in the pure from what it is in the applied branch.

3. In Pure Positive Economics (where, as will be remembered, we assume a *given* type of organization) it is necessary, if the equilibrium assumption is to be justified, that we should be able to assert the existence of a *tendency* to equilibrium; and indeed, if the assumption is to be usable, it must be a strong tendency. There are several questions here to be distinguished.

In the first place, it is by no means inevitable, in an arbitrarily given form of organization, that an equilibrium should exist at all. In the simple cases with which we are most familiar (such as the Marshallian case of a single industry—the production of a single product considered in isolation) there may be no doubt about it; but even there we have to be careful. There is no question, in the case of the single market, that under perfect competition, under monopoly, and under imperfect competition without oligopoly, equilibrium does exist; but one has only to point to the tortured history of duopoly theory to show that there are market forms, not necessarily unrealistic or unimportant, where the mere existence of equilibrium, even in a single market, is doubtful, and perhaps more than doubtful. In the case of the whole (closed) economy, it is only quite recently that the necessary existence of an equilibrium has been established, even for the simplest form of organization, that in which perfect competition is taken for granted.[1] For what forms of imperfect competition (if there are any) a similar necessity can be established is still (I believe) an open question.

But let that pass. Even if the equilibrium exists, it has still to be shown that there is a tendency towards it. This, as Samuelson has (rightly) emphasized, is not a matter that can be settled, once for all, as soon as the type of economic organization (according to the usual *static* classification) has been decided. A perfectly competitive system, for instance, may have a strong tendency to equilibrium, or it may not. The simplest example of this (sufficient to establish the point) is the 'cobweb theorem'. Even in the single market, under perfect competition, and such that the existence of equilibrium is indubitable, there may be no *tendency* to equilibrium, if speeds of reaction to price change are perverse. Something has to be specified about reactions to disequilibrium before the existence of a tendency to equilibrium can be asserted. The tendency to (static) equilibrium is itself a dynamic matter.[2]

[1] An outline of the proof, and of the steps by which it was accomplished, is given in Dorfman, Samuelson, and Solow, *Linear Programming and Economic Analysis*, pp. 366 ff. A still briefer outline, which does still (I think) bring out the main points, is given in my 'Survey of Linear Theory' (*Economic Journal*, December 1960).

[2] A word may usefully be inserted here (though it can do no more than skirt the fringe of a large subject) about the relation between this tendency to equilibrium and the stability of equilibrium, which has been intensively treated by mathematical economists. There is just one point that I want to make; and I shall only take the simplest case in which it arises.

In a perfectly competitive market, an ordinary downward-sloping demand curve for a product (say a farm product) may be confronted with a 'backward-sloping' supply curve—because (to follow the old story) farmers consume more of their own product when they can satisfy their rudimentary demands for the products of urban industry more easily. Supply and demand curves may then have multiple intersections, of which some (so we are informed by the textbooks) are 'unstable'. What exactly does this mean?

The property (it will be noticed) is a purely static property; it can be read off from the diagram, without any information about speeds of reaction, or anything about patterns of reaction that cannot be expressed in static terms. (If we did have information about speeds of reaction, we might find, on 'cobweb' lines, that some of the 'statically stable' positions were in fact unstable.) What

Let that pass again. Even if the equilibrium exists, and the tendency to equilibrium exists, we may still have insufficient ground to justify the equilibrium assumption if the convergence to equilibrium is very slow. For then, in any period of reasonable length that begins from a position which is out of equilibrium, the time that is occupied in approaching equilibrium (and still remaining, perhaps, quite far away from it) will be long in proportion to the length of the later phase, in which an equilibrium position is (approximately) realized. It is true that we can always, in a sense, overcome this last difficulty by lengthening the period of time for which tastes and resources are to be kept static; but static comparisons, which relate to average states over very long periods of time, will not often be very interesting.

There is, however, an alternative procedure which in such cases one would expect to be more promising. It will be remembered that we have some liberty to select the constraints which, in a particular model, are to be treated as *external*; or, what comes to the same thing, that we have some liberty to specify the choices which are to be regarded as 'open' choices, so that to them the equilibrium assumption is to be applied. If, with respect to some particular choices, convergence to equilibrium is very slow, it may be better

is it that distinguishes the 'statically unstable' position (or positions) in the absence of such information?

The 'statically unstable' position is itself an equilibrium; if it were hit upon, buyers and sellers would be making the offers which they preferred, at the price in question, and these offers would fit together. The only thing which can distinguish it from a 'statically stable' position is that it is an equilibrium which can only be reached *by accident.* If there is any rule for the correction of disequilibrium positions—so long as that rule incorporates the merely *directional* provision that the price is to be raised when demand exceeds supply, lowered when supply exceeds demand—it will not be possible for the statically unstable position to be reached as the terminus of a process of adjustment. A correction of a disequilibrium position in its neighbourhood will always lead *away* from it.

By this distinction the contrast between the 'statically stable' and 'statically unstable' position is (I think) made clear. It is not true that *any* rule of adjustment, which incorporates the directional provision, must lead to a 'statically stable' position; for the rule may be such (as in the case of the 'explosive cobweb') that every correction that is made, though it is the 'right' direction, will always overshoot the mark. What is true is that the statically unstable position cannot be reached by any such correction, since the correction goes, in principle, the wrong way. It can be hit upon by accident, but not by a process of correction, so long as that process has the merely directional provision in it.

I believe that this argument can be generalized to cover cases of multiple markets; but I shall not go into that here.

not to regard such choices as open choices. What we then get is a less 'general' or less 'full' equilibrium than we should have got if we had left them open; it may nevertheless be more interesting and more useful.

An obvious example of this device is Marshall's 'short-period equilibrium', in which the fixed equipment of the (single industry) economy is kept constant; choices that relate to the structure and to the size of that equipment are not, within the 'short-period' model, regarded as being 'open'. But it is not hard to find other examples; and (as we shall see when we come back to it in Chapter V) Marshall's device has other aspects which will concern us very seriously, as well as this.

4. It is the Pure Positive branch of Economic Dynamics which will be our main concern in the following chapters (III–XVI); the main thing that is still to be done in this is to commence consideration of the equilibrium concept in that territory. But before proceeding to that topic, a word should be inserted about the remaining branch of static theory, the 'applied' branch.

This, it will be remembered, is theory that is to be applied to actual facts: to the performance of an actual economy over a particular historical period. The form of organization that is assumed is chosen to fit those facts; it is not examined for its own sake, for its intrinsic intellectual interest or as an organization that might be brought into being in conditions that we wish to suppose. Here, then, it can only be a question of applying the equilibrium concept to such choices as, in the particular economy under consideration, may reasonably be regarded as 'open'; these, in some economies, may have quite a restricted scope. (We may, and commonly do, limit it still further in the interest of simplification.) But whether the scope of the open choices is wide or narrow, we are here committed, by the mere decision to apply a static model, to the choice of a model which satisfies the requirements that we have been laying down. The equilibrium must exist, and there must be a tendency to it; if these conditions do not hold in the model that has been selected, it cannot be used for the static analysis of the facts in question, and must be rejected. A model which satisfies these conditions must be found.

The actual fitting of the model to the facts is a statistical (or econometric) question with which we are not here concerned. It is nevertheless important, even from our present point of view, to emphasize that the actual data, to which the static model is to be fitted, will not themselves be static. Even if we take the existence and stability of the model equilibrium for granted, we have still to ask how far the actual observed averages can be expected to correspond with the stationary values of the equilibrium model.

There are two questions here. One (the less important) is a matter of averaging. Consider the following illustration:

Let y_t be an index of production at time t. We are fitting a production function, so that y_t is supposed to be a function of quantities of factors of production, which at time t may be written x_{it} ($i = 1, 2,..., m$). If this function were a linear function, such as

$$y_t = \sum_i a_i x_{it} + b$$

(a's and b constant), we could sum over time and take a mean value, giving

$$\text{mean } y = \sum_i a_i (\text{mean } x_i) + b$$

so that there would be the same relation between the mean y and the means of the x's as we should have got if the x's had been constant at their mean values. But if the function is not linear, this is not so. If it is log-linear (as with the Cobb–Douglas function)

$$\log y_t = \sum_i a_i \log x_{it} + b$$

the same procedure will give a relation between means of logs; and mean log y_t is the log of the geometric mean of the y's, so that the relation only comes out right if we take geometric means as our averages.

This is not to say that one mean is better than the other; the point is that averaging is itself a source of error, greater (of course) if the data (which are being treated as constant, though they are not constant) are in fact varying a good deal during the period under consideration. There is nothing surprising about that, but it is one thing to be remembered.

averaging as error

The more important question concerns the tendency to equilibrium. What exactly, when the data are changing, is this to be taken to mean? A natural interpretation would be something as follows.

Suppose that y_t^* is the equilibrium value of the variable y at time t, depending on parameters x_{it} as before. But now suppose that the actual value y_t does not necessarily equal y_t^*, but is merely drawn towards it, from its preceding value. We might then write

$$y_t - y_{t-1} = k(y_t^* - y_{t-1})$$

so that if $k = 1$ we have instantaneous adjustment, while if $k < 1$, there is only a tendency to equilibrium.

There is of course no reason in general why k should not be variable; but it is rather instructive to see what happens in the simplest case, when it does not vary. Then, if we sum over n periods, and divide by n, we have

$$\frac{y_n - y_0}{n} = k \, (\text{mean } y_t^* - \text{mean } y_{t-1})$$

$$= k \left(\text{mean } y_t^* - \text{mean } y_t + \frac{y_n - y_0}{n} \right),$$

so that $\text{mean } y_t^* - \text{mean } y_t = \left(\frac{1-k}{k} \right) \cdot \left(\frac{y_n - y_0}{n} \right).$

It follows that there is no discrepancy, either if $k = 1$ (so that there is instantaneous adjustment), or if $y_n = y_0$ (so that the end value is the same as the initial value). If k is much less than unity, and if the economy is (say) an expanding economy, with y_n much larger than y_0, there may be a considerable discrepancy. The observed average is brought below the equilibrium average because of the *lag*.

5. With this last illustration, simple though it is, we are well on the way to dynamics. For suppose that instead of concentrating attention, as we have so far been doing, on the *average* performance of the economy during the n periods that have just been considered, we face up to the variations that occur in the course of those n periods, and bring them in as part of the phenomenon we are concerned to understand and explain. It would be possible to proceed as we have just been proceeding; and (as we shall see in more detail, in the next chapter and in some of those that follow it) this is in fact the kind of procedure that is implied in the older work on Economic Dynamics, and in some (even) of contemporary work. For reasons which I shall explain, I am myself convinced that this procedure is inadequate. But it does already throw up some of the problems of equilibrium in dynamics; it is a *half-way house* with which we shall in fact have to be much concerned.

We have found ourselves, in the course of our attempt to find a theoretical basis for the fitting of a static model to changing data, having to interpret that model in the sense of making equilibrium values of time t dependent upon parameters that belong to time t, and upon those parameters only. Yet we have found that in the *actual* process, values at time t do not so depend. There is a 'moving equilibrium'; but actual values are 'lagged' behind the equilibrium values. Thus we have (1) a set of rules by which the equilibrium values depend upon the parameters, and (2) a distinct set of rules by which the actual values are drawn towards the equilibrium values. This is the same kind of distinction as we found ourselves making when we were considering the *tendency* to a static equilibrium (in the Pure Positive static theory); it begins to look as if some such distinction is going to persist right through the dynamic field.

But what are these equilibrium values? I began with the assertion that there is equilibrium when all 'individuals' are choosing the quantities, to produce and to consume, which they prefer. To a conception of equilibrium that is of this type we must hold fast. But how can we make these quantities dependent (in a dynamic economy) upon current parameters—the equilibrium values of time t upon the parameters of time t—and upon those only? The question did not arise in a static model, since the parameters, on which the equilibrium depended, were at all dates the same. Here they are not the same. If (say) population is increasing, an 'equilibrium' that is based upon present population, paying no attention to the increase of population, will not even be a transitory equilibrium; there will be no reason why the 'individuals' should leave the population movement out of account in their investment decisions; there will be no reason why there should be even a 'tendency' in the direction of an equilibrium that is solely based upon present population. Similarly for other variables. The static equilibrium, entirely based upon current parameters, is in strictness irrelevant to the dynamic process.

That is why the picture, of actual values chasing a 'moving equilibrium' (the equilibrium values of which are determined statically), has to be abandoned. There was a stage in the development of dynamic theory when it was a tempting picture; but it will not do. As soon as we face the problem of analysing a process, even its equilibrium values must be determined, somehow or other, in relation to the process. But how is this to be done?

6. The process is a process in time; time goes only one way. Past and future must be distinguished. Parameters that refer to the past, and those that refer to the future, each may enter into the determination of equilibrium values, but they will do so in different ways. The past, so far as it is relevant, is embodied in the *results* of past decisions: the physical capital of the economy and the acquired skills of labour.[1] Instead of introducing past parameters explicitly, we can use the current resources that embody them. But the future is also relevant, and the future has no such *current* representative. We must introduce expectations of the future, of the future after time t, if the equilibrium values of time t are to be properly determined.

Expectations may be wrong or right; this simple consideration has a vital effect upon the kind of equilibrium concept (or concepts) that we require in dynamics. We need (1) *equilibrium at a point of time*; the system is in equilibrium in this sense, if 'individuals' are reaching a preferred position, with respect to their expectations, as they are at that point. It is only to such an equilibrium that there can be a tendency. We also need (2) *equilibrium over a period of time*. If there is to be equilibrium over a period there must be equilibrium at every point of time within the period—an equilibrium which is of course based, as every point-of-time equilibrium must be based, upon its own expectations. But for period equilibrium there is the additional condition that these expectations must be consistent with one another and with what actually happens within the period. Period equilibrium is essential, in dynamic theory, as a standard of reference; but it is hard to see how there can, in general, be any 'tendency' to it.

The relation between the two conceptions can be spelled out in more detail as follows. Suppose that at t_1 (a point of time) there is 'point-of-time equilibrium'. It must be based upon expectations of the movement of parameters, some of which belong to the *period t_1 to t_2*, some of which belong after t_2. Suppose that at t_2 (the end of the period) there is again point-of-time equilibrium, based (of

---

[1] It may be necessary, for some purposes, to allow for 'learning by experience' —the influence of past experience upon expectations of the future. This is another way in which past parameters may come in, or be brought in.

course) upon expectations of movement after t_2. If these expectations (about $post\text{-}t_2$) are different at t_2 from what they were at t_1, it will appear that the expectations of t_1 were wrong. So that although the system was in point-of-time equilibrium at t_1 *ex ante*, it does not appear to *have been* in point-of-time equilibrium at t_1, when it is looked at from t_2, *ex post*. And if actual events between t_1 and t_2 were different from what was expected at t_1, these t_1 expectations will similarly be shown to be wrong.[1] What this means is that from the point of view of t_2, the system was not in point-of-time equilibrium at t_1, nor on the course between t_1 and t_2. In order that there should be equilibrium *over the period*, there must be equilibrium at every point within the period, looked at both ways.

Static equilibrium is of course, by necessity, equilibrium over time; but there are other interesting examples of equilibrium over time that are not static. One is the Growth Equilibrium of the regularly progressive economy, to which allusion was made at the end of Chapter I, and which will be examined in detail in Part II, below. More generally, every optimum path must be in equilibrium over time. It may indeed be said—it is not inconsistent with the proposed terminology that we should allow ourselves to say— that every path which is in equilibrium over time is an optimum path, under the 'constraint' of the particular organization that it assumes; but a path which was in equilibrium over time, under a non-optimum (say a monopolistically exploitative) form of organization, would not be an optimum path in a more general sense.

7. Some such distinctions as we have been making in this chapter seem to be unavoidable if we are to tidy up what has been a very untidy matter; but it is not to be denied that they can themselves

---

[1] There is indeed a fundamental difference between what happens to the *post-t_2* expectations, between t_1 and t_2, and what happens to the t_1-t_2 expectations. The former still relate to the future, at t_2 as at t_1, but the latter (at t_2) have been converted into facts. Expectations may (and probably will) be uncertain; there is nothing that has here been said about *point-of-time equilibrium* which makes it necessary that they should be certain. But for period equilibrium expectations that relate *within the period* will have to be certain. This may seem awkward, but I think it has to be faced. After all, it enables us to say that risk and uncertainty are one of the causes of period disequilibrium; and that is one of the things which we shall want to say.

I shall be returning to this matter in Chapter VI.

be confusing. It is only by using them (as I plan to do in subsequent chapters) that we can really get them straight. But I may conclude this chapter by giving some preliminary warnings.

The temporal distinction which we have just been making (equilibrium *at a point of time* and equilibrium *over a period of time*) looks very like 'short period–long period', the Marshallian distinction that is so familiar. But it is not at all the same thing. The Marshallian distinction (as explained) belongs to the class of 're-stricted-full' distinctions—a type of distinction which is valid, even in statics, where the temporal distinction does not occur. There is of course no reason why 'restricted-full' distinctions should not be made in dynamics also; the choices which we regard as 'open' may still be restricted, for particular purposes, in suitable ways.

It is indeed true that a restricted equilibrium, which is not a full equilibrium, becomes a disequilibrium position, from the point of view of the 'fuller' analysis, where the restriction has been removed. (The short-period equilibrium, which is not a long-period equilibrium, is a disequilibrium, from the point of view of the long period.) And it is similarly true that an equilibrium at a point of time, which is not an equilibrium over the period in which that point of time occurs, is a disequilibrium position, from the point of view of the period. (It is better to say that the path, on which the disequilibrium position occurs, is not an equilibrium path, over the period.) But an equilibrium over time may still be a restricted equilibrium. So far as the 'open' choices are concerned, there is equilibrium over time; but not all choices that might be open (or that we might want to consider as being open) are open. A full (or fuller) equilibrium may still have to be considered.

This last point has a particular bearing upon Welfare Economics (or Optimum theory). As was stated at the beginning of this chapter, a static welfare optimum has to be an equilibrium; we now see that the same must be true of a welfare optimum, in dynamics as in statics. It is nevertheless still possible (in both statics and dynamics) to distinguish between a restricted optimum and a full (or fuller) optimum. The distinction is the same as that between a restricted and a full equilibrium; the restricted optimum is a restricted equilibrium, and the full optimum is a full equilibrium. From the point of view of the full equilibrium (or optimum) the restricted optimum is not an equilibrium. It is an equilibrium, subject to its limitations, but it is not an equilibrium when those limitations are removed. Thus when we are concerned[1] with the relation between the restricted optimum and the fuller optimum, it need not be confusing if we refer to the latter only as an 'equilibrium'. The practice of doing so is in fact well established; if it is understood in this way it does not need to cause trouble.

[1] As in the Turnpike theory (Chapters XVIII–XIX, below) to which these concluding remarks refer.

III

STATIC METHOD IN DYNAMIC THEORY

1. THE point has now been reached at which we may take a preliminary glance at the road which lies before us. I am going to distinguish four 'methods' of Dynamic Economics, which may be listed as follows:

(1) the Static (or Classical) method—Chapters III to V;
(2) the Temporary Equilibrium method—Chapter VI;
(3) the Fixprice method—Chapters VII to XI;
(4) the Growth Equilibrium method—Chapters XII to XVI.

In the present chapter I shall be mainly concerned with introducing the Static method; but before I come to that, it will be well to say a word about the meaning which I here give to the term 'method', and about the relations which I conceive these four methods to bear to one another.

A method, in the sense here used, is a family of models. A model may be defined as a construction, in which certain elements of the state (or process) that we desire to examine (or to contemplate) are selected, such that the interrelations and interactions of those elements may be deduced by reasoning (especially, but not necessarily, mathematical reasoning): in the hope that our general understanding of the state (or process) may be enhanced by an understanding of that aspect of it which is presented by these particular elements. For certain purposes, it is true, we can do with a narrower definition. An econometric model is a model that is to be fitted to actual phenomena; it is a successful model if the discrepancies between actual values and model values are such that they can be ascribed to random errors. But not all economic models are econometric models. Econometric theory, as explained above,[1] is applied theory. There are models in Pure Positive theory, and there are models in Optimum theory; to cover all these models some such wide definition as has just been given (which would also cover the econometric models) seems to be required.

[1] p. 9.

Models, of course, can be grouped in various ways; most obviously by the content of the phenomena to which they refer. There are models of the national economy, of international trade, two-sector models, and so on. A group of models, in this sense, would not conveniently be called a 'method'. The particular grouping which I have in mind relates particularly to the *dynamic* character of the model. It is a classification of models according to the way in which they handle time and change.

Time + Change

2. It is my contention that this is a centrally important classification, which sheds light in several ways. I begin with the light that it throws on the history of economic thought.

It is not true that the 'classical' economists of the eighteenth and nineteenth centuries were uninterested in dynamic problems; the causes of economic progress (as they called it) were one of their main concerns. It is not even true that the 'neo-classical' economists of 1870–1920 were without that interest. What is true is that they had a very special approach to dynamic problems; their *method* of treating them was by the tools of static theory. That, as we shall see, was a most inadequate treatment. Though it is not without its uses, even now, there are respects in which it is most seriously misleading.

It is commonly supposed that we have put all that behind us, by the 'Keynesian Revolution'. But this again is an over-simplification. There was not one Keynesian Revolution; there were several. In place of the old 'static' method (or better, in addition to it) we now have several dynamic methods. And we need them. For no one has yet found a single method which is ideal for use on all of the dynamic problems of economics. Every known method is imperfect; it gives, at the best, a very partial illumination. We need to have all the methods at our disposal, and to be aware of their weaknesses, as well as of their strengths.

Among the 'dynamic' methods, it is my third (the Fixprice method, as we shall call it) which the reader will probably feel, when he comes to it, to be the most characteristically Keynesian. But even that is only the method to which the *General Theory* was tending; it is not at all straightforwardly in the *General Theory* itself. There are elements in Keynes (more, perhaps, in the *Treatise on Money* than in the *General Theory*) which are nearer to my second (Temporary Equilibrium) method. Even the fourth

(Growth Equilibrium) method, though it is (I would say) very un-Keynesian in spirit, has been largely the creation of economists who would reckon themselves to be followers of Keynes.

As between these methods, then, I am not proposing anything novel in suggesting that they should share our allegiance. I think, however, that we shall live with them more happily if we keep them distinct. They really are very different. We need them all, sometimes one, sometimes another (and I would not exclude the possibility that we can devise crosses); but whichever we use, we should know what we are using, and why we are using it.

3. I pass to the proper subject of this chapter. The static (or classical) method is one that we have met before—it figures as the 'half-way house'[1] in the last chapter; but we can deepen our understanding of it, and prepare ourselves to understand its relation with other methods, if we now approach it in rather a different manner.

Every method of analysis of a process of change can be exhibited, if we choose, as a sequence analysis. The process is divided into steps, or stages, which are analysed separately, and then (as best we may) fitted together. It is not indeed necessary to proceed in this manner; there are purposes, as we shall find in later chapters,[2] for which it is more convenient to work with continuous time; but it is probably wise to regard the analysis by stages as the more fundamental. It is certainly my experience that it is the better method of statement with which to begin. Distinctions which need to be made, and which come out clearly in period analysis, are not always so clear when we take time to be continuous. Besides, if one starts with stages, one can always proceed to the continuous statement by shrinking the duration of the stages; and it is not so easy to proceed the other way round. We cannot wholly dispense with the discontinuous treatment; for business men think in time periods, and it is in terms of time periods that they do their accounts.[3]

In the discontinuous treatment we begin with the working of the

---

[1] p. 23, above.

[2] Chapter XXI and Appendix D (to Chapter XX).

[3] It may be added that there is good mathematical precedent for the procedure proposed. How is one to understand (say) an infinite integral, except by approaching it through a limiting process from an infinite series? It is the *logic* of the calculus that we are in fact following.

model in a unit period (week, or month, or year); then we proceed to a sequence of such periods. There is of course a sense in which we do the same thing in statics; only in statics the periods are exactly alike, so one will serve for all. In dynamics the single periods (as we shall call them)[1] will not be alike, or not exactly alike; but they will still have some common features, so that much of the analysis can be made repetitive. Much of the work can be done on a *representative* single period; this single-period analysis is always a first step. But it is never the only step in a dynamic theory; some means of linkage between successive single periods must also be provided.

4. Some such layout as this is needed for every method of analysis of a dynamic problem, if it is taken sequentially. Thus what in the last chapter we called 'equilibrium at a point of time' becomes the equilibrium of the single period; what we called 'equilibrium over a period' becomes equilibrium over a sequence of single periods. The particular characteristic of the static method is to be identified within this general framework. It is simply this: that static theory is used as the single-period theory of the dynamic process. In each single period, the model is taken to be in static equilibrium. The process is reduced to a sequence of static equilibria.

Now it may well seem (and has obviously seemed to many people) that there is nothing very bad about this; that it is no worse than the things that have already been swallowed in static theory. Even in the purely static comparison of states, we do not (as shown)[2] have to believe that the economies under comparison are in fact unchanging; all that we do is to represent their average performance over time by that of a model economy which is unchanging at this average. Are we doing anything different here? It is certainly true that an actual economy will be changing all the time; however we divide its story up into subperiods, they will be periods during which change continually occurs. Is it any more than a natural simplification to make the period uniform, and to concentrate change at the junctions? Are we doing any more than that when we take the single period to be in static equilibrium?

If we were doing no more, the procedure would indeed be harmless; uniformity of that sort must be supposed in any dynamic

---

[1] We need some special term for them; they must *not* be called 'short periods'.
[2] See above, p. 12.

method, that analyses change sequentially. The crucial characteristic of what we are calling the static method is different from that.
It is (as it was expressed in the last chapter) that the equilibrium of
time t could be taken to be determined by *current* parameters only;
or, as we may put it now that we are using a sequential framework,
that the equilibrium of the single period may be treated as *self-
contained*. In a fully static theory this is a perfectly harmless
assumption. Nothing has to be said, in statics, about the obvious
point that production takes time, so that it must be oriented, not
towards the present, but towards the future; for if present and
future are identical we can substitute one for the other without
making any difference. We can take a demand curve (for instance)
which reflects current wants, and set against it a supply curve that
refers to current production; for the same demand curve will still
be 'there' when the process of production is completed; we do not
have to bother about the fact that they refer to different *times*. But
in dynamics these things do matter; it is of the essence of the
dynamic problem that present and future are not identical.

Proper dynamic theory, even at its single-period stage, must
take account of the fact that many activities that go on within the
period are oriented outside the period; so that what goes on, even
within the period, is not only a matter of tastes and resources, but
also of plans and expectations. In statics there is no planning;
mere repetition of what has been done before does not need to
be planned. It is accordingly possible, in static theory, to treat the
single period as a closed system, the working of which can be
examined without reference to anything that goes on outside it (in
the temporal sense). But this is not possible in dynamics. Even at
the single-period stage, the links which relate the single period to
the rest of the dynamic process cannot be neglected.

In general, there are many such links; but the most important
of them (in the sense that attention to it is hardest to avoid) is the
stock of physical capital that is handed on from one single period
to its successor. I shall confine attention, in the rest of this chapter,
to some questions of this physical carry-over.

5. If the single period is treated as being in static equilibrium, the
new investment that is undertaken in that period is not significantly distinguished from the rest of production; the relative
values of the new investment goods are determined, in static

manner, by supply and demand conditions, in terms of the tastes and resources of that single period.[1] The relative values of old capital goods (those inherited by this single period from its predecessor) are also determined as part of the general equilibrium of the single-period system; and it will usually be implied, as a condition of static equilibrium, that these should be consistent with the values of the new investment goods. But the value of a capital good, considered as a means of production, depends upon the return that is expected from it over its whole life. If this is reckoned as determinable from the conditions of the single period, the assumption has been allowed to creep in that the conditions of the single period are expected to remain unchanged in future periods. This assumption can only be avoided if we can stretch out the single period to cover so long a time that the useful lives of the capital goods, that are used in the period, fall altogether within it. But it will usually be impossible to do this by any stretching out; and it will always be true that by lengthening the single period we make it less fitted to play its part as an element in a dynamic process.

There is indeed just one case in which we can use this device effectively, and it so happens that it is a case that is of historical importance. Suppose that none of the capital goods that are used are seriously long-lasting; or (what comes to much the same thing) that the only capital that is used is circulating capital. And suppose that production has a regular cycle (such as the annual cycle of agriculture) so that the periods of utilization of the various capital goods fit together. Such an economy has a natural, largely self-contained, single period. When economists were dealing with a world in which production on this pattern was of dominating importance, they had a standing invitation to the use (even in their theory of economic progress) of static method.

As we shall see in the next chapter, it is their use of a model of this kind which goes a long way to explain the special characteristics of the 'growth theories' of Adam Smith and Ricardo; but even with them it cannot be the whole story. And when we pass to consider the use of static method by later economists, it gives us little help. Even today, when the properly dynamic methods have become more or less familiar, there are economists who allow

---

[1] A model that fits the above description rather exactly is the theory of capital of Walras.

themselves to slip back into the use of what is clearly our static method. It cannot be suggested that this has anything to do with the use of a circulating capital model. An 'agricultural' model of this kind is certainly not one that a modern economist would care to put as the centre-piece of a dynamic theory.

6. There must be something else. I will try to suggest what I think it is.

Dynamic theory is inherently difficult; we can never hope to grasp with our analysis all aspects of a dynamic process. In order to bring out the important things (what we think to be the important things) we must simplify. Now there is one kind of simplification which is particularly tempting, so tempting that it is almost impossible not to use it (as we ourselves shall find ourselves using it) at some stage in the process of working out our ideas. Though one may start with the intention of removing it later, it carries one away, and one never gets round to doing so. (Or, if one is working in aggregates, with a 'macro' model, one may make it without realizing that one is doing so.) This is the simplification of assuming that there is just one capital good in the economy; that capital has been made, by some device, *homogeneous*.

If the single capital good is a circulating capital good, the period of its circulation is conveniently taken as the unit period; we then have a single period which has automatically become self-contained, and the way is clear for the application of static method. This leads straight to the theories of Smith and Ricardo. As we shall see in the next chapter, nothing more is needed to lead one their way.

If the single capital good is a fixed capital good (a 'machine') as a modern economist would be likely to make it, the way is not so clear; it needs, at the least, a bit of clearing. For something must then be done about old, as well as about new, machines. New machines may be treated as homogeneous with one another, but old machines can hardly be treated as homogeneous with them—straight off. Yet even this is a difficulty which one can avoid, or can make a show of avoiding. We have in any case to introduce some rule according to which the ageing of a machine affects its productivity. If we work with a rule that makes this effect a pure effect of time, it is only a step to say that a machine, manufactured *n* periods ago, is to be taken as equivalent to some fraction (depending on *n*) of a new machine. The old machine, as well as the new, are thus reduced to definite quantities of the same 'capital substance'. Homogeneity has been reintroduced, and the way has been cleared for the use of static method.

I am not going to say that this is wrong. Neither the classical (circulating capital) nor the neo-classical (fixed capital) version is wrong if it is regarded as no more than a device for preliminary exploration. So regarded, the device is a useful device, which has positive achievements to its credit. It was, however, a disaster that economists remained for so long in the case that this preliminary step was their only capital theory. For when a model of this kind (of either of these kinds) is directly applied to real problems, the result is likely to be most misleading. The 'capital substance', which has a definite meaning *in the model* (so many bushels of corn, so many machines), becomes in application a metaphysical entity. Like other metaphysical entities, it is a boat that is loose from its moorings. It is the big thing that was wrong with classical theory.

If there is just one homogeneous 'capital', there is nothing to do with our savings but to invest them in this 'capital'; there can be no problem of malinvestment—or of saving going to waste. The static method, misapplied, lies at the root of what was wrong in 'classical' economics—to use that term, for once, in Keynes's inclusive sense. The point is already clear, as we shall see, in Adam Smith.

IV

PRIMITIVE 'GROWTH MODELS'—
ADAM SMITH AND RICARDO

1. THE text to which I now desire to direct the reader's attention is the third chapter of the second book of the *Wealth of Nations*— the famous chapter entitled 'Of the Accumulation of Capital, or of Productive and Unproductive Labour'. There can, I think, be little doubt that Smith intended this chapter to be regarded as the centre-piece of his whole work. Book I and the earlier chapters of Book II lead up to it; the rest of the work consists, in large part, of applications of it. And the principles that are laid down in this chapter—'Parsimony, and not industry, is the immediate cause of the increase of capital',[1] 'every prodigal a public enemy and every frugal man a public benefactor'[2]—have been distinguishing marks of 'classical' doctrine, from his day, almost (if not quite) to ours.

Apart from its crystallization in such easy-to-be-remembered epigrams, it is indeed not so easy to make out just what it is that Smith is saying. There are two difficulties which beset the modern reader. One is the fact that distinction between branches of economics, or kinds of economic argument, was still in its infancy. Though (as I shall show) he is in fact working with a much simplified pure theoretical model, he writes as if there was no gap between this and almost bare description. Something which is almost algebra in one sentence passes into sage remarks about the populations of Rouen and Bordeaux in the next. For the purpose of the present discussion I shall discard these realistic remarks, and look solely at the pure model.

Secondly, the pure model is consistently carried through on the assumption that the only form of capital (or the only form that matters) is circulating capital. This assumption is nowadays so unfamiliar (at least to those who have been brought up in the Anglo-American tradition of economics) that the sectorization— for that is what it is—which Smith bases upon it looks quite esoteric.

---

[1] *Wealth of Nations*, Cannan edition, p. 320.   [2] Ibid., p. 323.

He is, however, being perfectly logical; he is in fact doing the
same thing with his schema as we are accustomed to do with ours.

We concentrate attention upon fixed capital. Thus we define
gross investment as being equal to net investment (the increment
of the whole capital stock) *plus* replacement of the using up of old
fixed capital. There is no fixed capital in Smith's (formal) model;
but he does have something that corresponds to gross investment.
This 'gross investment' is (it has to be) net investment plus replacement of the using up of circulating capital. The labour which is
employed in this 'gross investment' he calls 'productive labour'.

Thus it is productive labour that plays the same part in his
system as gross investment does in ours. It is unproductive labour
which corresponds to our consumption sector (though it has, of
course, a much narrower coverage).

2. The single period is the agricultural year. The initial capital
stock is last year's harvest, a certain quantity of 'corn'. The 'productive' sector (in Smith's sense) transforms that corn into more
corn. It does so (he would doubtless have admitted) in two ways:
by natural reproduction (the use of corn for seed), and by employing labour in cultivation. But it is not in fact of much importance
to distinguish between these uses. For we can simply add the corn
which the labourer sows to that which he consumes; the total is
the amount of corn that is used up in employing him. He is
himself (in terms of the model) simply a part of the process by
which the harvest of one year is transformed into that of the next.
So that the whole of the corn that the labourer absorbs may just
as well be reckoned as his *wage*.

If the wage (in this sense) is given, the number of labourers who
can be employed will be determined by the size of the capital
stock—which is therefore, in this model, a wage fund. If they were
all employed in growing corn, the whole economy would be
reduced to its productive sector, and that sector would reduce to
an apparatus for making corn out of corn. Consider the working
of the economy in period (year) t. Let X_{t-1} be last year's output of
corn; let w be the given wage (measured in terms of corn); the
number of labourers employed will then equal X_{t-1}/w. If p is
labour productivity (the amount of corn produced by one labourer),
this year's output will be pX_{t-1}/w; so that

$$X_t = (p/w)X_{t-1}.$$

k = wage fund

The growth rate of the economy (measured in terms of this *gross* output) accordingly equals $(p/w)-1$.

This is what happens when the whole of the corn output is used as a (direct or indirect) input into corn production; when nothing escapes outside. But that is no more than a limiting case. Ordinarily there will be a 'leak'. Some part of the corn output will be used for paying wages to non-corn producers ('unproductive labourers'); some may even be consumed directly by non-labourers.[1] The capital that is used in corn production in year t (K_t) will then not be the whole of the previous year's production, but only a part of it. Write $K_t = kX_{t-1}$ (where $k < 1$). The number of labourers employed in corn production will now be K_t/w.

So $X_t = (p/w)K_t = k(p/w)X_{t-1}.$

The growth rate of the economy is now no more than $k(p/w)-1$ so that the growth of the economy is slowed down by its unproductive consumption.

3. There can, I think, be no doubt that this is the model that was in Smith's mind. At the time when he wrote agriculture was still (in all countries) far and away the most important of activities; to fit the case of agriculture naturally seemed to be the prime necessity. I have thought it worth while to write it out algebraically, in order to show how very close it is to the models that have been advanced by contemporary growth theorists; it almost goes into their form.[2] It is, nevertheless, a quite special model; it is quite difficult to generalize it; if it is generalized, without due circumspection, the results can be quite dangerous.

Its peculiarities are precisely those to which attention was drawn in the last chapter. Its method is static; static method has been made to seem applicable, by the two simplifications which we there identified—the confinement to circulating capital, and the single capital good. By means of these simplifications the single period (the year) has been made to be self-contained. How self-contained it is has not been generally noticed; there has in consequence been misapprehension of what Smith was saying.

[1] Adam Smith and his followers did not always draw attention to this possibility. But it makes better sense of the story to put it in, and the model can absorb it without any inconvenience.

[2] As we shall see in Chapter XVIII, it has a particularly close association with the Von Neumann 'equilibrium'.

It is very natural (with Cassel, and Harrod and Domar, in our minds) to suppose that the Smith model is a model of a regularly progressive economy—with p, w, and k constant from year to year: whence (as follows from the above) the growth rate will be constant. One may indeed doubt (when the point is put) whether anything so abstract as this is at all consistent with the general tenor of Smith's thinking; but it is of more importance to notice that he was not obliged to any such interpretation. For the crucial proportions (p, w, and k) relate only to the events of the year (the single period); there is no reason why they should not vary from one year to another. If they are different next year, the growth rate next year will be different; expansion will accelerate, or slow up. And why not? It is what seems to happen (I am sure Smith would say) in most 'opulent countries'.[1]

One of the troubles that we create for ourselves if we insist on interpretation as a regularly progressive economy relates to the real wage (w). If p, and k, and w are all of them constant from year to year, the employment of labour must continually expand; but where is the additional labour to come from? Smith was writing before Malthus; though he often writes in such a way as to lead one to attribute to him some foretaste of a Malthusian theory, it is dangerous to press that interpretation too far. It was, however, usual among eighteenth-century writers to assume the existence of a reserve of labour which could be called into employment (not merely into productive employment, in the technical sense) if there was a demand for its services; probably we should not think of this labour as wholly unemployed, but as under-employed, seasonally unemployed, and so on.[2] In such terms the assumption was no doubt quite realistic. But the amount of labour that would be available in this way would always be limited. There are plenty of passages in which Smith makes it clear that accumulation of capital (expansion of the wage fund) is taken to increase the real wage of labour; presumably because it creates a labour shortage.[3] It

[1] It follows that Smith's model, though it looks like a growth model, is not a growth model in the modern sense. It does not exhibit a sequence. The same is true, we shall find, of Ricardo.

[2] 'Our ancestors were idle for want of a sufficient encouragement to industry. It is better, says the proverb, to play for nothing than to work for nothing' (Cannan edition, p. 318).

[3] 'It is not the actual greatness of national wealth, but its continual increase, which occasions a rise in the wages of labour' (ibid., p. 71).

follows from the model that this rise in wages will diminish the rate of growth (making it, that is, less than it would have been if w had remained unchanged). I do not think that Smith would, or could, have rejected this conclusion; if he does not stress it, there is a clear reason for that. This is his conviction that it is not only w that would rise, if the force of the expansion were strong enough, but also p; the productivity of labour would increase in the course of expansion, since the division of labour would call forth increasing returns.

4. It may well appear, from what has been said so far, as if the crucial assumption, which enabled Smith to keep his single period self-contained, was the confinement to circulating capital; that the other assumption, of capital homogeneity, had nothing to do with it. On the surface, of course, Smith is not regarding capital as homogeneous; he has plenty to say about different uses of capital; he does not, when he is being realistic, think of agriculture as the only capital-using industry. I would still maintain that in his pure theory homogeneity is present; and that the peculiarity of his model cannot be fully understood unless we allow for that aspect too.

In a model with more than one kind of capital good, even though all of them are circulating capital (with—to make things easy—the same period of circulation), something has to be decided about the form in which the savings of the current period (and the reinvestment of the current period) are to be embodied. Suppose that there are two goods, which play the same part as the corn of the previous model; call them corn and chickens. There are, we may suppose, various ways (including feeding to labour) in which corn may be converted into corn, chickens into chickens, corn into chickens, and even (by feeding to labour) chickens into corn. The initial stock includes both articles, in a proportion determined by past decisions. The final stock also consists of both articles, in a proportion determined by the decisions of this period. But what governs those decisions? All that Smith could have done, if the point had been put to him, would have been to point to the condition that the rate of profit should be the same in each activity; but this, though it may be accepted as an equilibrium condition, does not solve the problem. (I do not suppose that Smith would have thought that it did; for he was well aware that he was using profit-equalization to determine *prices*.) The distribution of the final capital stock between 'corn' and 'chickens' would still remain to be explained.

There is of course no difficulty if we are assuming a regularly progressive economy. The initial proportion is then taken to be adjusted to the needs of the economy, and the final proportion must be the same as the initial proportion. But if data are changing from period to period (and I have insisted that the natural way to take the Smith model would require them to be changeable—that possibility is included), then the choice of final proportions must depend, even in a circulating capital model, upon the conditions that are *expected* to rule in future periods, or at least in the next period. Expectations which may be wrong, or right! The big simplification which results from the assumption of homogeneous capital is that these expectations can be left out.[1]

If one is just making a first raid into (admittedly) difficult territory, such a simplification (like many other simplifications) is readily justified; but as a matter of history this particular simplification was disastrous. For by overlooking the problem of the distribution of (gross) investment, it was easy to jump to the conclusion that saving is necessarily invested. The 'frugal man' must put his savings into 'corn'; for, in the model, there is nowhere else to put them.

It is generally recognized (Keynes himself recognized)[2] that in the age of Adam Smith there was an 'anti-Keynesian Revolution'; that it was at this period that the 'classical' doctrine of savings and investment (using 'classical' in Keynes's sense) took shape. But it does not seem to be so generally appreciated that the main agent of the 'Revolution' was Adam Smith himself. More, I think, would have been made of his responsibility if it had not

---

[1] There is indeed a sense in which even the model with homogeneous capital does not quite dispense with expectations, so that its single period may not be quite so self-contained as I have represented it to be. Saving, it may well be maintained, is inherently oriented towards the future; some view must be taken of future wants and future resources in order that there should be an incentive to save. There are undoubtedly certain purposes (primarily, if not entirely, of Welfare Economics) for which we need to make much of this point (as will be shown in Chapter XXI below). But I do not think that in Positive Economics it has ever been found to be very impressive. 'Frugality' (Smith), 'abstinence' (Senior), 'lacking' (Robertson); it is the negative aspect on which economists have insisted, and that is wholly contained with the single period.

[2] See his writings on Mercantilism.

seemed to be out of character; Smith was not at all a dogmatically minded man, and that he should be the source of such dogmatism! How is it to be explained? It is not simply the reaction against Mercantilism; Hume was equally against Mercantilism, but Hume's Essay on Money is not 'anti-Keynesian' in the way that Smith is. Nor can it be explained (or at least it cannot be sufficiently explained) by the 'monetary dichotomy', the habit of thinking in real terms and dealing with money separately; that went with it, but that is itself a part of the phenomenon that requires explanation. I believe that it is to be explained—that the whole change is to be explained—if we attribute it to the power of a model:[1] of a light that illumined much, but left things outside its beam in such darkness that their very existence was forgotten.

The 'dichotomy' was a *result* of the static character of the model. It was because the model paid no attention to plans and expectations that it neglected uncertainty and liquidity; so that the bridge between real theory and monetary theory, of the possibility of which Hume had had some inkling, remained unbuilt. The only monetary theory which could match the static real theory was one which concentrated upon the more mechanical aspects of the monetary system; this is just what the 'classical' Quantity Theory was. The responsibility for all this goes back to Adam Smith; it is the reverse side of his great achievement.

5. I turn to Ricardo. Ricardo was much more explicitly a model-builder than Smith; it follows that the interpretation of what he had to say is a less controversial matter. (It may be a difficult matter, but when we have got there we are sure we are home!) Ricardo is difficult, because his style in models is not ours; we have to translate him into our language. But now that Mr. Sraffa has found the key,[2] the translation is just like any other translation.

I shall only do a small bit of that translation here, a part which has a close connexion with what I have been saying about Smith. One must suppose that the young Ricardo, when he studied the *Wealth of Nations*, would have wanted to formalize it, just as we have been formalizing it (though his manner of doing so would

---

[1] 'An apparatus of the mind, a technique of thinking'—but it is just too hackneyed to quote.

[2] See his Introduction to the *Principles*, Ricardo, *Works* (ed. Sraffa), vol. i, especially pp. xxxi–xxxvii.

have been very different). There would, that is, have been a stage in which Ricardo was working on Smith like Marshall working on Mill (turning him into 'differential equations'). If these exercises had survived we should have seen directly how Ricardo interpreted the Smith model; a piece of evidence that would certainly have had to be considered in relation to the interpretation of Smith which has here been given. Of course they have not survived; but something which is next door to them has. Supposing that Ricardo had started by interpreting Smith in something which would correspond with our way: what is the next thing which one would see him doing? Precisely what we do find him doing: writing the *Essay on the Influence of a Low Price of Corn on the Profits of Stock*, which Mr. Sraffa has taught us to call, for greater convenience, the *Essay on Profits*.

I shall not be concerned with the relation between the *Essay on Profits* and the first chapter ('On Value') of the *Principles*; for that matter reference must be made to Mr. Sraffa himself. Nor shall I be much concerned with the topical aspects of the *Essay*. Mr. Sraffa conjectures (and the conjecture seems very plausible) that the *Essay*, as we have it, is a somewhat hasty rewriting of an earlier draft, prompted by the publication of the Malthus pamphlets which are mentioned on its title-page; references to Malthus, which would have been more digestible if they had appeared as footnotes, are worked into the text and confuse the argument. When these are cut away, the remainder is found to centre upon one of the most formidable of Ricardo's arithmetical tables; it is that table, and its implications, which chiefly concerns us here. The modern reader is accustomed, at the corresponding stage of an argument, to look for help to a diagram, or to a piece of algebra, rather than to a table of arithmetic. It is in fact not difficult to express what Ricardo was saying in terms of a diagram; when we do so, its connexion with what we have been taking to be the Smith model is rather striking.

Since Ricardo's particular topic was the Corn Laws,[1] he was obliged to distinguish the agricultural sector from the rest of the economy; he could not take that sector to be representative of the

---

[1] It may be mentioned, in passing, that from this point of view the exact date of publication (February 1815) is rather interesting. Neither Ricardo nor Malthus knew that next month Napoleon was going to escape from Elba; so they were thinking about the 'Economic Consequences of the (already established) Peace'. After June (after Waterloo) their discussion was again topical.

whole, as Smith (I have been maintaining) would appear to have done. But his model of the *agricultural sector* is similar to Smith's. It is an apparatus for converting corn into corn, by feeding to labour, or otherwise. The only essential difference is that land is now taken to be a scarce factor (experience of the Napoleonic blockade having emphasized the fact that it was a scarce factor in

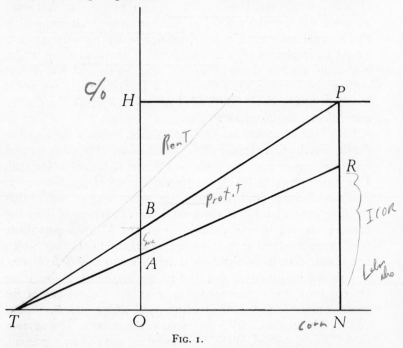

FIG. I.

Ricardo's England). What Ricardo was showing was how shortage of land would set a limit upon the expansion of agriculture, and therefore, by implication (but he never quite settled how far it was a sound implication), upon that of the economy generally.

As we have seen, it is consistent with the Smith theory that shortage of labour should set a restraint upon expansion; but the rise in real wages[1] through which this would occur is not a thing which to 'friends of humanity' (as Ricardo would say) would be distressing. It is otherwise in the case of rent; for with land defined as 'original and indestructible', the landlord is a parasite, at least economically. But I must turn to my diagram (Fig. I).

[1] In the modern sense; one had better be careful when talking about Ricardo.

6. Output (gross output) of corn is measured on the horizontal axis. On the vertical I measure the capital–gross output ratio. (Since both capital and output are measured in terms of corn, this, beyond any question, is a pure number.) The length OH is unity; so that the rectangle $OHPN$ represents the same quantity of corn, considered as capital (or input) as is measured by the length ON (when it is considered as output). Corresponding to the output ON, RN is the *marginal* capital–(gross) output ratio; that is to say, it is the quantity of corn that has to be used as input in order to produce an additional unit of corn output, when an output ON is already to be produced. The amount of land being fixed, diminishing returns can be expressed by making RN an increasing function of ON; thus we get the marginal 'curve' AR. As will be seen by checking through Ricardo's arithmetic, he takes this 'curve' to be a straight line—for no sufficient reason (this is of course a trick that is very liable to happen with arithmetical examples). I will follow him here in taking it to be a straight line.

At the margin, one unit of output ($PN = OH =$ one) requires RN of capital to produce it. Thus PR is the fraction of the marginal unit of output which is left as profit. The rate of profit on capital (at the margin) is thus equal to PR/RN. Now (says Ricardo) competition will keep the same rate of profit on capital being earned throughout the whole system; this will apply to inter-marginal units in agriculture, as one case of its general application. We may show this if we produce RA backwards to meet the horizontal axis at T; and then join TP, cutting the vertical axis at B. For BA/AO is then equal to PR/RN; the same rate of profit is shown to be earned all along the 'curve'. Total profit is then represented by the trapezium $BARP$. If we now take the rectangle $OHPN$ to represent total output (as is clearly permissible), we at once see it falling into three parts: (1) $OARN$, which is replacement of capital, (2) $BARP$, which is profit, and (3) HBP, which is rent.

When the model is put into this form it looks easy to 'work' it. If the expansion of employment makes it necessary to expand agricultural output, population will 'press upon the means of subsistence'. N will therefore move to the right. But the AR curve is unaffected, T is therefore unaffected; the line TP must therefore swing downwards, for P must move to the right along the horizontal HP. The rate of profit must therefore fall, while rent rises.

Improvements in agriculture, diminishing the capital–output

ratio, will cause the *AR* 'curve' to shift downwards, thus raising the rate of profit.[1] Importation from abroad, diminishing the output that has to be raised from domestic agriculture, will raise the rate of profit, since it will enable the *TP* line to swing to the left. And so on. But it is not for the sake of these deductions (important as they were for Ricardo and his followers) that I have introduced at this point a discussion of Ricardo's model.[2]

7. The things that are interesting about it, from our present point of view, are quite different. So far as the agricultural sector is concerned, Ricardo's analysis is closely in line with Smith's, excepting for the explicit introduction of diminishing returns (land scarcity). It can be written out in exactly the same terms as we have formerly used for Smith, except that p (the productivity of labour) is made to depend upon output; apart from that, everything that was said about Smith will still apply. We have the same confinement to circulating capital, and the same capital homogeneity; so the single period remains self-contained, and the static method can be used for the analysis of a dynamic process. It will be noticed that the Ricardian model is quite clearly *not* one of a regularly progressive economy; in the Ricardian model the economy is grinding to a halt. Still, in view of the self-contained-ness, the same method can be used, as long as we are looking only at the agricultural sector.

Where the trouble comes, as Ricardo himself came abundantly to realize, is outside the agricultural sector. The weak point in the *Essay on Profits* is the proposition, so casually slipped in, that competition will maintain the same rate of profit throughout the economy, in agricultural and non-agricultural sectors alike. (The equalization would of course be qualified by reservations about 'net advantages' of particular investments, qualifications which had been set out by Smith, and which Ricardo took over.) But what—outside agriculture—did one really mean by the *rate of profit*? Could the rest of the economy be fitted into the scheme of single-period self-containedness, in which that question had an evident answer?

[1] There is of course no reason (as is at once apparent when the matter is looked at diagrammatically) why the curve should shift downwards *uniformly*. (See Cannan, *Theories of Production and Distribution*, pp. 323 ff.)

[2] We shall find ourselves coming back to it, or to something like it, in quite a different connexion, in Chapter XXII.

In the more industrialized economy of 1815 it was no longer tolerable, even as an approximation, to assume that all capital was circulating capital; nor that, even in a metaphysical sense, all capital was 'corn'. The self-containedness of the single period was nevertheless so powerful an instrument, and so much depended upon it, that herculean efforts had to be made to retain it. What Ricardo did, in his efforts to retain it, can now be understood (thanks to Mr. Sraffa) by readers of the *Principles*. Homogeneity was to be retained by reducing capital to its labour content (the *labour theory of value*); fixed capital was to be reduced to circulating by consideration of periods of production (in the manner that was to be worked out more fully, decades later, by Jevons and Böhm-Bawerk). But all the power of these devices (and they had considerable power) could not save the self-containedness. It is apparent from Ricardo's own work that even in his hands the static method is already confining itself to its proper place—to the comparison of static equilibria, even of stationary states; it cannot extend to the analysis of a dynamic process. In the light of the subsequent developments there is nothing surprising about that.

For consider, in the light of this interpretation of Ricardo, what happened to capital theory in the rest of the nineteenth century. There is no need to consider it in detail, for it does not have much to do with the matters which concern us in this book. There is just one thing that must be said. The firm point, there as elsewhere, was the static method, continually refined upon, and more carefully applied. What could be done with the static method was done; but when it came to capital theory (self-containedness being no longer hoped for) all that could be done was the analysis of a stationary state, in which data do not change, and in which (therefore) there is no accumulation of capital.

This was so in fact, ever since Ricardo. The more precise capital theory became, the more static it became; the study of equilibrium conditions only resulted in the study of stationary conditions. But it was many years before anyone saw what was happening. Marshall saw it:

A theoretically perfect long period . . . will be found to involve the supposition of a stationary state of industry, in which the requirements of a future age can be anticipated an indefinite time beforehand. Some such assumption is indeed unconsciously implied in many popular renderings of Ricardo's theory of value, if not in his own versions of it;

and it is to this cause more than to any other that we must attribute that simplicity and sharpness of outline, from which the economic doctrines in fashion in the first half of this century derived some of their seductive charm, as well as most of whatever tendency they may have to lead to false practical conclusions.[1]

Wicksell saw it; it is marked in the very structure of his book. After concluding his Part II (in the first volume of his *Lectures*) in which he has set out his capital theory (his *stationary* capital theory), he passes to a third part (on accumulation) which is to be more 'dynamic'. But the third part is a mere fragment; though Wicksell saw the need for a more dynamic method, he did not go on to develop it himself. His successors did; but before we proceed to consider their contribution, we must examine how Marshall reacted to what he had seen.

---

[1] Marshall, *Principles*, 8th (or Variorum) edition, p. 379, note 1. It is interesting to find, from Mr. Guillebaud's collation, that the second sentence of the above quotation read originally:

'Some such assumption is really contained in many popular renderings of Ricardo's doctrines, which give them a sharpness of outline that he had never intended.'

The change was made in the second edition (1891). On reflection, it will be noticed, Marshall did not feel that he could throw the whole of the responsibility on to Ricardo's followers. And surely, in these second thoughts, Marshall was right.

V

THE METHOD OF MARSHALL

1. MARSHALL, it has just been shown, perceived the main issue with perfect clarity. He knew that static method (hitherto the only method of economic theory) led, when carried right through, to the stationary state, and no further. (The possible extension to a regularly progressive economy did indeed occur to him,[1] but he did not follow it up.) The theory of a stationary state seemed to him to be of little interest; if it was worth while to elaborate it at all, that was chiefly in order that it should not be mistaken for something else. What then was to be done?

There was, he thought, no alternative to statics. If a complete static theory led nowhere, we must make do with an incomplete static theory. We must lock up our difficulties in 'the pound of *ceteris paribus*'.

That, in short, is the method of Marshall. There is no question that it is a powerful method; for many problems of economics, it is as good a method as we are likely to get. It is not at all a dynamic method; it is a resuscitation of statics. Adam Smith had found one way of applying static method to dynamic problems; Ricardo had outgrown the Smith method, but had failed to find another. Marshall did find another; but again it was a special method which would only work in special cases (by Marshall's time, it is true, they were much more important cases). It would only work so long as the things that had been put into the 'pound' would stay there.

2. It may be observed that this same method was used by Marshall in at least two different ways.

The first was to fix attention (at least by preference) not upon the whole economy, but on a sector (it had better be a rather small sector) of it: the partial equilibrium of the single 'industry'. In this, as in many other instances (it seems plausible to maintain) he got a hint from Ricardo. So long as Ricardo had stuck to his

[1] *Principles*, 8th edition, p. 368.

agricultural sector, his static method had served him well; it was
when he tried to go beyond it that he got into trouble. Marshall
would adopt the same device. Well aware that full static equilibrium
meant stationariness, and believing that complete stationariness
meant sterility, he would seek a way out by concentrating upon the
'industry'. It would not be so uninteresting to inquire into the
conditions which would keep the single industry in full equilibrium.
It would not then be necessary to postulate a complete cessation
of change; it would be enough if the technique of the industry
was not (autonomously) changing, if the terms on which the factors
of production could be acquired were not changing, and if the
demand curve for the product of the industry were to remain fixed.
These, in particular cases, would not be such unrealistic assumptions; besides, as Marshall never tired of emphasizing, the theory
made no claim to be a *precise* theory; it would be quite sufficient
if the assumptions just listed were very approximately true.

That is one way in which Marshall applied his method; the
other is the device (as I think it is proper to call it) of the *short* and
of the *long period*. These, it will perhaps be as well to re-emphasize,
have nothing to do with the sense of 'period' as it appears in
truly dynamic economics (or as we have used it in our discussion
of Smith). They are technical terms of Marshallian economics;
when they are used by a modern economist one should look for
a Marshallian reference. The 'long-period equilibrium' of the
industry is the full equilibrium of the industry, with nothing
more 'impounded' than the things that were listed in the previous
paragraph. In the 'short period' impounding has been taken one
stage further.

The supply of specialized skill and ability, of suitable machinery and
other material capital, and of the appropriate organization has not time
to be fully adapted to demand; but the producers have to adjust their
supply to the demand as best they can with the appliances already at their
disposal.[1]

It will be important to look closely at this concept and to appreciate,
as exactly as we can, the use (as we shall see, the very peculiar
use) that Marshall made of it.

3. There is of course no question that (when 'period' is taken in its
natural, non-technical, sense) there is always more flexibility in

---

[1] Marshall, p. 376.

production when a long period is allowed for adjustment. If we take our stand at a particular historical date and look forward, the things that are to be produced in the following month have already been largely determined by past decisions; no change in demand can make much impression upon them. If we lengthen the 'short period' to three months, there is more flexibility. That is true; but it was much more than that that Marshall was saying.

The crucial assumption, which is the distinguishing mark of Marshall's method, is that the *industry* in the *short period* can be treated as if it were in static equilibrium. (Marshall, it should be noted, only made this assumption with respect to the partial equilibrium of the industry;[1] its extension, to the whole of a closed economy, does not come until Keynes, and when it does so it raises other questions.[2]) In the *short period*, then, the fixed equipment of the industry being given (it will be sufficient to confine ourselves to the industry), the model has become similar to the agricultural sector of Ricardo. The fixed capital has become like land, 'original' and 'indestructible' *within the period*. Within the period, it earns a rent, *quasi-rent* as Marshall called it.

It will be helpful to look at this procedure in the light of our previous discussion. Marshall, we may say, was treating his *short period* as a single period, in the manner of Smith or Ricardo, and invoking the constancy (or approximate constancy) of the fixed capital stock of the industry, as a justification for treating the single period as self-contained. As he would doubtless have admitted, this could give him no means by which he could string his single periods together, so as to combine them into a dynamic process. In a dynamic economy there will be changes in the capital stock in any time period, however 'short'; these changes are an essential part of the linkage that ties one single period to another. Marshall's method just leaves them out.

Even apart from that, is he justified in taking his *short period* to be self-contained? It is implied by the self-containedness (and this agrees with Marshall's usage) that the output of the industry, in the *short period*, is solely determined by (1) the state of demand in that period, (2) the fixed capital stock, (3) the terms in which inputs, such as those of labour and of materials, can be acquired

[1] I dare say that there are passages where he allowed himself to slip into a wider application; but I am sure that the above statement is broadly true.
[2] See Chapter VII, below.

within the period. Now it is not to be denied that these things will often be the important things; whenever they are the important things, the *short-period equilibrium* will be a fair approximation to a complete analysis; and that is all that Marshall (no doubt) would have claimed it to be. There is, however, no reason in general why they should be the only important things; whenever they are not, the inadequacy of the Marshall method will be at once apparent.

One of the things which Marshall left out (which he had to leave out) was what Keynes was later to call *user cost*. If the rate of usage of the fixed capital has any effect (in either direction) upon the measures which will have to be taken for its future replacement, there is an element in cost of production which will not fit into the static scheme. For the valuation of this usage depends on what is to happen—what is expected to happen—outside the *short period*. It cannot be considered at all without introducing into the model something that is more *dynamic*.

Another is stocks (or inventories). It cannot be assumed that the values set, within the short period, upon materials absorbed are determined entirely within the period. That would only be so in an economy where there was no carry-over, so that everything that was absorbed within the period was produced within the period. This is almost nonsense, in view of the time taken in production (of which Marshall made so much). The values that are set upon materials, so long as they are durable enough to be stockable, must depend upon expectations.

The common element in these two omissions may be put in a more general way. Whenever there is a possibility of *substitution over time* (as I called it in *Value and Capital*[1]) the self-containedness of the *short period* will break down.

4. Nothing has so far been said, in this discussion of Marshall's *short period*, about the particular aspect of his analysis which has figured, more than any other, in later controversy: the question of the market form (competitive or monopolistic, more or less competitive or monopolistic) that is being assumed. I do not think that it has been necessary to say anything about that up to now; the status of the short-period equilibrium, from the points of view so far discussed, will be the same whatever is the market form. There is, however, another aspect from which a particular

[1] p. 208.

question form turns out to be of major importance; at the point we have now reached, where we are at the threshold of more genuinely dynamic theory, we must give it the most serious attention.

How equilibrium in shortperiod

What was Marshall's justification for treating his short-period model, not merely as being self-contained, but also as being in equilibrium? How far, that is, can we expect that the performance of an industry (for we had better keep to an *industry*), over a month (say) of time, will be reasonably well represented by its short-period equilibrium? Even if substitution over time is neglected, so that it is accepted that *current* demands (and so on) are the only things that determine what firms will want to produce, why should we assume that what they want to produce is the same as what they sell? Equality between demand and supply, in the sense of amount bought and amount sold, is an identity, which has nothing to do with the equilibrium assumption. Equality between amount sold and the amount which, in the given circumstances, sellers will want to sell is quite a different matter. Sense can be made of it over a long period; but when it is applied to a short period, it looks a very dubious assumption indeed.

Nevertheless, Marshall made it; and I am not suggesting that he did not know what he was doing.[1] There is a way in which his procedure can be justified, for his own purposes; but the justification does not extend to the use which has been made of his procedure by later economists.[2] There is a distinction which it is most important to make.

In order to see how Marshall himself would have justified his procedure, we must turn to a part of his argument which has so far been left out. This is the theory of price determination in the 'ultra-short period': market equilibrium when the quantity to be sold is itself a part of the data, having been determined by decisions that, when the market opens, are already in the past. This is expressed, in Marshall's manner, in the form of an analysis of a 'corn market in a country town'. (It is rather a curious corn market, in that the corn is rather oddly assumed to be non-storable; for this reason it became common, in later Cambridge tradition, to

---

[1] He might, admittedly, have explained himself more fully; he would have spared his successors a lot of worry if he had done so.

[2] For instance by Keynes in the *Treatise on Money*. I believe that it was just at this point that the fundamental equation of the *Treatise* went wrong.

replace 'corn' by 'fish'.) Buyers and sellers are supposed to come to the market without knowledge of the equilibrium price—the price that will equate supply to demand. Transactions may thus take place, initially, at arbitrary prices. But it is Marshall's contention that the final price, at which the last transactions will take place, will be approximately the same as the equilibrium price. Even though there are initial sales at 'false' prices, the final price will be much the same as that which, if it had been fixed at the start, would in fact have proved to be capable of being carried through.

It is by benefit of this principle that Marshall's 'corn market' is enabled to dispense with artificial arrangements, like Edgeworth's 'recontract' or the 'crying of prices' of Walras. The purpose of these was to find a way by which early bargains could be undone if the prices at which they were made did not correspond with the equilibrium price. Marshall maintains that, even if they cannot be undone, it does not matter. For the effect of a bargain at a 'false' price is just to redistribute purchasing power from buyer to seller, or from seller to buyer, according as the 'false' price is too high or too low. The effect of that redistribution is an income effect; all that matters (from the point of view of price determination) is the shift which it produces in the demand curve for the 'corn'. If expenditure on 'corn' is only a small part of total expenditure, that shift is unlikely to be considerable. Therefore, in this 'ultra-short' period, the static determination of the price by equilibrium of demand and supply will give a fair approximation to what is likely to happen in practice.

5. It is unnecessary to go into any greater detail about the 'corn market';[1] I have not introduced it here for its own sake but for what follows on from it. Something very similar must have been supposed by Marshall to hold for the *short period* proper. (There can really be no doubt about that; otherwise why should he have bothered about the 'corn market'?) It is not output only, *it is also price*, which is supposed to be determined by equilibrium of demand and supply, in the short period.

This is where the question of what is implied about market form becomes important. The distinction which I have in mind is not

---

[1] I have myself discussed it in more detail elsewhere. See the Note to chapter ix of *Value and Capital* (pp. 127–9).

quite the same as the usual distinction between perfect and imperfect (or monopolistic) competition; but it is nearly the same— the one distinction very often corresponds to the other. There has been much discussion[1] about the precise character of the competition that is assumed by Marshall. It is now accepted that his model is not a strict perfect competition model, like that of Walras. His firms experience internal as well as external economies; they hold back for fear of 'spoiling the market'. That is true, but it is also true that in the particular respect that concerns us here Marshall is on the perfect competition side of the fence. His firms are not 'price-makers', as we have learned to think firms to be when they operate in an imperfect market. Prices are not set by firms and then altered if they turn out to be 'wrong'. They are more flexible than that; so they can be *determined* by demand and supply, by the bargaining of the market.

I suggest that this aspect of Marshall's model is nothing else but a straightforward reflection of actual conditions in England in the late nineteenth century: at the time, that is to say, when Marshall was writing. The standardized and branded goods, which are the typical consumers' goods of present-day economic organization, had not then appeared, though they were perhaps on the point of appearing.[2] The modern economist takes for granted that it is the manufacturer who fixes the price that the consumer is to pay; but in those days even manufactured goods usually passed along a chain of wholesalers and retailers, each of whom was likely to have some independent price-making opportunity. Nowadays, when demand increases, it is the manufacturer who decides whether (or when) to raise his price; when demand falls off, whether (or when) to lower it. In Marshall's day it will quite usually have been the case that he had no such choice.

An increase in demand would not be allowed to remain unsatisfied or to run down stocks unduly. Price would rise, not because of any action by the manufacturer, nor indeed by the ultimate consumer (who, then as now, would normally be a passive party); the initiative would come from the wholesaler or shopkeeper, who would offer higher prices in order to get the goods which, even at

---

[1] Since the days of the 'Cost Controversy' (*Economic Journal*, 1926 and after).
[2] For a detailed description of the transition, in one particular case, see C. Wilson, *History of Unilever*, vol. ii, pp. 64 ff. (See also B. S. Yamey, 'Origins of Resale Price Maintenance', *Economic Journal*, 1952.) These, it will be noticed, were developments of the period between 1890 and 1914.

the higher price, he could re-sell at a profit. Similarly, when demand fell, it would be the wholesaler who would offer a lower price. The manufacturer would have to accept that price, if he could get no better, or else he must refuse the business for fear of 'spoiling the market' (as Marshall says).

This, I believe, is the kind of market form that Marshall was envisaging. It will be noticed that it does not much resemble the (Walrasian) model of *perfect competition*. It is consistent with a good deal of ignorance, not only on the part of the ultimate consumer but also on the part of the manufacturers, and even (but to a lesser degree) on the part of the intermediary traders themselves. Plenty of trading will then go on at 'false' prices. It will nevertheless be true that in the *short period* (substitution over time being neglected) price is determined, at least roughly, by 'equilibrium of demand and supply'. That is all that Marshall needs for the applicability of his particular sort of static method.

6. Marshall was indeed a great economist. If, in this chapter, attention has been mainly directed to some limitations of his analysis, I hope it has been done in a way which makes it clear how much he could do in the directions in which (naturally enough, at his date) he preferred to work. Our problems, however, are not his; we must not expect to be able to use his methods for purposes for which they were not designed.

One of the reasons why we need other methods (as we shall see, more specifically dynamic methods) is that we are now more interested in macro-economic problems, from which (for reasons that have been explained) Marshall had, on the whole, to turn aside. But there is also another reason: that the market forms in which we are especially interested are different from that which he took as typical. It will nevertheless prove to be useful to have unearthed this point about market forms; for we shall need to have it before us when we are considering Dynamic Theory proper. It is desirable that Dynamic Economics (or that branch of it which is a part of Pure Economics)[1] should be able to deal with a variety of market forms. Marshall's form is thus still worthy of study, though we should study it in a way which makes it possible to study other forms too.

----

[1] See above, p. 8.

Though the method of Marshall can be regarded, as I have (on the whole) regarded it here, as a last stage in the evolution of static method, it gets very near to dynamics. The Fixprice method, which I shall be discussing in Chapter VII and its successors, though its characteristic assumption is the abandonment of Marshall's kind of price flexibility, owes much, in many ways, to Marshall. But before I come to that, I shall consider a method that retains price flexibility, though the form in which it is commonly put is more Wicksellian than Marshallian. We shall find that it poses some essential questions in a way that is rather clear-cut.

VI

THE TEMPORARY EQUILIBRIUM
METHOD

1. THE first of the (properly) dynamic methods which I shall consider is that which was developed (very deliberately developed) by Erik Lindahl[1] in 1929–30. I take this first, not on grounds of temporal priority (for I do not suppose that there is any priority over the work of others, over Robertson, or over Keynes), but because the Lindahl presentation is so good at isolating the central issues. Some of Lindahl's ideas have already been used in this book (Chapter III, above); consideration of his method will join on very easily to what we have been saying.[2]

Lindahl was himself quite a bit of a methodologist; he was fond of reflecting on what he himself had been doing. He thus came to be perfectly conscious that it was a new dynamic method that he was devising. But that, of course, was after the event. The method would not have been devised because there was a methodologist's pigeon-hole for it; it was devised because there was a need for it. The particular place where the need was felt—in Sweden, as in contemporary England—was in monetary economics.

The phase in monetary thinking to which I am referring is (as should be evident by dates) antecedent to the World Depression. It was the collapse of the pre-1914 International Gold Standard, and the conviction (which gradually prevailed) that that old 'monetary constitution' could not be restored, which had made the whole character of the monetary system an open question, as it had not been before, at least since the days of Thornton and Ricardo. Money was being looked at in a new way; new questions were

---

[1] The substance of his *Penningspolitikens Medel* (to which I refer) appears in English as Part II of his Studies in the *Theory of Money and Capital*. My own direct knowledge of it is derived from this English version.

[2] I have one special difficulty in discussing Lindahl. I have myself been responsible (in Parts III and IV of *Value and Capital*) for a 'dynamic' theory which claimed to be based upon Lindahl's work. I then supposed that I was treading, quite closely, in Lindahl's footsteps; he himself held that we were further apart. As will be seen in what follows, I have become convinced, in the end, that he was right.

being asked, and (almost from the start) they were what we have called dynamic questions. The stability that was sought—the monetary stability, stability of one variable (e.g. the price level) when other related variables are changing—is itself a dynamic property. It slips through the fingers when we try to deal with it by static methods. It requires, in order that we should be able to treat it, some way of analysing a process.

2. Swedish economists, coming to monetary theory in the nineteen-twenties, had an advantage in beginning from Wicksell; for in the doctrine of 'Interest and Prices'[1] they had a key that would open many doors, and (for a while) it remained very nearly their private possession. Even afterwards, when Keynes[2] and Hayek[3] had made Wicksell world famous, it was an advantage to the Swedes that for them his work was not a novelty. They did not over-estimate it, as those to whom it was new were at first tempted to do. In strictness, all that Wicksell had done (in the monetary field as in others) was confined to the analysis of stationary equilibrium. Something like what he had found for that case must (fairly obviously) be true much more generally. But *exactly* what would be true in non-stationary conditions was a thing that Wicksell had left for his successors to discover.

In Wicksell's stationary state, relative prices remain constant over time; and there is a rate of interest (Wicksell's *natural rate*) which is determined as part of this system of relative prices. Being part of the 'real' price system, which is closed and complete, without mention of money, so long as the economy is stationary, the natural rate is strictly to be interpreted as a rate of exchange between 'wine' now and 'wine' a 'year' hence; or, since relative prices are unchanging, between any good now and the same good a 'year' hence. It is only when we impose the extra condition that *money prices* should be unchanging that it becomes necessary to equate this natural rate of interest to the market rate (which is a rate of exchange between money now and money a 'year' hence). Equality between market rate and natural rate then emerges as a condition of price stability.

That was what Wicksell taught; but how is it to be generalized

---

[1] And of the second volume of the *Lectures*.
[2] *Treatise on Money* (1930).   [3] *Prices and Production* (1931).

for an economy which is not stationary? In such an economy it will usually be true that relative prices will be varying over time, quite apart from any question of monetary disturbance. It is then impossible that there should be any rate of interest which will keep *all* money prices from changing. The most that could conceivably be stabilized would be an index number of prices, but there are many possible index numbers: does this mean that there is a different natural rate for each index number? Or should we say that, excepting in a stationary state, *the* natural rate of interest does not exist?

It is unnecessary even to list the further questions which arose along this line of thought (the problem of short and long rates of interest will serve as a sufficient example). For the main thing which concerns us here is that these questions could not usefully be considered at all until the Wicksell theory had been given a new look.

3. To make things easy, let us start by maintaining Wicksell's assumption that the underlying 'real' economy is stationary; so that 'in a condition of barter' it would in fact be stationary, or (as a money-using economy) it could be kept stationary, even with respect to money prices, by keeping the market rate equal to the natural rate. But now suppose that the market rate is reduced below the natural rate—whereat, according to Wicksell, prices will rise. But how can this happen—how can the market rate be reduced below the natural rate? And how will prices rise? What will be the time-path of the 'cumulative process'? The 'cumulative process' is not a stationary equilibrium; it is a process of change, which needs to be analysed dynamically. The questions which we have been listing are dynamic questions.

This is where we come to Lindahl. In terms of the concepts with which we are familiar, his solution can readily be described. He reduced the process of change to a sequence of single periods, such that, in the interior of each, change could be neglected. Within the single period, quantities and prices could thus be determined in what resembles a static manner. Everything is just the same as with the 'static' kind of process analysis (which we have attributed to Smith or to Marshall) save for one thing: that expectations are explicitly introduced as independent variables in the determination of the single-period equilibrium. Wicksell himself had come near to this, but it had been concealed by his habit of working with a circulating capital model. In Lindahl it is at last quite clear that the single-period is not self-contained.

The case of the cumulative process is enough to show why expectations had to be brought in. However far we go in splitting up the sequence (of stationary economy subjected to monetary disturbance), we shall still find that each single period merely reproduces the old stationary equilibrium, so long as the single period is kept self-contained, and so long as the equilibrium conditions (of demands equal to supplies) are kept in force. Everything is just the same as regards all the *real* elements in the system; and the *rate* of interest (there can be only one rate of interest) must be equal to the natural rate. Splitting up merely reduces the difference between the price levels of the successive equilibria; it does not show the transition from one equilibrium to another. Only by explicit introduction of expectations can this Eleatic paradox[1] be resolved.

What we are effectively assuming, if expectations are not introduced explicitly, is that in each single period prices are expected to remain the same in future as they are in that period; the only difference between one single period and another must then be that prices are higher in the later period, so that (if there is any hard money in the system) the demand for money must be increased. The supply of money must be increased to match this demand; so that all that has happened is that the supply of money is increased, and prices have risen. We are back at a quantity equation, buttressed by a 'real balance effect'. But this is not what Wicksell had in mind. In spite of his occasional obeisances to quantity theory orthodoxy, his most characteristic model is that of an economy in which there is no hard money, not even such as may be kept as a reserve by a Central Bank. If there is such a reserve, and we are willing to suppose that the Central Bank endeavours to keep a constant 'real balance', then (with expectations tied, as before, to current prices) we again come back to the Quantity theory. But if there is no such reserve (or if we decline to make this special assumption about Central Bank behaviour) the position will be different—and more

---

[1] 'The moving Arrow, at an indivisible instant, must either be at rest or in motion. Now the arrow cannot move in the instant, supposed indivisible, for if it changed its position, the instant would at once be divided. If, however, it is not in motion in the instant, it must be at rest, and, as time is made up of such instants, it must always remain at rest.' (T. L. Heath, *Manual of Greek Mathematics*, p. 192.)

interesting. If there is no reserve (Wicksell's case), bank credit appears as a liability of the banking system, a debt from the banking system to the public, which is matched by debts from the public to the banking system; these can be matched *at any level*. The system can then be in equilibrium at any level of prices; there is no question of a relation between prices and the supply of money. All that is left is Wicksell's relation between prices and the rate of interest; but that is a relation that still needs to be tidied up.

4. Let us now proceed to see how the 'cumulative process' would be analysed—on Lindahl's method.

Let period (o) be that of the old (stationary) equilibrium, with market rate equal to the natural rate, r_n. In this old equilibrium, expected prices were equal to current prices. In period (1) the monetary authority reduces the market rate of interest, and (as is agreed) prices, or at least some prices, will rise. If, however, when these prices rise, expected prices rise equally, there can be no equilibrium in period (1) until the market rate is again equal to r_n. But as soon as we allow expected prices to diverge from current prices the difficulty disappears.

The simplest rule by which a determinate *cumulative process* may then be engendered is the following. Suppose that the money prices which, in period (t), are expected to rule in all future periods ($t+1$, $t+2$,...) are the money prices that did actually rule in period ($t-1$). There is a *lag* in the adjustment of expectations. Then in period (1), expected prices are (o) prices; any change in prices that occurs in (1) is taken to be temporary. There is then no difficulty in establishing, by a natural extension of static method, what will be the behaviour of the economy in (1), even though it is laid down that in (1) the rate of interest is to be reduced below r_n. If expected prices are unchanged, but the rate of interest is lower, current prices (or, at the least, some current prices) must be higher. There must be some tendency for the prices of (1) to be higher than the prices of (o). Current prices being adjusted, but expected prices not being adjusted, the rate of interest can be lower than r_n, and there can still be equilibrium.

Now pass to period (2), in which the market rate of interest is still maintained as in (1), being still less than r_n. There are just two things which can make prices in (2) different from what they were in (1). One is the fact that the system was not in stationary equilibrium in period (1)—for relative prices in (1) would not (or not all) have been the same as the stationary relative prices (of period (0)). Thus the capital stock which (2) inherits from (1) may be different from that which (1) inherited from (0). There may, that is to say, be a change in real resources. The other is the fact that, according to our rule, there will be a change in price expectations.

The prices which, in period (1), were expected to rule in the future were (0) prices; in period (2) they are (1) prices. (1) prices were, on the whole, higher than (0) prices, so that in (2) price expectations will, on the whole, be higher than they were in (1). Other things being equal, this will tend to make actual prices higher in (2) than in (1). And other things are equal (in particular, the rate of interest is the same as it was); there is just the possible effect of the change in real resources. Apart from this, prices will be higher in (2) than in (1), and for the same reason they will be higher in (3) than in (2). The cumulative process will continue, as Wicksell said, so long as the market rate of interest is less than r_n.

But will there in fact be an offsetting effect from the change in real resources? This is a question that has been much discussed, but it is unnecessary for us to go into it deeply here.[1] From the point of view of the present chapter it is sufficient to observe that, even if there is such an effect, its ability to offset depends upon timing. By the 'rule' that we are using, expectations adjust themselves in one unit period; that is to say, the length of the period has been chosen so as to equal the expectational lag. The speedier the adjustment of expectations, the shorter the unit period must be. But such shortening of the unit period is bound to reduce the change in real resources that can occur within the period; for the speed of the real change is determined, at least in part, by technology—by the calendar time that production processes take. Generally, therefore, the possibility of offsetting depends upon relative speeds of adjustment in these two directions; and these speeds are largely independent of one another. If expectations are

---

[1] As will appear in Chapter XXII, below, an increase in real capital in period (1), making possible an increase in supplies of products in period (2), may conceivably diminish the rate of interest that is appropriate for period (2), so that actual prices in (2) will fail to rise in the manner described. But in order for this to be possible at all, there must be some fixed factor (land or labour) the supply of which is not extensible to match the increase in the stock of real capital. Even so, one would surely expect that the fall would occur rather slowly.

sensitive, with a short adjustment period, changes in resources cannot make much difference to the Wicksellian cumulative process. If expectations are very sluggish things may be different.

5. I have chosen this particular example of the Lindahl method for hardly any better reason than that one had to have an example. It must, however, have been something like this line of thought that convinced Lindahl himself that expectations had to be explicitly introduced. From now on I want to consider the method more generally.

When I do so, I do not find it easy to proceed without some reference to the closely related theory which I gave myself in *Value and Capital* (based, as it was, upon conversations which I had had with Lindahl himself). The *Value and Capital* model is worked out in much greater detail than Lindahl's; for the sake of that detail I allowed myself a number of restrictive assumptions, some of which I have now come to think were unnecessary. I shall come back to these in later sections. It is more important, for the moment, to comment upon a point where I took a different direction from Lindahl's, under the influence (this time) of Keynes.

I was writing this part of my book in 1937-8, at a time when battle was raging over the *General Theory*. I was myself writing about Keynes in the intervals of working at my own book;[1] to clear up the relation between Keynes's approach and my own seemed (I think understandably) to be a necessary part of the task I had set myself. It had to come sooner or later, but I am now inclined to believe that I let it come too soon. I should have let my own argument develop at least one or two steps further before I looked up to see where I was in relation to the Keynes theory.

It is one of the major difficulties of the Keynes theory (a difficulty that was acutely felt by its first readers, though it has now been lulled to sleep by long familiarity) that it works with a *period* which is taken to be one of equilibrium (investment being equal to saving, saving that is a function of *current* income), and which is nevertheless identified with the Marshallian 'short period', in which capital equipment (now the capital equipment of the whole economy) remains unchanged. The second seems to require that the period should not be too long, but the first requires that it

---

[1] 'Mr. Keynes's Theory of Employment' (*Economic Journal*, 1936); 'Mr. Keynes and the Classics' (*Econometrica*, 1937).

should not be too short; for the *process* of getting into the equilibrium in question (the multiplier process) must occupy a length of time that is by no means negligible. It is not easy to see that there can be any length of time that will adequately satisfy both of these requirements.

A reservation on this point has always, I think, been at the backs of the minds of critical readers; but we have agreed to suspend our doubts because of the power of the analysis which Keynes constructed on this (perhaps) shaky foundation. Once the point is granted, the way is open for the use of familiar methods (methods that differ little, in essence, from those of comparative statics), so that the state of the economy in one 'short-period equilibrium' can be compared with its state in another. For many purposes (as the whole subsequent history of the Keynes theory shows) that is all that we want.

But it is not dynamics. It is not the analysis of a process; no means has been provided by which we can pass from one Keynesian period to the next. There are indeed versions of the Keynes theory which do provide such means. The Kahn multiplier theory is a piece of dynamic analysis in the way that the Keynes multiplier theory is not. (Thus it is from the Kahn multiplier that 'Keynesian' dynamic theories commonly begin, not from the Keynes multiplier.) The Keynes theory, it has often been observed, is not a dynamic theory; in one sense, at least, it is still 'quasi-static'.

The Temporary Equilibrium model of *Value and Capital*, also, is 'quasi-static'—in just the same sense. The reason why I was contented with such a model was because I had my eyes fixed on Keynes.

6. Both the Keynes theory, and the *Value and Capital* theory, are dynamic to the extent that their temporary equilibrium is governed by expectations. (Keynes locked them up in the 'marginal efficiency of capital', but they are there all the same.) But they are not used in the way Lindahl used them. In Lindahl's case, as appears from our example of the cumulative process, the single periods link on. In the others, they do not. What is the difference?

The place where I myself departed from Lindahl (and so moved in the direction of Keynes) was with respect to the things which I allowed to happen within the single period. According to Lindahl (I think one may safely say) the expectations that rule in the current period are based upon *past* experience; they are uninfluenced by what happens in the market during the current period itself. It is this which enables them to form a link between periods—a link, which, once we allow them to be based on current experience, is bound to disappear.[1] It was because I did allow them to be influenced (even, on occasion, to be chiefly influenced) by current experience, that my model was moved in a 'quasi-static' direction.

It will be well, in order to explain how this happened, to go into a little more detail about the structure of the model that I was using.

During the 'week' (as I called the single period) production and consumption proceed at prices that are established by trading on its first 'day' (Monday). Monday's trading proceeds until prices are established that equate demands and supplies, for goods and services to be delivered within the 'week'. It is not supposed that equilibrium prices are established at once; there may be a good deal of 'false' trading before they are established. While they are being found, expectations are adjusting themselves to the information that comes up in the course of this trading. Every change in prices, even if it is only a tentative change in prices, carries with it an adjustment of expectations; equilibrium is not established until a set of prices is reached which (together with the expectations that it engenders) determines demands and supplies that are equal to one another. This was the concept of equilibrium that I was using —made precise (indeed much too precise) by the notion of 'elasticity of expectations' (responsiveness of price expectations to current prices) which has been more of a success than I would have desired. In this equilibrium prices and price expectations are, at least to some extent, reciprocally determined.

Such reciprocal determination is, however, a piece of telescoping; in dynamic analysis, telescoping is dangerous. It is essential to keep the time-sequence right. Though changes in actual prices do affect expectations, and changes in expectations do affect actual prices, cause precedes effect. The *lag* may be short, but (in principle) it is always there. In truly dynamic analysis (of which Lindahl's is our first specimen) there must be lags.[2]

[1] The corresponding link was dropped by Keynes when he made consumption (i.e. the output of consumption goods) depend upon *current* income.

[2] This (I take it) is what Frisch meant when he defined a dynamic theory as one in which 'we consider the magnitudes of certain variables at different points of time, and we introduce certain equations which embrace at the same time

It is indeed by no means necessary that the lags should be of an expectational character (as they are in the Lindahl theory). The case of the Kahn multiplier, to which reference has already been made, is already before us as evidence to the contrary. The point which I am making is not specifically concerned with any one sort of lag; it is simply that some sort of lag is required in any dynamic theory, if process *as such* is to be made intelligible.[1]

It is inevitable, when time is divided into single periods, that the lags should extend from one single period to another. Not necessarily from one to the next; rapidity of reaction can be varied by making the lags extend across a number of periods. The expectations of period t can be moulded, according to various possible rules, by actual experience in combinations of periods in the past. Numerous different reaction patterns can be represented in this manner; but it will usually be only very simple types that we shall care to handle.

7. Let us go back to Lindahl. All that has been worked out, so far, is the Lindahlian approach to a very formal problem—that of Wicksell's cumulative process; something must now be said about the way in which the model would deal with questions that are somewhat more realistic. We shall then not want to begin from a stationary state; and there is indeed no reason why we should. All that we have to require of our period (o) is that the system should be in temporary equilibrium in that period: that the prices that are established in that period are such as to equate supplies and demands. What these (supplies, demands, and prices) are will depend upon data—the real resources available, the tastes of 'individuals', the expectations that have been formed, and the rate of interest (supposed, as explained, to be under the control of the banking system). Production and consumption, in period (o), are then determined; and the capital equipment, which (o) will hand over to (1), is also determined. Granted a rule about the formation

several of these magnitudes belonging to different instants' ('Propagation and Impulse Problems' in *Essays in Honour of Gustav Cassel*, p. 171).

[1] I do not mean to deny that there may be advantages, for mathematical manipulation, in shutting up the length of the unit period so that it becomes infinitesimal and the lags evanescent. But this, I think, is an operation which we should only allow ourselves when we have begun by setting up the model in lagged form. Economic lags are always finite; we cannot understand what we are doing unless we show the consequence *following* the cause. (See above, p. 30.)

of expectations in period (1)—and, of course, with given tastes and so on in period (1)—the behaviour of the economy in period (1) is likewise determined. And so on for later periods.

This is a very general statement—not in itself of much use. It would not be possible to construct a 'growth model' on these lines without specifying much further. But I do not think that that was the main way in which the construction was intended to be used. After all, static theory is not ordinarily used in that way; it is not used for actual working out of the system of prices and production that corresponds to a particular set of data. The important application is to Comparative Statics—the study of the changes in production and prices which we should expect to occur when the data are changed. So it is here. The natural application of the Lindahl model is to Comparative Dynamics. We start from a *basic* Lindahl process, extending over a number of time periods, with the system (in each period) in temporary equilibrium with respect to its own data. We then ask: if the data had been changed, or amended, in some particular, how would the process have been changed? What would have been the change to the *amended* process? This, in some cases at least, is a question on which something can be said. And reflection would suggest that it is in fact one of the main questions to which we require an answer.

What has been said above about the cumulative process fits, it will be noticed, into this formulation. The basic process was in that case the stationary state with constant prices; the change in data was a change in the market rate of interest. The nature of the amended process, in that case, has been already examined. But it is now at once apparent, when we proceed to regard the 'cumulative process' analysis as an example of a general method, that essentially the same argument will apply much more generally. We can start with *any* basic process, and inquire into the consequences of reducing the market rate of interest to a lower level than it is in the basic process (it need not be constant over time in either process—it is just that the *amended* rate is below the *basic* rate in each period. If the difference in interest (in the course of interest rates) is the only difference in data between the two processes, the consequential differences must be analysable in terms of expectational lags, and changes in real resources, as before. As before, it will follow (at least in the case where expectations are sensitive) that in the amended process, where interest rates are systematically lower, prices will rise continuously *relatively* to the contemporary prices of the basic process. This will be true without our having to assume that, in either process, prices are stable. If, in the basic process, prices were stable, they would be rising in the amended process; if they had been falling in the basic process, then in the amended process they would, at least, be falling less.

Another important question, which can be dealt with in the same manner, is that of an *autonomous* change in expectations. Suppose that the only difference between the data of our two processes is that, in period (1), producers in the amended process are provided with some 'news' that makes them more optimistic (as regards price expectations) than the corresponding 'people' (also in period (1)) in the basic process. Past experience—in period (0) and its predecessors—is to be the same in both processes. What difference will be made?

It is evident that, in period (1), prices will be higher in the amended process. Accordingly, if we take it that current prices have the same (lagged) effect upon price expectations as we have hitherto been assuming, there will be (some) rise in price expectations, of a continuing character, in the amended process relatively to the basic process, even if the autonomous rise only affected the basic period. But there will then be no reason why the rise in price expectations, and the consequential rise in actual prices, should increase over time. Temporary optimism (at constant market rate of interest, and with the effect on real resources—real accumulation of capital—still neglected) will result in a *permanent* lift in the price level, relatively to that of the basic process; but it will not result in a continuing rise, relatively to the price level of the basic process.

An autonomous 'improvement' in expectations, that does persist from period to period, can of course be treated as a sequence of temporary 'improvements'. Thus on the same analysis, it *will* result in a continuing rise in prices, relatively to the price level of the basic process.

8. The analysis of the preceding section is important. We shall come back to it again, in other forms, in other contexts. But for the moment it is important to realize its limitations—what it does *not* give us. It is generally true of the Temporary Equilibrium method, as so far expounded, that it has serious defects, in at least three distinguishable directions. Some of these defects may be mendable to some extent; but their combined force is such that they make it impossible for us to rest content with the Temporary Equilibrium method as our only dynamic method. It is necessary, as we shall see in detail in later chapters, to have alternative approaches at our disposal as well.

The first of the defects which I shall consider concerns uncertainty. My 1939 analysis has often been criticized (and the same criticism could, I think, be directed against Lindahl's analysis) for its neglect of uncertainty, or rather for its inadequate treatment of uncertainty. Far more is known now than was known then about 'decision-making under uncertainty' (Theory of Games and all that!); what it is that is left out, on the uncertainty side, can now be more accurately defined.[1]

An uncertain expectation (of the price of a commodity, we may still allow ourselves to say, that is to rule at some future date) can be represented (more or less adequately) by a probability distribution; and this (in turn) is usually describable by a fairly small number of parameters. These may be the ordinary statistical parameters (mean value, variance, and so on); or it may be that there are others more appropriate to the particular matter in hand.[2] The important thing is that an uncertain expectation cannot be adequately described in terms of a single parameter. It is insufficient to consider the changes in production (or consumption) plans that result from changes in the prices that are 'expected' as most probable. Attention must also be given to the effects of changes in the confidence with which these values are expected.

When these are allowed for, the theory of the 'plan' becomes much more complicated; for it is necessary to take account of those adjustments in business organization which are undertaken in order to diminish risk—and which otherwise are only too likely to slip through our fingers.[3] But the temporary equilibrium itself would not appear, at first sight, to be much affected. Current prices (or, more generally, the character of the equilibrium that is established in the current period) may affect future planning by their

---

[1] Discussions of the uncertainty problem that are rather closely fitted to the *Value and Capital* analysis are to be found in A. G. Hart, *Anticipations, Uncertainty and Dynamic Planning*; and in F. Modigliani and K. J. Cohen, *Role of Anticipations and Plans in Economic Behaviour*.

[2] As Professor Shackle would have us believe.

[3] Hart, op. cit.; G. B. Richardson, *Information and Investment*, ch. 8.

effect on the confidence with which expectations are held, as well as by their effect on the most probable expected prices. But though that is a bother in the statement of the theory, it looks as if it could be worked in without too much trouble, and without changing much that is of substance.

What, however, about the rate of interest? This is where there is a real and important difference. So long as we assume (as we have hitherto been implicitly assuming) that expectations are single-valued, we can talk, as we have done, about a *single* rate of interest. It is indeed possible (as was shown in *Value and Capital*) to deal with differences in the rate of interest on loans of different maturities. This can be done (the method there adopted) by reducing long lending to a sequence of short lendings—so that a long rate is regarded as being compounded out of *the* short rate and a succession of expected rates); or it can be done (as many people would prefer to do it) by taking the longest of long rates to be *the* rate, and regarding short lending as long lending which is planned to be undone at the end of the period. So long as expectations are single-valued, there is no inherent difference in these methods. In either case, there is one rate of interest which is *the* rate of interest in the current period.

As soon as we allow for uncertainty of expectation, such simple reductions fail us. They fail us in two ways. First, because of default risk, there will be no uniformity in the rates of interest that are established, at the same time, even on loans of the same maturity. Secondly (and more importantly), the amount that a business can borrow, at *any* fixed rate of interest, will be limited by its *credit*; but this barrier can be relaxed, to an extent which varies greatly with confidence, by the raising of funds in other manners, on equities and the like. If these things were to be fully allowed for, the Temporary Equilibrium model would require considerable amendment—a formidable task that has never (to my knowledge) been seriously carried through. I shall not attempt it here, but shall merely mention one fairly obvious point which emerges as soon as one begins to think about the matter.[1]

In the Temporary Equilibrium model, as we have been describing it, the rate of interest is under the control of the Monetary Authority. But as soon as we admit the existence of a spectrum of interest rates (and 'pseudo' interest rates, such as expected yields on equities) the direct control of the Monetary Authority over

[1] But see below, Chapter XXIII.

interest must be limited to a part (perhaps a quite small part) of the spectrum. How far the rest of the spectrum can be influenced depends not so much on arithmetical relations between rates— the extent to which one comes down just because another comes down may be infinitesimal; it is a matter of backwashes on confidence that do not proceed by any simple rule. We may still derive from the theory some useful knowledge of the way in which interest changes will affect production and prices, if they can be carried through; but we must not assume that they can always be carried through, just because the Monetary Authority desires it.

9. The second of the limitations which I want to discuss (but perhaps it is only a limitation of the *Value and Capital* model) is the confinement to the case of perfect competition. *Value and Capital* was of course throughout a perfect competition book; it was confined to the study of the pure theory of the perfect competition model. In such a model prices are the variables on which the working of the whole economy depends; supplies and demands are functions of prices. When expectations are introduced into analysis of this sort, it is natural to introduce them as price expectations. Supplies and demands have been taken to be dependent (statically) upon current prices; dynamically they should be dependent upon expected prices also.

Even in the present chapter (though I have not been supposing myself to be referring so expressly to the perfect competition model) I have allowed myself to drop into this familiar representation of expectations as *price* expectations; this is indeed very often a convenient simplification, but I do not think that it need be any more than that. There is no reason in principle why we should not have a Temporary Equilibrium theory of Imperfect Competition, in which the prices at which the firm sells are not independent of the quantities that it offers for sale. What it must then 'expect' is not a price, but a relation between quantities and prices (demand curve or demand function). It is this which will be determined from outside, when it becomes actual, and must in the meantime be estimated from such evidence as there is.

The simplest (but not the most interesting) form of this dynamic Imperfect Competition theory would make expected demand, in each future period, depend upon the price to be fixed in that future period, but on nothing else that was under the control of the seller.

The forms which such a relation could take might then be sufficiently distinguished by the values of quite a small number of parameters (if the 'curve' were linear, or log-linear, two would suffice). Changes in these parameters would then correspond exactly to the change in price expectations of the Perfect Competition theory. We could substitute these parameters for the price expectations; otherwise we should proceed in almost the same way as we have done before.

The interesting form of the theory, however, is more complex. It is not in general to be expected that the price fixed in any period will affect sales in that period alone; if 'news' takes time to travel, the price in one period will affect sales in later periods also. Demand functions, that is, will be temporally interrelated. It is then more difficult to reduce demand behaviour into terms of changes in a small number of parameters. In order to make the problem manageable, we are likely to have to confine ourselves to the study of simple cases. Some of these, however, seem to be by no means uninstructive.[1]

10. Neither of the two limitations, so far discussed, is inherent; either can be removed, or partially removed, if we are willing to take the trouble to do so; but the third, to which I now come, is inherent in the Temporary Equilibrium method itself. Both in the Lindahl version and in the *Value and Capital* version (and in the version given to this chapter, if that is to be distinguished from them) it is necessary to assume that prices remain unchanged throughout the single period; and that these prices are equilibrium prices which, within the single period, equate supplies and demands. In order to visualize this, some such construction as my 'week' and my 'Monday' appears to be necessary; but the artificiality of such constructions is only too obvious. They do deliberate violence to the *order* in which in the real world (in *any* real world) events occur.

It is no doubt true that the violence is greater with some market forms than it is with others. Though the Lindahl theory sprang from Wicksell, its conception of the working of the market is essentially Marshallian (in the *Value and Capital* version, the Marshallian affiliation is made explicit). We (Lindahl and I) were

[1] A particularly simple case of this kind is explored in my article *The Process of Imperfect Competition* (Oxford Economic Papers, 1954).

following Marshall in treating prices as determined (in the short period, or single period) by 'equilibrium of demand and supply'. Our single period (or 'week') was shorter than Marshall's 'short period'; this made the equilibrium assumption still more dangerous. Marshall, it was argued above,[1] may have been justified in the use that he made of it, in 1890; but to continue with it in the nineteen-thirties, and to make an even stronger use of it, was very dangerous indeed.

One of the reasons for this is that which came to be emphasized by Keynes: that there are markets, especially the labour market, in which prices are 'sticky'. The assumption of demand and supply equality, in every period, must for such markets be peculiarly un-satisfactory. In Keynesian terms, the Temporary Equilibrium Theory is a Full-Employment theory. But this is not all. There are many non-labour markets, in which Temporary Equilibrium gives a wrong impression of the market's working, in which it does not tell the story right. As a consequence, it leaves out parts of the dynamic problem in which we have a right to be interested. We have got to find some way of dealing with them.

Lindahl himself came to recognize this; in his later work he moved away from the Temporary Equilibrium method. In my own later work (and not only in this book[2]) I have done the same. But I do not wish to relinquish it entirely. I have not presented it here as an historical curiosity. For, as I have repeatedly insisted, it is not enough to have an economics which is committed to some particular market form; even if it is the form which happens to be dominant at the time, and in the country, in which we are living. We need something more than that. As a theory of its own market form the Temporary Equilibrium method is valid enough. But that is not all that there is to be said.

For one thing, even in the twentieth century there are markets (speculative markets in particular) which do work in a way that is near enough to what has been described. If we cannot give ourselves up to the Temporary Equilibrium model we can make some use of it as an ingredient. That is one way in which it can be used, but there is another way which is perhaps still more important.

Throughout this chapter I have been discussing the Temporary Equilibrium method as a method of Positive Economics—Pure

[1] pp. 54–56.
[2] In my *Trade Cycle* (1950) I did not use the Temporary Equilibrium method.

Positive Economics it may be (to revert to the distinction which I made in Chapter I) but Positive Economics all the same. What about Welfare Economics? The supply–demand equalization, which has been causing us such disquiet, when it is taken as a characteristic of a Positive Economic model, is, when it comes to Welfare Economics, perfectly at home.[1] If we are studying the properties of an optimum growth path, one of the things on which we shall insist is that, in each single period, it is to be in temporary equilibrium; and in this application even the other 'limitations' of the simple Temporary Equilibrium model (risklessness and perfect competition) may actually be found to be acceptable. If we are concerned with Welfare Economics, the Temporary Equilibrium model, or something very like it, should be just what we want.

And not temporary equilibrium only. What, it may be asked, has happened in the foregoing to an equilibrium that is more than temporary? Is there no equilibrium over time, equilibrium over a sequence of single periods, here at all? Temporary equilibrium is such that all are reaching their 'best' positions, subject to the constraints by which they are bound, and with the expectations that they have at the moment. Equilibrium over time, if it is to be defined in a corresponding manner, must be such that it is maintainable over a sequence, the expectations on which it is based, in each single period, being consistent with one another. When it is described as an 'equilibrium of perfect foresight', this equilibrium over time may hardly appear to be an interesting concept. But when it is looked at the other way, as a means of studying the properties of an optimum growth path, it may possibly appear to be less of a chimera.

---

[1] The qualifications about free goods, on which the 'linear programmers' (rightly) insist, do not here concern us.

VII

THE FIXPRICE METHOD

1. THE fundamental weakness of the Temporary Equilibrium method is the assumption, which it is obliged to make, that the market is in equilibrium—actual demand equals desired demand, actual supply equals desired supply—even in the *very* short period, which is what its single period must be taken to be. This assumption comes down from Marshall, but even in a very competitive economy, such very short-run equilibration is hard to swallow; in relation to modern manufacturing industry, it is very hard to swallow indeed. It was inevitable that the time should come when it had to be dropped.

The consequences of dropping it are quite far-reaching. We shall be able to do no more than begin to explore them in this chapter. They will occupy us far beyond it; indeed, in a sense, they will occupy us for much of the rest of this book. For this is the point at which we begin to enter the peculiar territory of modern growth theory and of modern cycle theory. The putting of that theory into its place, in relation to other parts of economics, will be our principal concern, and it is unnecessary to emphasize that this is no easy task. Besides, we have not only to clear up the external relations of growth and cycle theory with the rest of economics; we have also to clear up their mutual relations, and the relations of parts of each to one another. All this will spring from a consideration of the alternative 'method' which we are now to examine; but we must not expect that the whole of this large territory will come into sight at once. I believe that the route which we shall pursue is such that it will bring most (if not all) in the end into sight; but there is much that we shall not be able to perceive until we have passed the first stage.

At the first stage, I shall take the new method in rather a stark form. In that form it is sharply contrasted with the Temporary Equilibrium method; more sharply (perhaps) than we shall ultimately desire it to be. I do not think that there is any harm in this. The Temporary Equilibrium method (as we have enunciated it) was itself a 'pure' method, in which all markets were supposed to work in one way—a way that may be realistic for some markets, but is certainly not realistic for most. We shall best get a grip on the alternative method if we start by taking it also in a pure form. Though our ultimate preference may be for something which lies between, anything which does so must partake to some extent of the difficulties of both. It is the extremes which are (relatively) simple, so that it is with them that it is best to begin.

To pass from the one *pure* method to the other is quite a revolution. It is a revolution that is mixed up with the so-called 'Keynesian Revolution'; but I do not think that it is accurate to identify them. Though the 'methods' that are used in the *Treatise on Money* and in the *General Theory* are different, neither of them is a *pure* method; it is even doubtful (as we have seen) whether either of them can be called a dynamic method, in the strict sense that we are using here. There is, however, no question that, as between his two works, Keynes was moving in the direction of the new method; and it is in the work of his interpreters and successors that the clearest examples of the new method are to be found. In their hands the method is often presented as a Keynesian method; but it is wiser, in my view, to avoid committing ourselves to taking it as such. It is better to recognize that the direction of movement is one that is very widespread in contemporary economics, both through the influence of Keynes and otherwise.[1]

2. On the Temporary Equilibrium method, the system is in equilibrium in every single period; and it is by this equilibrium that prices are determined. If we abandon the demand–supply equation, how are prices to be determined? The answer, which must be faced, is that the new method does not have any way of determining prices. There must be some way by which they are

[1] A corresponding change was occurring in Sweden. The original (1929–30) form of Lindahl's theory, which we have been discussing, was pure Temporary Equilibrium. But in Myrdal's *Monetary Equilibrium* (1933), in spite of its title, the change is beginning. In Lundberg's *Economic Expansion* (1937) it is fairly complete. In Lindahl's later work, as previously noted, he also moved in the same direction. (See the first essay in his *Studies*—this was actually the last to be written.)

That, however, is not all. When the change is defined as widely as we are defining it, it links up with micro-economic work, such (for instance) as that of Mr. Andrews. It would also be interesting to examine the influence of Marx in impelling thought in the same direction.

determined, but it is exogenous. The determination of prices is taken right outside the model.[1]

All that is said about prices is that they must cover costs; more strictly, that a thing will not be produced unless it is profitable to produce it. Subject to this condition, prices can be what they like. It is not a very stringent condition, if it is unaccompanied by any rule about profits being normal; and the normalization of profits (equalization between different sectors) is a complicated process, for which it is difficult to give sufficient time during the lapse of a single period.

If there is no more than that to be said about prices, it is natural to assume that they remain unchanged throughout the sequence that is being analysed. If prices are fixed exogenously, one will naturally begin by assuming them to be constant. The model becomes a Fixprice model. Fixity of prices is in fact the characteristic feature of the models to which we now come, so characteristic that it will be convenient to use it as a name for the method. (The Temporary Equilibrium method can then be referred to, by contrast, as a Flexprice method.) It is not implied by the description Fixprice method that prices are never to be allowed to change—only that they do not necessarily change whenever there is demand–supply disequilibrium.

When prices are constant, quantities of goods and services can be added by adding their money values; money values become volume indexes. By its own inner logic, and without any deliberate decision having been taken to slew it in that direction, the model becomes a macro-model. The Fixprice method has an inherent tendency to 'go macro'; a tendency which there is now much experience to confirm.

3. It would, however, be unwise to rush too quickly into macro-economics. If a model of the whole economy is to be securely based, it must be grounded in an intelligible account of how a single market is supposed to work. What is the Fixprice theory of the working of a single market? In what ways does it differ from a Flexprice theory, such (for instance) as Marshall's?

The standard case of Marshallian micro-theory (as previously noticed)[2] assumes that the traded commodity is non-storable ('fish')

[1] 'Cost Push', with prices ultimately set by trade unions, is thus an hypothesis that fits very neatly into a model of this kind.
[2] pp. 52–54.

so that there can be no carry-over from one period to another. This is not, in practice, a particularly important case; the products of manufacturing industry, at least, do commonly have a greater durability; but it has been handed down from textbook to textbook as a standard case, merely because, in Flexprice terms, it is easy to handle. Having once got that case clear, one can go on to work out the Flexprice theory of a storable commodity without essential change in principle. When price is rigid, the advantage of beginning in this way is, however, less obvious. The existence of stocks has a great deal to do, in practice, with the possibility of keeping prices fixed. If, when demand exceeds output, there are stocks that can be thrown in to fill the gap, it is obvious that the price does not have to rise; a market in which stock changes substitute for price changes (at least up to a point) is readily intelligible. If there are no stocks to take the strain, it is harder to stick to the assumption of rigid prices. A market in which sellers leave demand unsatisfied without raising prices is certainly not a 'perfect' market—but it is quite a familiar sort of market in the real world all the same! The Fixprice assumption is more awkward in the case of non-storable than in that of storable commodities; but it is an assumption which even there we can bring ourselves, at least provisionally, to accept.

Let us therefore begin by reminding ourselves of Marshall's story. The price that actually rules for a perishable, price-flexible commodity of Marshall's type is that which equates current demand with current output. The commodity being perishable, the supply cannot include any stock element (positive or negative); it is 'flow demand' and 'flow supply' that are equated at the price that is established. If, however, they are only equated at a high price (at a price that is high relatively to 'normal cost of production') there is a signal for an increase in output; though the increase can only materialize at a later date, that is to say, in a later period. If they are equated at a price that is low in relation to cost, output will (similarly) tend to decrease. That is what we read in Marshall, or (indeed) in Adam Smith.

Now suppose that the price is rigid. There is then no reason why demand and supply (or output) should be equated—should be in equilibrium—in the current period. The commodity being perishable, an excess of demand over output cannot be met from stocks; it must simply go unsatisfied. An excess of output over demand cannot be added to stocks; it must simply be wasted. But that is

Fixprice
still adequate

Flow
+
Stock

not all that there is to be said. An excess of demand over output will still give the same sort of signal to increase future output—for we are assuming that if output can be sold, it will be profitable to produce it; an excess of output over demand still gives a signal to contract. Even in a Fixprice market the signalling does occur. The economy is not deprived of a means of adjustment, at least so far as the 'micro' level is concerned. If producers read the signals correctly (and even in the Flexprice market they still need to read the signals correctly) there can still be a 'tendency to equilibrium'.

When stocks are carried, the position is more complicated—much more complicated. For in that case (as we shall see in detail later)[1] it is not sufficient that producers should *on the whole* read the signals correctly. A fair adjustment of flow output to flow demand is not sufficient to ensure a fair adaptation to equilibrium. Exact adjustment cannot be expected; mistakes are bound to be made; but whereas in the case of the non-storable commodity mistakes are not carried forward, in the case of the storable commodity they are. Even a mere lag in adjustment (and the absence of any lag is hardly conceivable) will leave its mark upon the level of stocks. Thus as soon as we allow for carry-forward of stocks, the problem of equilibration in a Fixprice model is fundamentally transformed. We may express the transformation, at least provisionally, by saying that we do not only have to attend to the flow equilibrium of current demand and current output; we must also attend to the question of stock equilibrium.

4. The concept of 'stock equilibrium' is becoming familiar to economists;[2] but to give a general definition of it is by no means a simple matter. There is a crying need for such a definition if we are to make orderly progress in Fixprice theory; the matter needs a thorough investigation, so that I propose to give it a chapter to itself. It will, however, be useful, before we proceed to that inquiry, to look once again at the 'micro-model' of the single market. For there is one way in which our discussion of it may have given a wrong impression. By looking at the single market so much in isolation, we have failed to bring out how central, for all Fixprice analysis, the concept of stock equilibrium really is. If we had looked

[1] Especially in Chapter IX, below.
[2] It is sufficient to cite the 'portfolio equilibrium' of Liquidity Preference theory as an example.

at the same story in a wider way we should have found that we could not do without stock equilibrium, even if we began by considering the market for a perishable good.

Suppose that demand for butter has exceeded output of butter, and there are no stocks, so that butter, which people would have been willing to purchase, could not be bought. How will these consumers react? (There is no problem of the sellers' reaction, beyond that on their decisions to undertake future production; this we have already taken into account.) But what about the buyers? Their obvious reaction is to go away and buy something else. It is conceivable that this may be the whole answer. If the consumers had simply shifted their demands, requiring more butter and less of other perishables, they may just be obliged to go back to those other perishables; they may just be unable to shift their demand in the way that they desired. But suppose that there is an expansion of demand as a whole beyond what had been expected, the expansion of demand for butter being just a part of that general increase; there may then be no surpluses of other commodities waiting to be picked up. Consumers may still shift their demands to other commodities, but only in so far as there are stocks of those commodities available for sale. Once again we are back at the question of stock equilibrium; it is only the place where the stock equilibrium has to be considered that has changed.

There is a further possibility, which in a full analysis must be included. Suppose that the unsatisfied demand cannot be shifted at all, since there are no available surpluses of substitute commodities, either from stocks or from current output. The only thing that can then be done with the money that cannot be spent is to carry it forward. But the carrying-forward of unspent balances, when their owners would have wished to spend them, and do not desire to carry them forward, is the same kind of thing as occurs on the other side, when supplies that a seller desired to sell could not be sold. The seller is left with stocks that he does not desire to hold; the consumer (or buyer) is left with money that he does not desire to keep—in exactly the same sense. In both cases there is the same kind of stock disequilibrium.

Having got so far, let us look back at the case of the seller with the perishable product, who, if demand does not come up to expectations, has to 'waste' it or throw it away. We have said that in this case the disequilibrium is not carried forward. If we are solely considering the market for the product, that is correct; but if we widen our view, as we have just been doing in considering the consumer's position, it is not correct. Goods have been produced which could not be sold; the funds that were invested in those goods must therefore have been lost. What this means, in balance-sheet terms, is that the producer is left with a debt (or liability) against which there is no corresponding asset—a debt which he presumably owes to the same creditor to whom he owed it initially, for it is not the debt that has changed, it is the asset that has disappeared. Accordingly, just as we found (on the other side of the market) that there were 'surplus' money balances in the hands of consumers—debts owing to them which they did not desire at that time to have owing to them—so in this case we have a corresponding debt owed by producers, a debt which they do not (now) willingly assume, for there is no productive asset corresponding to it.

That, of course, is not the end of the story; it is indeed the main point that it is not the end of the story. Any economic entity which is left in a state of disequilibrium will take steps to right that disequilibrium; that is the characteristic effect of disequilibrium; it is the way in which disequilibrium carries its effect down the sequence. In this particular case, moderate losses can be offset by a reduction in dividends (or other withdrawals); that is one way in which the disequilibrium can be corrected (from the firm's point of view). It is, however, convenient not to rush on, so as to bring the reduction in dividend into the same period as that in which the loss is incurred. For we can then say that a demand–supply inequality, in the period in which it occurs, always shows itself in someone's stock (or balance-sheet) disequilibrium. There is great theoretical convenience to be got from unifying our treatment by adhering to this principle. And, after all, it is not an unrealistic convention: there is commonly quite a lag between the incurring of losses and the cutting of dividends (or, in worse cases, the 'reconstruction') that follows.

5. A general framework for Fixprice analysis is now beginning to show itself. Though we no longer assume that the system is in equilibrium in every single period, it could be in equilibrium (in some sense) under appropriate conditions; the conditions under which it could be in equilibrium are no less worthy of study than they were before. It is, however, impossible to deduce the actual path of the economy from a knowledge of these equilibrium conditions, and nothing more. The equilibrium conditions do not determine the actual path; all that they determine (or the most that they can determine) is an equilibrium path that we can use as a standard of reference. There will always be deviations from the equilibrium path. Some of these are simply due to imperfect planning (lack of foresight). But once a deviation has occurred, it leaves those affected in a state of stock disequilibrium; and their endeavours to right that disequilibrium are a main determinant of the next steps on the actual path. They are not the only determinant; the usual static propensities and technical restraints, all the things that are alone at work on the equilibrium path, are also present. It is, however, of the greatest importance to distinguish these two elements, which work in a distinctly different manner.[1] The 'equilibrium' forces are (relatively) dependable; the 'disequilibrium' forces are much less dependable. We can invent rules for their working, and calculate the behaviour of the resulting models; but such calculations are of illustrative value only. This is where 'states of mind' are of dominating importance; and states of mind cannot readily be reduced to rule.

These are things that will be worked out in some detail in the following chapters. Their full significance will only appear when they have been worked out. In the meantime what has been said may be useful as giving some indication of the way we are going.

---

[1] See also p. 18 above. In many cycle theories (including my own *Contribution to the Theory of the Trade Cycle*) these two elements are quite insufficiently distinguished.

VIII

STOCKS AND FLOWS

1. THE point has now arrived at which we must attempt a definition (a general definition) of the concept of stock equilibrium.[1] It is evident that this is going to be a key point of the Fixprice theory to which we have now come.

Stock equilibrium is an equilibrium at a point of time; in accounting terms, it is an equilibrium of the balance-sheet. That sounds simple; but the balance-sheet of a business, even as it is in practice, is quite a peculiar construction. It is important to realize that its counterpart in economic theory is also a peculiar construction, in much the same way.

The solid information on which a firm's accounts are constructed consists in records of the actual purchases and sales that it makes, goods and services that have actually been acquired or disposed of at prices that have been recorded. The 'transactions' or 'cash book' account that includes all such transactions over a period, and nothing else, is the unanalysed account from which the accountant starts. To that account the balance-sheet is in strong contrast. At the point of time to which the balance-sheet refers, the items that figure upon it are being held by the firm—that is to say, they are *not* being exchanged. Some may be near to being exchanged; they may have been recently purchased, or may be intended to be sold in the near future; values that are reasonably secure may then be placed upon this. (It should, however, be noticed that even in these cases these values are not necessarily firm values; an article may lose value very rapidly after it has been purchased; an expectation of sale, even in the near future, is not the same thing as an actual sale.) More importantly, perhaps, there are some assets (liquid assets) which are effectively identical with things (including securities) that are currently being bought and sold by others; they have a firm *market* price. Characteristically, however, the values that are set upon the items (the positive and even the negative items) in

---

[1] A point which (the reader may have noticed) was missing from our general discussion of the concept of equilibrium in Chapter II.

a balance-sheet are not firm figures. They are estimates, accountant's estimates; of a different *quality* from the items in the transactions account, which can normally be taken to be *firm*.

This distinction—this eminently practical distinction—between transactions accounting and balance-sheet accounting reflects itself in dynamic theory. The items on which a firm makes its practical decisions are the transactions items; a theory which is solely concerned with these voluntary decisions had better run, so far as it can, in terms of transactions alone. That, essentially, is what we do—what we find ourselves doing—in a Temporary Equilibrium theory. That theory can be set out (as it was in Chapter VI, above, and as it was in *Value and Capital*) without attention to balance-sheets—without, accordingly, any specific mention of stocks and flows. As long as we hold to the principle of price determination by 'equilibrium of demand and supply', on which that theory is based, we have no call to attend to anything but transactions. We do not need to distinguish between stocks and flows; for stocks and flows enter into the determination of equilibrium in exactly the same way.

There can, in competitive conditions, be no more than one price for the same commodity at the same time; and even in conditions that are only partially competitive, it does not have one price as stock and another as flow. The supply and the demand that are equated, in the single period of Temporary Equilibrium theory, may (and probably will) contain stock elements as well as flow elements. Supply comes partly from stock carried over, partly from new production; demand is partly a demand for use, partly a demand for carry-forward. Expectations of future prices affect both elements; interest affects both elements. The analysis does not require that stock and flow should be separated into compartments. It is not the case that there is one stock equilibrium and one flow equilibrium. There is one 'stock–flow' equilibrium of the single period; and that is all.[1]

---

[1] In a paper entitled 'Methods of Dynamic Analysis' which I contributed in 1956 to a Festschrift in honour of Lindahl (*25 Economic Essays*, published by Ekonomisk Tidsckrift) I suggested that Lindahl himself may have come to the method of working with a transactions account (taken *ex ante* and *ex post*) as a result of preoccupation with the problems of public finance. It is the fact that he had this background; and it is certainly true that capital–income accounting is less natural in the field of national budgeting than it is in private industry—where, indeed, its use is made compulsory by company legislation.

There may be something in this point, as something that contributed to the

The essential difference, when we pass to Fixprice theory, is that the position in which the firm finds itself at a point of time (at significant points of time) does not have to be a position that is *chosen*. It is the position which would have been chosen that is the equilibrium position; the divergence from that measures the extent of disequilibrium. The important thing is the extent of disequilibrium at the end of the single period—at the junction, that is, between one single period and the next.

That is why it is that in Fixprice theory we do have to use the concept of stock equilibrium; for it is by the absence of stock equilibrium that disequilibrium itself is carried forward. And it is the carrying-forward of disequilibrium which is the interesting thing. If it were possible for disequilibrium to be confined within the single period, its existence would do no more than mark a failure to attain a static optimum; we could say all we had to say about it by static methods. It has, however, been shown (in the preceding chapter) that even in the simplest conceivable cases it cannot be so confined. It will always leave a trail behind it. The way in which it hands itself on to the succeeding period is by leaving the firm (or other unit) and therefore the economy, at the junction, in a state of stock disequilibrium.

2. It is clearly desirable that our definition of 'stock equilibrium' should be usable (or as usable as possible) in Flexprice as in Fixprice theory; but we shall not be surprised to find that it is in Fixprice theory that the concept is more at home. Let us begin by getting it into a form which is suitable for Fixprice theory; and then see how much of it we can keep for the other case.

It is tempting to say that a firm is in stock (or balance-sheet) equilibrium if the assets (the physical assets) that it holds, the

evolution of ideas; but it does not get to the root of the matter. The important thing is that when one is using the Temporary Equilibrium method, the capital-income (or stock–flow) distinction is irrelevant; one can bring it in if one chooses, but the only reasons there can be for bringing it in are essentially extraneous to the model itself. I had found this, in my own experience, when I was writing *Value and Capital*; and I feel sure that when I relegated the concept of income to a separate, and logically dispensable, chapter of that book (chapter 14) I was not being influenced by any considerations of national budgeting. What I was saying—and what I would now say again—is that the capital-income dichotomy does not belong to the Temporary Equilibrium method; but of course I did not then realize (as I now realize) the scope of the other method where it does belong.

debts that it owes, and the debts (including money) that are owing to it, form a combination that is in some sense the best out of alternative combinations. But what alternatives? Any balance-sheet change (purchase or sale of assets, raising of new credits and even repayment of old) takes time to arrange; how are such changes to be made 'at a point of time'? If 'point of time' is taken strictly, there can be no alternative to what is actual. So, at first, one is tempted to argue; but this is a form of argument which is appropriate to Flexprice, not to Fixprice, theory. If the actual position may be a disequilibrium position, it is not necessarily one that has been voluntarily taken. It is itself not necessarily a *chosen* position; the alternatives to it are not choices that could have been made but are rejected. They must be alternatives in some other sense.

The fact is that in following the accountants in looking at the balance-sheet alone, we are (like the accountants) abstracting. We are deliberately looking at a part, not at the whole, of the firm's (or other unit's) position. The alternatives are not alternatives that are now available, nor do they even define alternatives that might have been available if in the past some different policy had been followed. They are simply the alternative balance-sheets (supposing actual physical assets to be listed on the balance-sheet) which, at current prices, would show the same 'net worth'. ('Net worth' is simply the balance of assets over liabilities—nominal 'liabilities', such as those that the firm owes to its own shareholders, being of course excluded.) One may perhaps say that they are the alternatives that 'look as if they were available' when one considers the balance-sheet alone—the balance-sheet *in itself*.

The use of such a concept as this in a Flexprice theory will evidently present difficulties—confirming our suspicion that stock equilibrium is not a concept that in a Flexprice theory it will often be convenient to use. In fact, it is only usable in such theory to a very limited extent. There are some balance-sheet changes (changes that only affect the more 'liquid' end of the balance-sheet) which, though they take some time to arrange, do not take much time; so that the time which is taken for them may justifiably (for appropriate purposes) be neglected. It is then permissible to say (as in Liquidity Preference and such-like 'portfolio equilibrium' theories one does say) that, so far as this part of the balance-sheet is concerned, a unit will be all the time (or practically all the time) in

stock equilibrium. But it is much more difficult to extend such analysis to the whole of the balance-sheet. For if changes take time, and prices may change during that time, the line between 'capital' and 'income' becomes hard to draw. We cannot firmly separate 'capital' from 'income' items unless we have begun by solving the baffling problem of 'maintaining capital—*real* capital—intact'.

In Fixprice theory there is no such difficulty. The fixing of prices gives a firm line between capital and income. The alternative balance-sheets are simply alternative forms in which the capital of the unit (or its 'net worth') might *apparently* be held. A change from one to another is an exchange of equal value (at the ruling prices) for equal value. But because the system is a disequilibrium system, such exchanges cannot necessarily be made. At the best they take time. The comparison between the 'alternatives' is nevertheless significant. For if the situation of the unit is in this sense one of stock disequilibrium, we may assume that it will endeavour to get out of that disequilibrium, when and as it can.

3. A firm is in stock equilibrium if its balance-sheet is the 'best' of such alternative balance-sheets; but what do we mean by 'best'? A firm is a producing unit; 'best' must be best with respect to plans and expectations. The equilibrium balance-sheet is that which is most appropriate to expectations—in one or other of the senses in which we have used that term.

In Temporary Equilibrium theory (where, as explained, the concept of stock equilibrium can only be applied at all conveniently if its application is restricted to the more liquid end of the balance-sheet) expectations will, as usual, be price expectations; expectations of yields, interest rates, and so on. The equilibrium balance-sheet is that which gives the most favourable expectation of yield (with allowance for risk). This, I think, is in full accordance with usual practice in Liquidity Preference theory.

In a Fixprice model, on the other hand, the expectations (as we have formerly found) must be expectations of demand—of amount that will be demanded. The equilibrium stock (which now includes the less marketable assets) must be one which will fully satisfy expected demand (for any inability to satisfy demand involves loss of profit); and of those that do so it must be that which is expected to satisfy this demand at least cost.

It is common to say (and one easily falls into saying) that the equilibrium stock is that which is adjusted to *current* demand; this, indeed, is pretty much what Marshall said. But in general it is by no means adequate to say this. For the capital stock which is appropriate to a demand which is constant at its current level is one thing; the stock which is appropriate to a demand which is increasing from its present level at a certain growth rate will ordinarily be quite different. It can be a source of great confusion if this distinction is not borne in mind. We must, in general, be prepared to think of the equilibrium stock in the broader way.[1]

4. The point has come when we must turn to the other side. What of 'flow equilibrium'? We are accustomed, working in terms of Marshallian theory, to think of flow equilibrium as something rather simple; and this notion did not have to be disturbed so long as we were dealing with a perishable product. But in general things are by no means so simple. The flow aspect of equilibrium is treacherous in the extreme.

Let us try to pass from the concept of stock equilibrium, as we have been defining it, into period analysis. If a unit is in stock equilibrium at the beginning of the period, and is still in stock equilibrium at the end, we shall want to say that it is in flow equilibrium during the period. There is no harm in that; but do we gain anything from it? Will it not be better, and more in accordance with our former terminology,[2] to say that it is in equilibrium over time *during the period*? It is in equilibrium over time if there is both stock equilibrium and flow equilibrium; but is that a helpful statement? Should we not just say that equilibrium over time requires a maintenance of stock equilibrium—which is all that needs to be said?

Even so, there are qualifications. For now that we have two stock equilibria to take account of (or to contend with) we have to consider whether the assumptions under which these stock equilibria are constructed (in particular, the expectations on which they are based) are consistent with one another. It would be wrong to say that a unit was in equilibrium over time during the period if it was in stock equilibrium at the beginning, and in stock equilibrium at

---

[1] This is a matter which will be worked out in detail in Chapters XII–XIV, below.

[2] See above, p. 26.

the end, but these equilibria were based upon different expectations, so that the end-stock equilibrium came about, as it were, by accident. There is no difficulty about this if we restrict ourselves to taking flow equilibrium *ex ante*; if we say that the unit is in flow equilibrium if it is in stock equilibrium at the beginning, and *expects* to be in stock equilibrium at the end. But this, though useful in its way, is hardly sufficient.

We can cut the knot if we recall the convention, which we have used on other occasions, that the single period is such that changes in expectations do not occur within it; they only occur at the junction from one single period to the next. The *end* of the one period is then to be distinguished from the beginning of the next by the change in expectations which may occur when this same instant of time 'puts on its other hat'. It will follow that in each single period, taken by itself, expectations (of demand in later periods) will remain unchanged; so the end-stock can be compared with the beginning-stock in a consistent manner. We can then stick to the statement that there is flow equilibrium when there is stock equilibrium at the beginning of the single period, and there is also stock equilibrium at the end. This flow equilibrium is also equilibrium over time during the period; there does not, so far, seem to be any adequate reason to distinguish.

There is nevertheless one reason why we need some sort of a distinction. Even though we insist upon defining flow equilibrium as a *maintenance* of stock equilibrium, additional conditions are necessary, in addition to the stock equilibrium conditions, in order that stock equilibrium should be maintained. These conditions are quite properly described as *conditions of flow equilibrium*. But they are necessary, not sufficient conditions. If they are satisfied, in addition to the stock conditions, there is (we may now safely say) equilibrium over time. But if they are satisfied, while the stock conditions are not satisfied, it seems doubtful whether the resulting situation should be described as one of equilibrium at all.

5. Let us now proceed to test these definitions by considering some examples—first of all, our familiar examples.

The stationary economy is in equilibrium over time, we may now say, because it is in stock equilibrium (the same stock equilibrium) at every point of time. Expectations are stationary, and the stock conditions indicate that balance-sheets are adjusted to these stationary expectations. The flow conditions (that production equals consumption, or—better—that current demands are equal to new outputs) ensure that stock equilibrium can be maintained. In this simplest of all cases, that is all that there is to be said.

The regularly progressive economy, as always, has much more to it. It also, we may now say, is in equilibrium over time—because it is in stock equilibrium throughout. But its stock equilibrium, at the beginning and end of each single period, will not be the same. For now it is expected that demand will be continuing to expand (at a constant rate). Expected demand will therefore be greater at the end of a period than it was at the beginning. (The demand that is now expected t periods hence will be what was then demanded $t+1$ periods hence; which is greater than what was then demanded t periods hence.) The capital stock must be expanded to be appropriate to this increased demand, if stock equilibrium is to be maintained. There can be no equilibrium over time unless there is this expansion of the capital stock. Flow conditions will therefore include the condition that production should just cover consumption demand plus this required investment. $cg = s$. The Harrod condition emerges as a flow condition of equilibrium over time, in the regularly progressive case. It is then a necessary condition, in order that stock equilibrium should be maintained.

Harrod

Even the regularly progressive economy is a simplified case; our definitions should have a wider scope. It is not necessary that demand expectations should have either of the simple forms so far discussed. More complex cases will soon become very complex; but it is necessary to peer at them a little in order to understand more fully what it is that we have been doing.

Let us suppose—just to get a manageable example—that consumption demand is expected to remain stationary for so many periods, and after that to increase at a given (constant) rate. At the end of the current period, the up-turn will have come one period nearer; end-stock equilibrium will thus require a larger capital than beginning-stock equilibrium; the flow conditions will accordingly entail some positive investment, and hence some positive saving, even in the current period, in which consumption demand is not expanding. Under this condition the economy can be in equilibrium over time, with its capital continually adjusted (as well as it can be adjusted) to these (perhaps anomalous) expectations. And so on for similar cases.

6. A word should perhaps be added on a question that may have been troubling the reader: is the use that we have just been making of the concept of equilibrium over time consistent with our earlier usage? We have here been taking expectations as given, and have been confining equilibrium over time *during the period* to an organization of the economy (both stock and flow) that is consistent with those given expectations. Should we not proceed the other way? Should we not say that an economy is in equilibrium over time if (and only if) expectations are *right*: if the expectations on which plans are based yield consistent plans—plans that can be carried through? This was a line of thought that arose naturally out of Temporary Equilibrium theory. There (as shown)[1] we do come naturally to a concept of long-period equilibrium over time, of which the accordance of expectation with realization is the distinguishing mark. What we say here must be kept in line with it.

The equilibrium over time that we have been discussing in this chapter is an equilibrium of the single period. If the single period is to have no more than a short duration (as we have usually implied to be the case) it can only be a short-period equilibrium over time. There is no reason why the period over which the equilibrium over time extends should not sometimes be short, sometimes long. We can get a long-period equilibrium over time by stringing several short equilibria together.

Even the longest period must be taken to have an end. Appropriate organization during the period must still depend upon the stock that is to be left at the end of the period. If there is to be equilibrium over time, even over a long period, there must be an end-stock equilibrium which is governed by expectations of what is to come afterwards. Such expectations must, in some sense, be data; they cannot be determined as consequences of what goes on within the period. This is true whether we are working with a Fixprice or with a Flexprice model. Something must always be assumed about the further future; in that sense there must always be some residual expectations that must be taken as exogenous.

I have said that equilibrium over time requires the maintenance of stock equilibrium; this may be interpreted as meaning that there is stock equilibrium, not only at the beginning and at the end of the period, but throughout its course. Thus when we regard a 'long' period as a sequence of 'short' periods, the 'long' period

---

[1] p. 75.

can only be in equilibrium over time if every 'short' period in it is in equilibrium over time. Since expectations are to be kept self-consistent, there can be no revision of expectations at the junction between one 'short' period and its successor. The system is in stock equilibrium at each of these junctions; and is in stock equilibrium with respect to these consistent expectations. That can only by possible if expectations—with respect to demands that accrue within the 'long' period—are right. Equilibrium over time does imply consistency between expectations and realizations within the period; it is only the expectations of the further future that are arbitrary—as they must be.

7. So much for stock equilibrium—and for flow equilibrium. It has taken us much trouble to get them right: trouble which the reader may have felt that they hardly deserved, for in Fixprice theory (our main concern) they are little more than bench-marks or standards of reference. What bearing does all this have upon disequilibrium? The main point that has emerged is negative; but it is a negative point of much importance.

If we start from a condition in which there is stock equilibrium (for the 'unit', such as a firm, or for the economy) flow equilibrium conditions ensure its maintenance; but what happens in the more important case when we do not start from stock equilibrium? Flow equilibrium conditions can still be written down (or can usually be written down); but what is their significance? All that they can determine (if they are sufficient to determine it) is the path that the economy would follow if it began with a capital stock that was appropriate to a position upon that path. In that sense the path that is determined is an *equilibrium path*. But if the initial position is not one of stock equilibrium it is not the path that will be followed, nor can we assume that there will be any tendency for it to be approached. It is, at the best, the 'long-period equilibrium' of the system; but whether there is any tendency for that long-period equilibrium to be approached, if we do not start from a position upon its path, is a question that must be left, for the present, entirely open.

IX

A PROBLEM IN STOCK ADJUSTMENT

1. IT will probably assist understanding of the distinctions which have been drawn in the preceding chapter if we see in detail how they work out in a simple case. I shall pursue this simple case rather far, and (as will be seen) the further working out of it is by no means simple. I am not suggesting that this working out is of more than illustrative importance. When the reader has had enough of it he will doubtless pass on. But some sort of illustration, at this point, does seem to be required.

The problem which I shall take is entirely 'micro'. It solely concerns the behaviour of the individual producer (or stock-holder). And it solely concerns that part of his behaviour which relates to the stock (or inventory) of finished product. In particular, the whole question of investment in fixed capital is left entirely on one side.

Prices being fixed, the state of demand is given from outside—it is an exogenous variable. The backwash of changes in production on demand (the multiplier effects which are so important in macro-analysis) is entirely neglected.

2. Let us suppose that our single producer has a single (storable) product, that takes n periods to produce. A decision about the amount to produce, or rather to begin producing, can be taken, according to our usual convention, once a period. (It does not matter whether the process of production is or is not carried on in the same firm as that in which the stocks are held. If it is in a different firm, then the assumption is that orders take n periods to execute.) These assumptions give a convenient framework within which to operate; I do not think that they are unduly restrictive.

As a preliminary, consider what happens when there is a once-for-all increase in demand. We then begin (as is commonly done) from a state of stationary equilibrium in this particular market. If it were certain that demand would remain stationary, no stock (or inventory) would be required. We may, however, admit some degree of uncertainty, so that even in stationary equilibrium there should be some positive stock, related in some manner to the level of demand. The stock-equilibrium condition (the only stock-equilibrium condition which is here of significance) is that the actual stock should equal this desired stock. The flow-equilibrium condition is that current output should equal current demand, so that the producer can *remain* in stock equilibrium. These two conditions being satisfied, there is equilibrium over time (as far as our particular producer is concerned).

Now suppose that there supervenes a significant rise in demand (an unexpected rise), after which demand remains constant at the new level. During the time that elapses before increased output can be ready, there *must* be a fall in stock—an increasing degree of stock disequilibrium. But it is by no means necessary that increased production should be started as soon as the increase in demand shows itself; some time may have to elapse before it is clear that what has occurred is a permanent rise, not a mere random variation. The longer this delay, the larger will be the fall in stock. But even when production is increased, if it is only increased enough to restore the flow condition of equilibrium (so that production again becomes equal to demand when the new output is ready), full equilibrium will not be restored. The state will still be one of stock disequilibrium; all that will have happened, by the adjustment that has so far occurred, is that the stock disequilibrium will be prevented from getting worse. Stock equilibrium will only be restored when the stock has been rebuilt; after there has been an additional (temporary) increase in output to replenish the depleted stock.

This is a situation which continually arises in practice; and in so simple a case as this the producer would certainly have no difficulty in making his adjustment. Knowing how long production takes, and how long he has himself delayed before taking action, he has only to decide in how much of a hurry he is, and so whether to spread the temporary expansion over a shorter or longer time, and his task is done. More generally, indeed, it is by no means so simple. The adjustment of stock to a fluctuating demand will need quite a bit of steering. There is always the double problem: on the one hand he must estimate what the future course of demand will be, and on the other he must correct the excesses and deficiencies of stock that result from past mistakes. Neither of these is an easy problem to solve; but they are nevertheless problems that are solved, more or less well, in the ordinary course of business management.

It is the second of these problems on which I am concentrating in this chapter. It would be immensely convenient, for the purpose of economic analysis, if we could find some way of representing a reasonable reaction to stock disequilibrium by a *rule* of conduct. We could then incorporate that rule into our models; this would enable us to calculate not merely the equilibrium path of the model, but something which might prove to be a good representation of the actual path which (under the conditions proposed) would be likely to be followed. The cycle models which have been constructed by economists[1] do generally incorporate (more or less explicitly) some such rule. But when one tries out these rules, even on so simple a 'micro' problem as that with which we are at present concerned, they do not seem to give good results. By deliberate steering, the ordinary business should usually be able to do better than it appears to do in such a mechanical model. The mechanical models are certainly suggestive, but it is not clear that we are wise to take them as anything more than that.

3. In order to show this I need some notation. Let D_t be the demand, O_t the output, of period t. Let I_t be production *started* in period t, so that $O_t = I_{t-n}$ (for production takes n periods). Let S_t be the actual stock, S_t^* the desired stock, at the *beginning* of period t. It is clearly necessary that

$$S_{t+1} - S_t = O_t - D_t.$$

I shall write

$$S_t^* - S_t = E_t$$

so that in stock equilibrium $E_t = 0$.

(1) The first rule to be considered is the 'Stock Adjustment Principle',[2] according to which the production started in any period is equal to a flow component F (based on what demand is expected to be when the output is ready) plus some fraction of the deficiency E. That is to say,

$$I_t = F_t + \lambda E_t$$

[1] By myself and by many others
[2] I borrow this term from R. C. O. Matthews (*The Trade Cycle*, p. 49). As Matthews observes, the Acceleration Principle, as commonly understood, is a special case of this more general principle.

whence $\qquad O_t = I_{t-n} = F_{t-n} + \lambda E_{t-n}$

$$S_{t+1} - S_t = F_{t-n} - D_t + \lambda E_{t-n}$$

$$E_{t+1} - E_t = (S_{t+1}^* - S_t^*) - (F_{t-n} - D_t + \lambda E_{t-n})$$

or $\qquad E_{t+1} - E_t + \lambda E_{t-n} = S_{t+1}^* - S_t^* + D_t - F_{t-n},$

the *fundamental difference equation* of this method of adjustment.

If equilibrium were maintained throughout, the left-hand side of this fundamental equation would be zero; the right-hand side must therefore be zero. Now all the components of the right-hand side depend in some way upon the manner in which demand (D) moves over time. Corresponding to any given movement of demand, there will be certain movements of F and S^* which will maintain equilibrium. If, for instance, demand was completely stationary, equilibrium would be maintained if S^* were stationary (so that $S_{t+1}^* = S_t^*$), and if production started were always equal to demand ($F_{t-n} = D_t$). If demand was expanding at a constant rate, and S^* was expanding with it, F_{t-n} would have to exceed D_t by an amount sufficient to supply this *equilibrium* increase in stock—so that the increase in demand would have to be foreseen accurately, and the equilibrium increase in stock would also have to be provided for. And so on, if demand were varying in other (foreseen) manners.

Thus if the firm were in equilibrium in time, the right-hand side of our fundamental equation would be zero; but the vanishing of the right-hand side is not a sufficient condition of equilibrium; it is simply what we have been calling the flow condition. If (as in our elementary case of a once-for-all increase in demand) there is a disturbance of equilibrium, there will be initial (disequilibrium) positions in which the E's will not be zero; afterwards, when demand has settled down on to its new path, the right-hand side should again be zero, so that we must have

$$E_{t+1} - E_t + \lambda E_{t-n} = 0$$

though the individual E's are not necessarily zero. This is a difference equation in the E's, the solution of which must depend upon n (the period of production) and upon λ, and upon them only. We can examine whether the 'Stock Adjustment Principle' (as defined) will lead back to equilibrium (or on to the equilibrium path) by asking whether this difference equation, starting from arbitrary values of the E's, will converge to a zero solution.

This is a purely mathematical question which can be explored by the methods that I have described elsewhere.[1] The equation is more difficult than that which gives the 'elementary case' of Accelerator theory, but it turns out to have very similar properties. There are two critical values of λ, which we may call λ_1 and λ_2. If $0 < \lambda < \lambda_1$, there will be a straightforward convergence to equilibrium, without any fluctuations save those that arise as a consequence of the arbitrary initial values. If $\lambda_1 < \lambda < \lambda_2$, there will be damped fluctuations. If $\lambda > \lambda_2$, the fluctuations will be explosive.

Mathematical formulae for λ_1 and λ_2 will be given in Appendix A; their general significance can, however, be explained in simpler terms.

It is obvious that if $\lambda = 1$, while $n > 1$, far too much new production would be started. Enough processes would be started in each single period to fill the whole gap between actual and desired stock that existed in that period; there would thus be a whole series of new startings, one after another, all effectively directed at filling the same gap. That is nonsense; a sensible value of λ must be far smaller than that. A value which naturally suggests itself is $(1/n)$; for 'induced investment', repeated at this rate, would just suffice to close the gap over the whole period of production. But even that, it is not surprising to discover, is too much. For if $\lambda = (1/n)$ is applied to the example with which we began, of the single increase in demand which runs down inventories during the period of production, it becomes apparent that the same fall in inventories is corrected more than once. In fact, it turns out that $\lambda = (1/n)$ gives a fluctuating solution, which is indeed damped, but not very heavily damped. We get a good idea of the values of λ_1 and λ_2 if we take them as

$$\lambda_1 = (1/3)(1/n), \qquad \lambda_2 = (3/2)(1/n)$$

so that $\lambda = (1/n)$ lies between the two critical values, but much nearer to the second than to the first.[2]

I conclude that if, on this principle, there is to be a smooth convergence to equilibrium, the induced investment must be spread

---

[1] *Contribution to the Theory of the Trade Cycle*, Appendix, esp. pp. 187 ff.

[2] If n is large, λ_1 tends to $e^{-1}(1/n)$, and λ_2 to $(\pi/2)(1/n)$; the approximation to values close to these, even for small n, is rather surprisingly fast. (It is easily seen that if $n = 1$, $\lambda_1 = \frac{1}{4}$, $\lambda_2 = 1$.)

very thinly; and (of course) if it is spread very thinly, it will take a long time before equilibrium is restored.

(2) This being so, it is natural to ask whether we could not get a better result from a different rule. The tendency to fluctuation (or rather the *kind* of fluctuation) which we have found to result from the Stock Adjustment Principle, was basically due to the translation of a stock condition into a flow condition: the *flow* of induced investment being made dependent upon the *state* of stock. It might be thought that this could be avoided, if induced investment were made to depend upon *changes* in stock: or, more strictly, on changes in E, the excess of desired stock over actual. It would be a plausible ingredient in a stock policy to suppose that replacement would be stepped up when E was rising; and vice versa.

If this were the only factor affecting the induced investment, we should find (on working through the analysis in the same way as we did with the first rule) that the λE_{t-n} of the former equation was replaced by a difference term, so that the critical difference equation took the form

$$E_{t+1}-E_t+\lambda(E_{t-n}-E_{t-n-1}) = 0$$

and this is an equation which is very easily solved. For it simply means that $E_{t+1}-E_t$ is $(-\lambda)$ of what it was $(n+1)$ periods before. Thus if $\lambda < 1$ (as we may again, but perhaps not so confidently, suppose) $E_{t+1}-E_t$ must converge to zero, though (in view of the negative sign of the multiplier) only after fluctuations. Even so, this does not mean that E_t will converge to zero; it only means that E_t will converge to a constant value (a constant that will depend upon initial conditions). There is no convergence to equilibrium, only to a constant degree of disequilibrium. As a rule that is to be taken by itself, this rule is even less attractive than its predecessor.

There is, however, of course no reason why it should be taken by itself. A producer might quite possibly work mainly on the Stock Adjustment Principle, but might also be influenced to some extent by the way in which his E was rising or falling. (One would indeed think that this would be a very natural thing to happen.) The tendencies to fluctuation which are due to the two components would then be superposed. In superposition they might offset one another, but there does not seem to be any general reason why they should do so. It is difficult to give a mathematical demonstration;

one would, however, guess that they would be more likely to reinforce one another.

(3) There is still another rule which deserves investigation. The defect in the 'Stock Adjustment Principle', as we have so far taken it, is that (as has been explained) it sets the producer filling what is essentially the same gap more than once. (This defect is of course not noticeable if, as is common in trade cycle models, decisions are only supposed to be taken once in every period of production—if the period of production and the decision period are taken to be the same. But as soon as we distinguish the two periods—and surely we ought to distinguish them—we have to face up to it.)

Now it may fairly be maintained that businesses do not in practice make this fault, because they know that the production which is designed to fill the gap is already in the pipe-line. We have left that knowledge out of account, but in practice it is bound to be taken into account. It could formally be taken into account if the Stock Adjustment Principle were *enlarged*; if it were applied, not simply (as we have so far applied it) to the inventory of finished product, but to the whole of the circulating capital—inventory *plus* goods in process.

This enlarged rule could formally be worked out in the same way as we have worked out the other; but as soon as we make the attempt we run into a difficulty. How do we value the goods in process? They would of course be valued in practice in terms of the labour and materials that had been put into them at each stage, a profit to cover overheads not being added until sale (so that it has nothing to do with the *relative* values of goods in process and final inventory). Now there is no reason why these labour and materials should be applied at a constant rate; all sorts of patterns of time application are possible. The proportion of the total prime cost that will be attributed to the unfinished product, when a given fraction of its total production time has elapsed, may thus vary quite considerably for this purely technical reason. But such differences have nothing to do with the question that here concerns us. It is entirely possible that there might be one productive process, with one time-shape of application, where the use of the enlarged rule made for an easy convergence to equilibrium, while there was another, with a different time weighting, where it did not. Thus it looks unlikely that we can give a general verdict on the enlarged principle. The best that we can hope to do is to work out special cases.

One special case which looks as if it would deserve discussion is the 'point-input' case, in which the whole value is put into the article as soon as it is started, so that goods in process are valued as equivalent to finished products. Though this is not a realistic assumption, it puts the maximum possible weight upon the 'goods in process' component, so that it should be the limiting case, at the other extreme from that which we began by examining (when no weight at all was placed upon them). Let us see how this case would come out, if we submitted it to the same analysis as we did the other.

The enlarged Stock Adjustment Principle may still be expressed as $I_t = F_t + \lambda E_t$, where F_t is the same flow component, but E_t, the excess of desired over actual, is now to relate to the _whole circulating capital_. That is to say, $E_t = K_t^* - K_t$, where $K_t = S_t + C_t$, in which S_t (as before) is the inventory, while C_t is goods in process. Our _special_ 'point-input' assumption will now be expressed by putting.

$$C_t = I_{t-1} + I_{t-2} + \dots + I_{t-n+1}$$

(on any other assumption about time-shape the I's would have weights that were less than 1, increasing from left to right).

Thus $E_t = K_t^* - (S_t + I_{t-1} + I_{t-2} + \dots I_{t-n+1})$.

As before $S_{t+1} - S_t = O_t - D_t = I_{t-n} - D_t$

and so

$$\begin{aligned}
E_{t+1} - E_t &= K_{t+1}^* - K_t^* - (S_{t+1} - S_t) - (I_t - I_{t-n+1}) \\
&= K_{t+1}^* - K_t^* - (I_{t-n} - D_t) - (I_t - I_{t-n+1}) \\
&= K_{t+1}^* - K_t^* + D_t - F_{t-n} - F_t + F_{t-n+1} - \\
&\qquad - \lambda(E_{t-n} + E_t - E_{t-n+1}),
\end{aligned}$$

an equation which is now in a form which is suitable for the same treatment as we gave to the corresponding equation in the 'unenlarged' case.

Putting all E's $= 0$, we get the flow condition; then, supposing the flow condition of equilibrium to be already established, we get the critical difference equation

$$E_{t+1} - (1 - \lambda)E_t - \lambda(E_{t-n+1} - E_{t-n}) = 0.$$

The effectiveness for equilibration of the enlarged Stock Adjustment Principle (on our particular assumption about time-shape of inputs) can then be tested, as in the other case, by inquiring whether the sequence defined by this equation, if it starts from arbitrary E's, will converge to $E = 0$.

An analysis of this equation (perhaps a little less complete than that which I give for its predecessor) will be found in the second section of Appendix A. From this the following conclusions appear to follow.

It should first be noticed that if $n = 1$, this equation is the same as its predecessor; for (of course) if $n = 1$, 'enlargement' makes no difference. Accordingly, for $n = 1$, $\lambda_1 = (1/4)$ and $\lambda_2 = 1$, as before.

For any value of n greater than 1, either $\lambda_2 = (2/3)$ or it is so little above $(2/3)$ as hardly to signify. This restriction is much less drastic than the corresponding restriction in the 'unenlarged' case, but that (of course) is as it should be. There ought now to be no question of filling the same gap more than once. Even so, the induced investment must be somewhat spread out if there is to be a convergence to equilibrium, even after fluctuations.

As for λ_1, it is larger than in the 'unenlarged' case, as we should expect, but it remains fairly small. It diminishes as n rises; for any value of n greater than 2, it is less than $(1/6)$. The induced investment must still be very gentle indeed if there is to be no tendency for (even damped) fluctuation.

4. It is unnecessary to take this particular investigation any further; the reader may indeed feel that we have already taken it quite far enough. It is hardly a discovery that to find that we are unable to 'simulate' the behaviour of intelligent business management by any simple rule. But I have thought it worth while to work the matter out in detail, for another reason. We needed an exercise in the working of the stock and flow analysis that was described in principle, but only in principle, in the preceding chapter. Instead of beginning with its application to the 'macro' problems, where it (or something like it) is most familiar, I thought it well to begin by trying it out on the 'micro' scale. We then keep close to the kind of thing which we can test out by our imagination—by putting ourselves in the position of the 'people' whose actions we are trying to represent. If we find—as we do find—that mechanical principles

of adjustment do not offer a good representation, we shall have gained something in the way of scepticism about the use of such principles in more ambitious undertakings. And this (I think we shall find) will be quite useful to us later on.

X

KEYNES-TYPE MACRODYNAMICS

1. IN this chapter, and in that which follows, I shall be considering the application of stock and flow analysis to Fixprice macroeconomics. Even within this limited field there are two kinds of model to be considered.

The first, with which in this chapter I shall be wholly concerned, is based upon that which was used by Keynes in the *General Theory* It is not the same as the Keynes model (which, as I have repeatedly emphasized, is not strictly a dynamic model); but it has an unmistakable relation to the Keynes model, and it is by that relation that it is easiest to recognize and remember it.[1]

In Keynes, the volume of investment depends upon the rate of interest; it is read off from the 'marginal efficiency of capital' schedule. As soon as we interpret Keynes in a Fixprice sense (as many of his successors have been inclined to do), the rate of interest becomes an exogenous variable (like other prices), so that the *given* marginal efficiency of capital schedule becomes a *given* volume of investment. But to go so far as that, in a properly dynamic model, will be very inconvenient; if actual (*ex post*) investment is given, there is no room for a dynamic process to work. It is accordingly inevitable, when one is concerned with dynamic analysis, that the strict Keynes assumption should be relaxed in some way or other. It may be done by introducing lags, or by distinguishing between *ex ante* and *ex post* investment. I am going to suggest a rather different way, which leads to a form of analysis that seems to have a place in the present discussion.

2. Instead of supposing that the volume of investment, as a whole, is given exogenously, let us suppose that a part only is so given. Formally, it might be a large part or a small part. We might simply mark off some sort of 'long-range investment' as autonomous

---

[1] I am tempted to follow the (undoubtedly appropriate) precedent of Professor Kahn who in his article on Duopoly (*Economic Journal*, 1938) used 'Cournotesque' in just the way that I have in mind. But 'Keynesesque' is too clumsy; 'Keynes-type' (like a 'claret-type' wine) will have to do.

investment; or we might reckon as autonomous the whole of that investment which is the object of deliberate policy decisions, excluding only that part which takes place 'passively' (as a difference between *ex ante* and *ex post*). The choice which we make on this matter cannot be decided by an appeal to facts. It is not a question of fact; it is a question of what we are trying to do. One might use one classification for one purpose and one for another.[1]

The particular line which I shall use in this chapter will leave a big part of investment as autonomous—nothing less than the whole of investment in fixed capital. This is quite a convenient line in practical application. It is in fact the common practice of business to take decisions about investment in fixed capital in a different way, and on a different level, from decisions about investment in working capital and stocks—the former being a matter for the board of directors, the latter (since it is a resultant of innumerable day-to-day decisions) being only influenced indirectly by major decisions that are made 'at the top'. Thus the division at this line makes quite good sense. It is an interesting question to inquire into the working of an economy in which fixed capital investment is planned—along lines that are determined outside the model—while the rest of investment adjusts itself, as best it can, to that given pattern of autonomous fixed capital investment.

The initial stock of fixed capital, at the beginning of the process under consideration, must of course be assumed to be given; if *net* fixed capital investment in every capital good is also given, the size and composition of the fixed capital stock will be given, throughout the whole of the process. It may, however, be maintained that it would be more sensible to take *gross* investment in fixed capital to be given autonomously, the extent of depreciation (or using-up) being left to be determined as a function of output as a whole. But if it is simply proportional to output as a whole there is no difficulty; I shall therefore simplify presentation by taking it that what is given is *net* fixed capital investment.

3. The working of a Keynes-type model, such as has been described, is mostly familiar; but it will be useful to set it down in

---

[1] In my *Trade Cycle* book I confined autonomous investment to the long-range variety; but it makes little difference to the formal argument whether a wide or a narrow definition is used.

the standard form to which we have been coming. One begins, of course, from the saving-investment *identity*. If A_t is net investment in fixed capital in period t, Y_t is income (or net output), and K_t is *working capital* (including stocks) at the commencement of period t, the identity can be written

$$A_t + (K_{t+1} - K_t) = sY_t$$

where s is the proportion of income saved. If, however, we write K_t^* for *desired* working capital, and $E_t = K_t^* - K_t$ (as in the previous chapter) the identity takes the form

$$A_t + (K_{t+1}^* - K_t^*) - sY_t = E_{t+1} - E_t$$

and a *flow condition of equilibrium* can be derived from it by setting E_{t+1} and E_t equal to zero.

Desired working capital must clearly depend upon the expected level of output; it should thus (in equilibrium) depend upon Y_t, $Y_{t+1}, ..., Y_{t+n}$, where n is the number of periods that are taken by that process of production (starting from original factors, including fixed capital as an original factor) that takes longest. It is a simplification (though a very usual simplification) to make it depend upon Y_t alone. I shall, however, make use of this simplification, along with others, since it is irrelevant to the main points which I want to make.

Let us therefore put $K_t^* = cY_t$, so that c is a *working-capital–output ratio*. Our *flow condition of equilibrium* accordingly becomes

$$A_t + c(Y_{t+1} - Y_t) = sY_t$$

and this, it must be observed, is a *difference equation*. Even if c and s are taken to be constants, it will not, by itself, determine an equilibrium path. It is simply a rule by which, if Y_t is given, Y_{t+1} can be determined. Thus it only determines a particular equilibrium path if we are also supplied with an *initial condition*; for instance, if we are given a value for Y_0.

Once that initial value is provided, the difference equation will determine the *equilibrium* course of output, corresponding to *any* given movement of A_t. There is no need for us to assume that autonomous investment is increasing at a constant growth rate; it may follow any *given* path. It is indeed possible, with the simplifications that we have made, for the difference equation to be solved, rather easily, whatever the path of A_t. The general solution is

$$Y_t = \left(1 + \frac{s}{c}\right)^t Y_0 - \frac{1}{c}\left\{A_{t-1} + \left(1 + \frac{s}{c}\right)A_{t-2} + \dots + \left(1 + \frac{s}{c}\right)^{t-1} A_0\right\}.$$

Thus Y_t will always have a growth rate which is less than s/c; remembering that c is the *working* capital–output ratio, this makes good sense.

Let us look for a moment at the special case where autonomous investment has a constant growth rate g; so that $A_t = A_0 (1+g)^t$. (Though this is a case that is easy to over-use, it has its uses as an important example.) The series in the square bracket then becomes a geometrical progression, and can be summed by the usual rule, giving

$$Y_t = \left(1 + \frac{s}{c}\right)^t \left(Y_0 - \frac{A_0}{s - cg}\right) + \frac{A_0}{s - cg} (1+g)^t.$$

In this case, then, equilibrium output has two components, one with the growth rate s/c, one with the growth rate g. Now it is clear that s/c must be greater than g. For if it were not so, though the first component would be positive, the second would be negative; and it would be this negative second component the size of which would be increasing faster. After a while, therefore, Y_t would certainly become negative—a possibility that must be ruled out. With constantly increasing (positive) autonomous investment, equilibrium output cannot be allowed to behave so badly. The condition $s > cg$ in fact says no more than that there is enough saving to support the increase in fixed capital and the consequential increase in working capital.

If $s > cg$, the second component is necessarily positive; but now it is the first component which has the faster rate of growth. Accordingly, if $Y_0 < A_0/(s-cg)$, we shall again find that Y_t becomes negative for large t. It follows that we cannot impose *any* initial Y_0 and get a sensible sequence for Y_t. We must have either Y_0 greater than or equal to $A_0/(s-cg)$.

In the former case, both components in Y_t will be positive, but the first will be growing faster. The growth rate of Y_t will therefore be rising towards the growth rate of this first component, which is s/c. But if investment in fixed capital is growing at a growth rate g, the total stock of fixed capital (though its initial growth rate may be in excess of g) must ultimately tend to rise at a growth rate g.

Output will then be trying to rise at a growth rate s/c, which is larger than g. There must therefore, sooner or later, be a shortage of fixed capital. If there is not to be a shortage, the growth rate of Y_t must not be larger than g. And this can only happen (we now see) if $Y_0 = A_0/(s-cg)$, so that $Y_t = Y_0 (1+g)^t$.

Thus there is, after all, only one equilibrium path of output—in this particular case.

$$Y_T = Y_0 (1+g)^?$$

4. What has happened? In the light of our general principles about stock and flow conditions it is not hard to locate the trouble. As I have repeatedly insisted, the flow condition is not a sufficient condition of equilibrium; thus it is not surprising to find that the equilibrium path cannot be adequately identified by mere manipulation of the flow condition. In order to determine the equilibrium path, stock conditions as well as flow conditions must be considered.

It may nevertheless be objected—have we not already made use of the stock condition? We have already taken it that desired capital (K_t^*) depends upon expected output (Y_t on our simplification). Surely this is a stock condition: yet it appears that it does not do its job. The answer, I think we must conclude, is that this condition is not the only stock condition. Though we have assumed that investment in fixed capital is given autonomously, it remains true that its holding of fixed assets is a part of the balance-sheet of the representative firm; a balance between holdings of fixed capital assets and of working capital assets is still to be required, as a necessary element in stock (or balance-sheet) equilibrium. The holding of fixed capital assets is, by assumption, a given magnitude, at each stage of the process; but the holding of working capital assets is a variable, which must nevertheless bear a certain relation to the holding of fixed capital assets, if equilibrium is to be maintained. One may indeed not wish to press this proportionality too exactly; for the ratio is not one that firms may be expected, in practice, to watch very closely. But, as is already apparent from our study of the particular case of the constant autonomous investment growth rate, any significant departure from a normal ratio is likely to build up. What began as a tolerable discrepancy builds up into something that is quite intolerable. I therefore include that proportionality (or approximate proportionality) between investment in working capital and in fixed capital is a condition that we ought to impose, when we are seeking to determine the Equilibrium Path of a Keynes-type model.

With this additional condition, everything becomes very simple. The flow condition of equilibrium is just the saving-investment equation, with the whole of investment (in equilibrium) deducible from autonomous investment, so that Y_t (in equilibrium) is then deducible from the saving propensity (just the old multiplier). The Keynes-type model reduces to the familiar form, after all.[1]

5. But, from all that has so far been said, all we have got is the equilibrium path. It is an equilibrium path (it must be insisted) only in the sense that *if* the initial stock of working capital is appropriate, and *if* demand-expectations are right, it is the path that will be followed. Nothing has been said about any tendency towards this equilibrium—from a disequilibrium position. It is the common practice, in Keynesian Economics, to take it for granted that there will be a rapid movement to equilibrium; so that the equilibrium position of an economy can be taken to represent its actual position, to be at least a fair approximation to it. But it will not be supposed, after our discussion of the corresponding micro-problem in the preceding chapter, that we shall here be able to make any confident statement about a tendency to the equilibrium that has been here described.

Let us proceed in the conventional manner with an equilibrium motion that is *disturbed*. That is to say, we start with an economy that is in equilibrium with respect to a given path of autonomous investment; expectations are right, and the stocks of working capital are such as to be appropriate to this particular path. We need not assume (any more than we did in Chapter IX) that the stocks are no more than are technologically necessary to support this growth path; the stocks that are necessary to permit a 'normal'

---

[1] It may perhaps have been noticed by some readers that in the last two sections I have been trying to mend a hole (of which I have for years been conscious) in the argument of my book on the *Trade Cycle*. The Equilibrium Path (as it appears, for example, in the diagram on p. 97 of that book) has long seemed to me to be inadequately defined. Even in the mathematical treatment (pp. 174–6 and 197–8 of the Appendix) it only appears as the limit to which the 'actual' process will converge, if it converges; but what if (as I frequently wanted to suppose) it does not converge? I still wanted to have an equilibrium path, if only for purposes of reference. I am now convinced that the trouble arose from inadequate attention to stock conditions; this is what I am now trying to explain.

degree of flexibility may also be supposed to be carried. Then, in a particular period, there is a shift in autonomous investment. It increases (we will first suppose) beyond what it was expected in the past to be for the current period. Is it *possible* that there can be an immediate (or nearly immediate) adjustment to a new equilibrium, that which corresponds to the new autonomous investment path?

I will begin by constructing a case in which it is possible that there could be a very direct adjustment. Suppose that production (both of fixed capital goods and of consumption goods) takes place in a series of stages, of equal length, each stage using the product of the preceding as raw material. Say that each stage lasts one month. Then, if there is an unforeseen spurt in autonomous investment—more new production of fixed capital goods is started in a particular month than was expected—there will be a direct increase in the employment of labour in that month (on the new fixed capital good production), and a consequential increase in demand for consumption goods, which we shall suppose to take place within the same month (there is no consumption lag). During the month that increased demand for consumption goods can only be met out of stocks; and it can be so met, if it is not too large, for we are taking it for granted that there are 'normal' stocks of consumption goods that can be run down.

Now it is just conceivable that at the moment when the additional consumption demand appears, production in the final stage should be increased. The deficiency in stocks of consumption goods might then be remedied within the month, so that, at the end of the month, the stock of the final product would already have reached its new equilibrium. But in order for this to be, even technically, possible, there must have been a stock of the raw material of the final stage; otherwise the production of the final stage could not have been stepped up. We may suppose (in accordance with our 'normal stock' hypothesis) that this stock does exist. But then, if final stage production is stepped up, and nothing else happens, the fall in stocks is simply passed one stage further back. Again, however, it is just conceivable (though with even more difficulty conceivable) that as soon as the increase in demand for the product of the penultimate stage began to declare itself, production in that stage also would be stepped up; but for this to be possible there must again be a stock of the raw material of the penultimate stage on which that stage can work. And so on, right back to the beginning.[1]

It seems to follow that if production is divided into equal stages, and if response to a change in demand is immediate all along the line, it is possible that stock equilibrium may be restored at the end of the 'month'. From that point onwards, there is of course no difficulty. Accordingly, if we take the single period to be one month, and if these conditions are satisfied, the system is again in equilibrium at the end of the single period.

But it is only too obvious what drastic assumptions we have to make in order that this should be possible. The necessary reaction is (as I have said elsewhere)[2] 'unbelievably quick'. But even that is not enough. It is also necessary that stocks should be held at regular intervals in the production process; and it will ordinarily be impossible technologically that they should be so held. It is of course always possible to divide a production process, arbitrarily, into equal-length stages; but some (perhaps many) of them will then be stages at which it is technologically impossible to hold stocks. It will then be impossible that equilibrium should be restored, after a disturbance, until quite a long interval has elapsed. And this is apart from the question of lags in adjustment. If there is a lag, the time taken for adjustment must be even longer.

It is in fact unreasonable to suppose that there will not be a lag. Accordingly, in the first period after autonomous investment has increased, there will be a fall in stocks, either entirely at the final stage of consumption goods production, or (in part) at earlier stages. At this point the rise in autonomous investment is partially offset by a fall in working capital (induced) investment, so that total output (Y) rises only to something short of its new equilibrium level. But so long as actual output remains, in this manner, below its equilibrium path, stocks will be falling, and ever more falling, below their equilibrium level; sooner or later this gap must be made up. As soon as an attempt is made to fill this gap, output will rise relatively to its equilibrium path, and will then rise above the equilibrium path, remaining above it until the gap has been filled.

---

[1] If there is a beginning. It is not unrealistic to suppose that there is; we can have a first stage in which there is no raw material, since we are assuming that there is a given stock of fixed capital, which may include land. The first stage may be extractive. But I do not think that this is essential to the argument.

[2] *Trade Cycle*, p. 50.

Now it is tempting to treat this 'spurt' or 'hump' in induced investment as if it were wholly analogous to the original rise in autonomous investment, so that it will lead to consequences of a similar character. It is certainly true that it also involves a rise in inputs, with a consequent effect upon the demand for finished products; it will therefore induce a 'multiplier' expansion of its own, on the top of that engendered by the original expansion (the expansion of output that was incorporated in the equilibrium path). But, especially in view of what we have learned (in the preceding chapter) about the corresponding disequilibrium on the micro-level, it would seem unwise to be dogmatic about the form which this secondary expansion *must* take. In particular, it would be unwise to assume that it must take the form which can be deduced by mechanical application of an 'Accelerator' or 'Stock Adjustment Principle'.

This is not to say that calculation of the cyclical movements, which emerge when we 'turn the handle' according to such rules, is a pure waste of time. It does unquestionably have an illustrative value; it is a useful indicator of the kind of thing that can happen. But one should not put too much weight upon it.[1] There is a most important distinction between the induced investment which is allowed for in the determination of the equilibrium path, and that which arises in the process of equilibration. The former is a technical necessity; it arises out of permanent factors in the technique of production, such as are expressible in a capital–output ratio. The latter is much more 'psychological' in character. It depends, first of all, on the amount of initial divergence from the equilibrium path; and this, though (as we have seen) it is partly a matter of technology, is mainly a matter of the way the change in demand is interpreted, of the way it is read, of the expectations which it engenders. As soon as there is a gap—as soon as actual stock falls, significantly, below desired stock—the deficiency must somehow, sooner or later, be made up. But how quickly it has to be made up depends upon the degree of discomfort which businesses experience when they are out of stock equilibrium; and that is a thing which has been left quite undetermined by the things that have been taken into account in the model under discussion.

It is not surprising, in the light of the foregoing, to find that

---

[1] Work upon the periods of the cycles that are generated by such mechanisms is (I have now come to think) particularly a waste of time.

simple Accelerator formulae rarely provide a good fit to the time-shape of actual cycles. The forces which the formulae take into account may still be the main forces at work; but the things which determine the time-shape of the cycles which they produce are of a more complex character.

6. If, still starting from an equilibrium position, one had worked out the effects of a downward (instead of an upward) shift in autonomous investment, most of the preceding analysis could have been put, without qualification, into reverse. There is more possibility of interrupting in the middle a process that has been begun than of starting in the middle a process that has not been begun; but the loss involved in such interruption is usually severe, so that it will not occur unless prospects are rather desperate. In all but such extreme cases, we must expect that there will be some unwanted accumulation of stocks, as a result of the initial downward shift—some necessary accumulation, but an actual accumulation that goes beyond what is technologically necessary. There will then be a surplus that has to be worked off—sooner or later, quickly or slowly.

What, however, if (as will surely be the case in application) we do not start from an equilibrium position? If, initially, the stock of working capital is too large, relatively to its equilibrium amount, the excess will be due to be worked off, with the consequences with which we are now familiar. A fall in autonomous investment, below what was expected, if it occurred in that case, would have an additive effect; but a rise in autonomous investment would diminish the surplus, so that a movement into equilibrium would be easier than it was before. Similarly if the initial disequilibrium was the other way. These (of course) were the situations with which Keynes (writing when he did) was most immediately concerned; but the others, that are more likely to give rise to inventory cycles, would deserve, in a truly 'general' theory, at least equal attention.

XI

HARROD-TYPE MACRODYNAMICS

1. THE Keynes-type theory, if it is formulated in the way that we have been formulating it, obviously needs to be completed by a consideration of what happens when fixed capital investment is not given autonomously, but is itself dependent, in whole or in part, on changes in output. I am still inclined to believe that there are purposes for which it is wise to leave a part of fixed capital investment autonomous (as I did in my *Trade Cycle* book); if one is thinking of a model that is to throw light on actual historical experience, it is as well that there should be a part of the phenomena which one's model does not attempt to explain. But for purposes of pure theory, where our object is the understanding of the principles on which economic processes work, it may be better to be more extreme. The working of an economy, in which all investment is induced investment, is one of the things which we should like to understand. It is a model of this kind which I shall call a Harrod-type model.[1]

The basic algebra of such a model is very familiar, but we had better write it out, in our own terms. Prices, as usual, are taken to be fixed, and there is no shortage of labour. Let K_t (now) be the whole stock of capital at the commencement of period t (fixed capital as well as working capital being included). Then the saving-investment identity is merely

$$K_{t+1} - K_t = sY_t$$

without any autonomous term. If the desired capital (K_t^*) bears a constant proportion (c) to output (Y_t), then, in equilibrium (where $K_t = K_t^*$ and $K_{t+1} = K_{t+1}^*$)

$$c(Y_{t+1} - Y_t) = sY_t$$

[1] I use this expression, as I have done the corresponding expression in the other case, so as to allow myself the liberty of neglecting qualifications, very properly introduced by Harrod (and by Domar) in their relevant writings, but which for my present purpose do not signify. The relation of my Harrod-type model to Harrod's own will nevertheless be recognized to be closer than that which my Keynes-type model bore to Keynes's.

so that the growth rate of output is s/c. $cg = s$, as (by now) everybody knows.

But before we can use this equation, before we can set it to work, there are several things about it that need to be noticed.

(1) K_t is the value of capital, measured at the fixed prices; we do not need to make any artificial assumption about capital being homogeneous, in order to be able—in this sense—to add capital goods together. But if we interpret K_t in this sense, then $K_t = K_t^*$ is a necessary, but not sufficient, condition of stock equilibrium; for it is possible that the aggregates might be equal, but that the actual stocks of some sorts of capital (in some or all industries) might be greater than desired, these excesses being offset by corresponding deficiencies of other sorts. This is a possibility which one tends to leave out, when one is thinking in 'macro' terms; but here, as we shall find, it is important to be able to refer to it on some occasions.

(2) We do not have to assume that s (the saving coefficient) is constant from period to period; but it is implied in the algebra that c (the capital–output ratio) is the same at the beginning of the period and at the end. In general, however, there is no need for desired capital to depend upon output in any simple manner.

(3) Even if these qualifications are neglected, all that is determined by the Harrod equation is the equilibrium (or 'warranted') rate of growth; but this is not sufficient to determine the equilibrium path. $cg = s$ is simply a flow condition, with the usual properties of flow conditions of equilibrium; in order that it should determine an equilibrium path completely, it needs to be filled out in some way or other. We cannot fill it out as we did in the Keynes-type theory, for there is now no part of the capital stock that is autonomously determined. Some further specification is needed if we are to have a determinate equilibrium path, if only as a standard of reference.

2. In order to see how this is, let us now suppose that s and c are constant over time. The Harrod equation, treated as a difference equation (just as simple a difference equation as can possibly be conceived), will then have the solution

$$Y_t = (1 + s/c)^t Y_0$$

but this is a path which is not determined until Y_0 is determined. What determines Y_0? As we shall see, this is a question that can be answered in more than one way.

An equilibrium path, let us remember, is a path that will (and can) be followed if expectations are appropriate to it, and if the initial capital stock is appropriate to it; both conditions are necessary. Now it is true that in any *actual* sequence (which may not be an equilibrium sequence) we must begin, at the commencement of period O, with a capital stock (K_0) that is inherited from the past; in the construction of an actual sequence, from that time onwards, this initial stock must be treated as a datum. But in the actual sequence Y_0 is not a datum in the same sense; it may be larger or smaller according as the initial stock is more or less fully employed. If the initial stock is a balanced stock, so that there is some output for which it is the desired stock, that will be the output that is given by the stock condition of equilibrium, $K_0 = cY_0$. One of the ways in which the Harrod equation can be interpreted is to take it as showing the equilibrium path that will be followed if the expectational condition is satisfied, if the initial capital is balanced, and if, in the initial period, it is fully used. The equation to this path might more appropriately be written

$$Y_t = (1+s/c)^t (K_0/c),$$

a path which (under the above assumptions) is unquestionably fully determined, once K_0 is given.

Such a 'full employment of capital' path is undoubtedly an important concept; we shall often be meeting it (and more complex developments of it) in later chapters. Here, however, I doubt if it is at home. I doubt if this path has any right to be selected as *the* equilibrium path of a Harrod-type model.

For consider what happens if, in the initial period, capital is not balanced, or is not fully employed. (We might alternatively have assumed that the capital stock was employed at more than optimum intensity, for there is no reason to suppose that optimum intensity is the same as maximum capacity.) There will still be an actual production (Y_0) in the initial period. And there will still be an equilibrium path starting from that actual output, the path that would be followed if expectations were right, and if the initial capital had been appropriate, in size and in composition, to this initial output.

But if this path is to be truly an equilibrium path, the initial output must surely be an equilibrium output. We have still not overcome the difficulty.

3. A possible way in which the difficulty might be overcome is the following.[1]

K_t, as has been said, is the capital stock at the commencement of period t; Y_t is output during period t. At the commencement of the period, output during the period is *future* output. This we have allowed for; there is stock equilibrium at the beginning of the period (I have repeatedly maintained) if the capital stock at that date is appropriate to this *expected* output. By our condition that in equilibrium expectations are right, we have brought 'expecteds' and 'actuals' together, *along the equilibrium path*. But if it is not an equilibrium path that is being followed, this identity cannot be assumed. It may nevertheless be granted that, even in general, expectations must be founded, in some way and to some extent, upon past experience. If expected output is based upon past output, it is a fair simplification[2] (comparable to that made when we assumed constancy in the original capital–output ratio itself) to reinterpret stock equilibrium to imply that there should be proportionality between the capital stock of time t and the realized output of period $t-1$. We then have

$$K_t = c^* Y_{t-1}$$

as our reinterpreted stock-equilibrium condition. (I mark the new capital–output ratio as c^*, in order to indicate that it is now to be taken in this *ex post* sense.)

It will, however, be noticed that we are making an additional assumption when we take it that expectations are formed in this simple manner. More complex assumptions of the same type (which may well be more realistic) are evidently possible. $K_t = c^* Y_{t-1}$ is merely the simplest form which this relation can take; it is sufficient for most present purposes to take it in this form, but we must not become too dependent on it.

If, however, we accept this relation, and if c^* is to be constant

---

[1] I think it is this which Harrod must have had in mind, though it is concealed by his habit of working with continuous time, not divided into periods.

[2] Cf. the assumption about price-expectations that was made in Chapter VI, above.

over time (another assumption!), maintenance of stock equilibrium will require that

$$K_{t+1} - K_t = c^*(Y_t - Y_{t-1}) = sY_t$$

whence it follows that

$$Y_t = \frac{c^*}{c^* - s} Y_{t-1}$$

or
$$c^* g = s(1 + g).$$

Mathematically, this looks hardly different from the Harrod formula; if we shrink the period, so as to work with continuous time, they become identical. But the significance of the revised formula is quite markedly different.

For if, as before, we take our start at time 0 (the beginning of period 0), stock equilibrium requires that $K_0 = c^* Y_{-1}$. And Y_{-1}, since it belongs to the past, is unquestionably given. If the initial K_0 is such as to satisfy this equation, then it is possible that the economy may proceed on an equilibrium path, given by

$$Y_t = (1 + g)^{t+1} Y_{-1}$$

(with g determined by the revised Harrod formula). But if the stock condition $K_0 = c^* Y_{-1}$ is not satisfied, it is not possible for the economy to follow an equilibrium path. If the flow condition is satisfied, the stock condition will never be satisfied. Both conditions must be satisfied if a true equilibrium path is to be followed.

4. It will be noticed that for this formulation to make sense it is necessary to have $c^* > s$. This looks a harmless condition, which one begins by feeling no difficulty in accepting; for s must be < 1, and one is used to values of the capital–output ratio which are much higher. It must, however, be observed that while s (being a ratio of flow to flow) is a pure number, the capital–output ratio is a ratio of stock to flow; thus the figure that we put upon it depends on the length of the unit period. If we are working with a period of (say) one month, c^* should be very large; but if we change to a 'long' period of (say) five years, the condition $c^* > s$ will be much less obviously satisfied.

It is nevertheless clear that we must have $c^* > s$, whatever the length of the period, if a Harrod-type equilibrium, interpreted as we have interpreted it, is to be possible at all.

This is an important matter; for (as we shall see) the celebrated 'instability' of the Harrod model depends upon it.

Consider an economy that, up to time t (the beginning of period t) has been pursuing an equilibrium path. At that point producers become more optimistic, so that they seek to expand the rate of growth (or, what comes to the same thing, the rate at which they are seeking to accumulate capital). This would be expressed, in the terms which we are now using, by a rise in the *desired* capital–output ratio c^*. The actual capital–output ratio at that time (which is K_t/Y_{t-1}, as we now reckon it) cannot of course be affected, since K_t and Y_{t-1} are already established. It is, however, to be expected that there will be a rise in actual accumulation during period t, above what it would have been if the access of optimism had not occurred. Producers will endeavour to raise K_{t+1}/Y_t towards the desired figure, and the only means that they have at their disposal to do so is to increase investment. But, under the conditions supposed, an increase in investment must have the wrong effect.

Whether or not the economy is in equilibrium, it must always be true that

$$K_{t+1} - K_t = sY_t$$

(for this is an identity). The same relation must hold, for the relevant magnitudes, in the new sequence and in the old (the sequence as it would have been if the access of optimism had not occurred). In order to distinguish, let us say that the access of optimism changes Y_t into $Y_t + \delta Y_t$, and similarly for the other variables. We must then have, in the new sequence

$$K_{t+1} + \delta K_{t+1} - K_t = s(Y_t + \delta Y_t)$$

(for K_t, being the actual capital stock at the moment when the access of optimism occurs, must be unaffected).

Taking the difference of these two equations,

$$\delta K_{t+1} = s\delta Y_t.$$

The realized increase in capital, in the one path over the other, is simply equal to the extra saving. It follows that the realized capital–output ratio, at time $t+1$, must be less, not only than the desired ratio ($c^* + \delta c^*$), but than the old ratio (c^*). For (along the old sequence) $K_{t+1} = c^*Y_t$ (the old path was an equilibrium path). Therefore

$$\frac{K_{t+1} + \delta K_{t+1}}{Y_t + \delta Y_t} = \frac{c^*Y_t + s\delta Y_t}{Y_t + \delta Y_t}$$

and this must be $< c^*$, since $s < c^*$.

It accordingly follows that in attempting to raise c^*, producers will only have succeeded in lowering it. They will thus, in period $t+1$, have an increased incentive to expand investment, which may be expected to lead to a further movement away from the equilibrium path. There is a cumulative divergence from equilibrium.

5. It is interesting to notice that this 'proof' of instability is not seriously affected if we abandon the assumption that the desired capital depends, in the simple way that we have hitherto taken it to do, upon the output of the previous period only. Suppose, for instance, that it depends upon the average of the outputs of the two preceding periods. We have only to take those two periods together, forming a 'long' period out of them; we can then let the 'long' period stand for the previous period of the model. The whole of the preceding argument will still hold. It must nevertheless be noticed that by lengthening the period, we diminish c^*. On the other hand, however much we lengthen the period in this manner, we must still have $c^* > s$; otherwise it would be impossible that an equilibrium path, for a model of this character, should exist at all.

Lagging of this kind does not diminish the instability; it may slow it up (in initial stages), but that is all. It is different if we drop the assumption (on which the whole argument has hitherto depended) that s (the *average* propensity to save) is unaffected by the change in income. That s should be constant along an equilibrium path is perhaps acceptable; but that it should be unaffected when there is a disturbance of equilibrium is rather a different matter. If we rework the equations for the difference between two paths, making s variable, the saving–investment identities will give

$$\delta K_{t+1} = \delta(sY_t)$$

so that the realized capital–output ratio will only fall if

$$c^* > \delta(sY_t)/\delta Y_t$$

which is the *marginal* saving-propensity. It is hardly possible that even this marginal propensity can be greater than unity; thus for a 'short' period (even of quite moderate length), even this stronger condition should be quite readily satisfied. But it is clearly possible that for a 'long' period it might not be; c^* might be less than the marginal, even though it was greater than the average propensity to save. Accordingly, given sufficient lagging, *and* a tendency for saving to rise with income (at least when out of equilibrium) the instability of the Harrod-type model could be removed.

A tendency for saving to rise with income (when out of equilibrium) could alternatively be expressed in terms of consumption lags. As is found by other methods, such lags do have a tendency to have a stabilizing effect.[1] But it would certainly appear from the foregoing that, in a Harrod-type model, they would have to be very strong in order to be effective.

6. There is a remarkable correspondence between the instability of the Harrod-type model, when it is established in this manner, and that of the Wicksell–Lindahl model, when that is established in the manner that was adopted in Chapter VI of this book. The Wicksellian 'cumulative process' is a property of a Flexprice model, this is a property of a Fixprice model; the one disequilibrium is a price disequilibrium, the other is a quantity disequilibrium; these are exactly the relations that one would expect from 'duals', in something like the sense that Linear Programming theory has made familiar. The more one works it out, the clearer it becomes that there is in fact a duality relation between the two theories.

In the Harrod-type model prices are given exogenously; can one say that in the Wicksell theory quantities are given exogenously? I did not put it that way in Chapter VI (for it might there have appeared to be too paradoxical a way of putting the point). Something that is substantially equivalent did come up nevertheless. In order that the Wicksell theorem should be true without exception, it was necessary to assume that the 'change in real resources' (as I called it) could be neglected. This amounted to assuming that the sequence of quantities (of inputs and outputs) proceeded autonomously, the sole effect of the discrepancy between actual and 'natural' rates of interest being a movement of prices. That is exactly *dual* to what we have been assuming here.

We further found, in our discussion of the Wicksell theory, that we could not make sense of the sequence without introducing lags, at least to the extent of making price expectations depend upon past experience. So it has been here. We could not make sense of the present story without introducing a similar dependence of

[1] See, for instance, my *Trade Cycle*, p. 81.

expectations upon experience, of demand expectations upon previous output. Here again there is a perfect match.

In the Flexprice model there is cumulative inflation (or deflation) if the expected rate of profit is out of line with actual interest; in the Fixprice model there is cumulative expansion (or contraction) if the expected growth rate is out of line with that which saving makes attainable. The rate of interest in the one theory is dual to the rate of growth in the other.

Among the prices which, in a Fixprice model, are taken to be fixed, is the rate of interest. But the Wicksell model can also be read as a study of the effects of a fixed rate of interest—upon prices, which in its case are flexible. Fixity of the rate of interest (or rather of the whole system of interest and quasi-interest rates) at an arbitrary level is a common feature of both kinds of 'cumulative process'. In the one way or in the other, a system in which interest (in this wide sense) is insufficiently adaptable seems to be liable to go off the rails.

So far, however, this is a mere conjecture. We have much further to go before we can put substance into it.

7. Let us now return, in the rest of this chapter, to the Fixprice model. We are on the verge of having to abandon it, but there is still one matter which it will be useful to attempt to explore with its aid.

While it is possible for price inflation to proceed to any level,[1] there is ordinarily a limit upon quantity expansion; it must ordinarily be limited by scarcity of primary factors, of which shortage of labour can be taken to be a sufficient example. In practice, of course, such a shortage will have wage- and price-effects, which in a Fixprice theory are excluded from consideration. It is nevertheless useful to see how far we can work out the effects of the shortage entirely 'in real terms'—which is effectively what one does when one examines the problem in a Fixprice model.

Let us then suppose that in a certain period the expansionary path that we have been analysing encounters a full-employment-of-labour 'ceiling'. In order to sharpen the issue, let us take it (here)

---

[1] There is indeed an interesting correspondence between quantity-expansion arrested by labour shortage and price inflation brought to a stop by limitation of money supply.

that the ceiling is an absolute ceiling: the total labour available is absolutely fixed and unchanging over time. We may, I think, take it that once a desired (or optimum) capital–output ratio has been achieved, it will not be possible to increase output without employing more labour.[1] There will thus be an absolute ceiling upon possible output as well as upon labour supply.

Even under these (admittedly drastic) assumptions, there are several cases to be considered.

The first is that, made familiar by Harrod, in which output had been expanding, before the ceiling was reached, along an equilibrium path, more and more of the given supply of labour being absorbed in the course of the expansion. When the absorption is complete, this expansion cannot continue. The desired capital will accordingly cease to expand, and the system cannot remain in equilibrium on its ceiling unless saving halts. If savers attempt to save the same proportion of income as before, output is bound to fall. If the average propensity to save (the proportion of income saved) refuses to decline, output cannot stop falling until it has fallen to zero.

More plausible assumptions about saving behaviour will of course give less apocalyptic results. If the proportion of income saved rises (and falls) with income, there may well be an income (or output) level at which saving is zero; it is then in principle possible for the economy to find a stationary equilibrium at this (no doubt) low level. But it may not be easy to get into that equilibrium. The capital stock which is appropriate to that low level is less than the capital that is appropriate to full employment; thus it is not possible to get into this equilibrium without passing through a phase of decumulation, which will not occur unless output falls to a level which is even lower than its low-level equilibrium. Horrors such as these have been much discussed, and it is probable that they do have some relevance to slump economics. But it is hardly worth while to pursue them far in this place. Let us leave them until we can discuss them (or what corresponds to them) under less restrictive assumptions than those under which we are now working.

For there are other, more interesting, possibilities. One, which arises directly out of the preceding discussion, occurs when the path that has been followed, before the labour ceiling is encountered,

[1] The Fixprice assumption must be borne in mind.

is an 'over-optimistic' expansion with an attempted rate of growth which is more than the 'warranted' rate. In this case, as we have seen, actual capital must be less than desired capital, at the point when the labour ceiling is hit. It is then quite possible for the economy to remain in a state of full employment for a certain time, while the deficiency is being made up.[1] The capital–output ratio will then be rising, and output can continue to increase, even though the employment of labour does not increase. For, even at an unchanged output, there would still be an opportunity for the investment of capital to bring the capital–output ratio up to its 'normal' figure; but if investment proceeded in this way, without output rising, the employment of labour would fall. That, however, would leave labour available for an increase in output; the system would have moved down below its full-employment ceiling. There would thus be a further opportunity for productive investment to supply the capital for this increase in output (without further change in the capital–output ratio). As long as the capital–output ratio remains below its 'normal' level, such expansion as this can go on. It is in fact the sort of expansion which was supposed by neo-classical economists to take place while capital increased and the supply of labour remained constant.[2] But it should be emphasized that there is nothing in this argument to indicate that, in the conditions supposed, an expansion of this sort *must* occur; all that has been shown is that it is possible.

And a point must surely be reached (if the deficiency in capital had merely occurred because of over-optimistic investment) when the deficiency is made good. After that (at least so long as we continue to hold by our Fixprice assumptions) all must be as before.

8. Nevertheless, having got so far, should one not go further? The attribution of the disequilibrium, along the path that was followed (in this last case) before the ceiling was reached, to 'over-optimistic expectations', itself depended upon the assumption that at some date in the past the economy had been in an expanding equilibrium, growing at its 'warranted' rate. There is, in general, no need that this should be so. It is by no means necessary to assume that in the macro-economic sense appropriate to a Harrod-

---

[1] As Mr. Kaldor observed, in a justifiable criticism which he made of the corresponding passage in my *Trade Cycle*.

[2] As Mr. Kaldor has also observed.

type model, a state of stock equilibrium should ever have been attained.

In order to show how this is, something (a very little in this place) must be said about technology. It is only in relation to a given technology (in the sense of a given state of technical knowledge, or available 'spectrum of techniques') that there can be a desired capital corresponding to a particular output—a capital stock which would produce that output in an optimum (or in what is considered to be an optimum) manner. Certainly this is the case if we think of the capital stock in real terms, as consisting of actual capital goods (machines and what not); but even if we think of it in value terms (with the real goods valued at given prices) the truth of the statement is unaffected. It has been implicitly assumed in our analysis (so far) that technology is unchanging during the process under discussion. I do not in fact see how, in this sort of formal analysis, that assumption is to be avoided. There must nevertheless have been a moment at which this technology was introduced; and it is not interesting to suppose that this moment was in the very remote past. It is much more interesting to take the moment at which the new technology is introduced as the base date from which the process under analysis is to proceed.

The actual capital stock (K_0) at that date will thus have been inherited from the past, from a time at which the technology, under which the economy was working, was different. Whether or not it was appropriate to the old technology, it is inconceivable that it can be appropriate to the new. It cannot possibly be a balanced stock, in relation to the new technology, so that the path which is pursued (from time 0 onwards) cannot possibly be an equilibrium path. Even in value terms, it is entirely possible that K_0 may be greater or less than c^*Y_{-1}, where c^* is the desired (*ex post*) capital–output ratio of the new technology.

Now suppose (as we are surely entitled to suppose) that, at the moment when the new technology is introduced, full employment of labour had been reached (or almost reached). It does not matter how it was reached—whether along a 'warranted' growth path or in some other way. For all that that will now affect is the relation of actual capital to desired capital under the old technology; and, under the new technology, that is irrelevant. All that can now matter is the relation of K_0 to c^*Y_{-1}, the capital which (for the moment) is the desired capital under the new technology.

If, in this sense, $K_0 < c^*Y_{-1}$, we have the same situation as was previously analysed; a neo-classical expansion, up to the point where equality is restored, is clearly possible. But in the opposite case, where it is actual capital that is the greater, there would seem (at first sight) to be no help that way. Would there not then be the same immediate downturn as we deduced for the case in which there was an encounter with a ceiling, after expansion along a 'warranted' (or equilibrium) growth path? If so, we get little comfort from our present way of putting the problem; for it is not obvious that there is any reason (within a Fixprice model) why the crucial inequality should go one way rather than the other.

In fact, however, this is not right. For we have not yet taken into account the necessity (it surely is a necessity) that, in relation to the new technology, the composition of the inherited capital must be wrong. Even if the value of the stock is right, at the old output (if $K_0 = c^*Y_{-1}$), there will still be a potentiality of increased output, as soon as the capital can be replaced in a more suitable form. As that replacement occurs, either output increases or labour becomes unemployed. But if output is to increase, with labour fully employed, capital investment will be required. Thus even if $K_0 = c^*Y_{-1}$, at the moment of introduction of the new technology, there can be some scope for new investment. Some 'neo-classical' expansion is still possible in this case; and the same must presumably hold, though to a lesser extent, if the critical inequality goes, not too far, the 'wrong' way.

And there is (possibly) a further point. We have so far been holding, quite rigidly, to the Fixprice assumption—even so far as to assume that the prices at which capital goods are valued remain the same as they were before, after the new technology has been introduced. But this (surely) is to take 'Fixprice' a bit far. To keep prices fixed while technology is unchanged is (perhaps) tolerable; but it is much more difficult to make sense of the assumption when technology is changing. After all, it was in terms of the pricing of manufactured goods that we introduced the Fixprice assumption originally; but it is on account of changes in technology that the (relative) prices of manufactured goods do most obviously change. Thus we ought surely to go over, when technology changes, to prices that are in some sense more 'suitable' to the new technology. Now at such prices, it seems likely that there will be some existing capital goods (those which had been constructed for specific purposes associated with the old technology) which will be considerably devalued. It looks therefore more likely than it did before that K_0 will be $< c^*Y_{-1}$, when the valuation is made at prices that are 'suitable' to the new technology. Though we still cannot say without exception that active invention is conducive to the maintenance of full employment, it does begin to look as if there is a presumption in that direction.

9. But what are these 'suitable' prices? This is a question that we cannot answer—cannot even begin to answer—as long as we continue to take prices as given. We have reached the boundary of Fixprice Economics. We must look for a method (whether or not it is the old Flexprice method remains to be seen) which will at least enable us to call prices into question.

PART II

GROWTH EQUILIBRIUM

XII

THE MODEL IN OUTLINE

1. As soon as we decide that prices are again to be called in question, we must abandon the Fixprice assumption, under which we have for so long been working. Prices can no longer be given from outside, but must be determined, in some manner, as part of the system. At this point, therefore, we come to a new 'method'. I believe, as I have indicated previously, that it is essentially this method (with the developments in Optimum theory that spring from it, and which we shall be considering in Part III) which is the basis for what has been presented by a number of economists, during the last two decades, as *Growth Theory*: a general theory, as they would claim it to be, of Long-term Economic Growth. I would not myself claim for it that it is a theory of Economic Growth, if by that one means a theory that can hope to give at all an adequate explanation of actual Growth phenomena; it seems to me to have a much narrower scope. It is just one of the methods of Dynamic Economics, needing to be supplemented by the other methods which we have been examining (and possibly by still other methods not yet devised) if it is to be a theory of Economic Growth in the sense desired. It is nevertheless an important method; and since there is no connected statement of its theory to which one can refer (and certainly no statement which presents it with the limited claims for its scope which are all that I shall venture), an attempt will have to be made to set out its theory rather systematically. That is what I shall try to do (so far as the Pure Positive part of the theory is concerned) in this Part II of my book.

It might be thought that our abandonment of the Fixprice assumption, which (as stated) is essential for the new method, would lead us straight back to price flexibility, and so to the Temporary Equilibrium method, which we considered (rather briefly) in Chapter VI. But this is not so; there is a sharp distinction between the two methods. On the Temporary Equilibrium method, the economy is taken to be in temporary equilibrium in every single period; or (if we prefer to work in terms of continuous time) there is equilibrium at every point of time, with respect to the expectations ruling at that point of time, whether there is equilibrium over time or not. On the new method, we do not have to make that assumption. We do concern ourselves with the prices which will permit the establishment of equilibrium over time; in that sense, and in that sense only, prices are taken as flexible. Along an equilibrium path prices must be such that there can be equilibrium; but nothing is implied by that about the behaviour of prices when the system is out of equilibrium. Out of equilibrium, it may behave as the Fixprice model behaved; or it may behave in other ways. The question of the mechanism by which the economy can get into equilibrium—what things are needed for the existence of such a mechanism—is a separate question, which will have to be separately discussed.[1]

If we have to suspend judgement on the question of reaching equilibrium—if the means of attaining equilibrium is an issue that, for the time being, must be left open—the study of the equilibrium path, by itself, may seem to be a barren study. One must, however, be clear about the properties of the equilibrium path before one can face the question of how it is to be approached. There are several fundamental questions about capital-using production which can be cleared up by a theory of the properties of equilibrium paths; we shall need to have that theory at our disposal before going further.

2. It is possible for an economy to be in equilibrium over time, in the most general sense, however its activities are changing over time. So long as future developments (relevant future developments) are correctly foreseen, and current conduct is adjusted to those anticipations, the economy (in that wide sense) is in equilibrium. For the method that we are now to examine, equilibrium over time is to be taken in a more restricted sense. The fundamental data (tastes and technology) are to be taken as unchanging; the only change that is admitted is a uniform expansion. It is the equilibrium of such an economy, expanding at a constant growth rate, which I describe as a Growth Equilibrium.

The principal case of a Growth Equilibrium which we have encountered up to the present is that of the Harrod-type model, which (before it hits a full-employment ceiling) is expanding uniformly at

---

[1] See Chapter XVI, below.

its 'warranted' rate. If this is taken in a 'macro' sense, as it was of course originally intended by Harrod to be taken, it is not a very exacting concept. There is nothing very startling in the idea that an economy should have a constant growth rate (in the usual statistical meaning of that term) between one year and another. But for more precise analysis such a macro-economic interpretation is by no means sufficient. All the simplified growth models which represent the real capital of the economy by a single good (whether it be the 'corn' of Adam Smith, or the 'meccano sets' or 'machines' of contemporary economists) must, if they are to be taken strictly, be concerned with an economy which is maintaining uniformity in a more detailed sense.[1] What they offer, in their Growth Equilibrium, is the Equilibrium theory of the regularly progressive economy.

Such a growth equilibrium is a generalization of the 'stationary state'; or (put the other way) the stationary state is a growth equilibrium with a growth rate zero. In the stationary state outputs remain constant, because technology is unchanging, and factor supplies are constant; in the growth equilibrium all elements in the economy are growing at the same (constant) rate—so that, although there is an absolute expansion, every element remains in the same proportion to every other.[2]

That is the strict sense of growth equilibrium which I shall be using in this chapter; but we should notice, before going further, that there is quite a question whether such an equilibrium can exist. There was such a question about the stationary state; for that cannot exist except at such a set of prices and incomes as will make net saving zero, and (as we have seen) it is easy to construct assumptions which are such that net saving will not fall to zero as long as output remains positive. Growth equilibrium does not

---

[1] It is tempting (and even such economists as Professor Meade and Professor Swan have succumbed to the temptation) to suppose that we can avoid this uniformity by supposing capital to be 'malleable'—that one capital good can be converted into another (either way) at a constant rate of transformation. I believe that this device is seriously misleading. It is true that once a price system is established, a value equivalence between different capital goods comes into being. But this is a consequence of the price system; we have no business to introduce it at the start, as a technological datum, which it clearly is not.

[2] This proportionality becomes explicit in the von Neumann 'equilibrium' which we shall be discussing in Chapter XVIII, below. But I wish to avoid bringing that in here; for its proper place is in Optimum theory, not in the Pure Positive theory, with which we are (still) here concerned.

require us to beg that question, but it has other difficulties to face which are quite as serious. One, it is very well known, is the matter of land; it is only when land is in abundant supply that an economy can maintain itself in growth equilibrium with an unchanged technology. If one overrides this objection, one is following Smith, not Ricardo;[1] to go back to a state of innocence before diminishing returns is not a thing which one feels comfortable in doing. Nevertheless, for the time being, that is what we shall do here.[2]

There are other difficulties to be faced which are at least equally serious. Very drastic homogeneity assumptions are necessary before it is possible to have an economy that can expand in constant proportions. As is generally recognized, it is necessary that the production function of every industry should be linear and homogeneous (constant returns to scale); but this is not all. A similar homogeneity must be assumed on the consumption side also. It is in fact the usual experience that as people get richer, the proportions in which they divide their expenditure between different consumption goods will vary (and the proportions of income saved will vary also). Such variations as these must be forgotten (or neglected) if a growth equilibrium, with constant proportions, is to be possible at all.

3. In the rest of this Part (as well as in some chapters of Part III) I shall make all these simplifications; but, having made them, I shall try to take full advantage of them. Since, in growth equilibrium, the outputs of all consumption goods keep proportion with one another, the system will behave as if there was just one consumption good—the bundle of consumption goods, combined in constant proportions, can be treated as a single good. Similarly it will behave as if there was just one capital good—and one sort of labour. Purely because of the constant proportions, the model becomes a 'macro' model. But we should be careful to observe the precise sense in which this happens.

The principal use of Growth Equilibrium theory is for comparative analysis (the *comparative dynamics* that corresponds to comparative statics). We then have two distinct economies, each in growth equilibrium, but with different data (being data that are consistent with growth equilibrium in each case); we compare the

---

[1] See Chapter IV, above.
[2] Some attention will be paid to diminishing returns in Chapter XX, below.

courses of outputs and prices in the two equilibria. As between the two economies, there may be all sorts of differences, differences in technologies, differences in tastes, as well as differences in saving propensities. It will then not be necessary, even though the proportions between elements remain the same over time in each economy, that they should be the same proportions in the one economy as in the other. Therefore, although we can treat each economy as having its own single sort of consumption good and single sort of capital good, they need not be the same sort in the two economies. Even if the consumption goods are the same, the capital goods need not be the same. The 'macro' character of the model should therefore not be over-rated. We can work in aggregates, but they are not necessarily aggregates of the same things.

As long as we stick to this comparative equilibrium analysis, we do not need to distinguish between fixed and circulating capital; for there is no reason why both elements should not be contained in the capital-good bundle. And there is another (perhaps more surprising) simplification which is also at our disposal; we can neglect depreciation. As long as the economy is in growth equilibrium, the wastage of the capital stock (in any period) must be proportional to the other (physical) elements in the system; this is true, whether the wastage is due to direct using-up (as in the case of raw materials) or to pure passage of time. As long as the growth rate is positive (or, more strictly, non-negative) all such wastage must be made good—in a prescribed form—if the equilibrium is to continue; that part of the production of the capital good may therefore be reckoned as part of the process of production of the net output (consumption output plus net output of the capital good). We can, as it were, divide the economy into two 'industries' —a consumption good 'industry' and a net investment good 'industry'; the using-up of the capital good that occurs in each industry is to be reckoned as being made good within that industry, so that it forms part of the costs of that industry, just like any other cost. This is just the same as if we assumed that capital goods last for ever—but we do not need to express the assumption in that paradoxical form. It is an assumption to which we are entitled, in virtue of our other assumptions, so long as we are only concerned with the analysis of equilibrium paths. It is only at the point when we seek to prepare ourselves for the study of disequilibrium positions that it has to be withdrawn.

These simplifications, then, are harmless; but there is a further simplification, into which one is naturally led as soon as one has divided the economy into two industries, that turns out to be open to much graver objection. Constancy over time in the make-up of the capital good (i.e. the bundle of capital goods) that is employed in the economy as a whole does not entitle us to assume that 'the' capital good that is employed in the one industry and the other is the same. Yet if we do not make that assumption our other simplifications are of much less help to us. For if we must distinguish between the primary capital good that is used in the consumption goods industry and the secondary capital good that is used to make new primary goods, we cannot avoid introducing a tertiary good that is used to make secondary goods—and so on *ad infinitum*. The simplicity of the model is hopelessly lost. I shall, in the end, face up to this difficulty, for I am sure that it is a difficulty that it is incumbent on us to face. It is nevertheless a complication which we may usefully postpone. For the present I shall take it that we have only two 'industries' and that in both industries the same capital good is used. But I would wish the reader to notice that this is a dangerous simplification. Useful though it is, it is liable to lead us to some conclusions that are not generally valid. But these conclusions, we shall find, bear on their faces a mark of their suspect character.

4. As explained, there is no necessity, when we are comparing different equilibrium paths, that there should be the *same* consumption good and the *same* capital good in the two equilibria; but it will be convenient, as a first step, to suppose that they are the same. If we assume that, and also assume the same technology, we are almost obliged to assume that there are 'fixed coefficients of production': that so much labour and so much capital good are required to make a unit of the consumption good, and so much of each to make a unit of the capital good (depreciation, as has been explained, being supposed to be made good all the time). Variability of coefficients, as commonly assumed in marginal theory, is in fact more typical of land-using than of capital-using production; particular cases in which such variability occurs can no doubt be cited, but there is little to be gained by giving them special prominence. For we are not going to be impeded, by the assumption we shall make, from a consideration of choice of techniques, even

in a wider sense; we can consider it, in what is surely a more realistic manner, when we come to consider changes in the specification of *the* capital good that is used. (This is how we shall deal with the matter in the next chapter.) We can consider choice of techniques, as long as it is associated with different capital goods.

The exact nature of the 'fixed coefficients' which we assume needs, however, to be noticed. They are not fixed *technical* coefficients (as such coefficients are often called); they are not quantities of factors that are needed, by technical necessity, to make a given quantity of product. We are solely concerned with equilibrium positions, so that the quantities in question are the quantities that are needed *in equilibrium*. They are therefore to be taken in the same sense as the capital–output ratios (and suchlike) with which we have become familiar in Fixprice theory. We need not suppose that it would be impossible (at least in the short run) to produce more than 1,000 units of product from the capital stock that is appropriate to 1,000 units. The relation between capital (or, for that matter, labour) and output that is expressed in these coefficients is simply to be taken as a *normal* relation. There is therefore (for instance) no reason why a normal reserve of raw materials, that is required as a condition of equilibrium, should not be included in the make-up of *the* capital good.

5. Preliminaries being over, we can now get to work. The theory which emerges, if we allow ourselves all the assumptions and simplifications that have been listed, is so simple that it can be set out in words without any use of mathematics; if we prefer a mathematical expression, nothing more is involved but simple algebra. There are, I think, advantages in each method of presentation; I shall therefore use them both. The algebraic treatment will be convenient for later generalization; while the verbal is a real help in bringing out the economic meaning. It enables us to assure ourselves, as we go on, that we are not talking nonsense; it even suggests actual historical situations which our analysis, with all its simplifications, may nevertheless approximately fit.

Such a situation can occur in the settlement of a new country, or colony. Before settlement, the country is empty; land is (nearly) free; but it is not unreasonable to suppose that production will only be possible if some capital goods, as well as labour, are available. These capital goods we will call 'tractors' (for the reasons

stated we do not need to bother about working capital); with their
aid one consumption good is to be produced. This, following
precedent, we will call 'corn'.

The area of land that can be cultivated with one tractor may be
defined as a 'farm'. Anyone who possesses a tractor can set up
a farm, which will employ so much labour (not necessarily all
employed in driving tractors) and produce so much corn. Alternatively, he may set up a factory for the production of tractors
(tractors, I am afraid, must for the present be the sole capital good
that is employed in factories also). A given number of tractors will
have to be employed in each factory, which will employ just so
much labour, and produce (per period) just so many new tractors.
Tractors (in the sense explained) last for ever, so the new tractors
are net investment. There is no reason why the tractor–labour
ratio in farm and in factory should be the same.

Production (of either kind) cannot start without tractors being
available; the first settlers in the colony must have brought their
tractors with them. This, however, is an archaeological question
that is of no importance for present purposes; what interests us is
the Growth Equilibrium which may be attained when both farm
and factory are in operation.

In order that there should be a Growth Equilibrium, the stock of
tractors must be expanding; and the supply of labour must also be
expanding to keep pace with it. The labour force may expand by
natural increase, or by continued immigration; let us begin with
the case of immigration, which corresponds to the case of the
Harrod-type economy, expanding at its 'warranted' rate.

New immigrants are then to come in, to whatever extent is
necessary, as soon as employment can be found for them. If there
is more land (of uniform quality) than can be used, land will
command no rent; but it is not sensible to suppose that labour will
come in for no wage. It will be better to take it that the supply of
labour is perfectly elastic at some given wage. For employment at
that wage, as much labour as is required will come in; but if
the wage fell below that critical level, labour would leave the
colony.

This fixed wage must be fixed in terms of something; and here
there is only one thing in which it can be fixed, the single consumption good which is corn. But the fixing of the wage in terms of
corn has important consequences. For, with corn-wages given (and

the amount of labour that has to be employed with the single
tractor also given), the share of the farm's output which must be
paid to labour is fixed in terms of corn; the share which is left over
as profits (or as earnings of the tractor) is therefore also fixed in
terms of corn. But (with the same tractors being employed in each
industry) it may fairly be laid down as an equilibrium condition
that the earnings of a tractor in tractor production must be the same
as its earnings in corn production; therefore, since the amounts of
labour and of tractor needed for tractor production are given, the
cost (and so the price) of a new tractor is also fixed, in terms of
corn. If we *define* the rate of profit as the ratio of the earnings of
a tractor to the cost of a tractor (we do not have to attend to
depreciation), then this, by what precedes, is also fixed. Thus,
before we have said anything about saving, or about the growth
rate of the economy, the whole of the (relative) price system is
already determined.

6. Before going further, let us set out this part of the argument in
algebraic form. For this purpose we need some notation—and
I must ask the reader to pay special attention to this notation, for it
will be used (and developed) to support the argument of the whole
of Part II. I have taken some trouble with it, to make it coherent,
and easy to remember. In particular, the device of using Greek
letters to mark a reference to the consumption goods sector, and
the corresponding roman letters to refer to the capital goods sector,
is a point that should be watched.

It is convenient to take prices to be expressed in terms of an
arbitrary unit, not otherwise specified. For we can then change our
standard of value without trouble; when we select a particular
standard commodity (corn, or labour, or whatever it is), we have
merely to set the price of that commodity equal to 1.

With this understanding, let

π be the price of the consumption good (corn),
p be the price of the capital good (tractor),
w be the wage of labour,
q be the earnings (quasi-rent) of the capital good,
r be the rate of profit,
α (capital) } be production coefficients in consumption
β (labour) } good production,

a (capital) ⎫ be production coefficients in capital good
b (labour) ⎬   production.

That is all we need, just for the moment.

In equilibrium, since the earnings of the factors must be the same in both industries, we have the *price equations*

$$\pi = q\alpha + w\beta, \qquad p = qa + wb$$

and by definition (since depreciation is neglected)

$$q = rp.$$

It follows, by substituting this last in the capital-price equation,

$$\frac{p}{w} = \frac{b}{1-ra}, \qquad \frac{q}{w} = \frac{rb}{1-ra}$$

and then, from the consumption-price equation,

$$\frac{\pi}{w} = \beta + \frac{r\alpha b}{1-ra}$$

the *wage equation* (as, after much hesitation, I have decided to call it).[1] This is a most important relation, upon which much of the work, to which we are coming, will turn.

What the wage equation expresses is a relation between w/π (the corn wage, or real wage, of labour) and the rate of profit r. It is directly evident, from the capital-price equation, that $r < (1/a)$; for if it were not so, w would be negative. Thus we may take it that $ra < 1$. It is therefore permissible to write the wage equation as a (convergent) geometrical progression

$$\frac{\pi}{w} = \beta + r\alpha b\{1 + (ra) + (ra)^2 + \ldots\}.$$

Every term in this expansion is positive, so that it is at once apparent that (π/w) rises with r. The real wage (w/π) necessarily falls as r rises.[2] We can draw out the relation between the rate of profit

---

[1] Samuelson, I fancy, would call it the 'factor-price equation'. (For his 'factor-price frontier' see below, p. 150.) I do not, however, like the idea of regarding r, as well as w/π, as a factor price. It is q which is the factor price, to my way of thinking. (See, however, Chapter XXIV.)

[2] There are of course many other ways of proving this proposition. But the series proof, just given, is to be recommended, since (as will be shown in Appendix B) it is capable of a very wide generalization.

and the real wage (under given technique) in the form of a curve (see Fig. 2, pp. 150, 152). It is a curve that must slope downwards, and which must intersect both axes (for the maximum possible r is $1/a$, and the maximum possible real wage is where $r = 0$, so that $w/\pi = 1/\beta$).

Thus if (as we were previously assuming) the real wage is given from outside, the corresponding rate of profit can be read off from the curve. (The wage must be fixed at a level that is $< 1/\beta$, if the technique that is being assumed is to be possible at all. In terms of our colony story, if this was the only possible technique, and the supply price of labour was $> 1/\beta$, the colony could not be settled.) But with the rate of profit once established, all the other price-ratios follow at once.

7. Relative prices are thus established, independently of the rate of saving; but with relative prices fixed, we are back at the Fixprice system (so far as the equilibrium path is concerned). We can, if we choose, simply follow Harrod and argue that the equilibrium rate of growth (not, of course, the actual growth rate of an economy that does not have to be in equilibrium) will be higher, the higher is the propensity to save. But it will be useful to check this over in greater detail.

Let us begin by looking at it in terms of our parable. The rate of growth (in any period) is the ratio between the output of new tractors and the stock of tractors; the same rate of growth must hold (in equilibrium) for every element in the economy. The existing stock of tractors is partly used in corn production, partly for producing new tractors; in equilibrium, the existing stock must be that which is required (or desired) for the production of the current output (of both products together). There is a fixed proportion between the output of new tractors and that part of the stock of tractors which is used for tractor production; there is therefore a strict dependence of the rate of growth on the proportion in which the stock of tractors is divided between the two industries. But this proportion also governs the ratio between the (physical) outputs of the two industries; and (with relative prices already determined) the ratio between volumes implies a ratio between values. But this value ratio is the ratio between the value of investment and the value of consumption. The rate of growth is therefore determined—wholly determined, once corn wages are

given and (of course) the production coefficients are given, by the proportion of income saved.

Or again, let us look at it in algebra. We must first complete our notation. I shall write

ξ for the output of the consumption good (corn),
x for the output of the capital good (tractors),
L for the labour employed,
K for the stock of capital (number of tractors), and
g for the rate of growth.

In equilibrium, the stock of tractors must equal the desired employment of tractors[1] (and the employment of labour must of course equal the desired employment of labour) so that we have the *quantity equations*

$$K = \alpha\xi + ax, \qquad L = \beta\xi + bx$$

and again, by definition (since depreciation is neglected)

$$x = gK.$$

These equations can be manipulated in precisely the same way as we manipulated the price equations. Substituting in the capital-quantity equation,

$$\frac{K}{\xi} = \frac{\alpha}{1-ag}, \qquad \frac{x}{\xi} = \frac{\alpha g}{1-ag}, \qquad \frac{L}{\xi} = \beta + \frac{\alpha bg}{1-ag}.$$

It will be noticed that if consumption output is to be positive, we must have $g < (1/a)$. (We had $r < 1/a$ as the corresponding condition on the price side.) If g is given, at a level which satisfies this condition, all the quantity ratios follow from it.

There is thus a perfect symmetry (or duality) between the quantity equations and the price equations; they work in exactly the same way. But, even together, they do not suffice to determine the whole system; some assumption about saving is needed to serve as a bridge between them. When we have (i) the price equations, (ii) the quantity equations, (iii) some saving equation, the system is complete. The equilibrium of the economy, at its given rate of real wages, is completely determined.

If we assume (as we have done hitherto) that saving is a fixed proportion (s) of total income, this gives

$$px = s(px + \pi\xi)$$

---

[1] From the Fixprice point of view, this is a *stock equilibrium* condition.

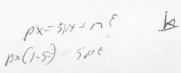

for saving ($=$ investment) is px, and consumption plus investment is total income. Accordingly

$$\frac{s}{1-s} = \frac{px}{\pi\xi}$$

a more convenient way of writing the *saving equation*. Now if the real wage is given, p/π is given; x/ξ will therefore be greater the larger is s. But (as we know from the quantity equations) the larger is x/ξ, the larger is g; so the equilibrium growth rate is larger the larger the saving propensity, the simple conclusion which we set out to confirm.

A more interesting question emerges when the real wage changes; but before we come to that it will be well to say something about the other case which we left over a few pages back—the case of the economy which is on its ceiling, expanding (for we will still allow it to expand) at a rate which is not set by saving, but determined in some other way.

8. This, in terms of the parable, is the case where there is no immigration, though the supply of labour is increasing—at a given 'natural rate'. If this economy is to remain in a constant-proportions Growth Equilibrium, with full employment of labour, everything must be expanding at the same rate as the labour supply is increasing. The tractor supply must be increasing at this same rate, which will determine a particular ratio between tractor output and corn output; if prices are fixed, so that p/π is fixed, it follows from the above saving equation that equilibrium can only be maintained if the saving propensity is adjusted to match. If it is not adjusted, and is less than required, the only equilibrium that is possible is an expansion at the corresponding 'warranted' rate—and expansion at that rate will leave a part of the labour force unemployed. If it is more than is required, the case is the same as that of the Harrod-type economy which hits its ceiling—with a constant saving propensity no equilibrium is possible at all.

But let us now suppose (it is the central question to which in this chapter we have been leading up) that prices can be adjusted. Does this release the jam? Does this make it possible to adjust to a change in the 'natural rate' of expansion of the economy, even though the saving propensity remains the same?

We have here, it is important to observe, two quite distinct questions. One is a question of existence. Can there exist another growth equilibrium, with the same production coefficients and the same saving propensity but with different prices, which will have the required different growth rate? That, in strictness, is the only question that can be answered within the framework of comparative equilibrium analysis. But even if that question is answered satisfactorily, it leaves another behind it. Is there a possible path— a tolerable path—from the one equilibrium to the other? What will be said in this chapter is only concerned with the first of these questions, and it is only terms of that question that what follows here must be understood.[1]

If the proportion of total income saved is to be kept constant, so that the ratio of investment to consumption $(px/\pi\xi)$ is to be kept constant, the growth rate can only vary (so that x/ξ varies) if p/π varies in the opposite direction. But, from the price equations

$$\frac{p}{\pi} = \frac{qa+wb}{q\alpha+w\beta}$$

so that a change in real wages, which changes q/w,[2] will only change p/π if the ratios of coefficients $(a/b, \alpha/\beta)$ are different from one another. If the ratios are the same, then (in the language of the parable) a change in corn wages leaves the corn price of the tractor unchanged; there is then no way out along the route of price changes. And even if the ratios are different there is only a limited way out. It is only within certain limits that it is possible for the system to accommodate itself to a change in the rate of growth by means of price changes.

The theoretical limits to the movement of real wages (the 'practical' limits must of course be much narrower) are when the wage is zero and when the profit rate is zero (when $w = 0$ and when $r = 0$). When $r = 0$, $p/\pi = b/\beta$; the corresponding growth rate (g_1) is given by

$$\frac{s}{1-s} = \frac{b}{\beta} \frac{\alpha g_1}{1-ag_1}.$$

If we put $m = \alpha b/a\beta$, so that m is the *ratio of the coefficient ratios* (an abbreviation of which we shall be able to make much use in the rest of this Part), this gives

$$g_1 = \frac{s}{a} \frac{1}{1+(m-1)(1-s)}.$$

[1] The second question will be discussed in Chapter XVI, below.
[2] For since $\pi = q\alpha+w\beta$, π/w and q/w move together.

When $w = 0$, $p/\pi = a/\alpha$; the corresponding growth rate (g_2) is given by

$$\frac{s}{1-s} = \frac{a}{\alpha} \cdot \frac{\alpha g_2}{1 - a g_2}$$

whence

$$g_2 = \frac{s}{a}.$$

With $s < 1$, each of these limits is $< 1/a$, as it should be (for m is > 0); and with $s > 0$, each of them is positive. It is only between these limits, which may be very near together if m is near to 1, that price changes can give any help.

But that is not all. Which of these limits is the greater depends upon the sign of $m - 1$. If $m > 1$, so that it is the farm (or consumption-good industry) which is the more capitalized, we have $g_1 < g_2$. A fall in wages (a rise in profits) will then make possible a faster growth rate. The fastest growth rate will occur when profit is as high as possible. But if it is the factory which is the more capitalized (why should it not be?) the fastest growth rate will be found at the other end, when profits are as low as possible. But this conclusion (agreeable as it may appear) is surely implausible. If profits are zero (or very low) so that the return to saving is very low, must not something happen to the incentive to save? Something, surely, has gone wrong.

9. I think myself that several things have gone wrong; it will take us much trouble to get them all sorted out. The simplest thing which has gone wrong is that we have carried the assumption of saving proportional to total income, over from the Harrod-type theory (where it belongs) to the present theory, where it is much less at home. As soon as we make a distinction between factor shares (as in the Harrod-type theory we did not have to do), the question must arise: will not the saving-income proportion be affected by income distribution? It may be affected in a 'classical' manner—that a lower rate of profit makes people less willing to save; in a Growth Equilibrium (which is quite different from Keynes's theory) that is by no means to be ruled out. But it is quite sufficient (as Kaldor has taught us)[1] to introduce a *direct*

---

[1] See his 'Alternative Theories of Distribution' (*Essays on Value and Distribution*, p. 209). I am entirely in agreement with Kaldor as long as we stick to the theory of Growth Equilibrium, in the sense I am here using that term. But it would appear that Kaldor would apply his principles more generally, and there I cannot follow him. (See, however, below, Chapter XV.)

effect of income distribution on saving. We may call it 'a different propensity to save out of profits and out of wages'; or, since we do not have to go into detail about who does the saving, we may simply make saving proportional to some weighted average of profits and wages, not simply to their sum.

The extreme case of Kaldor's assumption would make saving proportional to profits only.[1] This is a very convenient assumption, which simplifies things considerably, so that—purely in order to exhibit the properties of the model—it is one that I shall largely use. In using it, I do not mean to imply that 'saving out of wages' is practically unimportant. But the complications which it introduces are not matters of principle; they obscure our vision if we insist on taking them into account all the time.[2]

If we make saving a fixed proportion (s_1) of *profits*, the saving equation is much simplified. For we then have

$$\text{saving} = px = pgK = s_1(rpK)$$

so that

$$g = s_1 r$$

a relation that is becoming well known. The whole structure of the model is then vastly simplified. For many purposes there are just two equations that we have to hang on to—this *saving equation* and the *wage equation*, which (if we now allow ourselves to take the consumption good—corn—as our standard of value) may be written

$$\frac{1}{w} = \beta + \frac{r\alpha b}{1 - ra}.$$

(We still need other equations for particular purposes, but the general working of the system emerges sufficiently from these two equations alone.)

If the real wage (w) is given, the rate of profit is determined from the wage equation, and the rate of growth is then determined from the saving equation. The higher the real wage, the lower the rate of profit, and the lower (therefore) the rate of growth. If it is the rate of growth that is given, the same two equations work the

[1] It has been maintained by L. Pasinetti (*Review of Economic Studies*, October 1962) that this is the only assumption that we are entitled to make in a Growth Equilibrium model. If the model is considered as a long-period distribution theory there is much to be said for his view. But it does not seem to me that this is the only way of regarding it; it is not the aspect with which I am here principally concerned.

[2] They will be fully considered in Chapter XV.

other way round. The rate of profit (which is consistent with this rate of growth) is then determined by the saving equation, and the rate of real wage from the wage equation. The lower the rate of growth, the lower the rate of profit, and the higher the real wage. That is all that there is to be said.

The rate of growth is always less than the rate of profit (with $s_1 < 1$). The lowest growth that is consistent with equilibrium depends on the lowest profit that is acceptable; if the profit rate can fall to zero, the growth rate can fall to zero. The maximum possible growth rate is $s_1 \times$ the maximum possible profit rate; this, as we have seen, is limited by the technique and the limit (which must be presumed to exist) below which wages cannot fall. To compare these limits with the g_1 and g_2 at which we arrived under the other assumption about saving is not very meaningful; but there should certainly be more room, under the new assumption, at the lower end—and it is possible to argue, in a similar way, that there should be more room at the upper end (of the range of growth rates) also.

Everything that has been said in the latter part of this chapter has assumed that there is just one technique—that the specifications of *the* consumption good and *the* capital good are the same in the equilibria (or on the equilibrium paths) that we are comparing. That assumption (as was explained) could be only a first step; we must see what we can do about dropping it before going further.

XIII

CHOICE OF TECHNIQUE

1. THE single technique, to which our analysis of growth equilibrium has hitherto been confined, was represented, for purposes of verbal discussion, by the single consumption good of given specification (corn) and the single capital good of given specification (tractors) in which it was embodied. Algebraically, this amounts to representing the technique by the *set* of coefficients (α, β, a, b). Along any particular constant-proportions growth path, technique in this sense must remain unchanged. But when we come to comparing one equilibrium path with another, there is no reason why the techniques along the two paths should be the same. Even if the consumption good (consumption bundle) is the same, the capital good may be different. There are thus two kinds of changes in technique to be considered: (1) the simple kind, in which there is a change in the capital good only; (2) what looks like being a more complex kind, in which there is a change in the consumption good as well as in the capital good. (For it is hardly conceivable that the consumption good could vary without there being at the least some change in the proportions in which capital goods, as ordinarily understood, were used; and this would count, in our terminology, as a change in the specification of *the* capital good.)

In fact, when we have found a way of dealing with the first kind, to extend it to the second (so far as it can be extended to the second within a Growth Equilibrium theory) will give us little trouble. It is nevertheless convenient to begin by considering the first kind alone.

It should be understood that all we are now to consider is the response of technique to price changes. We still assume that technology is given: that there is a given range of techniques from which choice is to be made. The effects of changes in technology (changes in technical knowledge, or inventions) will not be considered until later chapters.[1]

---

[1] Especially Chapter XV (pp. 180–2) and Chapter XXII, below.

Even if the make-up (or specification) of the consumption good does not change, a change from one technique of production to another (involving a change in the make-up of the capital good) must be supposed to change *all* of the coefficients (α, β, a, b). For consider the matter in terms of the parable. The ultimate object remains the production of corn; but there is now a choice between using steam tractors (made by labour using steam tractors) and using oil tractors (made by labour using oil tractors). If there is only one capital good in each equilibrium, the two industries will have to change over from the one capital good to the other together.[1]

2. If we begin (as before) with the case of an elastic supply of labour (at a fixed real wage), there will (as we have seen) be a certain rate of profit that can be got from the one technique, and there will be a certain rate of profit to be got from the other technique (determined in the same way). If the first technique is chosen, when a higher rate of profit could be got from the other technique, there will be no equilibrium. The condition for a particular technique to be the equilibrium technique at given real wages is simply that it should be the technique which generates the highest rate of profit.

The relation between real wage (which in this chapter we will simply write as w) and rate of profit (r) for a particular technique is given by its wage equation. As we have seen, this equation can be represented by a curve, which will necessarily slope downwards, and must cut both axes (there being a maximum w and a maximum r that can be got with the particular technique). When there is a choice of techniques, there will be a wage curve of this sort for each technique, which may be drawn on the same diagram (Fig. 2(a)). At a given real wage it is the curve which is furthest out which will always be selected. It may conceivably be the case that it is the same curve that is furthest out, whatever w. But ordinarily some of the curves will intersect, so that it will be a different curve that is furthest out, at different levels of the real wage. The curve that is actually followed, when technique is

---

[1] One might conceivably consider a half-way house in which there was only a change in the (a, b) coefficients, involving a change in the method of production of the capital good without change in its specification. But nothing is gained in the way of simplicity by stopping, even for a moment, at this intermediate case.

variable, will thus be the 'outer frontier' or 'outer envelope' of the particular technique curves. Along the frontier the profit rate will fall more slowly (for a given rise in the real wage) than it would have done if technique had not been variable. Or, since the diagram can be read either way, this comes to the same thing as

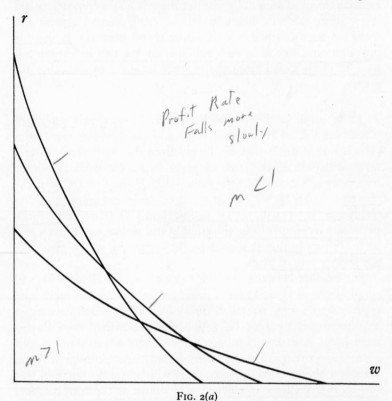

FIG. 2(a)

saying that the real wage can rise faster, for a given fall in the profit rate. We might indeed have got the same frontier by taking the choice of technique to be made on the basis of finding the highest real wage that could be offered, consistently with a given rate of profit.

3. This *wage frontier* (or 'factor price frontier', as Samuelson would prefer to call it) is the central concept of the theory of choice of techniques—along an equilibrium growth path. It is defined, and established, in this simple way; but it will be useful to examine its properties somewhat further.

The wage curve, for a single technique, is defined (as we saw in the last chapter) by the equation

$$\frac{1}{w} = \beta + \frac{r\alpha b}{1 - ra}.$$

Multiplying this out, we get

$$(\alpha b - a\beta)wr + \beta w + ar = 1$$

or, again putting m for $\alpha b / a\beta$ (the ratio of the coefficient ratios)

$$(m - 1)\beta w . ar + \beta w + ar = 1.$$

Whatever the value of m, this curve will always intersect the axes at the points where $w = 1/\beta$, $r = 1/a$. If $m = 1$, so that there is no difference in capital–labour ratios ·between the industries, it is simply the straight line joining these points. If m is not 1, the curve is a rectangular hyperbola, inward-bending if $m > 1$, outward-bending if $m < 1$. Thus when it is the 'farm' that is more mechanized, the curve is inward-bending; when the 'factory' is more mechanized the curve bends outwards.

(This is one of the results which we shall have to modify when we abandon the assumption that it is the same capital good that is used in both industries; but it will be useful, essentially as a piece of scaffolding, to let it stand for a while.)

Now it is evident geometrically (Fig. 2(b)) that if there were a number of alternative techniques, each of them being such that $m = 1$, so that their wage curves were straight lines, the form which the frontier would take would be that of an inward-bending polygon; if the successive techniques were close together, the frontier would approximate to the form of an inward-bending curve. Even though the individual technique curves were not inward-bending, the frontier curve would be. In the same way, if the individual curves were themselves inward-bending ($m > 1$), the envelope (though it might have kinks in it) would on the whole be inward-bending; if the individual curves were close together, the kinks would disappear, and the curve would take a smooth inward-bending form. Even if the individual curves were outward-bending ($m < 1$), it is possible that the envelope curve (in this sense) would be inward-bending (Fig. 2(c)). But it is not certain that it would be inward-bending; cases can be constructed, in which the

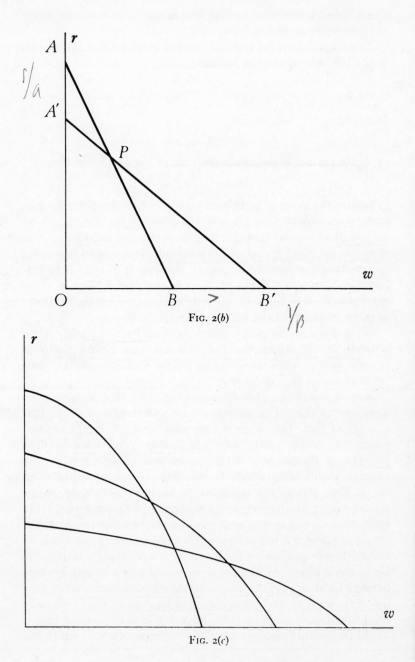

FIG. 2(b)

FIG. 2(c)

choice of techniques is rather narrow, where the possibility of shifting from one technique to another is not sufficient to prevent the envelope curve (based upon outward-bending individual curves) from itself being outward-bending.

It is nevertheless clear that variability of technique does work in the direction of making it more likely that the wage curve that will actually be followed will be inward-bending. Though the possibility that the envelope curve will be outward-bending is not removed, it looks less likely than it did in the case where there was only one technique that could be used.

4. Is there any general way in which we can specify the direction of the change in technique which will be likely to correspond to a lowering of the rate of profit (or to a raising of the level of real wages)? This is a snark which economists have been hunting ever since Ricardo. Can one say that a lowering of the rate of profit will indicate a change to more capital-intensive methods? So great a question cannot be completely answered under our present (much too limited) assumptions; but even within the present framework we have enough to throw some light upon it.

If the wage curves were all of them linear ($m = 1$) a fall in the rate of profit would lead to a shift in technique such as is represented by Fig. 2(b). There would then be quite definite things which we could say about the change in production coefficients. The old point of equilibrium was on AP (or AB); the new is on PB' (or $A'B'$). Since A' must be lower than A, $1/a' < 1/a$, so that $a < a'$; with the fall in profit the coefficient a (the capital-capital coefficient, we may call it) be raised. That is one sense in which (so it appears) the technique must become more capital-intensive. But further, since B' must lie to the right of B, $1/\beta' > 1/\beta$, so that $\beta > \beta'$; with the fall in the rate of profit the consumption-good industry must become less labour-intensive. Even here, it should be noticed, there are no similar rules about the coefficients α and b. That, perhaps, is hardly surprising, since—it will be remembered —the change in technique implies a change in the specification of the capital good; so that α and α', b and b' are not really comparable with one another. Even with linear wage-curves, we have just the two firm rules, about the capital-capital coefficient, and the labour-consumption good coefficient; and that is all.

How far can even these rules be preserved in non-linear cases?

If the wage equations are quadratic, the curves will in principle have two intersections; but it is not necessary that the other intersection should fall within the positive quadrant, which alone is relevant. It can indeed be shown that so long as *m* (the coefficient ratio) is the *same* along the two curves, they can have only one intersection within the positive quadrant;[1] thus if the shift is to another wage curve with the same *m*, the rules will necessarily hold. (This is true whether *m* is > or < 1.) The effect on technique of a change in the rate of profit (or real wage-rate) can thus be divided into two parts: (1) a straightforward 'substitution effect' due to the change in *a* and *β* (with constant *m*) for which the rules that we have been enunciating will hold quite strictly; and (2) an effect from the change in *m* (if there is one) which breeds exceptions. Not a very satisfactory situation, but one that has parallels in other parts of economic theory!

What will happen if there is a change in *m* sufficient to bring about a second intersection is shown in Fig. 3. A fall in the profit rate at the upper intersection will bring about a shift to a technique which has a higher 'capital-capital' coefficient (so that in that sense production becomes 'more capitalistic') but does not have a lower 'labour-corn' coefficient. One of the rules is satisfied, but not the other. Similarly, at the lower intersection, while the fall in the profit rate does lead to a shift to a technique with lower 'labour-corn' coefficient, the new technique does not have a higher 'capital-capital' coefficient. All that can be said in such cases is that at least one of the rules must hold. That is not much help; but for the reason stated, we do seem to be entitled to regard such cases as exceptional.

Of the two rules, that relating to the 'labour-corn' coefficient—that a rise in the rate of real wages (or a fall in the rate of profit) will tend to diminish the labour intensity of consumption-good production—looks as if it should be independent of our *dangerous*

---

[1] If the wage equations for two techniques (a, β, m) (a', β', m) for which *m* is the same, are written down and solved for *r* (the rate of profit at a point of intersection), we get a quadratic, which is such that the product of the roots is given by

$$aa' \, rr' = -1/(m-1).$$

If $m > 1$, this product is negative, so that only one of *r* and *r'* can be positive. If $m < 1$, the product is positive; but since $m > 0$, the right-hand side must be > 1. In that case then, either ar or $a'r'$ (or both) must be > 1; the corresponding *w* or *w'* will then be negative. In no case, if *m* is unchanged, can there be two intersections in the positive quadrant.

assumption, that it is the same capital good that is used in the two industries. The other, about the capital-capital coefficient, cannot have this kind of independence. If it generalizes at all, it cannot generalize just like that. How it does generalize, we shall see in the next chapter.[1]

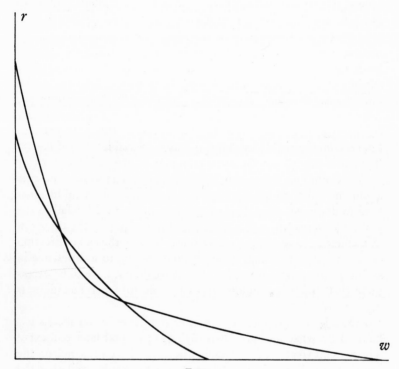

FIG. 3

5. Even before that, we have enough to make some progress with the question of adjustment to a change in the growth rate, which (when we last considered it)[2] we left in an unsatisfactory condition. What difference is made to that problem when we admit a choice of techniques? We found (it will be remembered) that if technique (a, β, m) was fixed, and the proportion of *total income* saved was also fixed, a change in prices (specifically a change in the rate of profit) could have no effect in facilitating a change in growth

[1] See below (Chapter XIV, pp. 165–6).
[2] See above (Chapter XII, pp. 143–5).

...e unless there was a difference in the coefficient ratios in the two industries. If there was no difference ($m = 1$), the price ratio (p/π) would be unchanged by a change in r, so that a change in r would be of no help in restoring equilibrium. We therefore looked for a way out (in Mr. Kaldor's manner) in terms of a difference in saving propensities between wage-earners and capitalists. We can now see that that is by no means the only way out.

It does indeed emerge from our present discussion that the case in which $m = 1$ (or is near to 1), which is the difficult case on the assumption of a given technique, is the easiest case as soon as we admit a choice of techniques within the technology. If $m = 1$, the limits between which the growth rate must lie (for equilibrium with a single technique) will coincide; we have $g = s/a$, for any (feasible) rate of profit. Now, however, even if s (the proportion of total income saved) is constant, a may be variable. And if $m = 1$ (for either the new or the old technique), or if m is near to 1 (for either technique), there can be no double intersection; the rule about the effect on a *must* hold. A rise in the rate of profit must tend to dominish a; thus a rise in the rate of profit (or fall in the real wage) must operate, by change of technique, in the direction of facilitating a rise in the growth rate. This is the same direction of effect as is attributed, in the Kaldor theory, to a difference in saving propensities; we now see that we do not have to lay stress upon that difference (unless we wish to do so) when technique is variable.

I shall be returning to this matter (which is by no means exhausted by what we have been saying) in several later contexts.[1] The present treatment is evidently defective by its reliance on the 'capital-capital' coefficient. It must also be emphasized that the change that is being considered is a change from one growth equilibrium to another; how it is possible to get from one such equilibrium to another is a question which we have not (so far) even approached.[2]

6. I conclude with a brief consideration of what happens when the specification of 'the' consumption good is variable. This will not give us much trouble, for most of what can be said can be treated

---

[1] Especially in Chapters XIV and XV, below.
[2] I shall say what I have to say about it in Chapter XVI, and (to some extent) in Chapter XXII.

by the same formal technique as we have been using on the other side.

All that we have to do is to establish some equivalence (on the demand side) between the new consumption good (or consumption bundle) and the old. In view of the homogeneity assumption, to which we are committed (as explained previously)[1] even on the side of consumers' wants, there is no difficulty about this. We are obliged to assume that the consumer's utility function (for some index of utility) obeys the law of constant returns to scale; that every indifference curve (of the representative consumer) can be derived from any other by simple magnification. It is then safe to say (though it would not be safe if we did not have this homogeneity) that a unit of one consumption good (or bundle) is equivalent to a unit of another if they are on the same indifference level. Starting with an arbitrary unit of the one, we have only to find the quantity of the other which is indifferent with it, and call that the unit of the other. Homogeneity ensures that if 1 of A is equivalent, on this test, to 1 of B, 2 of A will be equivalent to 2 of B.

Once this is granted, consumers' substitution and producers' substitution come, formally, to the same thing. We have only to think of consumption as consisting of various quantities of some abstract *consumption in general*, which is such that (1) an increase in the quantity consumed of *any* consumption bundle will increase *consumption in general* in the same proportion, and (2) *consumption in general* would remain the same if the actual bundle were replaced by another bundle (with a different 'mix') that was indifferent with it. Actual consumption goods then disappear from the picture; *consumption in general* takes the place of 'corn'; changes in the make-up of *consumption in general*, in response to price changes, will simply affect the specification of *the* capital good, in exactly the same way as it is affected by changes in the technique of production of a single consumption good, in the manner that was considered in the earlier part of this chapter. It becomes just the same story. All we have to remember is that a change in real wages (now to be understood as being expressed in terms of *consumption in general* or of a price index of consumption) may now affect production coefficients through consumers' substitution as well as through producers' substitution. The aggregate 'substitution effect' may thus be more important than it appeared while

[1] See above, p. 134.

we confined it to changes in production technique; but it works in substantially the same way.

That is all that need be said about substitution effects in consumption; income effects (it may appear at first sight) have been ruled out. But that is not altogether so. We are obliged to assume that the consumption bundle, of every consumer, remains unchanged in mix when his income changes (and there is no change in the prices confronting him); but we do not have to assume that the consumption-mix of every consumer is the same. For along a particular growth equilibrium, the distribution of income among consumers will remain unchanged over time; thus even if different kinds of consumers have different 'mixes', the 'mix' of total consumption will remain unchanged, so long as each consumer maintains his own 'mix'. But such differences in consumption patterns can be important, when one is comparing one equilibrium with another.

The difference in consumption patterns which it looks like being most interesting to introduce is that between the receivers of wages and of profits. If all wage-earners have the same consumption pattern, we can treat their consumption as consumption of a single *wage good*; if all capitalists have the same pattern, we can treat their consumption as consumption of a single *profit good*. We then have three goods in the system (wage good, profit good, and capital good); this looks like making things much more complicated, but in fact it is surprising how little difference is made. So long as there is no 'saving out of wages', we still have the saving equation $g = s_1 r$; this is indeed a powerful relation, which holds in many models, being very little dependent upon the simplifications which we introduced at the beginning of Chapter XII. And we still have the same wage equation, being a relation between the profit rate and the real wage rate (measured in terms of the wage good). We can use it to get a wage frontier (allowing for changes in technique) in very much the same way. For the wage equation is entirely derived from the costs of production of the wage good and of the capital good respectively; the profit good does not come into it. So that we can make this particular generalization, and still find that things remain much as before.

There is much more trouble when we permit 'saving out of wages'; but that is a hare which I shall not follow up in this particular direction.

For as soon as we contemplate splitting up the consumption good in this way, the question naturally arises: could we not also break up the capital good, and would it not be much to the advantage of the model if we did so? That, however, as we shall find, is a large question. It undoubtedly needs another chapter.

XIV

MANY CAPITAL GOODS

1. I HAVE thought it worth while to write out the Theory of Growth Equilibrium, as has been done in the last two chapters, in what is admittedly an over-simplified form, based upon assumptions which, just as they stand, cannot be accepted. For this is the easiest way of establishing the general outline. The outline does come out, in spite of the simplifications; once we have it we can proceed to elaborate it. We already have the 'boxes'; we can proceed to fill them in more satisfactory ways.

The particular simplification which in this chapter I shall seek to remove is the assumption that it is the same capital good that is used in both industries—that the capital good which is used in making tractors is nothing else but the tractor itself. All of the other assumptions, which we have been making, will still be retained. It is still the comparative analysis of constant-proportions equilibrium which is our sole concern. The problem of transition, from one such equilibrium to another, is still postponed.

It is possible (as previously noticed) to make the 'tractors out of tractors' assumption a little better by introducing a second capital good, and no more than that. Leaving tractors as the sole capital good in the 'corn' industry, we might introduce (say) lathes as the capital good in the tractor-making industry; but we should then have to have a third 'industry' to make the lathes. It would not sound so bad if the capital good that was used in the lathe-making industry was also a lathe. But though the model that can be constructed on that two-capital-good basis is fairly interesting, it is hardly worth while to stop at it. For it still leaves us with the dangerous persistence of an industry that uses the same capital good as input that it produces as output; and there is a serious temptation to attach too much importance to an industry of this peculiar kind.[1] It is better to go straight to the general case of many capital goods, so that this artificial 'industry' is cut right out.

[1] Ricardo himself (as Mr. Sraffa has shown us) went through all this. It was for exactly this reason that he abandoned his original model, in which agricultural production was reduced to the making of corn out of corn (Ricardo, ed. Sraffa, vol. i, Introduction, p. xxxi).

2. For the reason that was explained at the end of the last chapter, we need not trouble ourselves with more than one consumption good (one is enough to represent *consumption in general*). But we will now allow the employment (and production) of *n* capital goods, where *n* may be very large.[1] These capital goods are used for making each other, as well as for making the one consumption good. In spite of this enlargement of the problem, price equations and quantity equations (for a given technique) may still be written down in what is no more than a development of the form with which we are acquainted.

Consider the price equations first. There will be a price equation, expressing equality between price and unit cost, for the consumption good and for each of the capital goods that is in production. (In a constant-proportions growth equilibrium, all of the capital goods that are in existence must also be in production; so there will be just *n* of these capital-price equations.) There will be an equation of the type $q_i = rp_i$ for each capital good—it is a condition of equilibrium that the same rate of profit should be earned throughout the system.[2] But, now that we are disaggregating, it becomes inconvenient to make use of our former device for neglecting depreciation; we can hardly suppose that depreciation is being made good all the time within each of our many 'industries'. A more explicit method for dealing with depreciation (and with working capital) seems to be needed.

The following should suffice. Consider the use of the *i*th capital good in the making of the *j*th. If we followed our previous notation we should write a_{ij} as the quantity that is required (under the given technique) for making a unit of the *j*th. But we now wish to distinguish between the cases (i) in which the *i*th good is a permanent instrument that does not depreciate; (ii) in which it is a semi-permanent instrument of which some fixed proportion is used per period if it is used in *j* production;[3] (iii) in which it is a

---

[1] The possibility (a real one in practice) that the same good may be used for consumption and for capital purposes is neglected. I think I may be allowed this simplification.

[2] In Growth Equilibrium we are, I think, entitled to abstract from differences in risk; they have more relevance to questions of transition. But I fear that the reader will find that there is too little attention to risk in all this sort of Economic Dynamics.

[3] I do not think that this statement implies a confusion between depreciation in value terms and physical using-up; or that it involves us in a concept of 'evaporation', in the manner of Professor Meade. What it does imply is an

raw material or half-finished product that is wholly used up. The first of these cases fits exactly into our old formulation. The cost that is to be imputed, in the production of the jth good, to its use of the ith, is just $q_i a_{ij} (= r p_i a_{ij})$ as before. In the second case, it is $p_i(r+d_{ij})a_{ij}$, where d_{ij} is the proportion that is used up per period. (We can allow, without extra complication, for the possibility that the rate of using-up depends not only on the good i, but also on j, the good in the production of which it is being used.) In the third case we have merely to set $d_{ij} = 1$, and we get the imputed cost for a material that is used at the beginning of the period. In the first case, of course, $d_{ij} = 0$.

All three cases, therefore, are covered by the same formula. But since d_{ij} always appears with a_{ij}, we can take them together, writing the formula
$$p_i(ra_{ij}+e_{ij})$$
so that e_{ij} measures the using-up of the input, per unit of output, and a_{ij} measures the durable use that extends over the period.

3. With this understanding, we can write down a *capital-price* equation for each of the n capital goods. It will take the form
$$p_j = \sum p_i(ra_{ij}+e_{ij})+wb_j$$
where the sum is taken for $i = 1, 2, ..., n$, and b_j (of course) is the labour coefficient for good j. In any particular case, many of the coefficients a, b, e, will of course be zero; but if not zero, they must be positive. (There will also be one *consumption-price* equation, of similar form; but we will leave that over for the moment. In the first steps of our analysis we are only concerned with the capital-price equations.)

If (again for the moment) we take r to be given, the n capital-price equations form a system of linear equations, which should determine the n ratios (p_i/w)—the prices of the n capital goods in terms of the wage-unit. Indeed, I think we may say that in any case that is significant economically, they *will* determine the n price ratios (for the exceptions to which mathematicians rightly draw attention can only arise here through faulty classification—

absence of indivisibilities, so that in each period a part of the stock of each capital good is actually discarded. Such absence of indivisibility is of course unrealistic, but it is entirely in line with the other simplifications that are made in a Growth Equilibrium model.

the treatment as a different good of what is really no more than a bundle of goods that have been otherwise reckoned—and so on). But though we may take it that the n equations will determine the n price ratios, that is not enough. If a growth equilibrium is to exist under the technique proposed, every one of the n ratios must be positive; we cannot even allow any of them to be zero, unless some b is zero—and that is a thing which may fairly be excluded.[1]

In order to see what conditions are necessary for this to happen, let us begin by putting the e's on one side, so that the equations reduce to

$$p_j = r \sum p_i a_{ij} + w b_j.$$

If r also were zero, the solution of these equations is obviously $p_j = w b_j$ (pure labour cost); the b's being positive, these p's are certainly positive. If r is small, but not quite zero, it is clear that we must have $p_j > w b_j$ (for if it were not so, some of the p_i's would go negative). Nevertheless, if r is small enough, p's that are only a little above their corresponding wb's will do.

As r increases, the p's that are generated in this way must go on rising. For if $p_j > w b_j$ $(p_i > w b_i)$, it again follows from the above equation that

$$p_j > r \sum w b_i a_{ij} + w b_j$$

so that p_j goes on being pushed up as r increases. But with the p's all rising (albeit at different rates), a point must come, with rising r, when for some j, $r \sum p_i a_{ij}$ becomes $> p_j$. At that point it is w that goes negative. This is inadmissible, so that there is a *critical value* beyond which r cannot go.

Now let us put back the e's. Starting again with $r = 0$, let us multiply the e's by an arbitrary multiplier (μ) so that the equations become

$$p_j = \mu \sum p_i e_{ij} + w b_j.$$

This is formally just the same as before; so that we can only get positive p's from these equations if μ is less than a certain critical value. If this critical value (which now depends upon the e's) is < 1, the equations

$$p_j = \sum p_i e_{ij} + w b_j$$

[1] The properties of a set of equations of this type are becoming familiar to many economists through their occurrence in input-output theory and in the theory of the matrix multiplier. I think, however, that the intuitive explanation which follows (it has no claim to being a proof) will be found useful. It helps one to understand what one is at. For further discussion, see Appendix B.

(the original equations with $r = 0$) can have no admissible solution. But if it is > 1, they do have an admissible solution, by what precedes. This, then, is the condition for the technique to be a possible technique, with $r = 0$.[1]

Suppose that this condition is satisfied, so that the technique is a feasible technique, when $r = 0$. We can then take the original equations
$$p_j = \sum p_i(ra_{ij}+e_{ij})+wb_j$$
and let r rise, starting at zero. We know that there is a feasible solution when $r = 0$; as r rises, the price ratios p/w will increase; there must be a certain value of r at which this cannot go on any longer (by a slight adaptation of the former argument). At this value $w = 0$.

So *we may sum up* by saying that the conditions for the capital-price equations to have a feasible solution are two: in the first place, the e's must be such that the equations would have a feasible solution even if $r = 0$; and in the second place, r must be less than a certain critical value, or *critical rate of return*.

4. Granted that these conditions are satisfied, we can go back to the consumption-price equation. (This, it will be remembered, is a *single* equation.) We may write it, in accordance with our usual notation
$$\pi = \sum p_i(r\alpha_i+\epsilon_i)+w\beta$$
α's and ϵ's being coefficients of the uses of the n capital goods in the making of the consumption good, while the (single) β is the labour-coefficient in the making of the consumption good. If (as in the last chapter) we take the consumption good as standard of value, this becomes
$$(1/w) = \sum (p_i/w)(r\alpha_i+\epsilon_i)+\beta.$$

Now (as we have seen) so long as r is less than its critical value, each (p_i/w) increases with r. All α's and ϵ's are non-negative so it follows that $(1/w)$ increases with r. Thus there is a *wage curve* (for the particular technique) which slopes downwards from left to right, just like the curve which we have been using in the last two chapters.

So far, then, the simplification of 'tractors making tractors' does not do so badly after all. Even when we drop it, we still have a

---

[1] When $r = 0$ the capital-price equations become purely static; the system is the same as the static Leontief input-output system. The feasibility condition is therefore the same as that which has been called the Hawkins-Simon condition.

wage curve with properties that are broadly similar to those with which we are acquainted. There are just a few differences (or re-interpretations) which have to be noticed.[1]

The wage curve (for the particular technique) will still intersect both axes, as we are accustomed to find it doing (Fig. 2 above). But the meaning of the intercepts requires a bit of attention. The intercept on the w-axis, which we formerly expressed as $(1/\beta)$, will be less than our present $(1/\beta)$, because of the costs of using-up of capital which survive, even when profit is 0. This, however, is not a substantial difference—it is simply due to the fact that we are now allowing for depreciation explicitly, instead of treating it implicitly as in our former method. The making good of the depreciation is an *indirect* labour cost, which we are now showing separately. If indirect labour cost is included it is still true that the highest conceivable level to which the wage can rise, under the given technique, is set by the total labour cost of consumption-good production.

With regard to the intercept on the r-axis there is a more important change. In the one-capital-good model this intercept was $(1/a)$—the reciprocal of the capital-capital coefficient. That, inevitably, has to go. All that we can say about this intercept is that it marks the maximum to which the rate of profit can rise under this technique, even if labour was a free good. That, of course, is obvious on the diagram; but it is still an important point that we must draw the diagram to show such a maximum.

In the one-capital-good model the sign of the difference in co-efficient ratios (between the two 'industries') appeared to be a thing of much importance. According as the 'farm' or the 'factory' was more capital-intensive, so the curve would bend one way or the other. In the many-capital-good model, there can be nothing that corresponds to this at all closely. It is in fact no longer necessary that the curve should bend the same way throughout the whole of its length. It is normally a curve of higher degree than the second, so that it is perfectly capable of pursuing a serpentine course.[2]

[1] The generalization to n capital goods, worked out in this manner, is not completely general, since it assumes that every process of production has one product only (no joint supply). But I think I may make this simplification for the present purpose (see, however, Chapter XVIII, below).

[2] One must not beat too much of a retreat upon this matter. It is still true that the one-capital-good model is a fair simplification of the present more

5. Since (with our one consumption good) we have still got a wage curve that can be drawn upon a two-dimensional diagram, the theory of choice of techniques, which was elaborated in the last chapter, can be carried over in a very similar form. It is unnecessary to write it out again. All that has to be noticed is that in view of the possibility of 'serpentining', the possibility of the wage curves of different techniques intersecting more than once has to be taken rather (I do not think one need say more than *rather*)[1] more seriously; and that in consequence a lack of consonance between the two rules (derived from the two intercepts) is rather more likely to occur. The rules themselves must clearly be reinterpreted in accordance with what has been said about the intercepts in the preceding section.

Nevertheless, having got so far, there is a further question that arises. If it is only with this qualification that one can even say that a rise in real wages (and consequent fall in the rate of profit) favours the adoption of techniques that—with all indirect labour costs included—are less labour-intensive (and it is that rule which, in the light of the present discussion, must be accepted as the more interesting rule), does it not look as if we are putting the whole question the wrong way? It already appears that to distinguish techniques by reference to the maximum rate of profit they would permit, at a wage of zero, is not a very interesting way of distinguishing them; but is labour intensity, which amounts to distinguishing them on the basis of profit being zero, so very interesting, either? May not the whole trouble have arisen because we have asked the wrong question? Instead of looking at what might happen, in extreme positions, at the 'ends' of the curves, ought we not to fix our attention on what happens in the neighbourhood of the actual position where the change takes place?

Whether or not they have multiple intersections, the wage curves that correspond to preferred techniques are always related, at the point of change-over, in the same way. When there is a rise in the rate of real wages (or a fall in the rate of profit) there will always be a tendency to shift to a technique with a wage curve which (in

general model; there must be some sense in which a strong tendency to capital intensity in *net* investment makes the curve tend to be outward-bending, and vice versa. See Appendix B, p. 320.

[1] See previous footnote.

the way we have drawn our diagrams) is, at that level of wages, a curve with a slope that is less. That is to say, the new wage curve must be one on which, at that level, profits are less affected by a given rise in wages. In that sense, and in that sense only, the new technique must be one with a lower labour-intensity. And since the whole thing can be put the other way, it is also a technique in which wages are more affected by a given rise in profits. In that sense, and only in that sense, we can safely say that the new technique is one of greater capital-intensity.[1]

6. Here again I leave the question of changes in technique (within the technology). Everything that has so far been said in this chapter concerns the price equations. What of the others?

If all saving is 'out of profits' we still have the simple saving equation $g = s_1 r$, which remains entirely unaffected by the disaggregation that we have been performing. (It would of course be possible to disaggregate it by dividing our savers up into more classes; but that would be a different kind of disaggregation.) With the wage equation holding firm (as has been shown) and with this equation holding firm, our previous analysis of the effect of real wages on growth, and of growth on real wages, will hold good without any amendment at all. All is well so long as we can make this assumption about saving.

If some saving is 'out of wages', things are not so simple. Most of what I have to say about this case I shall hold over to the next chapter, but I must prepare for it here. If there is 'saving out of wages' the ratio of total saving to profits depends upon the ratio of total wages to profits; and this factor-share ratio (wL/rpK) depends upon quantities as well as prices. For the study of the factor-share ratio (and also for other problems, such as the transition problem to be discussed in Chapter XVI, below) we need the quantity equations. This is evidently the place where they should be put down in their general form.

7. It will be convenient to keep K to denote a general index of the quantity of capital in the system (when we can find such an index); so that the quantity of the ith capital good that is in stock at the beginning of the period under consideration will be written k_i. x_i will now be the gross output of the ith good during the period. The output of the (single) consumption good is ξ (as before).

In growth equilibrium the stocks of all capital goods increase at a growth rate g; so that gk_i is *net* investment in the ith good. With e's and ϵ's defined as before, the using-up of the ith good in production of the jth is $e_{ij}x_j$, and the using-up in consumption good production is $\epsilon_i \xi$. Thus we have the *accumulation equation* for each capital good

$$gk_i = x_i - \sum e_{ij} x_j - \epsilon_i \xi$$

(with the sum taken over all j). This corresponds to the equation $x = gK$ in the one-capital-good model.

In growth equilibrium the stock of each capital good must be that which is required for current production (of capital goods and of consumption goods); and the labour employed must be that which is required for the same production. So we have the *quantity equations*

$$k_i = \sum a_{ij} x_j + \alpha_i \xi \quad \text{(for each capital good)},$$
$$L = \sum b_j x_j + \beta \xi \quad \text{(for labour)}.$$

It is easiest to substitute the capital-quantity equations into the corresponding accumulation equations, so as to get a set of n equations to determine the ratios (x_i/ξ). Thus

$$x_i - \sum e_{ij} x_j - \epsilon_i \xi = g(\sum a_{ij} x_j + \alpha_i \xi)$$

or
$$x_i = \sum (ga_{ij} + e_{ij})x_j + (g\alpha_i + \epsilon_i)\xi.$$

Thus we come to equations that have exactly the same form as the capital-*price* equations; they can be discussed in exactly the same way. In equilibrium, all of the output-ratios (x_i/ξ) must be positive. Two conditions are necessary for this. First, a condition to ensure that all of the (x_i/ξ) can be positive when $g = 0$; but this is precisely the same as the first condition which we got on the price side; it is simply a question of the technique (for we are here working with a fixed technique) being feasible at all. In the second place, g must be less than a certain critical value—which turns out to be identical with the critical rate of return that we found for r.[1] If these conditions are satisfied, positive (x_i/ξ) can be found,

---

[1] Just as, in the one-capital-good model, the limit to r was $(1/a)$ and the limit to g was $(1/a)$.

depending on g; they will all of them be larger, the larger is g—for the same reason as we found for the corresponding theorem on the price side.

These values of (x_i/ξ) may now be substituted in the quantity equations, as written above, to give (k_i/ξ) and (L/ξ) in terms of g. Every kind of capital, and the employment of labour, will be larger, relatively to consumption output, the higher is the growth rate. This, I think, is what we should expect. But it is important to have shown that, in the comparative analysis of growth equilibrium paths, these rules are valid without exception.

8. The rules are concerned with the ratios of capital (and labour) to consumption output—not with the ratio of capital to net output (including net investment), which is the capital-output ratio, as commonly understood. Is there anything which follows from these rules about the capital-output ratio?

As before, let us take the consumption good as standard of value. Capital is then $\sum pk$, while net output (including net investment) is $\xi + g \sum pk$. Thus

$$\frac{\text{net output}}{\text{capital}} = g + \frac{\xi}{\sum pk}.$$

If prices are constant (as in a Fixprice model it would be appropriate to assume) the second of these terms diminishes with g (in accordance with the rule just enunciated). Thus a rise in g, which increases the first term, diminishes the second. It is possible that the two effects may offset one another, though there is no reason, in general, why they should. The net effect may go either way.

Thus it cannot be said that the capital-output ratio, in growth equilibrium, is independent of the rate of growth; but there is no theoretical reason why it should necessarily be affected in one direction. This being so, it may be a fair simplification to treat it as constant (within the technique, or—at constant prices—within the technology). In these terms, the assumption of constancy is defensible; but the defence is not one that goes very deep.

XV

FACTOR SHARES IN GROWTH
EQUILIBRIUM

1. THOUGH I have been taking all this trouble (from Chapter XII onwards) to set out in some detail a formal theory of Growth Equilibrium, I have been careful to set it out in such a way as to make clear what a restricted thing it is. It is simply a generalization of the Classical Stationary State. There is no more reason to suppose that we shall find actual economies that are (even approximately) in growth equilibrium than that we shall find fully organized competitive economies that are in a stationary state. We may perhaps be entitled to regard an actual economy as being, in some sense, in a transition to a growth equilibrium; but it is only in that way that Growth Equilibrium theory can have bearing upon what we find in practice.

It is true that there are devices by which we can make the state of an actual economy (especially if we are only concerned with trends—taken on the average over time) look more like our Growth Equilibrium than it appears at first sight. For formal purposes we have identified the 'natural' growth of the economy with the growth of its labour force; and we have allowed that growth to be understood in its obvious sense, of growth in the number of those who are available for employment. But it takes no more than a little reinterpretation to give it a wider meaning. We can include in the growth of the labour force a growth in the efficiency of labour—a growth in the efficiency of labour in collaboration with capital, in the sense that the same number of workers, provided that they have additional equipment, can produce more output at a later date than they could have done earlier on. The formal theory holds without change, after this reinterpretation; but there is of course a great difference in its look. For it now becomes perfectly possible that the constancy in the real wage, per *unit* of labour, which we have found to be a characteristic of an equilibrium path, should imply a rise in the real wage per *head*; the individual worker is simply supplying an increasing number of *units.* Capital is then not merely being saved and invested in order to employ an increasing population; it is also facilitating a rise in real wages per head. The 'progressive' economy is much more genuinely progressive.

There is no doubt that we can go that far; but there are many who would go further still. They would make much more general technical progress consistent with growth equilibrium, so long as it is of a 'neutral' character, so that it does not upset factor shares. Here, however, is a serious divide. If one adopts that view one is committed to 'macro' analysis; for the 'macro' magnitudes—saving, investment, wage bill, aggregate profits, and so on—cannot then be split up. Their separate components (industry by industry) have no precise meaning. This type of 'macro' analysis (which goes beyond the Fixprice territory, where I do not question the use of 'macro' magnitudes) seems to me to be distinctly suspect; it can let one down very badly. There is a constant temptation to import concepts from a disaggregated theory (labour productivities and the like) that do not really belong; with technique so fluid, they become impossible to define. It may indeed be possible, by taking sufficient pains, to overcome these difficulties;[1] but it cannot be right to elude them by assuming them away. I have therefore decided that in this work I will stop short of this kind of interpretation. I insist that any particular growth equilibrium path is an equilibrium *with respect to a given technology*; changes in technology (of which account must of course be taken in some way) must imply a shift from one equilibrium growth path to another.

2. It is clear that on my interpretation the question of factor shares does not have the same theoretical importance as it does for (say) Harrod or Kaldor; but it is of course an interesting question in its own right. It will be well, before going further, to bring together what we can say about it. Most of what follows is concerned with the problem of factor shares in growth equilibrium; a question which (in the light of what has just been said) is to be distinguished from the general question of factor distribution. When one is only concerned with the growth equilibrium question, one is comparing two paths, along each of which distribution among factors remains

[1] An example of what I have in mind is the device that is used by Solow ('Investment and Technical Progress', in *Mathematical Methods in the Social Sciences*, Stanford, 1959).

unchanged over time; one has therefore to explain the distribution (to analyse the difference between the two distributions) in terms of things which can remain constant over time along a particular equilibrium path. It is entirely possible to have one theory of distribution that is appropriate for this particular problem; and yet, when one is analysing a different problem, in which one does not wish to make the assumption that the economy is in growth equilibrium (and I should myself by chary of making this assumption in most practical applications), one may logically have a different theory, which explains factor distribution in other terms—in terms of things that do not stay constant on an equilibrium path. It is entirely possible to hold that in growth equilibrium, factor distribution must be determined in the kind of way that is described in the rest of this chapter; and yet to hold that there is another theory, at least equally valid, that runs in other terms. I would not now maintain that *the* theory of factor distribution is that which runs in terms of production functions and elasticities of substitution; but I would not abandon that theory altogether.[1] The light that it casts upon the practical problem may not be a very bright light, but neither is that which is cast by the Growth Equilibrium theory. We need, at the least, both of these approaches; and it is probable that the matter should also be approached from other directions as well.

3. Now for the formal analysis. I shall begin with our old simplified one-capital-good model; I shall then make a perfunctory attempt to extend it as far as I can.

If there is only one capital good (tractors) and (as in Chapters XII and XIII) depreciation is not explicitly considered, the ratio of profits to wages can readily be expressed in terms of r and g by the use of the price and quantity equations. If (as Kaldor would have us assume) g is given, what we get in this way is a relation between f (which I shall use to denote the *factor share* of profits in total income) and r (the *rate* of profit). It needs to be supplemented by a saving equation, if r is to be eliminated, so that the profit share is shown as dependent upon saving propensities, and upon g, only.

Since there are just two relations to be considered, it ought to be

---

[1] It does at the least require the elaboration which I have set out in the Commentary on my *Theory of Wages* (2nd edition, 1963, pp. 335–50). And see below, Chapter XXIV.

possible to exhibit the theory of the matter on a diagram (Fig. 4). I shall put f (the profit share) on the vertical, and r (the profit rate) on the horizontal axis. We have then two 'curves' connecting r and f—a 'price-quantity curve' derived from the price- and quantity-equations, and a 'saving curve' derived from the saving equation. In order to discover the properties of these curves, we need, I am afraid, a little algebra.

Take the price-quantity curve first. From the price and quantity equations (for a given technique)[1] we have

$$\frac{wL}{rpK} = \left(\frac{1}{r}\right)\left(\frac{w}{p}\right)\left(\frac{L}{K}\right) = \frac{1}{r}\left(\frac{1-ra}{b}\right)\left(\frac{\beta-a\beta g+\alpha bg}{\alpha}\right)$$

or, putting $m = (\alpha b/a\beta)$, as usual,

$$\frac{1}{f} - 1 = \left(\frac{1-ra}{ra}\right)\left(\frac{1+\overline{m-1}\,ag}{m}\right) = \frac{1}{M}\left(\frac{1-ra}{ra}\right)$$

as we shall find it convenient to write it. For the properties of the ratio which we are calling M turn out to be rather simple and manageable.

Since ag must be less than 1, M is always positive. It is greater or less than 1 according as m is greater or less than 1. Indeed, it always lies between m and 1, being nearer to 1 (for given m), the larger is ag. With given technique and given growth rate, M will be a constant.

If $r = (1/a)$, so that the profit rate has reached its maximum for the given technique, all income must be swallowed up in profits and $f = 1$, whatever M. (This is confirmed by the above equation.) If $r = 0$, $f = 0$, whatever M. Thus, whatever M, the curve will always pass through the points O and A $(1/a, 1)$ on the diagram. If $m = 1$, so that $M = 1$, the curve reduces to the straight line OA. If $m > 1$, so that $M > 1$, the curve will bulge upwards, as shown in the undotted curve on the diagram (Fig. 4). If $m < 1$, it will bulge downwards, as shown in the dotted curve.

Now let us turn to the saving curve. If all saving is 'out of profits', the saving equation is simply our old friend $g = s_1 r$; this, on the diagram will simply be a vertical line (S), which must of course[2] intersect the price-quantity curve to the left of A. An

[1] See pp. 140, 142.
[2] For $r = (1/a)$ is the maximum rate of profit that is consistent with this technique. If $r > (1/a)$ the technique could not be used.

increase in s_1 (with given g) will move S to the left, leaving the price-quantity curve unaffected; it must therefore lower the rate, and the share, of profit—so far as we can see at present. An increase in g will move S to the right, so that (so long as the price-quantity curve is unaffected) the profit rate, and the profit share, must both rise. And though it is here possible that the bulge in the price-quantity curve might be affected by the change in g, it seems safe to assume that the effect on the bulge would not be considerable. (It cannot be if m is at all near to 1.) The rules about the effect of changes in the growth rate and in the saving propensity (with all saving out of profits) seem therefore to be straightforward.

But all this assumes that technique is given. If technique is variable the price-quantity curve will be shifted when r changes; either of its parameters (a or M) may be affected. So far as M is concerned, the effect may go either way; there is nothing definite that we can say about it. But, at least when we are concerned with techniques with an m that is fairly near to 1, it seems safe to assume that the effect on M will be small. Even so, the effect on a remains.

If $m = 1$ (and so $M = 1$), we have the perfectly firm rule that a rise in r will tend to diminish a, so that, as r rises, the point A will move to the right along IA. Each r will then have its own technique, and its own technique curve; it will be just one point on each particular technique curve which will be an effective point. The price-quantity curve, for variable technique (within the technology) will be the locus of these effective points. The rightward movement of the particular curves as r rises will cause the locus to bend round, humping it upwards; and there is no reason why it should not bend round so much that at some stage (or stages) it turns downwards. It can perfectly well take the form that is shown in Fig. 5. And though, when M is not $= 1$, such bending round is not inevitable, it still looks likely; the form that is shown in Fig. 5 remains as an open (indeed a wide open) possibility.

Now it is true that if there are only a finite number of techniques from which choice is to be made (and I would myself prefer to assume that this is so), there will be some smallest and some largest value of a among these techniques. Thus when r has fallen so low that the smallest value of $(1/a)$ is selected, a further fall in r must reduce f, ultimately to zero. That is why I have drawn the 'variable technique curve' passing through the origin. But similarly, when r has risen so high that the largest value of $(1/a)$ is

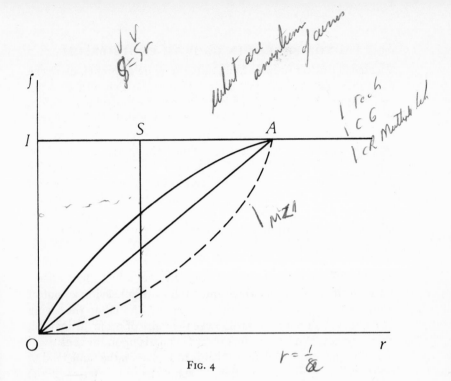

FIG. 4

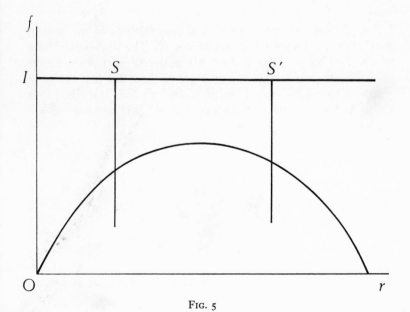

FIG. 5

selected, a further rise in r must raise the share of profits, up to the theoretical limit where that share $(f) = 1$. So that although the 'variable technique curve' may contain downward-sloping stretches, there must (so it would appear) be a kick-back at the end. Yet even this is not inevitable. There is in principle no reason why the smallest value of a (among the techniques) should not itself be zero—at a sufficiently high *rate* of profit (or, perhaps it would here be better to say, interest) capital ceases to be used at all. In that case (and I see no reason why we should refuse to include it) the *share* of profit falls to zero, when the *rate* of profit becomes too high. So why not draw the diagram (as I have done) to include that possibility?

If this is the form of the variable technique curve (and it is only the possibility of downward-sloping *stretches* which here arises) a rise in the profit rate (which must follow, if all saving is 'out of profits', from either a rise in the growth rate or a fall in the saving propensity) will not necessarily raise the *share* of profit. It may do, or it may not. Whether it does or not depends upon the sensitivity of technique to price changes: that is to say, upon the same kind of thing as was expressed (in the old static theory) in terms of the 'elasticity of substitution'.

4. Let us now attempt to make a similar analysis of the case in which there is some saving 'out of wages'. The interesting thing which then happens (as Kaldor has noticed)[1] is that the factor share comes directly into the saving equation. But that does not entitle us to use the saving equation alone to determine the profit share. As before, both equations (or curves) have to be used.

From the saving equation

$$gpK = s_1 rpK + s_2 wL$$

we have

$$\frac{g}{r} = s_1 + s_2 \frac{wL}{rpK} = s_1 + s_2\left(\frac{1}{f} - 1\right)$$

which is an equation of exactly the same form as that which we have been examining. If we write it

$$\frac{1}{f} - 1 = \frac{s_1}{s_2}\left(\frac{g}{s_1 r} - 1\right)$$

the correspondence is seen to be perfect. As before, the curve will

[1] 'Alternative Theories of Distribution' (in *Essays in Value and Distribution*).

pass through the origin, and through a point $r = g/s_1$ on the 'ceiling' $f = 1$. (This point is independent of s_2.) It is the ratio s_2/s_1 which corresponds to M in the other equation. Since we may take it that $s_2 < s_1$, the form of this curve will be that which was taken by the other when $M < 1$; that is to say, the saving curve must be a downward-bulging curve (Fig. 6).

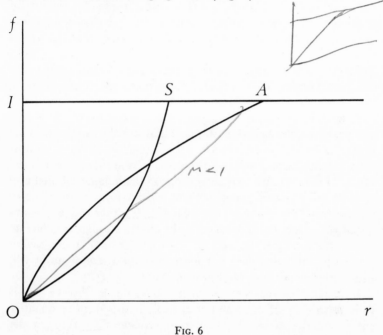

FIG. 6

If a particular technique is to be feasible, its 'particular technique' curve must intersect the saving curve below the ceiling.[1] If, for the particular technique, $m > 1$ and so $M > 1$, the curves will be bending in opposite directions; a leftward swing of the saving curve must then diminish the rate of profit—and, so long as the technique is fixed, it must diminish the share of profit also. That case is quite straightforward. If, on the other hand, we have $M < 1$, the two curves will be bending the same way; there are then two possibilities, according as the one or the other is the lower (at the origin). If M is only a little less than 1, the saving

---

[1] There can only be one intersection apart from the origin, since both curves are linear in $(1/r)$ and $(1/f)$.

curve will still be the lower, so we shall have the same relation as in the former case—there will be no exception here. But if M is much less than 1 (actually if it is less than s_2/s_1) the relation of the curves will be reversed. We shall then have an exception, but it is so extreme an exception that I do not think we need take much account of it.

For, in any case, if there is a reasonable degree of variability of technique, such an exception cannot occur. We shall always find that a leftward swing of the saving curve will diminish the *rate* of profit; but whether it also diminishes the *share* of profit depends, as before, on whether the 'variable technique' price-quantity curve has turned back or not. So the introduction of 'saving out of wages' does not make all that difference to our preceding results.

If, with given s_1, there is a rise in s_2, the bulging of the saving curve will be diminished; and this, in any but the exceptional case just mentioned, will reckon as a leftward swing. If there is a uniform rise in s_1 and s_2, this will show as a leftward movement of the point S towards I, without any change in the bulging. So that also reckons as a leftward swing. If there is a rise in s_1, without rise in s_2, there will be a leftward movement of S, together with a shallowing of the bulge. In all these cases the effects are similar. The rate of profit will tend to fall as a result of any increase in any saving propensity. But this does not mean that the share of profit will necessarily fall. It may do, but it may not.

In concluding this analysis, it is interesting to observe that if $m = 1$ (so that $M = 1$) and if $s_1 = s_2$, both the price-quantity curve and the saving curve become straight lines through the origin. Thus they cannot intersect again unless they have the same slope, when they become coincident. This merely verifies (very indirectly) a familiar conclusion: if there is no difference in saving propensities, no difference in coefficient ratios, and no variability in technique, growth equilibrium cannot be established merely by adjustment of the rate of profit.

5. Although I have written out this analysis of saving and factor shares in terms of the one-capital-good model, I think that the method of expression which we found ourselves adopting showed in itself that the analysis is not necessarily dependent on that simple assumption. The diagram in which the argument was expressed did not look as if it was so dependent; for the variables in

which it ran, the share of profit and the rate of profit, are variables
that will survive, however far we complicate the capital structure.
It is of course directly evident that everything that was said about
the saving curve is unaffected. It was only on the side of the price-
quantity curve that we made any real use of our simplification.

Even there the curve itself makes sense in the more general
system; it is only the machinery by which we established its properties that requires to be amended. If there are many capital
goods the ratio of profits to wages will have to be split up; it must
be written

$$\frac{f}{1-f} = \frac{r \sum pK}{wL} = \frac{1}{L} r \sum \left(\frac{p_i}{w}\right) K_i.$$

What we know of this sum is that[1] each (p_i/w) increases with r
(technique being given) and that each K_i (and also L) increase with
g. Thus if r is constant, the above ratio becomes a weighted sum of
K's divided by L; both numerator and denominator increase with
g; so that we may have a fair *central* case (corresponding to our
$M = 1$) in which when r is constant, f is constant. But in our
former model, when this was true, the price-quantity curve was
linear; here, however, though the price-quantity curve could be
linear, the conditions for independence of g and for linearity are
different.[2] In any case, however, we know that every (p_i/w) increases with r; so that if g is constant (and in the central case, even
if g is not constant) f must increase with r, as long as technique
remains unchanged. Something like the upward-sloping price-
quantity curve of our diagram must therefore continue to hold.
The main difference that is made when we confront it with the
saving curve (which, it will be remembered, has exactly the same
properties as before) is that we can be less confident of the absence
of multiple intersections.

There are similar complications when we come to changes in
technique. It is *possible*, in many-capital-good cases, that the wage
curve may be linear; if it were there would be similar rules about
a change in technique working clearly in one direction. But, here
again, the condition for the wage curve to be linear and the condition for the price-quantity factor-share curve to be linear are not
the same. In every way, the amount of 'play' in the system is
increased. All the same, since all that we have to do is to show that
the price-quantity curve (with variable technique) *can* turn back on

---

[1] See Chapter XIV, pp. 164, 169. [2] See Appendix B.

itself, these imperfections of fit are not desperate. The curve can still behave in much the same way, even if the arguments, by which we have established its behaviour, do not exactly hold. And that, I think, is all that is needed to clinch the preceding argument.

To sum up. What I have tried to show is that, even when one is only comparing growth equilibrium paths, the propensity to save (including inter-sectoral differences in the propensity to save) does not have any clear-cut bearing upon factor distribution. It may affect factor distribution, but so may (almost) anything else. An increase in saving (however distributed) must indeed tend to diminish the *rate* of profit; but (even so) its effect upon the *share* of profit is quite uncertain.

6. I turn, in the remainder of this chapter, to another question of factor shares. So far, we have been assuming, first technique, and then technology, to be constant; but what if technology is variable? There can then be no rules, only a classification. But the classification, of 'neutral', 'labour-saving', and 'capital-saving' inventions, has caused economists quite a lot of trouble.

All agree that an invention (a change in technology) is *neutral* if it leaves factor-shares unaffected—on some 'other things being equal' condition. The trouble is that there is more than one 'other thing being equal' condition that may be assumed. Even if we confine attention to the comparison of growth equilibria, it is still the case that specification of the technology[1] does not suffice to determine the equilibrium: something else must be given—such as the rate of real wages, the rate of profit, or the rate of growth. No one, to my knowledge, has attempted to define a neutral invention as one that leaves factor shares unchanged, if the rate of real wages remains unchanged; but there is in principle no reason why we should not define it that way, if we found it convenient to do so. It might indeed be quite useful to include it as a possibility, if we were attempting a more complete discussion of the subject. But it has (obviously) not been a popular alternative; so I shall not explore it here.

If saving propensities are given, constancy in the rate of growth and constancy in the rate of profit come to the same thing. For if all saving is 'out of profit', the saving equation $g = s_1 r$ has nothing to do with the technology; it must remain unchanged when the

---

[1] Including specification of the consumption good (or consumption bundle).

technology changes. If some saving is 'out of wages', g depends upon f (the profit share) as well as on r. But what we are looking for is a condition in which f can remain unchanged; in this condition the saving equation is still invariant. The Harrod definition of neutrality—that f is unchanged when r is unchanged—is accordingly a very natural definition, since it is a sound definition from either point of view.

Even so, there are other possibilities (quite apart from the wage possibility, which we have put on one side). It is possible to find one's 'other things being equal', not on the price side, but on the quantity side, by reference to some sort of capital-labour ratio. I do not know that anyone would make this choice if the theory of Growth Equilibrium were all that was in question; within that theory to define neutrality on the price side looks distinctly more useful. The possibility of a definition on the quantity side does nevertheless deserve to be considered: partly because it connects with the definition which seemed to be natural when one adopted a static approach;[1] partly because it may still have something for us when we have passed beyond the study of growth equilibrium.[2]

Even in a one-capital-good model, a comparison of equilibrium paths (with different technology) on the basis of constancy in K/L (in the sense of 'tractor'-labour ratio) would be meaningless. For, as has been repeatedly insisted, there is no reason why the specification of *the* capital good along one path should be the same as that along the other—even if technology is unchanged, and still more if technology is different. Some means of equating the different capitals must be found, and none can be found which is altogether without reference to prices.[3]

Even so, there is more than one possible measure that is open. Perhaps there are only two measures (as long as we maintain our conventions that there is just one consumption good, and one sort of labour, in the economy); but there are at least two. Equal capitals may be defined as being such that they have the same value

[1] As in my *Theory of Wages* (1932) where the invention was neutral if it left factor shares unchanged, when K *and* L were unchanged (begging questions about the measurement of K). See the Commentary included in the second (1963) edition, pp. 348–50.

[2] See below, Chapter XXIV, p. 302.

[3] When we are not concerned with growth equilibrium, it may sometimes be useful to insist that we must use a measure of capital by which an identical physical stock should always represent the same amount of capital; but such criteria are inapplicable here.

(1) relatively to the wage of labour, or (2) relatively to the price of the consumption good. Thus an unchanged capital-labour ratio might mean (1) that $(1/L)(pK/w)$ is unchanged, or (2) that $(1/L)$ (pK/π) is unchanged. These are not the same thing.

On interpretation (1), the capital-labour definition reduces, like the growth definition, to the Harrod definition. For if the factor-share ratio is constant—(rpK/wL) is constant—and if (pK/wL) is constant, r must be constant. It is as simple as that.[1]

On interpretation (2) there is no such reduction. For the ratio between capital in labour-terms and capital in consumption-good-terms is the real wage rate. With given technology this depends upon r (the wage curve); so that, with given technology, if r is constant, and the one measure of capital is constant, the other will be constant. But here we do not have the same technology along the two paths that are being compared. The wage curve will have shifted; as the result of an invention,[2] it will be shifted upwards (or outwards). Thus if the rate of profit is the same in the two equilibria, the real wage must be higher in the second; so that the value of capital deflated by wages will have fallen relatively to the value of capital deflated by the price of the consumption good. If the former is unchanged, the latter must have risen.

Thus an invention which was neutral in the sense of the Harrod definition (arrived at in any of the ways that lead to that definition) would if it left factor shares unchanged, only do so as a result of a *rise* in the capital-labour ratio, when that is taken in sense (2). In the static sense, then, it might not be a neutral invention. But would it be capital-saving or labour-saving? In view of what we have learned about a possible backward turn in the price-quantity curve of factor shares (Fig. 5, above) I do not think that we can give a straight answer to that question. The old static theory (which is feeling a bit better after what we have done in this chapter) would itself not have given a straight answer; it would have said that it all depends—upon the 'elasticity of substitution'.

[1] See Professor Kennedy's note in the *Economic Journal*, December 1962.
[2] A change in consumers' preferences will reckon, for almost all of this analysis, as a change in technology; but though it will in principle shift the wage curve, it will not necessarily shift it in any particular way.

XVI

TRAVERSE

1. Now at last we begin to emerge from Growth Equilibrium.
And—I expect the reader will be thinking—about time too! For
with every step that we have taken to define this Equilibrium
model more strictly, the closer has become its resemblance to the
old static (or even stationary) Equilibrium model; its bearing upon
reality must have come to seem even more remote. It has been
fertile in the generation of class-room exercises; but so far as we
can yet see, they are exercises, not real problems. They are not
even hypothetical real problems, of the type 'what would happen
if?' where the 'if' is something that could conceivably happen.
They are shadows of real problems, dressed up in such a way that
by pure logic we can find solutions for them.

Let us be clear what it is that has happened. The beginning
(both as a matter of history, and in the way the thing has been
arranged in this book) was with macro-analysis; for that analysis,
which worked solely in terms of the major economic aggregates,
the study of an expanding economy with a constant growth rate
was a natural—indeed an exciting—object. All is well as long as we
stick to aggregates. But if we really stick to aggregates then (as has
been shown) we are committing ourselves to a Fixprice theory—
meaning by that, as was insisted when we introduced the concept,
not a theory in which prices never change, but a theory in which
prices only change exogenously, not as consequence of changes in
other aspects of the system. So long as we admit this, we can content ourselves with a loose (or aggregative) concept of Growth
Equilibrium. It is when we pass beyond Fixprice theory, and
contemplate the occurrence of price changes as part of the economic
mechanism, that the trouble comes. At that point, if we are to deal
with the price changes properly, we have to disaggregate; and it is
the disaggregated growth equilibrium which is hard to stomach.

I have insisted that Growth Equilibrium (once we take it outside
the Fixprice territory) must be defined—can only be defined—
with reference to a *given* technology. But in the real world changes
in technology are incessant; there is no time for an economy to get

into equilibrium (if it was able to do so) with respect to January's technology, before that of February is upon it. It follows that at any actual moment, the existing capital cannot be that which is appropriate to the existing technology; it inevitably reflects past technology; to existing technology it is more or less inappropriate. Every actual situation differs from an equilibrium situation by reason of the inappropriateness of its capital stock. Once we turn our attention to the study of economies with inappropriate capitals, we shall (by that alone) have taken a big step nearer reality.

So that as much as possible of what we have learned about growth equilibrium should remain at our disposal, it is convenient to pose the problems of passage to equilibrium in the following terms. (They are, of course, derived from the way in which we are used to handle the corresponding problem in economic statics.) Suppose that we have an economy which has in the past been in equilibrium in one set of conditions; and that then, at time o, a new set of conditions is imposed; is it possible (or how is it possible) for the economy to get into the new equilibrium, which is appropriate to the new conditions? We do not greatly diminish the generality of our study of disequilibrium if we regard it in this way, as a Traverse from one path to another. And there is some advantage to be gained from greater specification of the initial position from which the Traverse takes off (that is what the point really is). Chiefly, it enables us to split up the kinds of adjustment that have to be made, so as to take different kinds separately.

2. There is one problem of this kind that we have already considered; we have already faced it when we were discussing the Harrod-type model (in Chapter XI, above). If an economy has been in growth equilibrium at a particular growth rate, and is required to adjust to a different growth rate (maintaining full employment of labour), it cannot do so unless the propensity to save is varied, or the capital-output ratio is varied. If (Kaldor's point, that has been fully allowed for in the present discussion) there is a difference in the propensities to save out of wages and out of profits (and it is *these* propensities that are fixed), a new equilibrium can be found, so long as there is a suitable change in the rate of profit. Indeed, if *anything* emerges to change the overall propensity to save out of income, along any channel, the Harrod difficulty can be got over. And (of course) if the change in the growth rate

affects the capital-output ratio in the right direction, that also will
help.[1]

But let us now suppose that this Harrod difficulty has been got
over: that a suitable change in the overall propensity to save, for
whatever reason, has occurred—will that be the end of the trouble?
There is a school of economists (whose voice has been almost
drowned in the fanfare of the Keynesian orchestra) which has been
maintaining, all the while, that it is not. Though their point has
rarely been put forward in such a way as to make it properly compelling, they do have something to say, and it will be worth our
while to examine it in some detail.[2]

3. Let us begin by looking at the matter (as we have on other
occasions found it useful to start by doing) in terms of our one-
capital-good model. We shall hardly be able to make progress unless
we have got that straight first, but we must not jump to the conclusion that the results we get from it have general application. In
fact, as we shall see subsequently, they are (when taken by themselves) quite seriously misleading.

In that model, as we found in Chapter XII, the equilibrium
ratio of 'tractors' to labour depends upon the rate of growth; with
given technique it depends upon the rate of growth only. Thus if,
at time o, the economy is in equilibrium with a growth rate g_0, it
will have to have a capital-labour ratio that corresponds. Now if the
rate of growth is changed (either upwards or downwards) and the
technique is unchanged, the equilibrium tractor-labour ratio will
be changed; so that the actual tractor-labour ratio, at time o,
will not be that which is appropriate to the new equilibrium. (I must
insist, for the moment, on the assumption that the technique, as
expressed in the production coefficients, is unchanged. It does not
much matter why it is unchanged. It may be unchanged because
there is no choice of technique—this is the only technique within
the technology; or it may be unchanged because the profit rate is
unchanged, so that the old technique is still that which is the most
profitable. In either case, it is probable that there will have to be an
adjustment in the *overall* saving-propensity, if there is to be a new

---

[1] See above, Chapter XIV, p. 169.
[2] The story goes back (at least) to Hayek, *Prices and Production* (1932). But
there are more recent statements, such as that of L. M. Lachmann, *Capital
and its Structure* (1956), which are more clearly what I have in mind.

equilibrium. I shall assume here that such an adjustment occurs. I want to concentrate on the problem of the Traverse.)

It will obviously be important to distinguish between upward and downward adjustments: when the initial capital-labour ratio (left over, we are supposing, from the old equilibrium) is less, and when it is greater, than that which is appropriate to equilibrium in the new conditions. This is not simply a matter of the way the growth rate changes. From the simple quantity-equations of the one-capital-good model—which we may begin by writing in the old form (with depreciation absorbed)

$$K = ax + \alpha\xi, \qquad L = bx + \beta\xi, \qquad x = gK$$

we have, as before

$$\frac{K}{L} = \frac{\alpha}{\beta + (\alpha b - a\beta)g} = \frac{\alpha}{\beta}\,\frac{1}{1 + (m-1)ag} = \frac{\alpha}{\beta}\,\frac{1}{1 + cg}$$

putting c for $(m-1)a$, a more convenient abbreviation in this case than the M which we used in the last chapter. Thus K/L is larger the smaller is $1 + cg$; but whether $1 + cg$ rises or falls with g depends on the sign of c, that is to say on whether $m >$ or < 1. There are thus four cases: according as g rises or falls, and according as $m >$ or < 1. It can in fact be shown that whether g rises or falls, there is a full-employment path to equilibrium, *provided that* $m > 1$. But if $m < 1$ (if the factory is more mechanized than the farm) such a full-employment path does not exist.

4. I begin with an algebraic proof, which the reader may omit if he does not care for it; I shall subsequently verify it by checking through the economics.

If there is full employment (of capital as well as labour) the above equation for K/L must hold *in any period*. As between periods t and $t+1$, the growth rate of capital is g_t, while that of labour is g^* (the new equilibrium rate). Thus if we divide the K/L equation of period $t+1$ by that of period t, we have

$$\frac{K_{t+1}}{K_t}\bigg/\frac{L_{t+1}}{L_t} = \frac{1 + cg_t}{1 + cg_{t+1}}$$

so that

$$\frac{1 + g_t}{1 + g^*} = \frac{1 + cg_t}{1 + cg_{t+1}}.$$

Rearranging,

$$\frac{c(1+g^*)}{1+cg_{t+1}} = \frac{c(1+g_t)}{1+cg_t} = 1 + \frac{c-1}{1+cg_t}$$

or

$$\frac{c(1+g^*)}{1+cg_{t+1}} - \frac{c-1}{1+cg_t} = 1 = \frac{c(1+g^*)}{1+cg^*} - \frac{c-1}{1+cg^*}$$

so that g_t converges to g^* if $(c-1)/c(1+g^*)$ is less than 1 in absolute value. From

$$-1 < \frac{1-c}{c(1+g^*)} < 1, \quad \text{we have} \quad 0 < \frac{1+cg^*}{c(1+g^*)} < 2$$

$1+cg^*$ is necessarily positive, since $ag^* < 1$. Thus the first inequality merely says that c must be positive. The second (with c positive) gives $1+cg^* < 2c(1+g^*)$

or

$$c > 1/(2+g^*).$$

This looks like being a stronger condition, but it does not invalidate the theorem. For if we write the condition in full, as

$$m-1 > 1/(2a+ag^*)$$

it becomes apparent that the expression on the right can be made as small as we like, by shortening the length of the unit period. a, the capital-capital coefficient, is a ratio of stock input to flow output; by shortening the length of the period, its numerical value is increased. The growth rate, g, is similarly a ratio of flow output to stock input; by diminishing the length of the period, its numerical value is diminished. Thus ag^* is unaffected, but a is increased, as the length of the period is diminished. If adjustment is continuous, $2a+ag^*$ becomes indefinitely large, so that the right-hand side of the last inequality tends to zero. The condition for convergence thus reduces to $m > 1$, on both sides. If, however, adjustment was not continuous, but was made at intervals, an m which was only a little greater than 1 might not be sufficient for convergence. There would not be a smooth passage to equilibrium, as the jerks might tend to overshoot the mark.

5. Alternatively, we might argue as follows. There are four cases to consider, according as $m >$ or < 1, and according as the growth rate in the new equilibrium is to be greater or less than in the old ($g_0 <$ or $> g^*$). We may take them separately.

    (1) $m > 1$; $g_0 > g^*$. Since the growth rate is to fall it will be

necessary, in the final equilibrium, that there should be a relative contraction of the investment industry; but the capital-labour ratio is higher in the consumption industry, so that if the shift to the new equilibrium structure took place instantaneously, there would not be enough tractors to employ the existing labour force; there would be unemployment of labour. Unemployment can, however, be avoided if the shift takes place gradually.

In period o, with K_0 and L_0 left over from the old equilibrium, full employment (of both factors) can only be maintained if the capital stock increases at the old rate g_0. But then, when we come to period 1, while capital will have increased at its old rate g_0, labour will only have increased at its new (lower) rate g^*; the overall K/L ratio must in consequence be *raised*. If there is to be full employment (of both factors) in period 1, some of the otherwise superfluous tractors must therefore be moved over to the consumption industry, where they can be absorbed—but at the expense of making the growth rate of capital lower in period 1 than it was in period o. If the adjustment is continuous (if, as we saw in the last section, the *period* is not too long) the growth rate of capital in period 1 will still be higher than the growth rate of labour, so that there can be a further rise in the K/L ratio in period 2. And so on through later periods. Full employment is maintained throughout, and the growth rate of the capital stock gradually falls towards its equilibrium level.[1]

(2) $m > 1$; $g_0 < g^*$. There will in this case be initially too many tractors to employ the initial supply of labour at the new growth rate. If there were an attempt to move instantaneously into the new equilibrium, a surplus of tractors would emerge, which could not be absorbed. And the existence of that surplus would make the new equilibrium impossible.

If full employment of both factors is to be preserved, it will be necessary, as in the first case, to begin with a period in which capital is accumulated at the old rate g_0. But then, in the next period, in order to employ the labour force (which has been increasing at a rate g^*, so that labour has become relatively more

---

[1] If (as we are supposing) equilibrium is maintained, on the new equilibrium path, by a saving propensity that is smaller than it was on the old, we must also assume that the fall takes place gradually, along the Traverse, if there is to be full employment all the time. There are obvious difficulties about this; but perhaps it is easier to suppose that the change takes place gradually than all of a sudden.

abundant, relatively, that is, to the supply of tractors) investment must be relatively increased. For since it is the investment 'industry' which has the lower capital-labour ratio ($m > 1$), it is the investment industry that must be expanded to absorb the relatively increased supply of labour. Thus the growth rate of capital will be greater in period 1 than in period 0; and if (as before) the adjustment is continuous, there will be a continual rise in the growth rate of capital, from period to period, gradually tending to the equilibrium rate g^*. Full employment of both factors will be achieved all the time. There is a full employment path to equilibrium, in both of these cases, if it is taken gently.

(3) $m < 1$; and here let us start with the case of a *rise* in the desired growth rate, so that $g_0 < g^*$; as in case (2).

With $m < 1$, K/L will rise with g; the initial capital will be insufficient to employ the initial labour at the new growth rate g^*. As before, if full employment is to be maintained in period 0, capital must be accumulated in that period 0 at the old rate g_0; but if labour is increasing at g^* (with $g^* > g_0$) this means that the K/L ratio, in period 1, will have fallen. Just as it fell in our second case; but this is now not a movement towards equilibrium—it is a movement in the wrong direction. If full employment is to be maintained in period 1, with this diminished K/L ratio, there must be a diversion of resources to that industry where the capital-labour ratio is lower; and that (with $m < 1$) is the *consumption* industry. If full employment is to be maintained the investment industry must go on (relatively) contracting; whereas the need is for it to expand. The point must be reached where the supply of tractors ceases altogether to expand; and beyond that point it will be impossible to employ the increment of labour.

What is the alternative? A gradual approach to Equilibrium, maintaining full employment, is here impossible; is it better to take a short cut? If the system adjusts itself immediately to the new equilibrium growth rate, accumulating capital at that rate, there will be an insufficiency of 'tractors' to support that growth rate with full employment of labour; some labour must therefore go unemployed. If there is continuance on that growth path, the proportion of labour that is unemployed will not increase; but the unemployed will not be absorbed. In order that they should ultimately be absorbed, there will have to be a temporary expansion in the investment industry to make up for the shortage of tractors.

But this means drawing more capital into that capital-intensive industry, so that the unemployment of labour must be temporarily increased, in order that it should be absorbed later on.

Before commenting, I turn to the fourth case.

(4) $m < 1$; $g_0 > g^*$. At the new growth rate initial capital will now be surplus. To maintain full employment expansion must proceed, in period 0, at the old rate g_0; this will now *raise* the K/L ratio. If full employment of both factors is to be maintained in period 1, the capital-intensive industry will have to be (relatively) expanded; this now means stepping up investment further. Continuance of the same process conducts further and further away from equilibrium—to a theoretical limit in the collapse of the consumption industry!

In fact, if the initial surplus of tractors is to be absorbed, there must be a (temporary) contraction in the investment industry. Unemployment of tractors must then be (temporarily) aggravated, in order that it should be ultimately absorbed (as with labour on the other tack). It is not, in principle, necessary that there should be unemployment of labour; for labour could be transferred to the consumption industry, where there would be plenty of tractors for it to use. But it is rather a lot to assume such easy transferability when it is a matter of a temporary adjustment; no such to-and-fro movement is required (so that the homogeneity of labour is a more tolerable assumption) so long as the economy can keep on an equilibrium path—or can move towards it smoothly. The chief lesson which we learn from these exercises is that smooth adjustment may not be possible.

6. But that is about all. I am not going to waste time in discussing whether conditions in which m is > 1, or < 1, are the more probable in practice; for it will be my contention that that question does not really arise. Our analysis of the Traverse, in the one-capital-case, is no more than a bogy. It is useful to work through it, since it should help towards an understanding of what follows. But in itself it is quite misleading. An actual economy—any actual economy—does not, indeed cannot, work just like that. It differs from the model described in quite essential respects. As soon as we take one or two steps nearer reality the situation is greatly transformed.

I do not believe (as I think that some economists believe) that the fixity of technique, under which we have been working, is the vital point. The big change occurs before we come to that—at the point where we abandon the single capital good. (It is not, or should not be, possible to deal with change of technique, except for comparative equilibrium purposes, before we have abandoned the single capital good; for, as I have often insisted, change of technique normally implies that there is a change in specification—that, at the least, the bundle of capital goods is combined in different proportions.) As was observed originally, the 'tractor' is a harmless assumption, so long as we are only concerned with comparison of equilibria; our preliminary abandonment of it (in Chapter XIV) did, I think, confirm that view. But when we leave Equilibrium, when we come to the Traverse, it will not do at all.

I shall confine attention, as before, to the question of a change in the equilibrium growth rate. Such a change (as we saw in Chapter XIV) will change the equilibrium ratios, not merely between labour and capital in general (whatever that is), but also between one kind of capital good and another. Thus it is not just a question of whether (K/L) rises or falls; it is a question of whether (k_i/L) rises or falls; and it will normally be the case that for different capital goods the answer will be different. It would indeed be surprising if (whether g is falling or rising) the equilibrium requirement for labour were to rise more, or fall less, than those for *all* capital goods. Such extreme cases (to which, presumably, the preceding analysis would most closely apply) are so extreme that they are hardly worth consideration. It is safe to assume that some (k_i/L) will rise, and some fall, whichever way the growth rate moves. So that, somewhat surprisingly, a more general theory may turn out to be more straightforward than the 'one capital good' theory.

As in the preceding analysis, we must start with a period o, in which (if full employment of labour and of all sorts of capital is to be maintained) capital must be accumulated at the same g_0 as in the old equilibrium. But then, at the beginning of period 1, while the capital goods are available in their old proportions, labour will have increased disproportionately (either up or down). Now if, with these quantities of factors, an attempt were to be made (in period 1) to maintain full employment of labour and of *all* capitals, it is most unlikely that the resultant production would be such as to tend towards equilibrium. It is indeed hardly probable that with

fixed coefficients, and with all the capital-quantity equations required to hold (essentially as before) but with labour appreciably
out of line, a set of positive outputs could be found at all. Something would have to give.

Now if the coefficients are really fixed (more of this in a moment)
the existing quantities of capital goods and of labour (still at the
beginning of period 1) set constraints on the amounts that can be
produced; if we insist on all-round full employment, we are in-
sisting that all of the constraints should be *operative*. If we waive
that condition, we can have some constraints operative, but some
not. Once there is a choice of the constraints that are to be operative, the set of outputs in period 1 ceases to be determinate; quite
a variety of alternatives should normally be open. And some, at
least, of these alternatives should be such as to conduct the economy
in the direction of an equilibrium.

There is one (sufficiently miserable) alternative which must be
open, and which it is useful to take as a standard of reference. If
no more than *one* constraint is made operative it is possible for the
economy to move on to a constant growth path, at the new equilibrium growth rate, at once. This one operative constraint must be
that which is set by the particular capital good for which the ratio
of (k_i/L) at the new growth rate and at the old is the lowest. An
expansion at the new growth rate, which is 'hinged' upon this particular capital good will certainly be feasible; but under-employ-
ment of labour will then be a permanency. This is a feasible path,
but it can hardly be called an equilibrium path.

Nevertheless, using this alternative as a basis, we can see what
is required in order that there should be a better performance.
Some of the labour and of the capital goods which, on this 'base'
plan are left unemployed, must be directed towards breaking the
bottlenecks. There must, that is to say, be a temporary expansion in
output, beyond the equilibrium proportion, of those goods that
are in shortest supply. Then, as the bottlenecks are relieved, the
'level' of the ultimate equilibrium can be lifted. There may well
be some route of this kind, even (I think) with fixed coefficients, by
which it can *ultimately* be lifted to a full employment of labour
equilibrium level.[1]

---

[1] I am well aware that this important matter deserves a more mathematical
analysis than I have been able to give it. Some further light upon it will, however,
be thrown in Chapter XIX.

Since this 'better' plan involves setting more labour (as well as capital goods) to work than would be set to work under the base plan, it is possible that there might be full employment of labour under the 'better' plan, even throughout. But one cannot be sure of this. There cannot be a 'better' plan unless some resources are under-employed; labour may be among those which are under-employed in the transitional phase, or it may not.

7. The picture which we have been drawing in this last section is still too dismal; there are several ways in which it needs to be amended, and they all work in the direction of making the Traverse easier. I do not think that these ways ought just to be summed up by saying that we ought to have worked with variable technique. There are variations which ought to be introduced, but they are not all of the same kind, nor do they work in the same way.

The first kind of variation is one that we ought (perhaps) to have kept more continuously in mind, even in the formal analysis of this chapter. When we first introduced our fixed coefficients (in Chapter XII) it was emphasized that what they represented were the *normal* quantities of inputs required for a given output. 'We need not suppose that it would be impossible (at least in the short run) to produce more than 1,000 units of output from the capital stock that is appropriate to 1,000 units.'[1] On this interpretation it was quite correct to treat coefficients as rigidly fixed (so long as there was no *change of technique*) while we were concerned (as in Chapters XII–XV) with Equilibrium theory; but this does not mean that on a Traverse they would have to be rigidly fixed. We have certainly been making them too fixed, so far, in this chapter.

If we bear in mind this interpretation, and rethink the work we have done in the light of it, it becomes evident that there should be a good deal of flexibility, along the Traverse, which has not so far been taken into account. When some capital goods are short, relatively to the normal requirement for them, production need not be held down by an insistence that these goods should not be used to more than a normal degree of utilization. They can, at least for a while, be over-used. This will raise the total amount of production that can be got from a capital stock that is inappropriately distributed, and in all probability raise it very considerably; for if

[1] See above, Chapter XII, p. 137. The capital-quantity equation is a stock-equilibrium condition.

the scarce goods are used at more than normal capacity, the surplus goods will be less under-utilized than would otherwise be the case.

That, however, leads on to the second point. If the scarce goods are over-utilized it is to be expected that they will be used up faster. In the case of circulating capital goods, over-utilization means reducing stocks below normal. There is a limit beyond which that process cannot be carried, and (even short of that limit) the deficiency must, sooner or later, be made up. In the case of fixed capital, there will also be some tendency to more rapid wear and tear; the future need for replacement will, at least to some extent, be increased. There is much the same effect on either side.

Nevertheless, even if one grants that over-utilization means 'borrowing from the future', it does facilitate greater flexibility. Indeed the whole process of using-up and replacement is a source of flexibility, since when additional supplies of some good are (for a time) no longer required, it is not merely net investment in that good, but gross investment, that can be cut down to zero. Too much, however, should not be made of this, since it cuts both ways. While it increases the resources that are made available for trans-ference, it also increases the resources which must be transferred, if idleness of capital is to be kept as low as possible. It may well be that a more important source of flexibility arises in connexion with those goods which are *in the middle*, being neither made par-ticularly scarce nor particularly surplus by the change that has occurred. Normal replacement of such goods (and a normal expan-sion in their supply) will indeed be required, if not now, then later; but if it is possible to postpone it, so that the resources which would be used for it can be (temporarily) employed elsewhere, bottlenecks which would otherwise have been cramping may be more speedily broken.

8. All this (as I think the reader will agree) does sound like sense— much more like sense than was the case with the 'simple' model with which we began this chapter. But (I expect he will be burning to ask) what about prices? Some of my equilibrium Chapters (XIII and XIV) were so occupied with prices that quantities seemed to slip into the background; here it has been the other way round. (Perhaps that is why the last page or two has begun to sound realistic; for in much of modern economics—as we have

seen—prices have been going out of fashion.) Surely, however, we must say something about prices if we are to tell anything like a full story.

I have deliberately posed the problem of this chapter in terms of a change in the (equilibrium) growth rate; for, in terms of equilibrium analysis, a change in g has the special quality that (if it is matched by a suitable change in the saving-propensity) prices do not *need* to be affected by it. In this case (and only, I think, in this case) prices in the new equilibrium can be the same as they were in the old. But does this mean that prices can remain unchanged on the way—along the Traverse?

It is by no means inconceivable that most prices might remain unchanged along the Traverse. For that, I think, is precisely the behaviour which is implied by 'full cost pricing' (or, as I would myself prefer to call it, *normal cost pricing*) in the present application. On this policy the prices which producers set are what they think to be equilibrium prices; they stick to those prices even when they are out of equilibrium.

With such behaviour, the account of adjustment which we gave when we were dealing with the Fixprice method[1] does (at least roughly) hold; the adjustment is being made in what is substantially a Fixprice manner, with prices playing no active part. And it is important to emphasize that adjustment can be made (some, at least, of the required adjustment can be made) even if it is only made in this particular way. For in the first place (since we are *not* assuming textbook perfect competition, such that marginal cost rises, immediately the equilibrium output is passed) there will be some output, beyond the equilibrium output, which producers will be only too glad to produce, once there is a demand for it. Secondly, even though they behave in a thoroughgoing Fixprice manner, setting (for accounting purposes) normal prices on their inputs as well as on their outputs, it will be a fact that capacity that is under-utilized will not be earning a full profit; if production can be stepped up profit will be increased. There is an incentive to bring unutilized capacity into production, and to extend production (when there is a demand) some way beyond optimum output, even when there is no movement in prices.

Yet if the adjustment proceeds entirely on this plan, there are limits to what can be done. Though there is an incentive, even in

[1] Above, pp. 78-82 (Chapter VII).

a Fixprice system, to bring into production unused capacity (not only fixed capital capacity, but surplus stocks of materials) when it can be utilized by its present proprietor; and though resources that are wholly unused may be transferred, since it is better to get the fixed price for them than to leave them idle; the mechanism of transference from those whose need is less to those whose need is more urgent must unquestionably be clogged. I am not thinking here of consumers' needs (all that is being taken for granted—formally, we still have our one consumption good!); the urgency in question is urgency in the breaking of bottlenecks. Flexibility along the Traverse is of major importance; an economy which insists upon making its transitions on a Fixprice basis is doing so with 'one hand tied behind its back'.

9. It is this that is the true function of price-flexibility along the Traverse: not, as economists have sometimes supposed, that it can itself give much guidance about the planning of production, about the choice of a path to equilibrium. This is another of the points that I have tried to bring out by my choice of a change in g as the key variable to be studied; for that is a case which is such that, even if there is a change in prices during the transition, the old price will have to be restored when equilibrium is restored.[1] If there is no change in prices during the transition, the choice of which path to pursue (out of the many paths that will be available, once we recognize that some capital goods will have to be surplus) depends entirely on the foresight of producers, on their skill in interpreting what has been happening to them, on their ability to forecast demand. If prices vary, during the transition, the position is not much better. For the changes in prices that will occur, during a transition of the kind that we are examining, are essentially temporary; operation with prices that are varying, and are (or ought to be) known to be varying, is a task that requires the same kind of skill as the corresponding operation on the quantity side.

When we are considering a different kind of Traverse, which is such that the price ratios that are appropriate to the new equilibrium and to the old are not the same, a corresponding *Fixprice* policy would presumably imply that prices are adapted at once (or sought to be adapted at once) to the new equilibrium; this is an

---

[1] I assume (as elsewhere in this chapter) that saving is adjusted to the new growth rate.

adjustment that could be made (if people were clever enough), unlike the corresponding adjustment on the quantity side which (in this case) probably could not be made at all.[1] But even if the 'right' prices could be reached immediately, and were then held, the position would be the same as with the Fixprice policy after the change in growth rate. The arguments about flexibility on the way to equilibrium remain substantially the same.

But there is a far larger question that then comes up. It is a condition for the establishment of the new equilibrium that the right prices should be found—for without the establishment of the right prices the right techniques will not be selected. If it is not just a matter of the maintenance of the old prices, but of the finding of new prices, this (in turn) cannot be an easy matter. If unsuitable prices are adopted, and adhered to for long, unsuitable techniques will be adopted; the problem of getting into equilibrium will be further complicated, and the approach to equilibrium will be retarded.[2]

In an actual economic situation, all these problems arise at once, while (because of the advance in technology) the equilibrium at which the economy is aiming is continually shifting. No wonder that there is a problem of business management!

[1] In the case of a change in the growth rate, it would be possible to move at once along the constant growth rate path which we took as 'base', though that would not be an equilibrium path. If the change was one (say) in technology, even that 'miserable' alternative would not be possible.

[2] I am thinking of the choice of techniques as being properly a matter of the long-term equilibrium; short-period adjustments being not so readily expressible in terms of production coefficients. But there can, of course, be no firm line. Cases may arise (they are not so infrequent in conditions of changing technology) in which an arrangement, which would quite conveniently be expressible in terms of production coefficients, may be temporarily adopted, to fill the gap until a superior technique has been more fully worked out, or until the new capital goods (which take long to produce) are ready.

PART III

OPTIMUM GROWTH

XVII

TYPES OF OPTIMUM THEORY

1. THE kind of analysis which has emerged from our discussion of the Traverse could no doubt be carried further; but I shall not make any serious attempt to carry it further in this book. It would evidently be necessary, if we were to elaborate it, to introduce some particular assumptions about investment policy: to assume that businesses, in carrying out their difficult task of adapting an inappropriate capital stock into something more appropriate, will go about that task in some particular way. But it is hard to see what particular assumption of this kind there can be that is especially deserving of study. Even in macro-analysis (as we found in Chapters VII–XI) there are no compelling principles that can be relied upon to perform this function; there, however, it was possible to find some simple rules (capital stock adjustment and so on), the consequences of which it was at least of some interest to work out. Similar exercises could presumably be performed, even with a disaggregated model; but it would be blatantly obvious that they would be no more than exercises. Perhaps this is unduly pessimistic; all I ought to say is that I myself do not see any interesting way of taking this analysis further. Henceforward, therefore, I shall leave it on one side.

We have nevertheless by no means completed our theoretical task. It is the dynamic problem of positive economics—of the actual behaviour of an economy, with imperfect foresight—that, when considered even in this much detail, becomes so baffling. The corresponding problem of Welfare Economics is appreciably more tractable. Though we cannot determine the actual path which the economy (even the model economy) will follow, we can say much more about its optimum path, about the path which will best satisfy some social objective. Much of the work that has been done in Dynamic Economics has in fact been Optimum theory; it has yet to be explained how it fits in.

2. Dynamic Welfare Economics ought, in principle, to face all the standard difficulties of Static Welfare Economics. Interpersonal

optimum = path best read objective

comparisons, increasing returns, external economies—the lions in the path of static theory—all remain with us. It is scarcely to be expected that they will be more tractable when they are taken in a dynamic setting. A general dynamic theory, which fits all these things into their places, is quite out of reach. It will certainly not be offered here. We shall have to content ourselves with something much simpler.

It may nevertheless be worth while to observe, before passing on, that some of these troubles look a little less worrying when they are put into a temporal context—not that they are really any easier to deal with, but that we are less likely to be tempted to exaggerate their importance.

Static Welfare theory leads up to a consideration of the gains and losses which accrue to the 'individuals' composing an economy, as a result of some feasible change in organization; and then, either by some system of weighting (difficult to make acceptable) or by some system of compensation (difficult to make plausible) it endeavours to set those gains and losses against one another. It is, however, to be noticed that the static approach carries with it an overtone of assumption that the gains and losses (and the compensation) are all of them *permanent*. As soon as we dynamize, it becomes essential to distinguish between permanent and temporary gains and losses. And as soon as we make that distinction we can add to the (probably almost empty) category of changes in which some gain while none lose, a more interesting category of changes which are such that losses are temporary, while gains are permanent. Compensation for temporary losses is more feasible than compensation for permanent losses. The former, indeed, is such that it can often be introduced by agreement; while the latter (suggestive of those 'compensations' given by the Courts for the loss of a limb, or the break-up of a marriage) has something inherently inadequate about it. This is not to say that economists may not find themselves obliged to consider the possibility of compensation for permanent losses; but even if we insist on valuing permanent losses very high (so that changes involving them are practically excluded from consideration), the field for 'reforms', which are free from any important element of permanent loss, is not impossibly restricted. A Compensation Principle, that was restricted in application to compensation for temporary losses, looks distinctly more acceptable than one that did not make this distinction.

The question may nevertheless arise: how are permanent and temporary gains and losses to be weighed against one another? It does not necessarily arise in an acute form, but it may do so. Suppose, to take the simplest possible case, that a particular *primary* change (as we may call it) confers a permanent benefit on A, and a temporary loss on B. If B's loss is offset by a temporary measure of compensation (at A's expense), A is left with a permanent gain, secured at a temporary cost; the only question which then arises is whether the 'investment', from A's point of view, is worth while. But if the time-shape of the compensation that is offered does not match that of the loss (and this is a matter on which there may well be differences of opinion) B's time-preferences as well as A's must be considered. To some extent it may be possible to avoid *this* interpersonal comparison by reference to opportunities for lending (and borrowing) on a market; but we cannot take it for granted that the opportunities for such intertemporal transactions that are open to A and to B are the same. If the market were perfect, there would be no problem; but that is no comfort, for on perfect markets (if they were conceivable) few of these issues would arise at all. And perhaps it is true that the imperfection of the capital market is the most fundamental of all kinds of market imperfection.

3. The points that I have been making in this last section are perhaps best regarded as an appendage to static, rather than as the beginning of dynamic Optimum theory; for the dynamic theory, at least as far as it has been developed up to the present, stops well short of this kind of complication. The central dynamic problem is indeed of quite sufficient difficulty to make it reasonable to begin by neglecting them. Here too, I shall mainly have to follow common practice in assuming a world in which there are constant returns to scale, and in which there is no problem of differences in wants—even, for the most part, to such an extent as will allow us to retain our assumption of a single consumption-good. I shall try to be on the look-out for ways in which these drastic assumptions can be relaxed; but I shall not be able to relax them to any great extent.

The central problem of dynamic Optimum theory is the planning problem. Given an initial endowment of capital, embodied in particular capital goods, and given an expected flow of labour, what is the plan of production, in present and future, which will

character of *path*

enable some given aim to be reached in the most efficient manner? At this point, it will be observed, we pass beyond the (more or less) competitive economy which has so far been mainly considered. The form of organization by which the optimum is to be reached is not prescribed; the question whether it can be reached by a competitive system is left open. The general character of the path which will satisfy optimum conditions is the sole question that is at issue.

Even so, the nature of the aim that is being sought must be prescribed; and it can be prescribed in several different ways. Some of the distinctions that may here be drawn are the same as in statics. We may, in the first place, either be seeking to maximize some objective measure of total output, or some subjective measure ('economic welfare'). If we select the former we have still to choose our objective measure: there are two main alternatives. Either we seek to maximize the *quantity* of some bundle of commodities, in which different outputs are to be combined in fixed proportions; or we seek to maximize the *value* of output, in which different commodities are reduced to a common measure by being valued at fixed prices. It is a fundamental theorem[1] that, given appropriate convexity conditions, these two procedures are equivalent: that there is a set of prices, corresponding to each possible commodity-bundle, such that maximization of the bundle is equivalent to maximization at the corresponding prices. 'Quantity-optimizing' and 'value-optimizing' (as we will call them) must nevertheless be distinguished, for there are other conditions in which they are not the same.

If we are to maximize the utility of output, we must have some overall 'social welfare function', or we must have some corresponding device by which the utilities of different individuals can be made comparable with one another. The role of the Compensation Principle is to provide a case in which we can establish a correspondence (similar to that established under convexity between quantity-optimizing and value-optimizing) between utility-optimizing and value-optimizing. If changes in which some gain and others lose are ruled out by compensation, maximization of the value of output, at any set of prices, and disposal to consumers at that same set of prices, will also maximize utility. But if our concept of 'social utility' is such that it can be increased by direct transfers,

---

[1] Koopmans, *Essays on the State of Economic Science* (first essay), gives a very careful statement.

such a value-optimum is not necessarily a utility-optimum. It is still probable that *the* utility-optimum will also be a value-optimum, but there will be many value-optima which are not utility-optima, because they have not excluded the increase of 'social utility' by direct transference.

4. All of these questions that arise in statics arise in dynamics also. But there is one special question which is basic in dynamics, though it has no static counterpart. This is the question of the 'horizon'. A production plan must normally extend over a definite period of time: it runs from time o ('now') to time T (five, it may be, or ten years hence). What is to happen after time T is not explicitly provided for. But some attention to the claims of that further future must still be paid. The plan, which begins with the given initial capital, must end with some terminal capital, to serve as the initial capital of the next planning period. The aim of the plan must be to maximize (in one or other of the above ways) the flow of 'consumption' outputs over the period o to T, *and* the terminal capital at time T.

Now the flow of consumption outputs can itself be regarded as a series of dated outputs. If it is to be maximized in any meaningful sense, the individual dated outputs

$$\xi_0, \xi_1, ..., \xi_{T-1}$$

must be reduced to a single variable, in one or other of the above manners. We can quantity-optimize by fixing the proportions in which these temporally distinguished outputs are to be combined; or we can value-optimize by fixing their relative values; or we can utility-optimize by introducing a utility function of these T variables, and maximizing that. But whichever of these courses is adopted something must be said, or implied, about the terminal capital. It will always be possible to increase flow output (in any of these senses) by raiding terminal capital; but a maximum flow output, that is reached by reducing terminal capital to the minimum that is possible technologically, is not a sensible aim of any planning.

The difficulty might (in principle) be overcome by bringing terminal capital, as well as flow output, into the maximand. Proportions between them might be fixed, or relative values for them might be prescribed, or they might be brought within the same utility function. A formal theory on these lines could readily be set down; but it would not make much sense. The proportions or values that would have to be fixed (between *flow* and *stock*) would have no simple meaning. Stock and flow are different; it is better to bring them into the problem, even into the optimum problem, in different ways.

5. At this point, therefore, roads again diverge. We can either fix our attention upon the flow of consumption outputs, seeking to maximize that—but if we do so we must set some constraint upon terminal capital, which must not be allowed to fall below a prescribed level (each of its components not to fall below a prescribed level). Or we can fix our attention upon the terminal capital, seeking to maximize that—but if we do so, if we are to pose that problem in a sensible manner, we must impose some constraint on the flow outputs, which in their turn may by no means be allowed to disappear. Every optimization problem is one of maximization under constraints; but we have a choice on what is to be included in the constraints, and what is to be included in the function that we are seeking to maximize.

The 'Turnpike' theory, which will be considered in the following two chapters, is concerned with an optimization problem of the second type. It is the terminal capital that is to be maximized; the flow of consumption outputs (so far as it appears at all) only appears in relation to constraints. Excess production of consumption goods (in excess of the prescribed minimum) during the period of the plan is treated as valueless; nothing (it is reckoned) is gained from it. The more completely it can be sacrificed to the final achievement, the more successful the plan is held to be.

The state of mind that conceives of planning in this manner is familiar enough; but it is a war mentality, a Stalinist mentality, and one may be forgiven for finding it distasteful. To confine our attention to this branch of Optimum theory, to the exclusion of the other, would indeed be a mistake. Yet if it is simply considered as a part of a more general theory, it does have something to offer. For the character of the optimum path, in terms of the adjustment of capital structure, can be worked out in more detail by this method than it can be by the alternative route. We can make some use of what we learn on that side, even if we prefer to proceed in the other manner. This is a good reason for beginning with the 'Turnpike' approach.

So long as we are content to think of the aim of the plan in terms of maximizing terminal capital, there is no question of intertemporal preference that can arise, since the components of the terminal capital are all available at the same date. Measurement of what is to be maximized raises no more than the usual static problems. But as soon as we make our maximand the consumption flow, with constituents that are differently dated, we are faced with questions of intertemporal pricing (interest and time-preference) much more centrally and immediately than in the 'Turnpike' theory. It is on that side that the flow theory has most to say. On the side of production structure it is relatively weak.

Each, therefore, has its merits and its defects. We cannot dispense with either.

XVIII

THE VON NEUMANN 'EQUILIBRIUM'

1. TURNPIKE theory (the theory of the optimum path when the terminal stock, at the end of a given period, is the sole maximand) falls into two parts, which it will be convenient to take in separate chapters. The first, which is due to von Neumann, establishes conditions for the existence of an 'equilibrium' path, together with certain properties of that path. In a sense that is not far from Marshall's, this 'equilibrium' (the Turnpike) is the *long-period* equilibrium of the system. It is an optimum path, if it is feasible, but in general it will not be feasible. The nature of the optimum path, when the problem is such that the equilibrium path cannot be followed, is the subject of the second part (to be considered in Chapter XIX). Its principal achievement (the Turnpike theorem proper) is to show that, if sufficient time is allowed, the optimum path will approximate to the equilibrium path, keeping close to it over the greater part of its course. That is to say, even in this field of Optimum theory, there is (in a sense) a 'tendency to equilibrium'.

Both parts of the theory are the work of mathematicians. The original von Neumann article,[1] on which all later work has been based, was a distinguished performance by a mathematician of the first rank. The Turnpike theorem, which originated in what mathematicians would call a 'conjecture' by Samuelson and Solow,[2] has been the object of abstruse mathematical investigations by these authors and by others.[3] I make no claim to be able to discuss the matter on their level. When I began to work on these chapters I planned to do no more than to show the relations between

---

[1] *A Model of General Economic Equilibrium* (to give it the title by which it is known to English readers). The original publication was in German (*Ergebnisse eines mathematischen Kolloquiums*, edited by Karl Menger, 1935–6). The English translation appeared in the *Review of Economic Studies*, no. 33, 1945–6.

[2] 'Balanced Growth under Constant Returns to Scale' (*Econometrica*, 1953).

[3] L. W. Mackenzie, 'Turnpike Theorem of Morishima' (*Review of Economic Studies*, October 1963) gives a recent bibliography. It was the version in Dorfman, Samuelson, and Solow, *Linear Programming and Economic Analysis*, chs. 11–12, which brought the Turnpike theorem (there for the first time so called) to the notice of less-mathematical economists.

Turnpike theory and the other 'methods of dynamic economics' which have been our concern in the other parts of this book. The theory itself I would just take over from the mathematicians. But as I proceeded I came to see that I could do rather better. It is possible, I now believe, to break up the mathematical argument so that much of it can be restated in a form which comes more naturally to economists. I do not claim that what I shall give is a 'proof of the Turnpike theorem'; but I do think that it is a useful way in which the nature of the argument can be explained.

2. There is a particular case of the von Neumann equilibrium which is also a particular case of our own Growth Equilibrium, with the properties of which we are by now well acquainted. Though there are other (perhaps better) ways by which von Neumann's construction can be approached, it is this which fits in best with our own former work, so that it is particularly suitable in the present context. We shall not need to use it as more than an introduction.

It was an essential point of our former analysis that to any technique of production there corresponded a 'critical rate of return' entirely determined by the technique. If the production coefficients (that expressed the technique) were given, the rate of return could be calculated.[1] It was this same rate of return which set a maximum (in growth equilibrium) both to the rate of profit and to the rate of growth. In the simplified model of Chapter XII, with tractors made by tractors, the rate of return was $(1/a)$, the limit beyond which neither r nor g could rise. It was shown in Chapter XIV that in the more general case of many capital goods, there is a corresponding limit.

Every feasible technique will have a rate of return, in this sense, that corresponds to it; when there is a choice of techniques, there should be some technique (the 'top technique', we shall call it) which has the highest rate of return—the highest return that can possibly be got, along a growth equilibrium path, within the technology. (It is of course conceivable that there may be two or more techniques that 'tie' for the top place; but I shall simplify by leaving that possibility out of account. It complicates the statement, without affecting the principle. I shall therefore assume

---

[1] The assumption of 'constant returns to scale', on which the whole argument hangs, is here essential.

that there is just one 'top' technique.) When we are concerned with Optimum theory, and particularly with that form of Optimum theory which sets as its aim the maximizing of accumulation, it is to be expected that this *top rate of return* will be of particular importance. The von Neumann equilibrium is a Growth Equilibrium at the top rate of return.

It will, however, be remembered that in order for the top return to be realized (as a rate of profit) it was necessary that the wage should be zero; and a return that is only attainable on that extreme (and indeed absurd) assumption may well appear to be of little interest. But this (as often happens in such cases) is an obstacle that can be overcome, at least to some extent, by suitable redefinition. We have only to adopt the device (which we have already encountered in our discussion of the Adam Smith model)[1] of treating a fixed real wage of labour as a cost, expressed in terms of the using-up of the goods consumed by labour. 'Corn' is then a circulating capital good, which by being 'fed to labour' reproduces itself (and produces other capital goods in the same way). Labour coefficients do not then appear explicitly among the production coefficients; the labour that is required for the production of a particular (capital) good appears in the form of the quantity of 'corn' required to 'pay' the necessary labour. This is a 'capital-capital' coefficient, just like other capital coefficients. A rise in real wages will of course increase these 'corn' coefficients; it will thus be shown as a change in technology, which diminishes the rate of return on any of the techniques that can be carried over. It will have to be implied that the supply of labour is perfectly elastic; that additional labour can be acquired, as required, as soon as there is the 'corn' to pay for it. This, it must be fully admitted, is quite a special assumption; but it is an assumption with which we have by now become very familiar.

With wages absorbed in this manner, the rate of profit, on any technique, is identified with its maximum rate of return. Wages have been made (by implication) identical with consumption out of wages; the only source that is left for saving is profits. If the rate of growth is to be as large as possible, saving 'out of profits' must be as large as possible; from $g = s_1 r$ (the saving equation which, on the present interpretation, is clearly still valid) we conclude that if all profits are saved ($s_1 = 1$) we must have $g = r$.

---

[1] Chapter IV above.

Rate of growth and rate of profit are equal, both being equal to the same rate of return. The technique with the highest rate of return will also have the highest growth rate.

3. That is the way in which one can proceed to the von Neumann equilibrium, starting from our previous model; von Neumann's own presentation, however, was considerably more general. We could only deal with fixed capital, on our method, by assuming constant rates of capital wastage (our d-coefficients); that device (though, as explained,[1] it is a defensible device when we are only concerned with the comparison of growth equilibrium) is not really good enough for the present problem, where paths that are not equilibrium paths have also to be considered. Von Neumann's own solution was to regard a used 'machine' as a different good from a new 'machine'; after every period in which it was used it would change its quality, and hence its specification. The range of phenomena that can be covered by this more elastic formulation is no doubt far wider.[2] But it involves an analytical difficulty that is very serious indeed.

We can no longer regard the production coefficients as quantities of inputs required for the production of some particular output; the outcome of a productive process will have to include, not only its regular output, in the ordinary sense of that term, but also the used (but not used-up) fixed capital goods that are left over. Almost all production, accordingly, is *joint production*. Even to show the existence of a von Neumann equilibrium path in a system of joint production is no easy matter; it does not follow from what has been said, from what could be said, in terms of our own model. And there are several other points (as we shall see) where the assumption of joint production is a source of difficulty.

It was for the purpose of dealing with joint production that von Neumann invented Activity Analysis (as it has since been called): what we now know as the theoretical basis of Linear Programming. This development, of great general importance in itself, appears in his paper, as a kind of by-product of his main investigation. I shall avoid going deeply into it here. What I shall do is to try to follow through the argument, fairly completely, for the case

[1] See above, Chapter XIV, p. 161, n. 3.
[2] But it still leaves one with qualms about discontinuities; the assumption of 'constant returns to scale' in these terms, is quite hard to swallow.

in which there is no joint production[1] (and by implication no fixed capital either). A purely circulating capital model, without joint production, is a special case of von Neumann's model, and it is a special case of our model also. Everything that we have established will apply to it, and everything that von Neumann established will apply to it also. But it is no more than a special case; it has some properties that do not generalize. I shall indicate what these properties are, but I shall make no attempt to discuss the general von Neumann case at all fully. When we come to the second part of the theory (the Turnpike theorem proper) the joint production complication will fall into its place.

4. Let us, however, fix our attention (for the present) upon the pure circulating capital case, in which (as Mr. Sraffa would say) *commodities are used to produce commodities*, all inputs (in each single period) being wholly used up in producing the outputs of that period. In our former presentation the available techniques were ultimately to be regarded as directed towards the production of the single consumption good (or, in the generalization to 'consumption in general', of any of a group of consumption goods, or consumption bundles, that could be substituted for one another). In the von Neumann system, consumption (in our former sense) has disappeared; products have no purpose except to serve as inputs into future production; for maximum growth, growth must be growth, just for its own sake! But this is not an aspect which one would desire to take seriously. In economics, production is oriented towards consumption; the no-consumption case, which the Turnpike theory (formally) studies, is only a limiting case of production with consumption. It is in that light that we shall regard it here.

In consumption-oriented production, the techniques that are reckoned as within the technology must be directed towards the production of the consumption good; thus, though there is a choice of techniques for the production of each capital good, all are *indirect* techniques for the production of the consumption good, and it was in that light that we found it most convenient to consider them. A particular technique of production for each capital good, and one for the consumption good, constituted a technique of production for the whole economy. Here, even though the

[1] In the sense of von Neumann.

consumption good has 'gone', it will be convenient to maintain continuity by using the same terminology. I shall therefore allow myself to refer to a group (or matrix) of techniques, one for each commodity, as a 'technique'.[1]

It is an essential assumption of the von Neumann theory (and of the Turnpike theory proper that follows from it) that there is a 'convexity' relation between techniques; that any combination of feasible techniques (with one sector of the economy organized on one technique and the rest upon another) is itself a feasible technique. This is another 'constant returns to scale' assumption, about which an economist may well feel reservations. In a circulating capital model it is fairly acceptable; but to carry it over to fixed capital techniques (as von Neumann did) raises questions about discontinuities which are left unanswered. Whether there is anything left of the whole Turnpike theory if we are unwilling to commit ourselves to such assumptions (or are unwilling to do so without reservations) is a question that ought to be faced. I hope to have a few remarks to make about it before I have done.

5. The 'existence' of an equilibrium path (on which the components of the capital stock remain in the same proportions over time) follows from our own work in the case of the circulating capital model; von Neumann's own general proof I shall not attempt to examine. There are, however, some theorems about this equilibrium which he also established, and which will be of particular concern to us in the next chapter. Their validity in the circulating capital model can be fairly easily seen; and we can get some idea of how they will work in the general case.

I. *The equilibrium path is a balanced growth path*. In the circulating capital model this follows at once from our former work on growth equilibrium.

In growth equilibrium with positive consumption (as was shown in Chapter XIV), when technique is given, and growth rate is given, the stock of every capital good must bear a determinate proportion to current consumption output; there was a formula

---

[1] It will be in this sense that I shall assume (as stated on p. 209) that there is just one 'top technique'. If there was more than one 'technique', with the same (top) growth rate, they might be utilized together in equilibrium, part of the economy being organized in the one way, part in the other. The matrix of techniques might then be 'decomposable', a possibility which has given much trouble to the mathematicians. Here, I think, we may allow ourselves to rule it out.

which would enable us to express the ratio (k_i/ξ) in terms of g, and of the production coefficients. It follows that the ratios between the stocks of pairs of capital goods (k_i/k_j) will be similarly expressible. In the 'circulating capital' von Neumann equilibrium, consumption output will have disappeared, and g will have risen to the full 'rate of return'; but (k_i/k_j) will still be determined in the same manner—only, since g itself is now dependent on the technique, the proportions (k_i/k_j) will now depend upon the technique alone. There is thus an equilibrium set of proportions for each technique; it is only if the goods are combined in these determinate ratios that constancy in the ratios over time can be preserved. To each technique there is a balanced growth path. The von Neumann path is the balanced growth path that corresponds to the top technique. Or—as we shall allow ourselves to say when we desire to emphasize this particular property—it is the top-balanced path.

I shall merely assert that the same proposition holds when joint production is admitted; but indeed it would be surprising if it did not—for joint production itself tends to tie proportions together.

II. *The equilibrium path is an optimum path.* What exactly does this mean? It is a statement about the growth rate of the equilibrium path; but just what statement? This is not a matter which we have previously considered; we shall have to go into it in some detail.

(1) That the top-balanced path has a higher growth rate than any other balanced growth path is obvious; that, in effect, is the way that the top technique has been defined. What von Neumann asserts is much more than that. There is a sense in which the top-balanced path has a top growth rate: a growth rate which is not exceeded by that of any other possible path, balanced or unbalanced. This is far from obvious; indeed, unless we are careful, we may find ourselves taking it in a sense in which it is not true.

What do we mean by a growth rate along a non-balanced path? There is only one kind of definition that can conceivably be relevant: and it is fortunate that it is one that comes very naturally to economists. We must value the capital stock, at each stage of the path, at constant prices, thus constructing an index-number of the 'quantity of capital'. The growth rate will have to be defined, as an economist would expect to define it, as the growth rate of that index.

Such an index (and the growth rate that is calculated from it) will have the usual weakness of index numbers, that it is not insensitive to the choice of the particular prices that are used as weights. So long as we confine ourselves to the comparison of balanced growth paths, this does not matter. For if all components are increasing in the same proportion, the growth rate of the index will be the same, whatever the weights that are used; the prices that are used for weighting simply cancel out. But as soon as we come to consider paths that are not balanced, the choice of weights becomes important. It is not possible to prove von Neumann's theorem for *any* weights, however arbitrarily chosen; it is indeed likely that in any instance we should be able to find weights for which it would not be true. All that he showed[1] is that there will be at least one set of weights for which it is true. That does not sound much; but (as we shall find, when we come to use it) it is sufficient.

I shall try to explain how these weights are found, and why they work in the way they do; I shall not attempt to do more than that.

(2) Along a non-balanced path the growth rate will (or at least may) be changing from period to period; but since all that we have to show is that the equilibrium path has a 'top' growth rate in any single period, it is only at what happens in one single-period that we need to look. The beginning-stock is the 'input' and the end-stock is the 'output' of the period. The growth rate on one path is higher than that on another if the value of output is higher, relatively to the value of input; thus if the value of input were the same, the value of output would have to be higher. Let us test this out, and see what it implies.

Suppose that input prices are given, and that the total *value* of input is given; but now suppose that inputs are freely exchangeable for one another on a market, so that the *composition* of input is variable. Consider the *quantities* of outputs that can be got by using different techniques—under the constraints of the given input prices and given value of input.

Composition of input being variable, the full value of input can be utilized, whatever quantities are to be produced, and whatever technique is adopted. (For if less than the whole value were utilized on any 'plan', production could be increased by increasing everything in the same proportion.) Corresponding to each technique,

---

[1] The crucial proposition is that marked (8**) in von Neumann's paper.

there will be a limit to the quantities of /outputs/ which can be produced from this given value of input. In our 'circulating capital' case, with no joint supply, this limit must take the form of a linear 'frontier'.[1] (What happens in the joint supply case we shall see later.) In the case of two commodities (useful, as usual, for

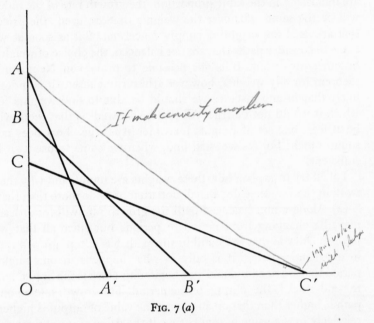

FIG. 7 (a)

illustration) the 'no joint supply' frontier will appear on a diagram as a downward-sloping straight line.

Each of the lines AA', BB', CC', ... (Fig. 7 (a) or (b)) is a frontier to the outputs that can be got from the given value of input, with a particular technique. Corresponding to any arbitrary set of input prices, there should (or so it appears at first sight) be a 'production possibility' diagram of the one kind or of the other.

But in fact, once we make the convexity assumption, Fig. 7 (a) is not possible. For if output A is feasible, and output C' is feasible, any combination of A and C' (any point on the straight line

[1] For the quantities of inputs (k_i) that are required to produce a bundle (x_j) of outputs by a given technique are then given by $k_i = \Sigma a_{ij} x_j$; if input prices (p_i) are fixed, the outputs that can be produced from a given input value are related by

$$\Sigma p_i k_i = \Sigma\Sigma p_i a_{ij} x_j = \Sigma(\Sigma p_i a_{ij})x_j = \text{constant.}$$

joining A and C') must be feasible. We can in fact construct a 'mixed' technique that has a frontier AC'. Thus it is only a situation such as is represented in Fig. 7 (b) with one technique 'covering' the others that is in fact admissible.

It is clear that this technique, which covers the others, must be the top technique. For if that were not so, we could select the

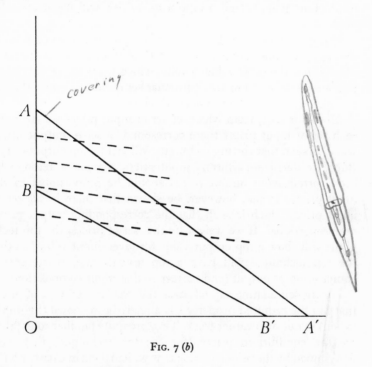

FIG. 7 (b)

point on the line which is such that input quantities and output quantities are in the same ratios; there must be such if a balanced growth rate (for the technique in question) exists. By shifting over to the top technique, we could then quite certainly increase the output value. A production-possibility line that did not belong to the top technique could not be 'covering'.

(3) It accordingly follows that for any input prices, and for any output prices (not necessarily proportional) there will always be a set of outputs, got by using the top technique, which has at least as high an output value as is attainable from given input value. That is true, but it is not sufficient. For suppose that we impose

(on Fig. 7 (*b*)) a set of parallel price-lines that represent output price-ratios (in the usual manner). A point between *A* and *A'* (which is where the balanced set of outputs is likely to be situated) will not necessarily have as high a value as could be attained, at those output prices, at *B* or at *C* using a non-top technique. For such output prices the superiority of the top technique, for the production of its balanced output quantities, will not necessarily hold.

There will, however, be *one* set of output prices which is such that the price lines are parallel to *AA'*; at those prices every point on *AA'* has the same value, a value which must 'cover' all others that are attainable. For this particular set of output prices the top technique must yield a top output-value.

All this is true, from whatever set of input prices we start. To each set of input prices there corresponds a set of output prices which is such that the top technique will yield a top output-value. But if we start from arbitrary input prices, there is no reason why these *corresponding* output prices should be proportional to the input prices. It can, however, be shown that there is *one* set of input prices which is such that the corresponding output prices *are* proportional. If we weight by that set of prices, the top technique will show a top output-value for given input-value; so that the top technique will have a top growth rate, whatever the composition of output (and corresponding input composition).

For the 'circulating capital' case, the existence of a set of prices that has the required property has already been shown (by implication) in our own earlier work. They are quite familiar to us; they are the equilibrium prices (for the top technique) that were determined by the price equations. As we had them in Chapter XIV, the prices of capital goods had to bear determinate ratios to the rate of wages; there was a formula for (p_i/w) which expressed each ratio in terms of the coefficients (of the technique) and of the rate of profit *r*. In the corresponding von Neumann equilibrium, the wage has fallen to 'zero', and the rate of profit has reached a maximum (determined by the coefficients); so that the relative prices of the capital goods are determined by the technique alone. At these prices, input prices and output prices will correspond (for that is what the equations say). So that it is these equilibrium prices which are the self-corresponding prices that we seek.

It has accordingly been shown, in the 'circulating capital' case, that when growth rates (along any path) are calculated by valuing at the equilibrium prices (of the top technique), production by the top technique must have a growth rate that is higher (or more strictly is at least as high) as is attainable in any other manner. How much of this is left when joint supply is admitted? A proper answer to that question must be left to the mathematicians;

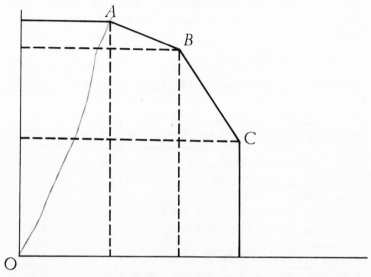

Fig. 8

but it is not hard to show, by our present method, just what the difficulty is.

(4) Suppose (to take the extreme case) that there is a technique (or activity) by which all the capital goods in the system are jointly produced. As inputs, they are used in fixed proportions; as outputs, they appear in fixed proportions. If (as before) input prices are fixed, and the total value of input is fixed, it would follow, if this technique were used, that fixed quantities of all outputs would emerge. The proportions would be fixed by the technique, and the scale (or 'intensity', as Activity Analysis would say) would be fixed by the constraint on the value of input. The production-possibility curve (for that technique) would apparently be reduced to a point (such as A, on Fig. 8). But it is better to say that the feasible outputs are anything less than these quantities, so that the feasible region is reduced to the 'box', on OA as diagonal.

The frontier of this is the frontier for the single technique (of this ultra-rigid character). But as soon as there is a choice of techniques (even of rigid techniques such as this) the character of the frontier changes. For if we continue (as von Neumann did) to assume convexity, once A is feasible and B is feasible any point on AB is feasible (the two techniques can be combined in any desired proportions). Thus the frontier builds up into a convex polygon, such as is shown in Fig. 8. The *general* difference that is made by joint supply is that the frontier ceases to be linear, but is liable to change direction from one 'facet' to another.

There is much of the preceding argument to which this does not make much difference. The convexity of the frontier enables us to argue, as before, that there will be some 'technique' (now to be interpreted as a 'facet' of the frontier) on which output value will be maximized, at any given output prices. And conversely: corresponding to any efficient combination of outputs (represented by a point on the frontier) there will be some set of output prices at which this combination of outputs maximizes output value. Thus, if we can prove that there exists a balanced growth path (under joint production) and if we can prove that there is a self-corresponding set of prices (under joint production), and if we can prove that these two belong together, on the same facet of the frontier, we are home. But these things cannot be proved by our former methods, for it is now impossible to consider prices and quantities separately, as we have hitherto been doing. This therefore (as far as I can see) is the point at which we have to hand over to the mathematicians. The second theorem, that the top-balanced path has a top growth rate (at least as high, if not higher, than that on any other feasible path) when it is reckoned at the right prices, is true, even under joint production; but it cannot be proved by methods that suffice for the 'no joint production' case.[1]

---

[1] I have taken it for granted, in the foregoing, that the equilibrium prices (at which the growth rate is to be reckoned for Theorem II) are all positive. (They must of course be non-negative.) In the case of 'no joint production' this is unquestionably a fair assumption; for a free good could not then be produced (in equilibrium) unless it was entirely made out of free goods; and this is a possibility which we are surely justified in leaving out. But under joint production, the position is not so clear. There might then be goods which were inherently surplus, appearing as by-products of profitable processes. The system could not help producing them, but would produce them in quantities which were in excess of what could be reused. The analysis has been extended, by

6. There is still a further point which in the 'no joint production' case is rather particularly worrying.[1] All that is shown, in that case, by the second theorem, is that (when valued at the right prices) a path which uses the top technique will have the top growth rate; this is true, it will be noticed, for *any* path that uses the top technique. What is it that distinguishes the top-balanced path from other top-technique paths? In what sense is it an equilibrium path, while they are not?

The answer to this question may not be the same when there is joint production as when there is no joint production. In the latter case (and in some of the former) it is given by the theorem:

III. *The equilibrium path is the only top-technique path that is continually viable.* When this theorem is true (as we shall find in the next chapter) it enables us to strengthen and to simplify the statement of the Turnpike theorem. Thus it is important to discover when it is true. We may begin by showing that it is true under 'no joint production'.

We are now solely concerned with top-technique paths, comparing one with another. But we have now to watch them for more than a single period. We can, however, begin from our single-period diagram (Fig. 7 (*b*)).

Starting, as before, from a given *value* of input (the input prices being now, we shall clearly want to assume, equilibrium prices) the range of possible outputs (using the top technique) is shown by AA' (or by what corresponds to that in many dimensions). That is to say (when there is no joint production) the whole range of output proportions is feasible, using the top technique. But to this there does not correspond the whole range of input proportions. For in order to produce at A (one output only) a certain combination of inputs will be required; in order to produce at A' another definite combination. In order to produce a combination of outputs *between* A and A' what will be required is something *between* these basic input combinations. That is to say, there will correspond to the whole range of output combinations a range of input combinations which is *narrower*; it will, for instance, be impossible

the mathematicians, to cover even this case; but in a simplified presentation, such as that attempted here, it seems reasonable to neglect it. I shall therefore assume throughout, in what follows, that all of the equilibrium prices are positive.

[1] When there is joint production, feasible top-technique outputs are restricted to those upon a single facet of the whole output frontier; under no joint production, there is no such restriction.

to use the top technique *at all* if only one sort of input is present, and that particular input can produce nothing by itself. It will only be if the available inputs lie within this narrower range that all of them (using the top technique) can be fully used.

Now consider a sequence of periods, each of which is to use as inputs the outputs of its predecessor. (The path to be followed need not be an equilibrium path.) The final outputs, at the end of the sequence, need not be balanced outputs; they may be in any proportions whatever. But the inputs of the last period cannot be in any proportions; their proportions must be within the range that has just been described. If the outputs of the penultimate period are to be fully used, they also must be in these narrower proportions; the inputs of the penultimate period must therefore be such as can produce this narrower range of outputs; this, it is to be expected, will restrict them *more* than the inputs of the last period were restricted. And so on. The further we take the sequence back, the narrower is the range of input proportions from which we can start.

If we start with balanced inputs, then (as we know) the process can be carried through, maintaining balance, for any number of periods. But if we do not start from balanced inputs, we must start from a composition that is very near to balance if it is to be capable of being carried through for a large number of periods without breaking down. (What is meant by breaking down is that the whole of the outputs of the period cannot be used as inputs of the following period, as they have been formerly; once this happens, the growth rate of the process—measured from output to output—must fall below the top rate.) Thus any divergence of the initial composition from a balanced composition must cause a breakdown, in this sense, sooner or later.

This is hardly a proof; for I have not attempted to define the 'narrowing' precisely. But it leads one to expect that it would be possible to define it precisely;[1] and so to show (what is in fact true) that our third theorem, in the 'no joint production' case, does—almost inevitably[2]—apply.

7. Now consider joint production. In that case, as we have seen, the production-possibility frontier is not *flat*. The only combinations

---

[1] For a more precise discussion, see Appendix C.
[2] 'Almost inevitably' because of the Morishima exception, for which see below.

of outputs that can be produced, at top growth rate, are those which lie upon some *facet* of the frontier, such as *AB* in Fig. 8. The outputs that can be produced on this facet are not combined in all proportions; there is a restriction upon the proportions in which they can be combined. Corresponding to these 'top facet' output-proportions there will (as before) be a range of input proportions; there will be a restriction on this range, as there was in the other case. But now there is a restriction upon both sides. We cannot therefore deduce, as we did in the 'no joint production' case, that there must be 'backward-narrowing'. It is possible here (as it was not possible there) that the input proportions might be *less* restricted than the output proportions. If that were to be so, what would happen to our theorem?

It is of course stood upon its head; but that is less defeating than might be expected. If it is the input proportions that have the wider range, the output proportions will have the narrower range; so there is still a convergence to equilibrium, but it goes the other way. We can start with any inputs which are in such proportions that they can be fully utilized on the top facet; the inputs of the next period, being outputs of the first, will then be more restricted than the inputs of the first. And so on. After a number of periods the inputs (and outputs) will be narrowly restricted; when they are narrowly restricted, they must have approached an equilibrium composition (for there is no other composition to which they can be restricted narrowly). Thus, though in this case the path may *begin* out of equilibrium, it must approach equilibrium.

We might restate our third theorem to cover this 'forward-narrowing' case by admitting the possiblity that the top-balanced path might be distinguished, not by being the only path that is continually viable, but by being the only path that is *ultimately* viable.

That, however, is by no means all. There are (in principle) four main possibilities. There is now a restricted set of (top technique) output proportions, and a (corresponding) restricted set of input proportions. It might happen (1) that the output set contained the input set—which is what happens under 'no joint production'; we then have *simple* backward-narrowing. (2) It might happen that the input set containing the output set, so that we had *simple* forward-narrowing. (3) It might happen that there was an overlap of the two sets. (4) It might happen that the two had nothing in common—but this last can be ruled out, for there would then be no balanced growth path with full utilization, and we are taking it that such a path exists. (1) and (2) have been discussed; but the third possibility (of the overlap) needs to be brought in; it looks like being an important case.

The simplest way of dealing with this third possibility is to take two single periods together.[1] If the (top technique) path is to be viable over the double period, the stock at the join (being both input and output) must belong to the overlap (as just defined). The input of the first single period must belong to the input range which has an output in this overlap; the output of the second must belong to the output range which has an input in this same overlap. Now consider the double period, of which those just defined are the input and output. For the double period we must (as before) have either (1) simple backward-narrowing, or (2) simple forward-narrowing, or (3) there is still an overlap. Cases (1) and (2) reduce to the former cases, beginning from the double period. In the third case we may argue as follows.

Every set of proportions that belongs to the second, or double period, overlap must belong to the first. The second overlap must therefore lie inside the first, so that by further lengthening (if the overlapping continues) we must again get a convergence to the equilibrium path—that being (as it were) shut up within a continually diminishing *overlap*. Thus there is still a convergence, though it is not done by simple backward-narrowing or by simple forward-narrowing. We may sum up (so far) by restating our third theorem in the form:

III. The top-balance path is the only top-technique path which is both *continually* and *ultimately* viable.

8. But even that is not all. There is still an exception, which has been explored (in several manners) by Professor Morishima. I shall not pay much attention to this exception in the following chapter; it must, however, be shown how it fits in.[2]

Every set of proportions that is feasible (either as input, or as output, or both) in a double period must be feasible in a single

---

[1] By the use of this device, the whole argument can be made more rigorous. For a restatement in these terms (which I owe to Professor Morishima) see Appendix C, sect. 5.

[2] For further discussion, see Appendix C.

period; thus the double-period range must, in some sense, be contained within the single-period range. It is, however, not necessary that it should be contained in the sense that is needed for the preceding argument. I will merely take one example. It might happen that the double-period range was the same as the single-period range, and that this continued to occur however far the doubling was carried. There would then be no convergence (any way) to the equilibrium path. We might begin with a set of proportions within this range (which were not equilibrium proportions); the sequence would stay within the range, but it would not converge to the equilibrium path, in either direction.

Fairly numerous examples of this character can be constructed. They are interesting in themsevles, but we should be clear that they are exceptions. They can be admitted, without it ceasing to be true that Theorem III (in its revised form) does give the right impression. In the 'no joint production' case, when the normal condition is backward-narrowing, a Morishima exception can only appear at a limit, when the backward-narrowing has become so small as to have disappeared. When there is joint production, it must be taken more seriously; it is nevertheless still true that it is a boundary possibility, which will only be hit if the parameters of the problem come out just right.

It might, for instance, happen that a particular top technique was backward-narrowing when some coefficient was less than c (a constant), forward-narrowing when this coefficient was greater than c (all others remaining unchanged). What is to happen when the coefficient equals c? This would not be a case of an overlap, nor would it be a case of forward- or of backward-narrowing; the only thing that can happen is for the range to remain unchanged when the period is lengthened. This is a simple case of the Morishima exception.

9. The Morishima exception is the only exception to the truth of the Turnpike theorem (as usually stated). So long as Theorem III holds, in the form that we finally gave it, the Turnpike theorem holds. Any kind of narrowing is sufficient. It will hold for forward-narrowing as well as for backward-narrowing; though the character of the convergence to the Turnpike is not the same in the one case as in the other. The possibility of taking them together makes, of course, for elegance in the mathematics. But for a presentation such as that at which we are aiming, it will be wise to distinguish. It will not be necessary, in the analysis that follows, to go on fussing about 'no joint production'; that is a ladder that can be kicked down. But we must still be prepared to distinguish between the various kinds of narrowing. In our first statement of the Turnpike argument, we shall assume that the top technique is backward-narrowing. When we have that behind us, it will not be hard to see what amendments are needed for the other cases.

XIX

THE TURNPIKE THEOREM AND ITS SIGNIFICANCE

1. I COME now to the second part of the theory—the Turnpike theorem itself. With the three von Neumann theorems behind us— the theorems that have been explained, though by no means fully proved, in the preceding chapter—the remainder of the argument can be set out, almost completely, in a relatively simple manner.

We are now to start from a stock that is not an equilibrium stock—that is not (as we have been saying) top-balanced. We are to aim to attain, at the end of a given number of periods (T), the largest possible stock of a given (also, in general, not top-balanced) composition. What can be said about the optimum path in this sense? What (that is to say) is the character of the optimum path when the von Neumann path (or Turnpike) cannot be followed?

It is strongly suggested by what we have said about the second von Neumann theorem that we should fix our attention upon the movement of an index, in which the components of the capital stock are weighted by their equilibrium prices. Since the terminal stock is to have a given composition, the largest stock of that composition will have the largest value, whatever price weights are chosen; to maximize the *value* of the stock, with the given composition, at any price weights, is an adequate formulation of the aim that has been set. The particular price weights which it will be most convenient to use are clearly the equilibrium prices, since it is in terms of these that the Optimum property of the von Neumann path is expressed.

This is the method which we shall follow; it is a clue which (as we shall find) simplifies things very much. But it is a little more helpful in one of the cases that were distinguished in the third theorem (as finally stated) than it is in the other; it will therefore be convenient to begin with that easier case—which is what we called the 'backward-narrowing' case. When we have that case behind us, the other can be dealt with more easily.

There is another simplification which we may permit ourselves—

at a first round. It is not in general necessary that all of the commodities which are included in the initial stock (or in the terminal stock) should be represented in the equilibrium stock; but if they are not, what are their prices? We are going to have trouble with this case, and worse trouble (for another reason) with goods that are not in the initial stock, but are in the equilibrium stock. These troubles, also, it will be convenient to postpone. I shall therefore begin with the preliminary simplifications:

(1) that there is backward-narrowing,

(2) that it is the same list of commodities that is represented, in positive quantities, in the initial stock, in the equilibrium stock, and in the terminal stock. The only differences in the composition of the three stocks are differences in proportions.

I make these simplifications for convenience in presentation; we shall remove them before we have done.

2. The index of the capital stock, got by weighting at von Neumann equilibrium prices, I shall call K. If log K is measured on the vertical axis of a diagram (Fig. 9), and time on the horizontal, exponential expansion, along a balanced growth path, will be represented by an upward-sloping straight line. Thus if the initial stock (index OA) was top-balanced, expansion could proceed along the von Neumann equilibrium path (or Turnpike), which would be represented by the line AU, of a greater slope (or growth rate) than that of any other *balanced* growth path that is technologically possible. But we are to suppose that the initial stock is not top-balanced. In that case, *since there is backward-narrowing*, we may invoke Theorem III in its first form. If the top technique were employed, making full utilization of the initial stock, and of the stocks into which it was transformed in subsequent periods,[1] though a path AU (with top growth rate) might be followed for a few periods, it would not be continually viable. The point would have to come at which the whole stock could not be employed at the top technique, so that the growth rate would have to fall below top. It must indeed be admitted to be possible, if the time (T) that is allowed for the whole process is a short one, that a particular

---

[1] We continue to assume (see above, Chapter XVIII, p. 220 n.) that the equilibrium prices of all commodities, that are represented (in positive quantities) in the equilibrium stock, are positive. It will then follow from our second simplification that there must be full utilization (at each stage) if a top growth rate, measured as we are measuring it, is to be attained.

initial stock might be converted into a terminal stock of particular composition, even though the initial stock was not top-balanced. But at the best, this is a very special case; when T is large, it is of negligible importance. For a large T (and it is a large T in which we are interested) the initial stock cannot differ significantly

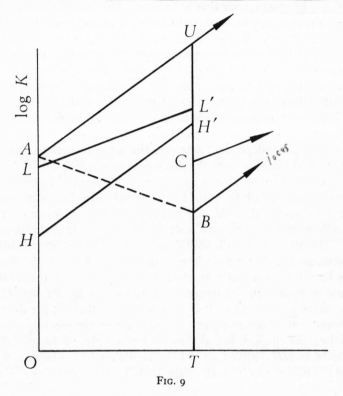

FIG. 9

from an equilibrium stock if the top technique is to be employed throughout. We may then allow ourselves to say that if the initial stock is not top-balanced, a path of top growth rate cannot be followed. Even so (it appears from Theorem II) the path AU is relevant, as setting an upper limit to the expansion that can be attained.

Though the path AU is out of reach, there is a path, from initial (non-top-balanced) stock to terminal (non-top-balanced) stock, which is certainly feasible (on our assumption that the compositions differ only in poportions); it can be constructed in the following way. First, the initial stock is reduced to a top-balanced stock by *discarding* surplus quantities. This can always be done if the difference is solely one of proportions; a top-balanced stock can always be found *inside* the initial stock. The discarding, we may suppose, is kept to a minimum; it is the largest top-balanced stock that can be found *inside* that is selected.[1] After this discarding the top technique can be used, until the final period (time T), when by a second discarding (of the same sort) the top-balanced stock is reduced to the terminal composition. Such a path is shown on the diagram by $AHH'B$. I shall call it a *quasi-balanced* path.

Since the discarding is a pure matter of change of composition, it will always reduce the value of the stock (at the given price-weights) in a proportion that is independent of the date at which it occurs. Thus, on our logarithmic diagram, the *distances AH* and $H'B$ are independent of time; the same reductions will be required at whatever date the discarding takes place.

It would of course have been possible to construct an alternative quasi-balanced path by initial and terminal discarding, with some other technique than the top technique being employed on the middle stretch. Such a path is shown by $ALL'C$. It could happen that the alternative path would gain over $AHH'B$ by requiring less discarding, but it must lose by its lower growth on LL'. Since the terminal stock that is reached by either route has to have the same composition, the terminal values (shown by BT and CT) are directly comparable. It is at once evident that if little time is allowed, the alternative path that uses a non-top technique may be the more efficient. But as T moves to the right, the locus of B is parallel to HH', while that of C is parallel to LL'. The path that has the higher growth rate on the middle stretch must ultimately win.

All that this shows is that $AHH'B$ will be more efficient (when sufficient time is allowed) than any other quasi-balanced path. It does not follow that it is an optimum path; it should indeed be possible to improve upon it quite considerably. Once we drop the condition that the same technique is to be employed throughout

---

[1] Suppose that the units in which the components are measured are chosen in such a way that one unit of each (and therefore any equal number of each) constitutes a top-balanced stock. Let the number of such units of the ith good in the initial stock be k_i. There will be some good (or goods) for which this k_i is smallest; let the first good be such a good. Then k_1 units of each good will be the largest top-balanced stock that can be found *inside*. (Cf. p. 192, above.)

(apart from the initial and terminal discarding), it should be possible to reduce the discarding losses at H and at H' by (perhaps quite temporary) adoption of non-top techniques, which are more suitable to the initial and terminal compositions, though they are such that if they were employed on the middle stretch they would be less productive. It certainly looks likely, when we 'build up' an optimum path in this way, that it will have to approximate to a von Neumann path on its middle stretch (as the Turnpike theorem maintains). But this is not a demonstration; we can do better.

Consider again the position at time T (T arbitrary). Since we know (by Theorem II) that AU is a ceiling beyond which it is not possible to expand, we can conclude that the terminal outcome of the optimum path, at time T, cannot be greater than that which is represented by UT. But it cannot be less than BT, which can be reached by a quasi-balanced path that is certainly feasible. Thus the average growth rate along the optimum path must lie between the slopes of AU and of AB. But as time increases, the locus of B is a line that is parallel to AU (as we have seen). Thus, as time increases, the difference between the slopes of AU and of AB must continually diminish. The average growth rate along the optimum path must lie between them. Thus the difference between the 'Turnpike' growth rate and the average growth rate along the optimum path must converge to zero. By taking sufficient time it can be made as small as we like.

Now we know (again from Theorem II) that the growth rate along the optimum path (measured as we are measuring it) can in no single period exceed the 'Turnpike' growth rate. Thus the differences between the Turnpike rate and the growth rate on the optimum path, period by period, are all non-negative; and their average, when a large number are taken, can be made as small as we like. It follows, rather obviously, that not more than a *small* number of these differences can be large. Over most of its course, the difference between the growth rate on the optimum path and the Turnpike growth rate must be small.

Over so long a period (still assuming backward-narrowing) a Turnpike growth rate is only attainable on the Turnpike itself. It would seem to follow (on this same assumption) that a growth rate which was very near to a Turnpike growth rate would only be attainable (if not actually on the Turnpike) then upon a path which lay in its immediate neighbourhood. If so—standing on the backs of the three theorems, and for the case which is delimited by the two simplifications—the Turnpike theorem is proved.

3. Now to drop the simplifications. I begin with backward-narrowing.

To most of the argument, as stated, the admission of forward-narrowing (or of overlapping, or indeed of the Morishima exception) makes remarkably little difference. It is always true that AU sets a ceiling to the growth rate that can be attained, in any period; and it is always true (so long as the other simplification is retained) that there is a feasible path ($AHH'B$) which can be reached by initial and terminal discarding. It is always possible to discard to the von Neumann composition, and then to discard from it to the terminal composition. The growth rate along the optimum path must always lie between these limits. We can argue, as before, that the average growth rate along the optimum path must approximate to the top growth rate, if sufficient time is allowed. It will follow, in the same way, that for most of the time the growth rate on the optimum path must be near to a top growth rate.

What may not follow, in quite the same way, is that the optimum path must, on that stretch, be near to an equilibrium path. It is here that we have to distinguish.

(*a*) It could happen, if there is simple *forward-narrowing*, that a top growth rate could be attained, with full utilization of the initial stock, even though the initial stock was not top-balanced. The initial stock would have to be such that the top technique could be employed with full utilization, but this condition could be satisfied without the necessity of initial top-balance. Such a path would be shown on our diagram as a movement along AU, though it would not be implied that the stock was a balanced stock along that path. But though it was not initially top-balanced, it would have to be moving into top-balance. If enough time were allowed, the stock would be near to top-balance over a large part of the course.

That is what would happen if the initial stock was such that the top technique could be used with full utilization. If it were not such, a path of that kind would not be feasible; and our former argument would hold without substantial change.

(*b*) The case of *narrowing by overlapping* will work in much the same way. Here, however, it will not be true that *any* initial composition, such that the top technique can be used with full utilization, will serve as the start of a viable path (moving into equilibrium) at the top technique. Some compositions will do this, but some will not. This, however, means no more than that we have to make the same qualification as under (*a*), but it has a more restricted scope.

(*c*) In the case of the Morishima exception, there will be *some* initial compositions which will serve as the start of an oscillatory path, fluctuating about the equilibrium path, but not converging to it, however much time is allowed. Such a path is a top technique path with full utilization; it also will appear on our diagram as a movement along *AU*. If the initial position is not such as to permit of full utilization at top technique, it may nevertheless be a path of the Morishima type which is the easiest top technique path to approach from it; there may then be an approximation (sufficient time being allowed) to the Morishima path, not to the von Neumann path. Here then there will be an exception to the Turnpike theorem.

The exception is there, and the qualification is there, but their importance should not be exaggerated. Suppose we restate the Turnpike theorem. Suppose we make it say that (sufficient time being allowed) the optimum path must (for most of the way) use the top technique, or something very near to the top technique. In that form it would be true, whatever the condition about 'narrowing'. It may well be that it is in this form that we shall find it most useful—in economics—to consider it.

4. Our other simplification—that it is the same list of goods that is represented, in positive quantities, in all of the three compositions—must now be removed. There is no doubt that it must be removed, if the theory is to have any hope of interesting economic application.

In order to construct our quasi-balanced path, we had (1) to convert the initial stock into an equilibrium stock, and (2) to convert the equilibrium stock into a stock of the terminal composition. If the commodities that occur in the three stocks are not all the same, there are problems of conversion at each of the two 'joins'.

If there are commodities in the initial stock which are not in the equilibrium stock, that creates no problem of conversion at the first 'join'; such commodities can readily be discarded. From the point of view of the equilibrium path, such commodities are surplus, and should therefore be valued at zero prices. They can be discarded without loss of value; but this makes no formal difference to the preceding argument.[1]

If there are commodities that are in the equilibrium stock but are not in the terminal stock, there is again no problem about discarding; but when such commodities are discarded there will be a loss of value.

Where there is difficulty is in the converse cases, of commodities that are in the equilibrium stock but are not in the initial stock, or of commodities that are in the terminal stock but are not in the equilibrium stock. In these cases there is no stock of the required composition *inside* the previous stock. We cannot proceed by simple discarding. And this, in economic applications, is surely a thing that is very likely to happen.

To deal with these cases we must make some amendment; but it need not be very considerable.

We must suppose that there is some way of getting from the initial stock to the top-balanced stock, by some process of production that is feasible. For if there were no such way, that 'top' technique would be irrelevant to the optimization problem; it could not be the top technique for the purpose in hand. The top technique must be defined in such a way that it is *accessible* from the initial stock, and that the terminal stock is *accessible* from it. Granted that, though it will not be possible to proceed from the initial stock to the top-balanced by simple discarding, there will be a way in which it is possible to proceed. There is no reason why we should not incorporate such a transformation into our quasi-balanced path—at the cost of a very simple adjustment.

Consider the *quickest possible* transformation of the initial stock into a top-balanced stock, which may include as much discarding as is necessary in order to make the transformaton as quick as possible. The first element of the quasi-balanced path (corresponding to the discarding from A to H) will have to consist of this

---

[1] It should, however, be emphasized that there may well be ways in which commodities that do have positive prices on the equilibrium path, but which have to be discarded between A and H (so that there is a loss of value in their discarding) can nevertheless be utilized, in a preliminary phase, by combining with them some of these 'surplus' commodities. Thus, though the 'surplus' commodities are not used on the quasi-balanced path, they may be used on the optimum path—to diminish the loss of value on the co-operating commodities.

quickest transformation. It cannot be done instantaneously but it can be done in a finite time. The final element (corresponding to the discarding from H' to B) may also have to be a quickest transformation, of similar character. The condition that the transformation is to be carried through in minimum time may not restrict it to one technique (or sequence of techniques); but there must be one which (for that minimum time) gives the least loss of value. The loss of value (on that transformation) is therefore determinate. As soon, therefore, as we allow a sufficient time, over the whole process, for the double transformation to be carried through, the proportional loss of value (represented by UB on the diagram) is determinate; it is independent of any further extension of time. The locus of B is still a straight line parallel to AU. The average growth rate on the optimum path must still approximate to that on the Turnpike if sufficient time is allowed.

5. *If sufficient time is allowed.* Surely it is the case that with this last amendment we are emerging from our mathematical tunnel; we are coming out into economic daylight. In any practical economic problem, although plans must be drawn up on the basis of existing technology, that technology will not be the same as the technology that existed in the past. The initial stock must have been constructed under past technology; so that the *present* top-balanced stock must almost certainly contain goods that are not present in the initial stock. The minimum length of time which will be needed for the production of such goods—even if everything that can be sacrificed is sacrificed to their production—is by no means negligible. Suppose—it does not seem an unplausible figure—that this minimum length of time is three years.[1] The transformation (corresponding to the discarding) at the beginning *and* at the end of the process may well take a time that is something like that.[2] The total length of time that is necessary for the whole process, in order that we should be able to affirm the approach to the Turnpike with any confidence, must therefore be *large* relatively to $3+3$ years. Half a century? And what will have happened to technology by that time?

[1] Second World War experience (which is rather to the point) suggests such a figure.
[2] In a 'circulating capital' model, the final transformation might take no more than a single period; but when fixed capital (with joint production) is included, this will not (in general) be possible.

It is (admittedly) a jump to proceed from mathematical (or quasi-mathematical) analysis to such 'practical' considerations. But the particular method of exposition which we have used may help to justify it.

I have drawn a sharp line, in these chapters, between the original von Neumann theory (with its strict and elegant mathematical assumptions) and the Turnpike theory proper that is based upon it. All that we needed to carry over from the first to the second were (1) the existence, (2) the optimality, and (3) the viability of the balanced growth path. By the first, a particular structure of the capital stock was necessary for equilibrium. By the second, the growth rate of the equilibrium path (valued at suitable prices) was at least as great, *in any period*, as that of any alternative path that was feasible. By the third, it was only along the equilibrium path that a process of top growth rate could be continuously (or indefinitely) carried through. These were the only things which we needed to take over, in order that the main point of the Turnpike theorem should be established.

Now I am inclined to think that an economist would be prepared to guess that something like these three requirements would be satisfied, even in conditions where von Neumann's assumptions were not satisfied, or not satisfied completely. Even if there are significant discontinuities, so that there are exceptions to the rules of convexity and of constant returns to scale; or (again) if the real wage (or 'corn' coefficient) cannot be relied upon to remain constant in the course of development; there should still be some possibility of identifying an equilibrium path, in the sense of the optimum path *as it would be* if the composition of the capital stock were properly adjusted to the technology. And there is still a distinction, an important distinction, between that (generalized) 'Turnpike' path and the *actual* optimum path which is restricted by an initial stock that is inappropriate. It is a serious mistake (in development planning quite a tempting mistake) to confuse them.

But from this angle the significance of the Turnpike theorem (in so far as anything like it is valid) is almost the opposite of what first appears. If there were a rapid convergence of the actual optimum to the Turnpike, it might not much matter if we failed to distinguish between them. It might not much matter if we *began* by putting up the fine new steel mills which will be appropriate in the millennium, and discarded at once the bullock-carts which we plan to have outgrown. But if (as we have seen reason to believe) there is only a slow approximation, this by no means follows. The far future is vastly uncertain; it is the near future for which we are always (really) planning. For the determination of those first steps (even if we are to consider them as an approach to the Turnpike) consideration of the properties of the Turnpike is not much guide.

This is so (it will be noticed) even if we hold to the central directive of Turnpike theory: that the terminal stock, at the end of the planning process, is the only thing which is to have 'utility'. But if, after all, it is the first steps at which we ought to be looking, is it sense to take the consumption outputs during that phase as being of no importance? I hope that the reader will have come to agree with me that it is not. But if so, we cannot be content with the theory that has been set out in these chapters. It cannot do as our only Optimum theory.

XX

THE INTERTEMPORAL PRODUCTION
FRONTIER

1. I TURN to the alternative type of Optimum theory, which sets as its objective, not the terminal capital stock, but the stream of consumption outputs. This is a less difficult theory than the Turnpike theory; it can be tackled, for the most part, in quite a conventional manner. But it needs to be set out with some care, if it is to be properly valid, and is not to be misunderstood.[1]

There are some ways in which its assumptions are wider (or can be wider) than those which are necessary for the Turnpike theorem. Thus it is necessary for the Turnpike theorem that there should be unlimited labour: that the supply of labour should be perfectly elastic at a given real wage. This is more than was necessary for the existence of a growth equilibrium. There can be a growth equilibrium, as we found previously, if the supply of labour is increasing at a constant growth rate, given autonomously; but that is not enough for the Turnpike theorem. Not only on the Turnpike, but on the approach to the Turnpike, the real wage of labour must be fixed. All resources, indeed, must be reproducible—at a cost; not merely can there be no autonomously given labour supply, there can also be no fixed supply of land. If the supply of land is a significant restraint upon the expansion of production, there can indeed be no growth equilibrium with positive expansion (as Ricardo found).[2] The only full equilibrium which is then possible is the stationary state.

[1] This is the theory which I tried (not quite successfully) to set out in my paper 'A "Value and Capital" Growth Model' (*Review of Economic Studies*, 1958). I was unacquainted with Turnpike theory at the time when I wrote that paper; for that reason (and doubtless for others also) some of the argument is insufficiently guarded. I nevertheless still hold to the basic theorem which I was trying to express: a theorem which was in fact proved (though, as we shall see, it was very quaintly stated) in *Value and Capital* itself. What I shall try to do in this chapter is to translate the argument of Chapter XVII of *Value and Capital* into more modern terms.

[2] See Chapter IV, above. The theory to which we now come has much the same relation to Ricardo's model as the Turnpike has to Adam Smith's. But (as we shall see) it does not need to be taken in so 'pessimistic' a sense as Ricardo's.

There is now no reason why we should not include all these possibilities. There can be land which is fixed in supply, and there can be labour which is fixed in supply, if we choose to make those assumptions. But we are not obliged to make them; we can make them, or not make them, as we like. But it is convenient to begin by making them, at least in the sense that the movement of labour supply is given autonomously. There is a fixed supply of labour in every single period, though it need not be the same in different single periods. An autonomous growth rate of the labour force is therefore permitted. Even so, the supply of labour to the productive process as a whole is a datum; just as the supply of land and of initial capital (capital goods left over from the past, before time o) are data. The problem is one of maximizing output, over the whole planning period (from o to T) from these 'original factors'.

The outputs that correspond to these resources are the consumption outputs, over the planning period, and the terminal capital. It is the stream of consumption outputs which is now to move into the centre of the picture. Since we are mainly interested in the distribution of that stream over time, it will be convenient (and perhaps not too dangerous) to retain the simplification of a single consumption good. The stream of consumption outputs can therefore be written

$$(\xi_0, \xi_1, ..., \xi_{T-1})$$

but there are no firm constraints upon these outputs unless the terminal capital (at time T) can somehow be specified.

2. As was explained in Chapter XVII, we cannot do this merely by attaching the terminal capital to the end of the stream of consumption outputs; for there is no direct way in which we could value it in comparison with them. We need some device to help us round the difficulty. There seem to be two ways in which such a device could be found.

One way of proceeding is to treat the terminal capital as a constraint. That is to say, we seek for the 'maximum' stream of consumption which can be produced from the given resources, consistently with the condition that a given capital stock should be left over at the end of the process. Since it is the amount of every component of the terminal stock which must be prescribed in this manner (and must be prescribed in such a way as to be capable of being produced from the resources), this condition is, at least at first sight, very cramping indeed. If the whole composition of the terminal stock (to be reached at a given date) is prescribed in this manner, will not the whole course of the production plan (between 0 and T) be quite narrowly circumscribed? If both initial stock and terminal stock are to be tied down in this way, there will not be much scope for the choice of a 'best' sequence of consumption outputs.

The weight that has to be given to this objection depends, however, upon the length of time (to T) that is allowed. It is in the later stages of the plan (as time T is approached) that the rigid specification of terminal stock is most cramping; the effect which it has in those later stages is broadly similar to the effect of the given composition of initial stock in the opening stages. In the middle stages (if there are enough middle stages) there should be a greater freedom of choice. By extending the time which is allowed for the plan, we can indefinitely extend that part of the planning period over which the rigidity of terminal stock does not so much matter.

Taking this principle to the limit, we can (if we choose) push off the terminal date into the remote future, so that it is (effectively) an infinite stream of consumption outputs which is all that we have to consider. It has been shown[1] that this procedure is mathematically justifiable; and it has its attractions, since it enables us to evade the whole question of the terminus. I shall make some use of it in what follows; but I shall not rely on it entirely, since there is an alternative, which is perhaps more interesting from the economic point of view.

On this alternative procedure we do not entirely avert our eyes from the consumption outputs that are to be forthcoming after time T; we merely assume that they are to follow a predetermined pattern. It is then unnecessary to specify the size and composition of the terminal capital; all we have to do is to require that it shall be such as to produce future outputs, with a specified time-pattern, in an optimum manner. The specified pattern which it will obviously be most interesting to take is that of steady expansion; what we should then specify is that the terminal stock should be

---

[1] For the mathematical analysis, see Malinvaud: 'Capital Accumulation and Efficient Allocation of Resources', *Econometrica*, 1953; 'Analogy between Atemporal and Intertemporal Theories of Resource Allocation', *Review of Economic Studies*, 1961. A more summary treatment is in Koopmans, *Three Essays on the State of Economic Science*, pp. 105 ff.

Find path to equilibrium which is colour.

such that the economy is able, from that time onwards, to be in a growth equilibrium. The problem before us would then reduce to the selection of a path to equilibrium, which is an optimum path from the consumption point of view.

We must, however, be careful to see that the pattern of output which is prescribed for the 'epilogue' (as we may call it) is a feasible pattern. If there is a fixed supply of land (which is a continuing restraint upon output), *or* if there is a fixed supply of labour (constant over time), a Growth Equilibrium, with constantly expanding consumption output, will not be feasible. The only equilibrium pattern which can then be prescribed for the epilogue is a stationary output; the path to equilibrium must be a path to a stationary state. It can indeed be a stationary state at various levels; for we have not said anything (nor in this chapter shall we say anything) about saving propensities. The larger the consumption outputs during the planning period, the lower the stationary output in the epilogue will have to be.

If land is not a significant restraint, and if labour supply is increasing at a constant rate, a Growth Equilibrium, with a rate of expansion not greater than the growth rate of the labour supply, may be feasible. If we impose the condition that there should be a prospect of full employment of labour (in the epilogue), the growth rate which will have to be planned for (in the epilogue) will be fixed at this growth rate of labour. But it will still be the case that the level from which this expansion starts (and hence the consumption output, per unit of labour, throughout the epilogue) will be liable to be affected by the consumption outputs that are to emerge during the planning period.

It seems to follow from this discussion of the terminus that there are two formulations of consumption-oriented Optimum theory which look like being more interesting than any others. The first is that where we treat the planning process as extending into the indefinite future, so that choice is between *infinite* streams of consumption outputs—the streams

$$(\xi_0, \xi_1, \dots)$$

that can be produced from the given initial equipment, and given flow-of-labour supply. The second is that in which the consumption outputs, after time T, are to have a prescribed growth rate (which may be zero). Thus if $t > 0$, $\xi_{T+t} = \xi_T(1+\gamma)^t$ where γ

is given.[1] The stream of outputs that has to be determined is then reduced to the form

$$(\xi_0, \xi_1, ..., \xi_{T-1}, \xi_T)$$

with a finite number of variables, of which ξ_T stands for all outputs from time T onwards.

It will be these two formulations that I shall try to keep in play.

3. Whichever we adopt, the given resources set limits upon the output streams that are feasible.[2] If the number of variables in the stream is finite (as in our second formulation), the stream can be represented as a point in many dimensions; the feasible streams will be limited to a particular region on that many-dimensional 'diagram'. Such a region will have a production-possibility frontier of the usual type. Any stream that lies within the frontier is feasible; but only those that are on the frontier (so that production is maximized, when the time-shape of the stream is given) are optimal, from the quantity-optimizing point of view.[3]

If we adopt the first formulation, so that the number of variables is infinite, 'geometrical' representation fails; but there is a *frontier* all the same. For if the time-shape of the stream is given—if there is a rule by which the ratios of the consumption outputs in the various periods are given (and there is no reason why such a rule should not extend into infinite time, as for instance the prescription of a given growth rate would do)—there will still be a maximum to the amount that can be produced from the given resources. And that is all that is needed.

The feasible region must have a frontier; I shall further assume (as we did at a corresponding point in the Turnpike theory) that it is a convex region, in the usual sense. That is to say, if any two streams are feasible, any stream which lies *between* them is feasible. If it is possible to change over from one to the other, it will also be possible to change over part of the way.

It must indeed be admitted that this is an assumption about which one has considerable qualms. All-round convexity implies an absence of increasing returns; and in a theory of this sort to

[1] I use γ instead of g since this is now a growth rate of consumption outputs; the distinction is important, as we shall see in what follows. One might generalize a little by including γ as a variable; but I shall not trouble to do that.

[2] Assuming, of course (as always until Chapter XXII) that the technology is given.

[3] See above, Chapter XVII, p. 204.

assume an absence of increasing returns may be even less tolerable than it has been in our earlier work. Let us, however, remember that our single consumption good is standing for the whole range of consumption goods, reduced to homogeneity by one or other of the devices with which we are now familiar; it is not clear that increasing returns, important as they may be in particular sectors, must be so dominant as to override the convexity rule when that is applied to 'consumption in general'. Indeed as we have to use it, the convexity rule is not so strong an assumption as appears at first sight. So far as increasing returns are due to discontinuities (and it seems probable that discontinuities are the main, if not the only, cause of increasing returns phenomena) they may be thought of as causing 'holes' in the feasible region, with the possible consequence of 'dents' in the frontier. Such dents can nevertheless coexist with an overall tendency to convexity, a tendency which may well be sufficient for the purpose for which we require it.

The only purpose for which we require the convexity assumption is to assure ourselves that quantity-optimizing and value-optimizing come to the same thing. If there are no dents in the frontier, any position on the frontier will maximize the value of output at some set of prices;[1] if there are dents, the positions which maximize value will still be on the frontier, but there will be some positions on the frontier which will not maximize value. For a movement from one 'vertex' (between the dents) to another, the convexity rule will still hold. If we are content to confine choice to such 'vertex' positions (and though we may not always be content to confine it to them, we should often be willing to do so) we can go ahead, without too much regard to the dents.

4. What now are the prices that we are here to use for value-optimizing? They are values of consumption output at one date in terms of consumption output at another date; they are therefore expressible in terms of *real* rates of interest, interest measured in terms of the consumption good.[2] The value of the stream of consumption outputs is to be got by *discounting* back to some base

---

[1] On a two-dimensional diagram this is obvious geometrically. That the same principle holds for any number of dimensions is now well known. See for instance Koopmans, *Three Essays . . .*, pp. 23 ff.

[2] Such *real* rates of interest are of course to be sharply distinguished from *money* rates (rates of interest in the market sense). They are only the same if the money price of the consumption good is constant (over time).

date, most conveniently taken to be time o, the date of the start of the plan. The value of the plan, which for optimum production is to be maximized, is this discounted value.

Suppose that the rate of interest (r) is constant over time, and write λ for the discount factor $1/(1+r)$. The value of the plan is then given by the familiar formula

$$K = \xi_0 + \lambda\xi_1 + \lambda^2\xi_2 + \dots$$

extending to infinity if the plan is of indefinite duration. If K is to be finite, λ must not be too large, so that r must not be too small. What is the nature of this constraint becomes apparent if we adopt the alternative formulation. For then

$$K = \xi_0 + \lambda\xi_1 + \dots + \lambda^{T-1}\xi_{T-1} + \\ + \lambda^T\xi_T\{1 + \lambda(1+\gamma) + \lambda^2(1+\gamma)^2 + \dots\}$$

and the bracketed expression has a finite limit if $\lambda(1+\gamma) < 1$, so that $r > \gamma$. The rate of interest that is used for discounting must be greater than the growth rate to which the consumption plan *tends*.[1] If this condition is satisfied, the value of the plan, on the second formulation, becomes

$$K = \xi_0 + \lambda\xi_1 + \lambda^2\xi_2 + \dots + \lambda^{T-1}\left(\xi_{T-1} + \frac{\xi_T}{r-\gamma}\right)$$

which is clearly a finite value.

At an optimum position, the value of the plan is maximized; so that $K(\xi, \lambda) > K(\xi+\delta\xi, \lambda)$, where the change from ξ to $\xi+\delta\xi$ represents any feasible change in any of the elements (ξ_t). If ($\xi+\delta\xi$) is taken to be the stream at which value is maximized for the discount factor $\lambda+\delta\lambda$, we have similarly (for that other optimization)

$$K(\xi, \lambda+\delta\lambda) < K(\xi+\delta\xi, \lambda+\delta\lambda).$$

From these 'Samuelson inequalities' the basic property of the production frontier is easily derived.

Dividing the one by the other (as is permissible since all terms are positive, we have

$$\frac{K(\xi, \lambda+\delta\lambda)}{K(\xi, \lambda)} < \frac{K(\xi+\delta\xi, \lambda+\delta\lambda)}{K(\xi+\delta\xi, \lambda)}$$

[1] The necessity for this condition will not surprise us in view of our earlier work.

so that the effect on *outputs* when the rate of interest changes is such as to *increase* the ratio of $K(\xi, \lambda+\delta\lambda)$ to $K(\xi, \lambda)$. If $\delta\lambda$ is small, this ratio is approximately equal to $1+P(\delta\lambda/\lambda)$, where P is a measure which now depends upon the outputs and upon λ only. What has been shown is that a fall in the rate of interest (a rise in λ) has an effect on outputs which tends to increase this index P.

5. What is the meaning of this index? The best way of taking it, I now[1] suggest, is to regard it as an index of the average growth rate of the stream of outputs. So that *a fall in the rate of interest tends to increase the average growth rate of the stream of consumption outputs*. But this is a statement which needs justification.

If we calculate the value of P for a stream of infinite length and of constant growth rate γ, we find that $P = (1+\gamma)/(r-\gamma)$, an expression which (at constant r) evidently rises with γ. For the comparison of streams of this form, the truth of our proposition is at once established.

Usually, however (always, indeed, if there is a fixed supply of 'original factors') the streams which we should be comparing are not streams of constant growth rate. The average growth rate of such a stream remains to be defined. What I am saying is that there is a possible definition (it is a possible definition, since it gives the right meaning in the case of the constant growth rate, when average growth rate has an unambiguous meaning) which will make our proposition true. It is not surprising that we require to have a special definition to make the proposition true; one would not expect it to be true (any more than the rule about von Neumann optimality was true) for any definition of growth rate.

It is important to notice that the measurement of the average growth rate of a stream of consumption outputs is not the same problem as the measurement of the growth rate of a capital stock. In the latter case, we have only to look at the initial stock and at the terminal stock; all we have to determine is the 'annual' growth rate, which, when accumulated over the whole period, will account for the rise from one to the other. But in the case of a

---

[1] In *Value and Capital* (esp. pp. 184–8) I described it as the average period of the stream. But this was a reference to Böhm-Bawerk (though Schumpeter said it was 'not in Böhm-Bawerk's spirit') with which I do not now need to trouble the reader. I did, however, already observe that it had to do with growth rates—what I there called 'crescendo'.

consumption stream this will not do. We cannot measure from the consumption of the first period to that of the last; the first might have been abnormally low, the last abnormally high; a growth rate from one to the other might be quite unrepresentative. It is only possible to get an average growth rate for a flow magnitude of this kind if the whole of the flow is brought into the calculation. We must, that is, estimate some kind of a trend; it is the growth rate of the trend which we must take as the average growth rate of the flow magnitude over the whole period.

But to say that we must take a trend does not suffice to define the average growth rate completely; for trends can be estimated in different ways. In particular, there is a question of weighting. A regular way of fitting a trend would be to weight by undiscounted values; but there are at least two reasons why undiscounted values cannot here be appropriate. One is that the whole choice, that is here under consideration, runs in terms of discounted values; it is by discounting that the successive items are made comparable, one with another. Another is that we must have discounting, if changes in output in the far future (especially in the case of an infinite stream) are not to swamp everything else. It must therefore be concluded that the only kind of average growth rate, that can possibly be relevant to the present discussion, is a trend growth rate, with some sort of weighting by discounted values.

It is shown in Appendix D that straightforward calculation of a trend growth rate, weighted by discounted values, though it does not yield precisely the formula which is needed for our proposition, does yield something which is very similar. The difference between this trend formula and our formula is simply that in the trend formula the discounting that is taken is rather greater. When one allows for the ambiguity in the calculation of trend formulae, due to variability in weighting, it does not seem inappropriate to say that our formula is one possible trend formula. So that, for an appropriate sense of trend growth rate, the rule that a fall in the rate of interest tends to increase the trend growth rate does seem to hold.

6. But, after all, the reader may well be asking, why all this pother? That, at a lower rate of interest, there should be more investment (so that, with full employment, there should be less consumption in the present with more later on) is surely something that we knew already. What is the point of stating it in this complicated way?

There are, I think, two reasons. One is that it is useful, at least for certain purposes, to think of the whole production plan spread out through time, and not merely of the bit of it which comes into the present 'single period'. Effects on the whole stream (in terms of production-possibilities) are a matter on which it is useful to have knowledge. It is not merely the case that when (real) interest changes, present consumption should be diminished, in order that future consumption should be increased. With a *permanent* fall in interest (such as we are assuming) there should be a substitution of further for nearer outputs, all along the line. It may indeed happen (it is in practice very likely to happen) that present consumption output is so tied down by past production decisions that it can only be affected by interest changes (even by changes that are expected to be permanent) to quite a small extent. But this does not mean that the general effect of the interest change is correspondingly small. The substitution may still take effect when it can. Even if there is no substitution against present consumption output, there may still be a substitution against nearer, in favour of further, future outputs. This is covered, just as much as the other, by our rule about the effect on the growth rate.

It must of course be remembered that we are dealing with Optimum theory. That the optimum production plan will react in this way does not prove that actual production planning will react in the same manner. Actual planning has other things that affect it, in addition to the physical constraints, that are the only things here taken into account. It is affected by uncertainty about the future course of real interest (which is not only a matter of the future course of money interest rates, but of the future movement of prices). It is affected by the length of time that is taken to revise investment plans—to work out, and make arrangements for, the new plan, that has become the most profitable plan under the new conditions. Such 'frictions' are at least as important in practice (as a cause of lags) as the physical constraints that are set by past production. But even when these frictions are allowed for, our rule about the growth rate will continue to give the right impression.

7. The other way in which the rule is helpful concerns the second formulation with which I began this chapter. Even though it is laid down that after time T, the stream of consumption outputs that is planned for is to have a *given* growth rate, the rule will still hold. It will of course refer to the average growth rate over the whole period (before and after T); even if the growth rate after time T is fixed, the average can be raised, by a rise in the growth rate before time T. This is entirely consistent with what we have found by other methods.

The path which we are examining is an optimum path. After time T, when it has a given growth rate, it must be a growth equilibrium path, of the kind which we studied in Chapters XII–XIV. (It is not a von Neumann equilibrium, since the wage rate is not given.) The rules which we found about our former growth equilibrium will apply to it. The lower the rate of interest (or profit)[1] the higher will be the rate of real wages; a wage curve (of the form which we had in Chapter XIII, with variable technique) will be operating. It is almost inevitable that if the real wage is higher, consumption output will be higher; that is to say, the effect of the fall in interest, when we come to the growth equilibrium— though at that stage it cannot affect the growth rate—will be to raise the whole *level* of the path. In order to get to this higher level, at time T, there must be a faster growth up to time T. So that the characteristic effect of a fall in interest, in this case, is (1) to cause a drop in consumption output in the present or near future—there must be a drop in consumption somewhere, for resources are fully (and efficiently) employed, and there is to be a rise later on; (2) to cause a rise in the growth rate between time o and time T, (3) to cause a rise in the level of output after time T. The shift, in fact, is that which is represented by the move from the dotted to the continuous line on Fig. 10 (in which the logarithm of consumption output is measured on the vertical axis, in the manner with which we are familiar from Chapter XIX).

I have so far assumed that the time T, after which the system is to be in growth equilibrium, is given; but this is an assumption which we ought to be prepared to drop. When we are regarding the path to be determined as an approach to growth equilibrium, we should suppose that the growth equilibrium will be attained, not at an arbitrary date, but at the point when a capital has been

---

[1] It is immaterial, in growth equilibrium, what is the standard of value in terms of which the rate of interest is measured; for relative prices remain unchanged over time.

accumulated which is appropriate to the growth equilibrium of the system, whenever that is. It may come sooner, or later.

Suppose that the capital stock, at time 0, is such that the system is already in growth equilibrium, at the old (higher) rate of interest. When the rate of interest is reduced there must (in general) be

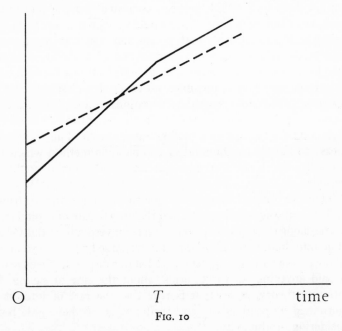

O   T   time

FIG. 10

a new growth equilibrium; but it will not be significantly different, in terms of the present theory, unless there is a change in technique from the one growth equilibrium path to the other.[1] The former capital stock will then have become inappropriate. It will take time for the capital to be transformed into a stock that is appropriate; during that time there should be a higher growth rate of consumption output, in the manner that has emerged from the present model. What we have in fact derived from the theory of this chapter, in this particular case, is an indication of the nature of the

---

[1] If there is no change in technique, the capital-labour ratio will be unaffected by the change in interest, so that the system can move into the new equilibrium at once. In terms of the present construction, the equilibrium is at a corner point of the production frontier, at which some change in interest is possible without a movement along the frontier being required. This is a limiting case, but it fits in.

optimum growth path (in the appropriate sense) during the Traverse.

8. There are doubtless other ways in which the theory of the intertemporal frontier could be developed, but I shall not do more than mention them here. We have been assuming that the rate of interest is constant over time; what would happen if it was variable? A shift from one variable path to another that was consistently lower would presumably work in much the same manner that has been described; but a uniform change such as this is by no means the only change that is possible. To cover the 'classical' case of a growth process that tended to a stationary state (in Ricardo's manner)—and this is one of the things that ought to be covered—we should have to introduce a falling rate of profit. This would not be easy to handle by the kind of comparative method which we have been following, but it is not impossible that it could be managed.

There are further interesting questions, about the distribution between wages and profits, and the growth rate of capital (and income) along the approach, which deserve investigation. But I shall not go into them here. They would in any case be better examined when we have a more complete model at our disposal. We have not yet said anything, in these terms, about the side of saving. In Optimum theory, at least, it is true that the rate of interest is determined by productivity and thrift; so far we have only been considering productivity.

Thus

XXI

OPTIMUM SAVING

1. If we are quantity-optimizing, any plan that is represented by a point on the production frontier is an optimum; but if we are utility-optimizing, only that point is optimum which maximizes utility. In terms of the conventional two-dimensional diagram, the utility optimum is that point on the frontier which lies on the highest of a set of indifference curves. Involved in this statement are (of course) all the troubles about distribution which have been made so familiar in Welfare Economics; but (as was explained in Chapter XVII) those matters will not be considered here. We shall suppose that a community indifference map is (somehow or other) definable: perhaps by a 'social welfare function' of Bergson's type, perhaps by the heroic assumptions that earning power is equally distributed, and that the indifference maps of all individuals (so far as they are concerned with intertemporal choices) are the same. A theory which is restricted in this manner should be no more than a first step; but there may be purposes for which it is sufficient. It serves, in any case, as a means of exploring the ground, of getting some preliminary acquaintance with things that ought to be discussed.

If we make no more than the usual 'diminishing marginal rate of substitution' assumption about the indifference map (or, to put the same assumption into a more modern form, if we merely assume that consumption plans *preferred or indifferent to* a given plan form a convex set),[1] there is really no more to be said about preference and utility than what will correspond to the central proposition of the preceding chapter. As between two indifferent positions, we can set up Samuelson inequalities. If the plan (ξ) is chosen at discount factor λ, and the plan $(\xi+\delta\lambda)$ at discount factor $\lambda+\delta\lambda$, and the two plans are on the same indifference level, we shall have

$$K(\xi, \lambda) < \text{ or } = K(\xi+\delta\xi, \lambda)$$

and

$$K(\xi+\delta\xi, \lambda+\delta\lambda) < \text{ or } = K(\xi, \lambda+\delta\lambda)$$

[1] See, for instance, Koopmans, *Three Essays* . . ., p. 26.

in just the same way as we have the corresponding inequalities in elementary demand theory.[1] If there is a non-zero substitution effect, both of these inequalities cannot be equations. If then we divide one by the other, as in the previous chapter, we find that the change in discount factor tends to cause a change in (ξ) which diminishes $K(\xi, \lambda+\delta\lambda)/K(\xi, \lambda)$, or $1+P(\delta\lambda/\lambda)$. Thus it is now a *rise* in the rate of interest (a fall in λ), which increases P. As between indifferent positions, a rise in the rate of interest tends to *increase* the trend growth rate of the stream of consumptions.

As we shall see later, there is quite a good deal to be made out of this proposition; but it must be accepted that it is a poor thing, on a first impression. It seems to tell us so very little. Consider its application to the comparison of growth equilibria. In growth equilibrium the growth rates of all elements are the same, and are constant over time; the trend growth rate may therefore be identified with the growth rate of the capital stock, the g of former chapters. For saving out of profits, we then have $g = sr$ (as is now familiar). If we suppose that this saving is determined by utility maximization, as here considered, the proposition before us merely states that g increases with r; but we cannot conclude from that that s (the saving/income ratio) increases with r. s may rise, or fall, or remain constant; the only thing that is ruled out is that s should fall so much (when r increases) that sr is diminished. And even this is only ruled out so long as we confine our attention to the substitution effect. There does not seem to be any reason why we should not have, on occasion, to include an 'income' effect, which would work an exception, even to our very weak proposition.

2. It must have been for some such reason as this (though of course they did not express it in our manner) that several writers on the theory of interest and saving (from Fisher and Ramsey[2] to Tinbergen and Frisch[3]) have sought to specify the utility function further. Are there any particular characteristics which we may assume for the utility function plausible enough to be reasonable in most (if not all) intertemporal utility problems, and strong enough to give more definite rules about behaviour? There is

[1] $K(\xi, \lambda)$ is the discounted value of the stream (ξ), as in the previous chapter.
[2] Irving Fisher, *Rate of Interest* (1907), *Theory of Interest* (1930); F. Ramsey, 'Mathematical Theory of Saving' (*Economic Journal*, 1928).
[3] J. Tinbergen, 'Optimum Savings' (*Econometrica*, 1960); R. Frisch, 'Dynamic Utility' (*Econometrica*, 1964).

a particular form of function, which has emerged from their work, and which is thought to satisfy these requirements. Certainly it does give a much stronger theory, if it is acceptable. It is tempting (and eminent economists, from Ramsey onwards, have succumbed to the temptation) to use it for making prescriptions about saving—for laying down rules of behaviour about saving, which (it is held) a rational community ought to follow. The belief that there are such rules (and that they have, at least, some degree of authority) has spread widely among economists; it is not without influence even on those who are unacquainted with the details of the Ramsey theory. The assumptions upon which the theory is based should therefore be given a close examination. I believe that I can show that they are in fact very fragile—much too fragile to stand the weight that has been put upon them.

For the simplest form of the theory, we need *three* special assumptions; it will be convenient to begin by setting it out on that basis. Not all of these assumptions, we shall subsequently find, are essential; but there is one that is essential—the whole theory collapses without it. And there is a quite simple reason why that assumption is very hard to accept. It is therefore not surprising (as we shall also find) that the theory itself has some odd features; not all of the consequences that must be drawn from it make as good sense as they should. But it will be best to let all these points appear as we proceed on the basis of the three assumptions.

(1) The first of the three assumptions is *stationariness* (as Koopmans[1] has called it). This 'stationariness', it must be emphasized, is a pure characteristic of the utility function; it has nothing (necessarily) to do with Stationary Equilibrium. What it means is that the (intertemporal) want-system remains unchanged over time; as time moves forward, the whole want-system moves forward with it. More precisely, the marginal rate of substitution, between consumption t_1 periods *hence* and consumption t_2 periods *hence*, remains the same at whatever date the choice between the two consumptions is made, provided that all the planned consumptions (dated so many periods *hence*) remain the same. Consumptions are valued according to their distance in time from the planning date, whatever the planning date may be. The stationariness assumption is that the system of wants is of this character, and that

[1] T. C. Koopmans, 'Stationary Ordinal Utility and Impatience' (*Econometrica*, 1960). As will be evident, I owe a great debt to this subtle paper.

the plan chosen is one that *continues* to maximize utility in terms of that want-system.

It is clearly by no means necessary, in a practical problem of planning, that this stationariness assumption should be valid. A simple case in which it would not be valid would occur with a plan which incorporated an extension of education, which will modify (and is expected to modify) the wants of the community as time goes on. But the existence of exceptions does not prevent the stationariness assumption from being an interesting assumption. It is not this assumption which I desire to criticize. What is the effect of assuming stationariness is one of the questions in this field to which we should certainly like an answer.

If the stationariness assumption (and nothing else) is incorporated into our analysis by Samuelson inequalities, we shall have to add to the inequalities (above written) which compare values discounted back to time 0, similar inequalities with values discounted back to each future date (only the consumptions subsequent to that date being included in each case). The plans will in fact have to be tested for indifference *all along the line*. Manipulating these in the same manner as before, we shall find that the substitution effect (of a rise in the rate of interest) must not only increase the trend growth rate of the whole stream

$$(\xi_0, \xi_1, \xi_2, \xi_3, \xi_4, \ldots);$$

it must also increase the trend growth rates of the remainder-streams

$$(\xi_1, \xi_2, \xi_3, \xi_4, \ldots)$$
$$(\xi_2, \xi_3, \xi_4, \ldots)$$

and so on. This is of course a stronger condition than that with which we started. But it does not, by itself, overcome the crucial weakness of the original proposition. For if we apply it, as before, to the comparison of constant growth paths, it tells us no more than the first pair of Samuelson inequalities did. If the paths under comparison are constant growth rate paths, the trend growth rates of the remainder streams will be the same as that of the original stream; so that if one condition is satisfied, all are satisfied. Taken by itself, the stationariness assumption gets us hardly any further.

(2) The second assumption to be introduced is *homogeneity*. What is meant by this is the same as what is meant by homogeneity in the case of the homogeneous production function—an increase

in consumptions (inputs) in the same proportion will increase utility (output) in a proportion that depends upon the utility (output) level, but is independent of the proportions in which the consumptions (inputs) are combined. (We have met this before, in the application to a utility function, when we were concerned with the definition of 'consumption in general'.[1]) Homogeneity of the utility function does not imply cardinality; it is a pure property of the indifference curves (or surfaces). Here, if (ξ) and (ξ') are two streams that are on the same indifference level, we are to get another pair of indifferent streams when we multiply every item in (ξ) and every item in (ξ') by any identical multiplier. It follows from this property that the marginal rate of substitution, between consumption at time t_1 and consumption at time t_2, is entirely determined by the *ratios* between consumptions at these and at other dates. Consequently, if the rate of interest (which plays the part of a price system) is given, the ratios between planned consumptions (at different dates) will be determined, irrespective of the general level of consumption that is attainable over the whole sequence. So long as the rate of interest remains unchanged, an increase in total wealth will increase planned consumption, in all periods, in the same proportion.

In itself, this homogeneity assumption looks harmless; it amounts to no more than a bracketing together of 'income' and substitution effect; the 'income effect' is made manageable by being reduced to the simplest form that it can possibly take. But when this assumption is combined with the stationariness assumption, the result is drastic.

If the want-system is stationary, and is also homogeneous, the only type of consumption plan that can be optimal, at a constant rate of interest, is a plan with a constant growth rate. For if

$$(\xi_0, \xi_1, \xi_2, \ldots)$$

the optimum plan at time o, and

$$(\xi_1, \xi_2, \ldots)$$

the optimum plan at time 1, are plans that maximize utility under the same want-system (stationariness), the only difference between them (when the rate of interest is constant) must be such as arise from the change in capital value, due to saving that has

---

[1] See above, Chapter XIII, p. 157.

occurred (or that may have occurred) in the period o to 1. If such a change in capital value changes all consumptions in the same proportion (homogeneity), it will follow at once that

$$\xi_1/\xi_0 = \xi_2/\xi_1 = \xi_3/\xi_2 = \ldots$$

so that the growth rate of consumption must be constant, from period to period. Only a constant growth rate plan can be chosen (at constant rate of interest) if there is stationariness and there is also homogeneity.

There is certainly no question that this is a convenient property; and to reach it in this way may perhaps persuade us to adopt it with a lighter heart. But even if we do accept it, it does not, in itself, give us any help in dealing with the problem with which we began. For it was precisely in relation to constant growth rate paths that our original difficulty came up most sharply. All that can be said, even when we have both of these first two assumptions, is that a rise in the rate of interest will tend to increase the growth rate of the optimum path—our former proposition, only made a little more precise, since we need no longer talk about 'trends' and have absorbed the old reservation about income effects. But the effect on the proportion of income saved remains as obscure as ever.

(3) The third assumption is that of *independence*. This is the point at which we go over to Cardinal Utility; but it is not the cardinality that is important—it is the independence which is taken to go with it. A general assumption of cardinality would itself impose no additional restriction; but there is an additional restriction when the cardinal utility function is assumed to take the particular form of a sum of *separated* utilities

$$U_0(\xi_0) + U_1(\xi_1) + U_2(\xi_2) + \ldots$$

so that the marginal utility of consumption in each single period is taken to depend upon consumption in that particular single period *only*. A cardinal measure of that particular form does imply an ordinal property: the marginal rate of substitution between consumption at time t_1 and consumption at time t_2 (being the ratio between the marginal utilities of these consumptions) is made to depend upon these two consumptions only; consumptions at other dates do not affect it. If we have that ordinal property, it must be possible to put the utility function (if we choose to do so) into the form which has just been given;[1] if we can have the separated form, we must have the ordinal property. The two are strictly equivalent.

It is independence (in this sense) which, when added to the other assumptions, works the transformation. The consequences of the combination are very far-reaching indeed.

3. Take homogeneity and independence together. Homogeneity says that all consumptions are to increase in the same proportion when there is a change in capital value (and no change in interest); independence says that the marginal utilities of the consumptions (which are to keep the same proportions to one another since there is no change in interest) are each of them dependent upon its own consumption only. These things can only happen together if all of the (separated) marginal utility curves have the same elasticity; and since we might have started from any combination of consumptions, they must have the same elasticities at all points of the curves, which can only happen if each curve is a curve of constant elasticity—the same constant elasticity for each separated curve. Thus the marginal utility of consumption at time t must be given by the formula

$$q_t \, \xi_t^{-(1/\eta)}$$

where η is the (common) constant elasticity, and q_t is a constant, that may vary from one curve to another.

At an optimum position, this is to be proportional to the discount factor, which we have been writing as λ^t. In this case, however, it is neater to work with continuous time. Let us accordingly write the discount factor as e^{-rt}, where r is (now) an *instantaneous* rate of interest. It follows at once that ξ_t must be proportional to

$$q_t^{\eta} e^{\eta rt}.$$

We must have a consumption path (at the optimum) such as can be represented by this formula, if there is to be homogeneity and also independence.

If there is also to be stationariness, the path must be a constant growth path; and this formula will only give a constant growth

---

[1] That the correspondence works both ways is becoming familiar through the use that is being made of the independence assumption in other connexions, by such writers as R. H. Strotz, 'The Utility Tree' (*Econometrica*, 1957), and I. F. Pearce, *A Contribution to Demand Analysis* (1964). A proof is, however, given in the Appendix to this chapter.

path if q_t itself has a constant rate of growth (or decline) over time. Now the q's are the weights that are given to future utilities to make them comparable with present; it follows from the stationariness assumption that these weights can only differ because of delay (as t increases). It is commonly accepted that the delay will diminish the (present) utility of future consumptions; let us grant that (at least provisionally). We may therefore write $q_t = Ce^{-pt}$, where p is to be constant (the rate of time-preference). Finally, therefore, we have

$$\xi_t = C^\eta e^{\eta(r-p)t}$$

so that the growth rate of the consumption stream emerges as

$$g = \eta(r-p),$$

an elegant formula which (it appears) is due to Champernowne.[1] In so far as this formula is acceptable, it is undoubtedly more informative than the bare rule that the growth rate rises with the rate of interest, with which we started.

But is it acceptable? Let us begin by noticing some of its implications.

4. The familiar $g = sr$ is still valid (along a constant growth path) even though we are using instantaneous rates.[2] Thus, for the proportion of income saved, we have (from the Champernowne formula)

$$s = \eta\left(1 - \frac{p}{r}\right)$$

from which there immediately follow the Ramsey properties: (1) that if there is no time-preference ($p = 0$) we have $s = \eta$, so that the proportion of income saved is independent of the rate of interest; (2) if p is positive, there will be zero saving when $r = p$, while if $r > p$, the saving-proportion will be larger, the larger r, up to a maximum at $s = \eta$, as before. These are quite sharp conclusions; but they are odd conclusions. The more one reflects upon them, the odder they seem.

[1] According to D. H. Robertson, *Lectures on Economic Principles*, vol. ii, p. 79. It is unnecessary, on a constant growth path, to distinguish between g and γ.

[2] See Appendix D. It will be remembered that we are not distinguishing between profits and wages; capital value is the discounted value of the whole stream of consumptions; income is the interest on this capital value.

It must surely be supposed that consumption must always be positive; $s < 1$. But it has just been shown that if $p = 0$, $s = \eta$; so that the model will only make sense, when $p = 0$, if $\eta < 1$; the marginal utility curves must be *inelastic*. If $p > 0$, we can have $s < 1$, with $\eta > 1$, if the rate of interest is not too high; but we shall find consumption going negative at high rates of interest. This is intolerable; it must therefore be concluded (and has been concluded in fact by Ramsey and his followers) that we must take $\eta < 1$. But there is no intuitive reason why the marginal utility curves should be inelastic; it is odd[1] that we should have to make them inelastic in order to make sense of the theory.

It further follows that if the marginal utility curves are inelastic, the total utility function (for the individual dated consumption) must be such that there is a limit beyond which utility cannot rise however much consumption increases; utility cannot increase indefinitely. Ramsey's 'Bliss' is an essential character of the model; the whole construction depends upon it. But (again) it is not obvious intuitively why the utility function must have this property.

There is a final point, which was not noticed by Ramsey.[2] If the utility function, $U_t(\xi_t)$, for the individual dated consumption must have this form, the utility of the whole stream, which is the sum of $U_t(\xi_t)$ from $t = 0$ to $t = $ infinity, will not be finite unless $p > 0$. But it is the total utility, in the sense of this sum, which is being maximized. One cannot maximize something which is infinite. So that unless $p > 0$, the whole construction breaks down.

Thus it is not fair to proceed as Ramsey did, to treat zero time-preference as a criterion for rationality, and to pour scorn upon the weakness of our telescopic vision which makes us unwilling to save at the high rates which (it is alleged) would be appropriate for $p = 0$. If there is no time-preference, then (on the theory) it is necessary that the curves should be inelastic; but if the curves are inelastic, it is impossible that $p = 0$.

5. What has happened? We must go back to the assumptions, and look at them again. One which is clearly weak is homogeneity. Can we drop that, and get something that is more acceptable?

---

[1] As Tinbergen has noticed (op. cit.).

[2] I owe it to the paper by Koopmans, where it is established in much more general terms.

If we drop homogeneity, but maintain stationariness, we shall drop the constant growth path. But perhaps it is that which ought to be abandoned.

If we drop homogeneity, but maintain independence, we are not tied down to a particular utility function; we can give the marginal utility curves another form. Quite general forms are hard to handle; but there is one (which was considered by Ramsey) which is quite simple, and which is surely an improvement. This would make the marginal utility of consumption become infinite, not at zero consumption, but at some positive 'subsistence' level. We can then keep something like the 'constant elasticity' form, but shift the whole curve to the right. That is to say, for the marginal utility of consumption at time t, we should have

$$q_t(\xi_t - A)^{-(1/\eta)}$$

which would give
$$\xi_t = A + Ce^{\eta(r-p)t}$$

if we stick to the constant rate of time-preference. The result is thus that it is not consumption as a whole, but the excess of consumption over subsistence, which has the constant growth rate, the rate that is given by the Champernowne formula.

It will be shown in Appendix D that if g is this growth rate, the proportion of income saved (at time t) is given by

$$\frac{s_t}{1 - s_t} = \frac{g}{r - g}\left(1 - \frac{A}{\xi_t}\right).$$

If (as we may suppose) consumption rises with time, this gives the proportion of income saved rising with time, being low when consumption (and therefore income) is low, but rising towards a limit, which is the same limit as was expressed by the former formula

$$s = (g/r) = \eta\left(1 - \frac{p}{r}\right).$$

Thus if we begin with a level of income that is near subsistence, there is no difficulty in admitting low rates of saving; but the same difficulties (essentially the same difficulties as before) emerge at high levels of income. An amendment of this kind does not seem to be much help; and it looks probable that the same sort of thing would happen if we changed over to any other plausible marginal utility function.

6. What then of independence? It is more and more apparent that it is independence that is the key assumption. As long as we maintain independence we are bound to get something like the Ramsey results; but what is the case for the independence assumption? As soon as we face up to it, and consider (quite directly) what it implies, it becomes apparent that the case for making it is very weak indeed.

If the successive consumptions (ξ_t) have independent utilities, the amount of present consumption which the chooser will be willing to give up, in order to be able to increase consumption in year 5 from so much to so much, will be independent of the consumptions that are planned for years 4 and 6. It will be just the same, whether the increase in year 5 is to be a sudden spurt, out of line with its neighbours; or if it is needed to fill a gap, to make up a deficiency (that would otherwise have occurred in year 5), so raising the consumption of year 5 up to the common level. This is what is implied by the independence assumption; when it is stated in those terms, surely it must be said that it cannot be accepted. The sacrifice which one would be willing to make to fill a gap must normally be much greater than what it would be worth while to incur for a mere extra. There is indeed a sense in which there is a rapidly falling 'marginal utility of consumption' in the particular period. But it is not due to the inelasticity of an independent 'marginal utility curve'; it is due to the complementarity between the consumption that is planned for the particular period and that which is planned for its neighbours. It is nonsense to assume that successive consumptions are independent; the normal condition is that there is a strong complementarity between them.

It is not to be denied that there are some kinds of saving which are directed towards particular future expenditures, so that the complementarity with neighbouring consumptions may for them be rather weak. But the clearest case of this is saving for a particular event (as for one's own old age, or for the marriage of one's children); and though there may be independence in these instances, it is abundantly clear that with them the stationariness assumption will not hold. Even with them we do not have independence and stationariness. Other sorts of saving-up, as for the purchase of durable consumer-goods (in the days before consumer credit) are not, I think, exceptions to the rule of complementarity.

Any saving which is not just saving-up—saving which is a pure exchange of present for future satisfactions, satisfactions that are not inherently different save that the one is present and the other is future—must, because of the complementarity, take the form of the substitution, for the present consumption, of some sort of a *flow* of consumption in the future. This is, surely, how it appears to the ordinary man; this is why what is offered to him (nearly always) is interest, or dividend, or annuity, on his savings. The institutional arrangements are a practical recognition of the complementarity that is in question. Saving of this kind (and it is the only kind for which the stationariness assumption is appropriate) cannot be adequately analysed by considering the present and *one particular future date* in isolation.

What are being compared are present sacrifice, and *flow* of future satisfaction. If the complementarity is perfect, so that the time-shape of the future consumption-flow is taken as fixed (and this, though an extreme assumption, is a better assumption than the assumption of independence), we can treat the planned future consumption as a single good, and represent the whole choice on a two-dimensional diagram. But it is then a choice between sharply different things: once-for-all consumption in the present period, and a stream of consumption extending into the indefinite future. Nothing more can be laid down about such a choice than we are accustomed to say about the choice between any two commodities (or commodity bundles). The supply curve of saving against the rate of interest may be rising from left to right or may turn back on itself (but for nothing more than the usual Walrasian reason).

When we particularize, splitting up the stream of consumptions into particular dated items, we do not change the situation fundamentally, once we allow for the complementarity. But there can be as much complementarity as is possible, and the Samuelson inequalities will still hold. Thus we come back to the rule about a rise in the rate of interest increasing the trend growth rate—the 'poor thing' with which we started.

7. I should like to emphasize, in conclusion, that we get no further than this by assuming 'rationality'. If the question is simply one of the choice between two 'commodities', it is equally rational to give a high value, or a low value, to one in terms of the other. The only thing that is irrational is to act in such a way as must result in future damage, and to leave it out of calculation. Thus it is

ordinarily irrational to 'waste one's substance'—to indulge in a high rate of current consumption, which must be followed, at some point, by a fall to a much lower level. Violent contractions are exceedingly painful, and it is foolish to expose oneself to such pain by lack of foresight. But as for the amount which should be sacrificed now in order to bring about a rise in the future *stream*— that is a matter on which wisdom may have more than one opinion.

XXII

INTEREST AND GROWTH

1. I T is strongly suggested, both by the positive and the negative results which have emerged in the last two chapters, that the key relation of intertemporal Optimum theory is a relation between the rate of interest and the rate of growth. This will not surprise us, after what we learned when we were solely concerned with the comparison of growth equilibria; for it was already the case in that equilibrium theory that the rate of profit (r) and the rate of growth (g) were occupying a similar position. Comparative equilibrium analysis can itself be regarded (from one angle) as a part of Optimum theory. When it is so regarded, we do not have to make a distinction between interest rate and profit rate; they are one and the same thing.[1] In the comparative theory, in the important case where all saving was 'out of profits', the saving equation $g = sr$ established a link which tied quantities (dependent on g) and prices (dependent on r) together. 'Saving out of wages' made things more complicated, so that when we took it seriously (as we did in Chapter XV), the factor-share ratio had to be introduced as a third key variable. But when, as seems appropriate in Optimum theory, we treat capital value as the capitalized value of the *whole* expected stream of consumptions, we are averting our eyes from the distinction between profits and wages; wages appear as interest on the 'capitalized value of labour', so that $g = sr$ becomes a valid equation for saving out of income as a whole. If then the rate of profit were given (as it could still be given in a model where the supply of original factors was perfectly elastic), the equilibrium rate of growth will be higher, the higher the propensity to save. But if the rate of growth is given (as it may be in a model where the rate of growth of an essential factor is given autonomously) it will be the equilibrium (real) rate of profit that will be lower, the higher is the propensity to save. But these are rules that refer to the comparative analysis of growth equilibrium,

$g = sr$
$s = 1$
$g = r$

[1] As soon as we cease to concern ourselves with Optimum theory (as in Chapter XVI, or as we shall do in Chapter XXIII) the distinction between interest and profit becomes of course of vital importance.

and to that only; outside Growth Equilibrium (and in any practical problem we are always outside Growth Equilibrium) the position is less simple.

When we are comparing optimum paths which do not have to be constant growth paths, we are left with the principles which have emerged from our studies of the intertemporal production frontier, and of intertemporal utility, in Chapters XX and XXI. These were summed up in the rules: (1) that on the productivity side, a rise in the (real) rate of interest tends to diminish the *trend* growth rate of the consumption flow; and (2) that on the side of saving, a rise in the rate of interest tends to increase this same *trend* growth rate. These rules are not (of course) inconsistent, any more than the contrary slopes of supply and demand curves are inconsistent. They are properties of two *curves*, one for productivity and one for 'thrift', which are related in much the same way as demand and supply curves are related. What remains to be said, in the field of Optimum theory, can be summed up on a diagram, in terms of these two curves.

The place of these curves in the intertemporal theory is indeed much the same as that of 'macro' supply and demand curves in static theory. When static Optimum theory is set out fully, it has to be expressed in the Paretian terms of 'tastes' and 'obstacles'— the maximization of a utility function against constraints; but we are accustomed to summarize, for particular purposes, by reductions such as the reduction to demand and supply for labour in general (even though the 'price' of that labour, its real wage, can only be defined, very roughly, in index-number terms). The static optimum is reached when the demand price for labour (its marginal product) equals its supply price (the real wage at which that quantity of labour will be supplied). Or we may put the same relation the other way up (as Keynes did)—supply and demand for 'output in general'. The relation between interest rate and growth rate is of the same character. If it is complained that our trend growth rate is elusive and ambiguous, one may reply that its chief ambiguity is just the same index-number ambiguity that afflicts all (or nearly all) macro-economic magnitudes.

2. Let us then try to draw the diagram (Fig. 11). It will, I think, be more natural to put r (since r belongs to the price-system) on the vertical axis, and γ (which belongs to the system of quantities) on

the horizontal. There must (by our rules) be a productivity curve which we shall expect to be downward-sloping, and a saving curve that is upward-sloping. Can we specify further? Not much, but there are a few things that can be said.

One is that the whole operative part of the diagram must lie to the left of the 45° line ($r = \gamma$). That, in growth equilibrium,

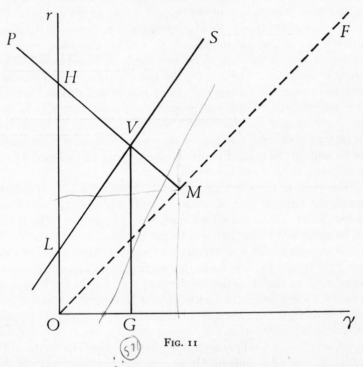

FIG. 11

$g = s r$

we cannot have $g > r$ is by now familiar; if it were, consumption (all consumption, on the present interpretation, not merely consumption out of profits) would be negative. That the same rule must hold, even out of growth equilibrium, is less obvious—though not surprising. In fact, it must hold, if the rate of interest is to perform its function of facilitating the selection of an optimum position; for if $\gamma > r$, or indeed if $\gamma = r$, the capitalized value of the stream of consumptions will not be finite. We must therefore conclude that always $r > \gamma$.

Both of the curves must therefore lie on that part of the diagram which is to the left of the 45° line (*OF*). So far as the (upward-sloping) saving curve is concerned, this does not appear (at first sight) to be of much significance; it is easy enough for this curve to keep within the permissible sector. But the productivity curve will meet *OF* at some point such as *M*; we must draw it cut off short at that point. What does *M* signify? The γ-coordinate of *M* (which is of course equal to the *r*-coordinate) represents the maximum consumption growth rate that is attainable under the constraints—that is to say, with the given technology, given initial equipment, and given flow of labour supply (varying, perhaps, over time, but varying in a given manner). That there should be such a maximum will now be expected. But it is not of negligible importance (what now appears) that this same maximum growth rate sets a minimum to the rate of interest that is consistent with optimality. So long as there is to be positive growth, no amount of saving can make the (optimum) rate of interest (or profit) fall to zero.

Is there any similar minimum on the side of saving? If we held to the Ramsey theory, we should say that the saving curve would cut the vertical axis at a point $r = p$ (*p* the rate of time-preference). If the rate of interest fell below that level there would be decumulation (negative growth). But we have seen reason not to put faith in that theory, so that we cannot subscribe to its reason for putting *L* above *O*. It does nevertheless appear that that is the right place to put it. For either *L* lies above *O*, or it coincides with *O*, or the saving curve meets *OF* in the positive quadrant. But this last possibility is hardly serious, since it would mean that at some *low* level of interest the *desire* to consume would become zero; so we may take it that either *L* lies above *O*, or coincides with it. The latter possibility is not excluded, but it would seem that to put *L* above *O* is the more general case.

Even if this is correct, *L* does not set a minimum to the rate of interest in the way that *M* does. The minimum that is set by *M* is a true minimum; there can be no optimum path at a lower rate of interest. But since we are not now confining attention to equilibrium paths, and are treating the intertemporal utility function of the community as something given, it is not excluded that there might be an optimum at negative growth—as might happen (on the Ramsey theory) if there was a very high rate of time-preference, so that the whole saving curve of our diagram was raised bodily, putting L above H. This is a possibility from which we shall usually avert our eyes, but theoretically it ought to be included. I have therefore drawn both curves extended to the left of the vertical axis, for an interesection to the left of that axis should be left as a possibility.

Normally, however, we should expect that there would be an intersection to the right of the axis (at a point V, as drawn). The optimum rate of interest and the optimum rate of growth (starting from the given initial equipment) would be determined by the coordinates of this point of intersection.

3. Let us now make an attempt to rework, in terms of this diagram, the analysis of a movement to equilibrium, such as we have already contemplated at the end of Chapter XX. It is too much to hope that the whole of that complicated story can be clearly set out in terms of the variables that are represented on such a diagram; the most that can be expected is that it will shed a certain amount of light upon the matter.

It is clearly possible, in the first place, that our optimum V might be a position of Full Growth Equilibrium; but for that to happen quite a number of conditions would be necessary. The optimum rate of growth (OG) would have to equal the natural growth rate of the economy (set, let us say as before, by the natural rate of increase of the labour force). The rate of interest (or profit) VG would have to be such as would call forth a rate of saving sufficient to support that rate of growth (V would have to lie on the saving curve). To that profit rate there would correspond an equilibrium technique; the capital stock of the economy would have to be of such a size, and of such a composition, as would employ the initial labour force at this equilibrium technique, and at the growth rate OG. If all of these conditions were satisfied, V would be an optimum point, and it would be a point of 'full growth equilibrium'.

Now suppose that we do have an initial capital of exactly this description, fitting the initial labour force with a growth rate OG and interest rate VG, but that the propensity to save is greater than that shown by SV—the saving curve is shifted to the right. This would have the kind of effect that was attributed to a fall in the rate of interest in our previous discussion. The optimum point would be moved downward along the productivity curve, to a point such as V' (Fig. 12). At V' the trend rate of growth is greater than the equilibrium rate of growth; but that (as we saw) is as it should be. For technique is being shifted in a more productive direction (in the sense of facilitating an ultimately higher level of consumption output); and during that shift the trend rate of growth must increase. There is certainly no reason why the rate of growth *in this sense* should be restricted to the equilibrium rate.

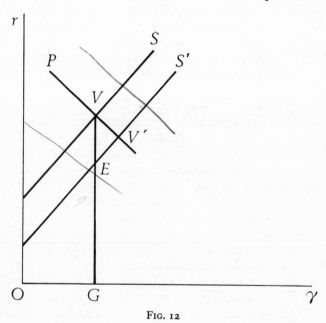

FIG. 12

In a process of adjustment, such as this, the trend rate would clearly rise above its equilibrium level.

This, however (again in terms of our previous analysis), will be only a passing phase; as time goes on the growth rate (in the sense of trend growth rate) must fall back to the equilibrium rate. This looks as if it should be represented on the diagram by a fall in the productivity curve, moving V' backwards along the (new) saving curve until it reaches a new equilibrium at E. I do not in fact doubt that a construction of this kind gives the right impression. It will, however, be noticed that between V' and E there would be a fall in the rate of interest. But our productivity curve (and also our saving curve) have been constructed on the supposition that the rate of interest is to remain constant over time. If V' is to be an optimum position, it should be constructed on the assumption of a movement of interest, such as is required along its optimum path; and here it is clear that it is falling interest, towards the rate at the 'ultimate' optimum E, which should be implied. Some correction on the position of V' ought in strictness to be required to allow for this. Yet it does not appear that it would invalidate the general impression that we get from the diagram. As a result of the shift in the saving curve, there would be a temporary rise in the growth rate above its equilibrium level; while the rate of interest would fall to its new equilibrium level, not immediately, but by degrees, as the process of adjustment worked itself out.

4. Let us now shift our viewpoint, and look at the same story from another angle. In the process of adjustment there has been a movement along the saving curve (from V' to E); there was a need for this movement, in the story as we have told it, because the initial capital (on which the productivity curve through V' was based) was appropriate to the (old) higher rate of interest VG, not to the (new) equilibrium rate EG. This, however, was a piece of scaffolding, which should now be taken down. More in general, the optimum path of the economy will differ from an equilibrium path because the initial stock is inappropriate—for one reason or another; the particular reason which was given as an exercise in the last section was not particularly plausible, and should henceforth be disregarded. Whatever the reason for the inappropriateness, there should be a movement to equilibrium, such as is (roughly) represented by the movement from V' to E along the saving curve (supposing that that curve, which is independent of the initial equipment, may be taken as given). A 'disequilibrium' optimum, in which both r and γ have values greater than their equilibrium values, may occur for all sorts of reasons.

But when we generalize in this way the question naturally arises: is there any reason why the disequilibrium position should always lie to the right of the equilibrium position, as I have drawn it? Is a movement to equilibrium, from a disequilibrium that lies to the left of E on the saving curve, ruled out? I do not think that it is ruled out; but there is a reason for thinking that it is very much less likely than a movement from the other side.

As I have repeatedly insisted, the chief reason, in practice, why the initial capital (from which the optimum path must set out) should not be of equilibrium composition is that technology is continually changing. The capital stock of the economy, as it exists at any particular time, has been built up in past technical conditions; it was constructed to meet the needs of a technology which is not that for which it has now to be used. Every change in technology displaces the production frontier (of a *given* capital stock); every gain in technical knowledge displaces it *outwards*. Every such displacement displaces the productivity curve that is derived from that frontier; but the fact of an outward displacement does not necessarily mean that the productivity curve is moved in any definite manner. There is, however, a strong presumption that the displacement of the frontier will have a bigger effect on further future outputs than upon outputs of the present or nearer future— merely because it takes time to put knowledge to use, and to incorporate it in the durable instruments which will usually be required if it is to be used effectively. It may not be universally necessary that technical advance should take this form; but we can hardly go wrong if we take it that it is this form which is dominant. The characteristic effect of technical progress must then be to raise the trend growth rate that is optimal, at a given rate of interest, starting from a given capital stock. That is to say, the effect of technical progress is to shift the productivity curve (in the sense that we are using it in this chapter) to the *right*.

5. These diagrams that we are using are horribly simplified; but they are (I think) beginning to make sense. We have to think of technical progress as a force that is continually pushing the optimal point to the right along the saving curve; while sheer lapse of time, with the opportunity which it gives for adjustment to past technical progress, is responsible for a movement that is always tending towards the equilibrium point. It is at once apparent why it is that optimum positions to the left of the equilibrium point are not very likely. For at any such point, both of these two forces would be working in the same direction; thus if (by chance) such an optimum did come about, it could hardly persist for long. But to the right of equilibrium the forces are working in opposite directions; it is therefore conceivable that they may balance one another. But it is better (I think) to say that to the right of equilibrium there will be some movements one way, some movements the other; so that *on the average* we shall expect to find the optimum point to the right of E, with optimum growth rate and optimum rate of interest above their equilibrium values.

This is the general conclusion to which we seem to come. It makes a simple and not unfamiliar picture, in spite of all the assumptions and qualifications which we have had to make on the road by which we have reached it. How does it square with what other economists have said, and with what we ourselves have been saying in other places?

(1) It may first be observed that it fits quite nicely with the Ricardian model, and with the 'classical' and 'neo-classical' models that later economists have built upon Ricardo's. The original Ricardian model, which was discussed in Chapter IV of this book, is just a special case of the present construction.

For Ricardo, the scarcity of land was *the* limiting factor. Land was essential, and was fixed in supply; so that the only possible growth equilibrium, with given technology, was the stationary state ($g = 0$). In the absence of technical progress this would be the equilibrium to which the system would tend. Thus (for Ricardo) the E of our diagram is on the vertical axis; its vertical coordinate is the *minimum rate of profit*, at which there is no incentive to accumulate or to decumulate. The actual position (not clearly distinguished, as we have been trying to distinguish it, as the *optimum* position for an actual situation) would have a higher rate of profit, and a positive (therefore higher than equilibrium) growth rate. There would be a tendency to stationariness (corresponding to our tendency to equilibrium) unless it was offset by improvements. This is Ricardo's theory; our present construction (it is now evident) is simply a generalization of it.

(2) Let us next consider the relation of our present model to the von Neumann model; this, at first sight, is a more mysterious matter. In so many respects the two appear to be opposite. For us (as for Ricardo) 'disequilibrium' growth rate and profit rate are above their equilibrium counterparts; for von Neumann (and for the Turnpikers) they are below. And it is the imperfect adjustment of the capital stock, to that which is required along the equilibrium path, which *in each case* causes the discrepancy. Only for the one theory it goes one way, in the other way in the other theory. What is the explanation?

It is, I think, twofold. The less important reason is that the von Neumann system has no limitational factor with a growth rate that is given exogenously. Everything is reproducible; the maximum growth rate is entirely determined by the technology. When that maximum rate is achieved, it can continue indefinitely (by constant returns to scale). The von Neumann model (as I have said before) belongs to the school of Adam Smith, not to that of Ricardo. But this, by itself, would not suffice to work the difference.

The more important reason is the difference in objective. If (as in von Neumann's case) it is the terminal stock, at the end of the process, which is the sole criterion of optimality, it will follow that in order to attain an optimum, the average growth rate over the whole process must be as great as possible. If the maximum growth rate—which has been made to exist—is attainable; if the initial capital is such that it is attainable; then that is the growth rate which must be achieved along the optimum path. If the initial capital is such that the top growth rate is not attainable, the optimum path must be a path which comes as near to it as it possibly can.

In the alternative theory, the objective is to maximize the 'utility' of the consumption flow; this does *not* imply maximizing the growth rate. (It may well be that this reminder that maximizing growth rate is not a sensible economic objective is the most important thing that is rubbed in by all our theorizing!) If there is a ceiling to the consumption output that is attainable in any period, and the ceiling is attainable, 'utility' will be maximized by attaining it. Utility will not be maximized by starting at a lower level, and working up to the ceiling—just in order to have a higher growth rate in the process of getting there! If one is obliged, by initial endowment, to start at a low level, and work up to the 'long run' ceiling gradually, one will have a higher growth rate; but it is *less good* to have to do that than to be on the ceiling all the time. The economic problems of reality are much more nearly of the latter character than they are like von Neumann's. While we may analyse them (if we choose) in terms of growth rates, we get them the wrong way up if we set the maximizing of growth rate as the objective to be attained.

(3) There is a more subtle distinction, which plays an important part in substantial differences among contemporary economists, on which our present construction appears to throw some light.

I have been very careful, from the beginning of the more

constructive Part II of this book, to work with concepts that were defined with reference to a *given* technology. Our original growth equilibrium was so defined; the von Neumann equilibrium was so defined; the intertemporal production frontier, on which these last three chapters have been based, was so defined. There have been several places where we have taken account of technical progress; but we have always brought it in from outside, as an exogenous change in data. Whatever one thinks of the importance of technical progress—and I am not in the least concerned to deny that it is of overwhelming importance, in modern conditions—the treatment of it in this way is, I am convinced, the right way of *arranging* the theory. One must arrange it in this way if one is to keep a sense of the identity of physical capital goods: goods that have been made for a purpose, and are being used for a purpose; goods that if their purpose disappears, may become valueless. I think I may claim that what has been done since Chapter XII is a justification of the decision to arrange things in this way; if we had not done so we could not have brought the different approaches, whose relations we have been exploring, into relation with one another.

It is nevertheless very tempting, when one is thinking in terms of macro-economic aggregates (but only when one is thinking in terms of such aggregates), to proceed otherwise. The constructions of the present chapter (which, as explained, are in substance macro-economic constructions) illustrate how this is.

If the 'actual' position V' (reverting to Fig. 12) is normally kept to the right of the equilibrium E by the force of technical progress—being further to the right when technical progress is strong, nearer to E when it is weak—would we not do better to redefine our *equilibrium*, so that we could have it as a *normal* state of the economy, instead of being kept, as it is on our construction, out at an extremity, only to be approached in quite exceptional conditions? This, I think, is what Mr. Kaldor has been trying to do in some of his papers;[1] and one sees the point of it. It is more convenient to base one's discussion upon a norm, from which variations take place each way. But can one regard that norm as an *equilibrium*?

In order that it should be correct to treat it as an equilibrium, one must suppose that technical progress occurs in response to economic forces: that if it is going 'too fast' or 'too slow', there are

[1] Such as 'A Model of Economic Growth' (in *Essays in Stability and Growth*).

forces (within the economic system—or price mechanism) which tend to bring it back to its equilibrium intensity. Such are the forces which are supposed to operate in Mr. Kaldor's 'technical progress function'. I would not myself deny that there are such forces, and that they do account for a part of the phenomenon of technical progress. I may indeed claim that I have long been willing to recognize their existence; they figure in my *Theory of Wages* (1932) as 'induced inventions'. It would perhaps be possible, if all technical progress was of the 'induced invention' type, to reckon the possibilities of such progress into the production frontier; for it is not to be supposed that all the techniques, that we reckon as belonging to the *current* technology, are written down in books, waiting to be taken from the shelves when the time comes for them to be used. On this interpretation, with the induced inventions brought inside the technology, and with no other kind of technical progress admitted, the 'norm' that has just been described would be identified with a growth equilibrium; there would be no distinction between V' and E; the economy would be in Growth Equilibrium all the time. This is indeed the picture which one does seem to get from some of Mr. Kaldor's writings. I reject it myself because I am unconvinced that the whole (or even a sufficiently large part) of the phenomenon of technical progress can be dealt with in that way.

Surely there is another part, which comes from non-economic causes, or which is dominated by non-economic causes, chiefly by the advancement of science. One scientific discovery leads to another: one leads to another for scientific reasons that have nothing to do with economic applications. Economic incentives do indeed determine what parts of the scientific corpus are developed for use in economic production; but the growth of the corpus, from which the economic opportunities are selected, is only to a limited extent an economic matter. The new opportunities, which result from scientific advance, may sometimes be large and abundant, sometimes much less abundant. Thus from the economic point of view there is in technical advance a random element; though (as is often maintained) this random element may be becoming less important, surely it is always there. Even a random element may show statistical uniformities; but the time which is taken for such uniformities to reveal themselves may be very long. Thus, even if it has a norm, our 'actual' V' may fluctuate markedly about it; and it is hard to make sense of history unless one supposes that such fluctuations occur. At the very least, it seems wise to leave the door open so that one can deal with that possibility. That is why I prefer a model of the kind that we have been constructing to one which would bring too much of the phenomenon into the strait-jacket of its 'equilibrium'.

PART IV

AFTER GROWTH THEORY

XXIII

KEYNES AFTER GROWTH THEORY[1]

1. MAJOR questions still lie ahead; but they will have to be treated in rather a perfunctory manner. If they were to be treated on the scale which they deserve, they would need (at least) another volume; and I do not know that it is a volume that I should be capable of writing. As it is, I shall do no more than peer a little into these further regions.

One of the questions on which the work we have been doing ought to throw light is the monetary question; I shall say what I now have to say about this in the present chapter. I shall not go into it deeply; I shall say no more than is necessary for the making of one distinction, which I think to be of central importance. It is the distinction which we owe (in substance) to the later work of Keynes; though (as will appear) it here emerges in rather a different light from that in which Keynes (mainly) saw it.

The basic model of Keynes's *General Theory* is a short-period (or even single-period) model; it is in that guise that we have considered it (or some aspects of it) in Chapters VII and X, above. There are, however, numerous passages in which Keynes appeared to be contemplating a more long-period application: Keynes's 'Vision of the Day of Judgement' as Pigou[2] called it. It is this part of Keynes's work which can be given some reconsideration, in the light of what we have been finding in Parts II and III of this book. We shall find that there is no need to take it in the rather apocalyptic manner in which Keynes (and Pigou) were inclined to take it. We shall nevertheless be able to distinguish an element in it which is true, and very important.

2. Throughout the whole of our own study of growth equilibrium and of optimal growth paths, we have abstracted from money: an abstraction which (I fear) the reader must often have felt to be nearly intolerable. Something, at the least, must be added

---

[1] Or Wicksell after Keynes, as it turns out!
[2] In *Economica*, 1936, p. 129.

somewhere (and this is the place for it) on how the use of money could be fitted in.

Let us go back to the regularly progressive economy, and its growth equilibrium (Chapters XII–XIV). There would have been little difficulty in making this into a money-using economy if the only money that was admitted was a commodity money (a metallic money, we should no doubt want to say). As so often, hardly more than a little reinterpretation would be needed. For the transactions involved in the 'corn' production and the 'tractor' production of our model, carried through at unchanging money prices, a certain quantity of gold (say) would be needed—a quantity that might be regarded as dependent upon the quantities produced, and upon the prices at which the exchanges were conducted. Now prices, as we saw, would be determined in such an economy independently of quantities; and the price of gold in terms of 'corn' would be no exception. It would be determined by the cost of production of gold (the 'cost of obtaining money' as Senior would say); the price of 'corn' (and of all other commodities) in terms of gold would follow. The quantity of gold needed to 'circulate' current output would then become proportional to current output; so that on the quantity-side gold would appear as a capital good like other capital goods—it could indeed be fitted into our algebra without substantial amendment. The growth rate of the gold stock would have to be the same as that of the other elements of the economy. The equilibrium quantity of gold (at any moment, or in any single-period) would be determined, as a proportion of current output, in just the same way as the proportion (k_i/ξ) of any ordinary capital good. On this 'Ricardo–Senior' assumption there is, in equilibrium, no particular problem of money.

Even so, there is one point that should be noticed. We cannot, when we are comparing one equilibrium growth path with another, get a rise in prices just by increasing the quantity of money. For if money prices (on another path) were higher, the price of gold (in terms, say, of labour) would not cover its cost of production, so that the gold supply would not increase, as in equilibrium it would be required to increase. There could only be higher money prices if the real cost of obtaining gold were lowered. There is an equilibrium quantity of money, and an equilibrium growth rate of the money supply, equal to the growth rate of everything else.

I am not of course suggesting that (even for a world for which the commodity money assumption was appropriate) this equilibrium condition would get one very far. As always, there is a problem of Traverse; and even nineteenth-century economists realized that this Traverse problem is very difficult. It is nevertheless useful to set out this equilibrium condition as a basis for comparison with other models. Many comparisons could be made; but it will be sufficient here to go to the other extreme.

3. A pure credit money, without commodity 'backing', is analytically nothing else but a part of the general system of debits and credits that exist between the 'individuals' or 'entities' that compose the economy, at any moment of time. (The Government, or Governments, reckon from this point of view as just one sort of entity; a bank is just one sort of entity; money is just one sort of debt due from certain sorts of entities; it is sufficient to regard it as just one sort of debt.) This is in fact the way in which Wicksell first taught us to think of money. There are doubtless many practical purposes for which it is too general; but there are others, equally practical (as the Radcliffe Report has made evident) for which it is unwise to stop much short, even, of this degree of generality.

If it is a pure credit money that is to be introduced into our equilibrium, we find (first of all) that there is no price equation to determine the value of money in terms of goods and services. It is impossible to determine the equilibrium price-level, as before, from the price side. On the quantity side we have to reinterpret the quantity equations, going into detail about the supplies and demands, from the individual entities, from which they are derived. These equations, it has been insisted, are always to be regarded as stock equilibrium equations. They imply equilibrium of the balance-sheets of the individual entities, and this means that the right kinds of debts and credits are found, in suitable amounts, in the balance-sheets; debts to and from the banks (and the Government) must be in some sort of equilibrium with one another. (The same must of course hold for the banks, and for Governments, themselves.) Thus we may generalize the conception of demand for money, and assert its equilibrium in the form of saying that the whole system of debits and credits must be in equilibrium. This was concealed by the quantity equations, in the way we wrote them; but the implication of an equilibrium of this sort was there all the time.

Even in a credit economy, a regularly progressive equilibrium at constant money prices is clearly conceivable; the condition for it (looking, as we are now doing, more closely) is that the system of debits and credits should remain in equilibrium, every item expanding at the same growth rate—the real growth rate of the economy, which we called g. It is of course assumed (as I think economists do implicitly assume) that such expansion at constant proportions will maintain equilibrium—there are 'constant returns to scale' (or something like it) here too.

When we make comparisons of equilibria, the difference between the commodity money economy and the pure credit economy emerges at once If there is commodity money, equilibrium money prices can only be different if there are differences in real costs (including the cost of obtaining money). But with credit money it is entirely possible that all *real* prices and quantities might be the same in the two economies, yet that money prices might be different. This cannot happen with commodity money, but it can happen with credit money.

It is further possible with credit money (but not with commodity money) that an economy might be in Growth Equilibrium, in real terms, while the money price-level was changing over time. Money prices could be rising over time, and everything else be as before; excepting that the rate of profit in *money terms* would have to be adjusted. If the real rate of profit (as previously calculated) were 10 per cent. per annum, and prices were rising at 5 per cent. per annum, the money rate of profit would have to be (approximately) 15 per cent. This (by now) is a familiar point; I do not think that I need to elaborate it. All that needs to be said is that, in order to maintain this (inflationary) equilibrium, the whole system of debits and credits must be expanding (in money terms) at a rate which is correspondingly in excess of the real growth rate of the economy. If there is some part of the system—particular sorts of debts from government, or particular sorts of debts due by banks—which we dignify by the title of money supply, that money supply must be correspondingly expanding. This, however, is true for any part of the debit-credit system; in itself it gives no reason for imputing to the money supply any special role. A special role has been attributed to it, essentially (I think) because the money supply, defined in some way that seems appropriate to the economy under consideration, is selected as that part of the whole debit-credit system which is especially capable of being controlled. Control the money supply, said Quantity theorists, and the rest of the debit-credit system must fall into line.

4. This, of course, is where we come to Keynes—and 'Liquidity preference'. It is no part of my intention to go over the well-trodden ground of Keynesian versus 'classical' theories of the mechanism of adjustment; the precise way in which the Keynesian amendment affects the determination of the equilibrium itself must nevertheless be noticed. I am myself quite clear that the main point which Keynes made in this connexion is valid, and is extremely important; but it is not unimportant that at the stage of analysis which we have now reached we can rewrite it in a new form, giving it a somewhat different 'long-period' appearance from that which it gets in the *General Theory*. There are real economic problems which have come up since 1936 to which this reformulation does not seem to be irrelevant.

Strictly interpreted, the Liquidity Preference Curve of the *General Theory* is a relation between the quantity of money (or the quantity of money available to be held in idle balances) and the rate of interest—the long-term rate of interest on government bonds. Money, presumably, is bank money; so that liquidity preference appears to be a matter of the choice between this money, and these bonds, at the margin. But it has long been recognized that the significance of liquidity preference is much wider than that. It is wider, in the *General Theory* itself; for (according to the usual economists' convention) the rate of interest on long-term bonds is taken to stand for the whole gamut of rates and yields, on securities of all kinds, that are established on the market. As soon as one begins to ask questions about the structure of these rates, it becomes apparent that the choice between money and bonds is only one of the many possible choices between forms of asset-holding into which similar considerations of liquidity enter.[1] The demand for money, it used to be said, arises out of the needs for convenience

---

[1] I may claim to have seen this even before I saw the *General Theory*; see my 'Simplification of the Theory of Money' (*Economica*, 1935). See also R. F. Kahn, *Notes on Liquidity Preference* (Manchester School) and my later paper on 'Liquidity' (*Economic Journal*, 1962).

and security; liquidity preference is an elaboration of the security motive; but the security motive in the demand for money is not fundamentally different from the security motive in the demand for safe securities—even though the latter do bear interest, while money (it is assumed) does not.

The theory of Liquidity Preference is conventionally approached by asking how it is possible that an individual (or entity) may simultaneously hold bonds (that do bear interest) and money (that does not). The theory of rational conduct under uncertainty does unquestionably provide an answer to this problem. But the same answer will apply to the related question: how is it possible that the individual may simultaneously hold assets with different yields? This latter question is overlaid in practice by the complication of maturities, which make comparable yields on securities of different types troublesome to calculate; but that this can be put aside, and simultaneous holding of assets with different yields can still be found, cannot be doubted. The condition that the Keynesian 'money' should be non-interest-bearing is not essential; there might be no money which did not bear interest, and a question of liquidity preference, between liquid assets bearing low interest, and less liquid assets of higher yield, would still arise.

Having gone so far, we can go further. This wider question, it is easy to see, is still no more than a part of a yet wider question: that of the coexistence of assets with different yields, available (even though not actually held) to the same entities on accessible markets—the influence, that is to say, of liquidity considerations (differing, inevitably, from one individual or entity to another) upon the whole structure of yields and interest rates. This is a large question on which to embark in the present chapter, which is only an epilogue (or a part of an epilogue); something of the model with which one might begin may nevertheless be sketched out.

5. We might start from an economy (rather of Wicksell type) in which there is just one bank, providing credit money (the only money there is), and no other financial institutions. There are then three parties, or sorts of parties, whose balance-sheet equilibrium has to be considered: firms (conducting real investment), private individuals (savers), and the bank itself. Savers can hold their assets in bank money, or in securities (loans or equities) of the producing firms; the liability side of the savers' balance-sheets does not have to be considered. Firms have real assets, and they may have bank money; they have debts to the bank, and to the savers. The bank has debts owing to it from the firms; it owes debts (bank money) to the firms and to the savers. There is a question of balance-sheet equilibrium in each case.

If the savers switch from bank money to securities of the firms their liquidity is diminished; they will therefore require a higher yield upon such securities than they get from the bank. If the firms expand their holding of real assets, by borrowing from the bank, or by borrowing directly from the savers, their liquidity is diminished; they will therefore be unwilling to pay interest on these loans which is as high as the return which they expect to get from their real investment (their rate of profit). The same is in fact true, though in a slightly more complicated way, even if the 'capital' is raised by the sale of equities; for to offer a yield on the new shares which is as high as that which is expected from the new investment would damage the position of present shareholders, whose interest may be identified (for the moment) with the interest of the firm. Thus we may summarize by saying that the rate of interest payable by the firms, to the savers and to the bank, must $r < \Pi$ be lower—and with a reasonable weight attached to liquidity quite significantly lower—than the profit rate which is expected by the firms.

What now of the bank? If, as we are supposing, there is only one bank in the economy, it has no problem of liquidity in the narrow sense; there can be no 'run' on this bank, for there is no more liquid asset into which claims on the bank can be turned. But there remains a wider sense in which even this bank may have a similar problem. Its assets are the debts that are due to it, but these are assets of uncertain value. There will be cases in which a firm is willing to borrow, at the usual rate of bank interest, but in which the bank will be unwilling to lend, because it is too uncertain of the firm's capacity to repay. Thus the bank's loans will be restricted, at any given rate of bank interest, by the bank's concern for the solvency of its debtors; and this will be reinforced by the concern of the borrowers for their own liquidity. However careful is the bank's choice of borrowers, there will be some bad debts. It will therefore be impossible for the bank to lend, except at a rate of interest which is in excess of what it pays; there must be a difference to cover bad debts, and also to cover administrative expenses.

The picture which emerges, in this first model, is therefore as follows. There is a maximum to all rates of interest, set by the expected rate of return on real investment (I simplify by the assumption that there is just one rate of return); there is a minimum which is set by the rate of interest *paid by* the bank. This latter rate may be zero, but it need not be zero. All other rates of interest (those paid by firms to savers, and those paid by firms to the bank) must lie, in equilibrium, between these limits. Where they will lie will be determined by a balance of liquidity considerations in the balance-sheets of lenders and borrowers respectively.

6. That is only a first model. We might proceed, as the textbooks usually proceed, to a multiplicity of banks. But the consequences of that are well known; it will be more instructive to take another route. A place is evidently left, within our first model, for the introduction of *financial intermediaries*; let us bring them in and see what difference is made.

The expansion of credit is restricted, in the first model, by several factors. It is restricted, in the first place, by liquidity considerations on the part of the borrowing firms; but we can probably ascribe more importance to uncertainty, on the part of the bank, about the prospects of the real investment which the firms propose to undertake; and to the effect on the liquidity of the savers, or on the general risk-position of the savers, if they expand their direct holdings of the firms' securities to more than a limited extent. The financial intermediary can prosper if it can make use of specialized knowledge about the prospects of particular kinds of real investment; so that it can make advances to firms, or investments in the securities of firms, which the bank would not know were sound investments; and if it can acquire resources which enable it to make these financial investments at a less loss of liquidity than they would entail upon the private saver. But it cannot prosper unless it makes a profit; this implies that it must borrow at a lower rate than that at which it lends, there being a sufficient difference to cover its administrative expenses, and to compensate it for the additional risk in which it (in its turn) is involved in every extension of its operations.

Thus its 'in-rate' (as we may call it—the rate at which it borrows) and also its 'out-rate' will have to be fitted into the structure of rates, as previously described. Its in-rate will have to be higher than the previous minimum, and its out-rate will have to be lower than the previous maximum. It is not necessary that the in-rate of the financial intermediary should be higher than the rate which is paid by the firms (directly) to the bank, or by the firms (directly) to the savers; for it is not unlikely that the intermediary may be able to attract funds from the bank and from the savers by offering a greater degree of liquidity (by pooling of risks) than the firms could do directly. And it need not necessarily charge a lower out-rate than that which is charged by the bank, since it will be willing to do business with the firms which the bank would not do. It is, however, clear that its in-rate must be appreciably in excess of the old minimum, and that its out-rate must be higher than its in-rate, if it is to function at all.

Just as we have superimposed our first financial intermediary upon the bank, so we might (quite realistically) superimpose a second intermediary upon the first. (There might, of course, be a series of intermediaries operating, perhaps in different markets, like our first intermediary; that is not the point to be considered here.) There is no reason why there should not develop a hierarchy of specializations, in which the intermediaries of higher order are largely (though not entirely) dependent for their funds on those of lower order. If this happens (and one would expect it to happen) the in-rate of the higher order is the out-rate of the lower order; so that the out-rate of the higher order, being higher than the in-rate of the higher order, is doubly higher than the in-rate of the lower order. All this has got to be squeezed in between the minimum and the maximum of the first model. It would certainly appear that there will be more room for that squeezing if the maximum (the rate of profit on real investment) is fairly high.

7. The model that has just been described should have its uses in the teaching of post-Keynesian (and 'post-Radcliffe') monetary theory; but the temptation to develop it in that direction is one that I must here resist. I have brought it in here solely because of the bearing that it may have upon the relation between interest (or profit) and growth, which emerged from the very different investigation which we were pursuing in the last chapter. One is naturally led to confront the one with the other, though it is

evident that it is quite dangerous to do so. The two belong to different families of assumption—in the terminology of this book they belong to different 'methods'. But they look as if they had something to say to one another all the same.

The former argument (of Chapter XXII) was a piece of Optimum theory; it was concerned with the relation between optimum growth and optimum interest in various conditions of 'productivity' and 'thrift'. Here we are no longer concerned with Optimum theory; we are back in Pure Positive Economics, examining how a system that was organized in a particular way could be expected to work. To take over results from one to the other is (in general) a fault—a fault, indeed, to which economists are peculiarly liable; it is responsible for some of the most foolish things that they have ever said. Here, I am afraid, we are going to commit it; but let us do so with open eyes. Let us simply assume that the relation between the optimum rates which we discovered (or appeared to have discovered) in the Optimum theory is valid, not indeed for actual rates as they have been in history, but for the rates which would have been established if the monetary system had been working 'perfectly'. That is to say, let us see what might have happened if the monetary system had been the only obstacle to optimum growth.

It is clear, in the light of the present discussion, that what we were calling (in the Optimum theory) a rate of interest must go back to its former name as a rate of profit; it is the rate of profit which arises out of the *real* relations which were considered in the Optimum theory, not the rates of interest which we must expect to be lower than the profit rate, to the extent of the liquidity margins that we have now been describing. It was the main (relevant) conclusion of our former analysis that the rate of profit (the optimum rate of profit) was likely to be higher, other things being equal, in conditions when the rate of technical progress was rapid than when it was slow. This, of course, is not an original conclusion; the main thing that can be claimed for the analysis by which we reached it is that the 'other things being equal' clause was fairly well defined. What has now to be considered is the bearing of this point upon the present (monetary) discussion.

8. Let us begin by looking at the matter (once again) in a rather Wicksellian manner. Let the rate of profit be determined by real factors (in the manner now supposed); and let there be a pure credit economy, such as has been described, with a single bank, together with financial intermediaries. There should then be a certain basic rate, payable *on deposits* by the bank, which will leave room for a structure of interest rates that is consistent with monetary equilibrium—using 'monetary equilibrium' to mean that there is a fair balance between the real assets which firms desire to hold and those that are available for them to hold, at the prices initially ruling. It is not to be expected that there will be any basic rate, which will leave all firms in the economy in stock equilibrium; but there should be some rate (or perhaps some band of rates) which will prevent the disequilibria that occur from being much more in one direction than in the other. That is as much as can be expected of a monetary equilibrium, which cannot be an equilibrium in any exact (or pedantic) sense.

This basic rate (we can now see) must be lower than the rate of profit, perhaps very much lower. There has got to be room for the whole spectrum of market rates of interest (and yields on equities) in between. If, for the moment, we suppose this *gap* to be fixed, there will be a minimum to the rate of profit at which the system can work. The bank (we may reasonably suppose) cannot reduce its basic rate (the rate which it pays) below zero; for if it did so it would be inviting some other body (perhaps one of the financial intermediaries) to take over its functions. For the purposes which we have here in mind, such a possibility is indeed not to be quite ruled out; it is better (and, it is also more significant) to say that there is a minimum to the rate of profit which is consistent with the maintenance of the particular set of financial institutions which we have posited. The *gap* itself is a matter of that particular set of financial institutions; with a different set of financial institutions there need not be the same gap. With a given set of financial institutions, including intermediaries, that have to earn their living and to satisfy their needs for liquidity, there must be a gap; it may be compressible to some extent, but it is not indefinitely compressible.

If the rate of profit is above the minimum, there will be room for the given set of financial institutions, and there will be some basic rate which is consistent with monetary equilibrium, in the loose sense in which we are using that term. If the rate that is fixed by the bank is lower than that *equilibrium rate*, the demands of firms for real assets will tend to be greater than what is available; an expansionary (and probably inflationary) process will begin to develop. (On the whole question of how it will work out, many of the things which have been said in Chapters VI to XI, above, are relevant; they need not be repeated here.) If the basic rate is significantly higher than the equilibrium rate, there will be a reverse tendency. All this much as in Wicksell's 'Interest and Prices'. We simply attribute less power to our bank than Wicksell did to his; it has less freedom to manœuvre (this is what we have learned from Keynes), and we may admit that the bank's policy has got to soak through the general financial structure before it can take full effect (either in an expansionary or contractionary direction).

Let us look, once again, at the *gap*. In a system with financial intermediaries, the size of the gap is set, quite largely, by the financial intermediaries—by their necessities of having out-rates above their in-rates, and by the 'pyramiding' of these margins which occurs when one tier of financial intermediaries is imposed upon another. It might therefore be thought that in the absence of intermediaries the gap could be narrowed. But that, I think, is not correct. If the intermediaries were removed, *and monetary equilibrium was to be maintained*, direct investment by the bank in the firms, and direct investment by the savers in the firms, would have to take over what had been done through the intermediaries; not the same investments, no doubt, but equivalent investments would have to be induced. The general liquidity of the system would be less; this would make for wider margins, a wider *gap*. The introduction of financial intermediaries narrows the gap, so that it makes it easier for the system to function. It is true that the constituents of the gap, after the financial intermediaries have come in, are more objective—they are more a matter of administrative costs, and less of subjective liquidity preferences; but this change in character does not imply that the width of the gap is not at the same time reduced.[1]

[1] I am prepared to believe that this last point has considerable historical importance. The beginning of a process of expansion (pretty much, I suppose, what Rostow means by 'take-off') might occur because of real factors (inventions and the like) raising the real (prospective) rate of profit. But it might also occur because of financial improvements, diminishing the size of our 'gap'; thereby permitting access to funds, for improvements which could have been made earlier, if the necessary funds had been forthcoming. It is not savings only that are required, but a channel of communication between potential savings and potential real investment.

9. What I have to say on these monetary matters is nearly complete. There does of course remain much more that could be said on the lines that we have been exploring; but I have said nearly as much as is suitable for inclusion in the present book. There is just one further point, that unquestionably belongs to the present argument, so that it must certainly be mentioned.

The rate of profit, as we have been considering it, is determined in real terms; but the rate of interest (both the basic rate and the rates that are built upon it) are in money terms—have we not done wrong in confronting one with the other? In order that the real rate of profit should be converted into a monetary rate, we must make some assumption about price expectations. If prices are (on the whole) expected to remain constant, the expected real rate of profit and the expected money rate of profit come to the same thing, and the preceding analysis will (on the whole) stand up. Monetary equilibrium is then a state of affairs in which the demands for real assets balance the supplies, given these stationary expectations; there is then a prospect of equilibrium over time with prices pursuing, on the whole, the course that they are expected to pursue. But suppose that prices are not expected to remain constant. Suppose that they are expected to rise—to go on rising for some exogenous reason, perhaps (for there is no reason why such a consideration should be excluded) because of 'cost-push' by trade unions. What difference would that make? What could then be said about monetary equilibrium?

There should be monetary equilibrium when there is equilibrium over time, when demands and supplies are consistent with a rise in prices, at about the rate at which they are expected to rise. But in such an equilibrium the money rate of profit would be higher than the real rate. Accordingly, even if growth were retarded, so that the real rate of profit sank towards its minimum, the system might still function, for the higher money rate would still leave a sufficient *gap*. Or so it would appear. Inflation might persist, but it need not be an uncontrolled inflation. By the maintenance of a suitable basic rate, the rate of inflation could be held down to that which was decreed by the 'cost-push'. From a narrowly monetary point of view (at least) equilibrium would be maintained.

This is evidently a point which is of much practical importance. It has obvious relevance to the conditions that exist, in many countries, at the time of writing, and which will doubtless continue to exist for many years to come. But there is one further thing which it seems to be necessary to say about it. It is not quite safe to assume that the money rate of profit can be put up, in this way, by inflationary expectations, while the size of the *gap* is entirely unchanged. Especially when the gap has been built up, in the way that has been described, from the costs and liquidity preferences of financial intermediaries, it is itself to some extent a *real* pheno-menon; it may therefore be expected to grow, in an inflationary atmosphere, at least to some extent. If it were to remain quite unchanged, it could only be as a consequence of 'money illusion'; and however important money illusion may be upon the path to equilibrium, it is not a reliable ingredient in the making of an equilibrium position. Thus while the possibility of an inflationary equilibrium is a qualification that needs to be made, in relation to the principle of a minimum rate of profit, it is a qualification upon which it would be unwise to rely very far.

The important conclusion which (in my view) emerges from this chapter is quite different. There is a place for monetary policy, as a smoother of the price effects of changes in the real rate of profit—changes that must be expected to occur. Too much should not be expected of it, but something can be expected. It can perform its function more satisfactorily—it can deal with wider swings in the real rate of return, and deal with them more quickly—if it is backed by an efficient system of financial intermediaries,[1] which will ensure that the gap (which *hampers* the efficiency of monetary policy) is not too wide. But the gap can never be abolished. It is therefore always possible that a situation will arise in which the efficacy of monetary policy (however well it is backed up by financial intermediaries) will fail. But such failure is less likely if technical innovation (in the widest sense) is in the full spate of activity than if it is in a sluggish condition.

That, I think, is what is left—in the end—of Keynes's 'Day of Judgement'.

---

[1] An alternative possibility, that the 'contact' (which I have ascribed in the above to financial intermediaries outside the Bank) might sometimes be estab-lished by specialized departments within the Bank (or banking system) itself, should not be overlooked. It would certainly need attention in a more extended treatment. I owe this reminder to Mr. J. Helliwell, of Nuffield College.

XXIV

THE PRODUCTION FUNCTION

1. THE other matter which I wish to discuss before concluding is the 'producion function' controversy. This, of course, is a question that belongs to the field of the 'Static Method in Dynamic Theory' with which we began. But the production function model is only one kind of static model; it has complications which in other static models are not felt so acutely. I therefore preferred to begin with the simpler static models of the 'classics'—Adam Smith and Ricardo; from these (as the reader will by now have appreciated) there is a clear line of descent to the Growth Equilibrium models to which we were to come. The 'neo-classical'[1] production function does not, in the same way, belong. It must be discussed, but it could not usefully be discussed until a later stage. I have indeed myself found that I had to go through a great deal of what we have been going through in this book before I was in a position to make up my mind about it.

The question is this. If production (in some sense) is X, labour (in some sense) is L, capital (in some sense) is K, is there any relation $X = F(L, K)$ which can be expected to hold, even very approximately, in a closed system, under a given technology? Are there any senses of X, L, K for which such a relation can be expected to hold? Only if that question is answered affirmatively can there be any scope for the other, that goes with it, but must not be confused with it. Can the shares of labour and capital, in the distribution of the product, be determined (even approximately) by marginal productivity—the share of labour being $L(\partial X/\partial L)$ and the share of capital being $K(\partial X/\partial K)$, the *quantity* of the other factor, in each case, being held constant while the *partial*

It is commonly called 'neo-classical' but the appropriateness of the description must surely be questioned. There is no 'production function' in Jevons or Marshall, Walras or Pareto, Menger or Böhm-Bawerk. There is in Wicksell, but he is careful to confine it to his model of 'production without capital'. J. B. Clark can hardly be regarded as a major neo-classical economist. The originators of the 'production function' theory of distribution (in the static sense, where I still think that it should be taken fairly seriously) were Wicksteed, Edgeworth, and Pigou.

derivatives are calculated? There are other interpretations of marginal productivity; it is only if it is taken in this 'macro' sense that it depends upon the production function. But if it is taken in that sense, the *existence* of the production function must be established before the question of distribution by marginal productivity can arise.

The existence question is a different question according as it is taken in a static or a dynamic context. There is a simple form of production function which still seems to me to be defensible as an instrument of static analysis; and (as I insisted in the first chapter of this book) there are real problems—static problems—for which static analysis is all we want. There can be no question that when we merely comparing the *states* of two economies, the differences between the sizes of their real products (almost however measured) must be attributed to differences in factor endowment (labour and physical capital), to differences in technical knowledge, or to differences in the efficiency with which the factors are applied. One has still to face the question of what different factor endowments are to be regarded as equivalent (so that they can be represented by the same K—or L); but this is an index-number kind of question, difficult but not insoluble. Provided that we are only interested in static comparisons—and are prepared to make the main static assumption that the economies under comparison can be treated as if they were in some sort of static equilibrium[1]—this production function can be allowed to pass.[2] It is at the point when we seek to use it in dynamic theory that the major troubles come.

2. In order to show just how this is, I am going to work through an exercise. I shall construct an imaginary economy, which is not utterly unlike an actual economy, though its experience will differ from actual experience in some important respects. These differences are deliberately chosen to 'show up' the production function. We can see precisely what happens when we try to interpret our imaginary economy in terms of a production function. It will be seen that the same difficulties that will arise in our

---

[1] See above, pp. 12, 16.

[2] Even the marginal productivity corollary may then possibly be allowed to pass. I have been into all this in the Commentary that is attached to the 1963 edition of my *Theory of Wages* (pp. 331–50). I shall not repeat it here.

imaginary economy will also arise in a real economy; the advantage of using the imaginary economy is that the difficulties are made more sharply defined.

The crucial assumption of the imaginary economy is that the technical advance which it experiences is discontinuous. It experiences a sequence of major inventions, but it has time to adjust itself to each before the next is upon it. The discontinuity itself is perhaps not so unrealistic; it is not so difficult to tell the actual story in terms of major inventions (electricity, the automobile, the aeroplane, plastics, the computer) with secondary improvements being treated as consequential from them. The whole of each new technology is not immediately revealed; it is discovered bit by bit in a process of working out. What is unrealistic is to suppose that the 'automobile age' is completed before the 'aeroplane age' begins. Yet that is a thing that could happen; it is not impossible that there could be an economy which periodically settled down into some sort of 'equilibrium'.

Let us begin by taking this equilibrium very strictly. There are inventions (let us say) in 1900, 1910, 1920; in 1909 and in 1919 the economy has settled into a *stationary state*. In that stationary state the labour supply must not be increasing; and it will be easiest to assume that there is no change in labour supply over the whole process. In the stationary state there must be no net saving, no net personal saving and no net business saving; the value of gross investment must equal the value of the resources currently used up. In the stationary state the meaning of this 'no net saving' condition is perfectly clear. But it is by no means so clear what we are to do with it when we take it over into the periods of adjustment— between 1900 and 1909, between 1910 and 1919, and so on. If there is to be 'no net saving' in equilibrium, it will be natural to assume that there is no net saving out of equilibrium; but the meaning that is to be given to this latter assumption requires to be very carefully defined.

A natural interpretation would (I think) be the following. Suppose that the price level of consumption (the price of *the* consumption good, as we have been saying in earlier chapters) is kept constant—somehow or other; that there is no net saving out of personal incomes; and that there is no net saving out of business incomes, in the sense that gross investment is equal to depreciation, *measured at historical cost*. A rule of this kind has the merit that it is consistent with the maintenance of equilibrium, if it continues to hold after equilibrium is reached; and it accords well enough with conventional business behaviour about the measurement of profit. It would therefore appear that it is a natural rule with which to begin.

How then would an economy, which had this experience, and behaved according to these assumptions, work? At the moment when 'electricity' is discovered, its entire capital equipment is non-electrical; it is in stationary equilibrium under its non-electrical technology. The mere access of knowledge that occurs in 'January 1900' can make little immediate difference to productivity. It may make some difference; the net product (which in our non-saving economy may be considered as consisting wholly of consumption goods) may be somewhat raised; but it is to be expected that the immediate rise will be small. In order that production should rise to the full extent that the new technology makes possible, a process of adjustment will be needed—a process that will take time. It will take time for the opportunities that the new technology opens up to be fully realized, for the ways in which it can be used to be worked out, and for the ideas that are generated in this manner to be transmitted from establishment to establishment, from firm to firm. We may speak of this as the time needed for 'informational diffusion'. But it will also take time for the capital stock to be transmuted into a form which is appropriate to the new technology, by the reinvestment of depreciation allowances in new forms; we may speak of this as 'capital transmutation'. Both informational diffusion and capital transmutation will be occurring, and will be influencing one another, over the whole period '1900-9'. It is optimistic to suppose that they can be completed within ten years—but let that pass.

There is no reason to suppose that the process of adjustment, in these two directions, will be a smooth process; there will be plenty of room for errors and mistakes. There must nevertheless be a general tendency for production to rise over the period of adjustment. Production must be higher in the new equilibrium than it was in the old; and it cannot rise fully straight away. A gradual rise to the new equilibrium level is the simplest thing that can happen.

3. All this is preparatory to our main question: how is this process

of adjustment to be described in terms of a production function? This is a question which divides up into several parts.

There is first of all the question of the *comparison* of the new equilibrium (1909) and the old (1899). There is stationary equilibrium at both dates, so that the comparison is almost a static comparison. Almost, but not quite. For the two equilibria are equilibria of the same economy; they are tied together by the condition that there has been no net saving in the interim. The value of capital (in terms of consumption, since there has been no change in the consumption price-level) is to be the same. Production has been increased by the change in technology; the supply of labour (by assumption) is unchanged; and the supply of capital is unchanged, in this particular sense. Can one properly express this change by a shift in a production function, which must now be written $X = F(L, pK/\pi)$, the supply of capital being now represented by its 'real' value? Can one treat the supply of capital as fixed, when capital has been transmuted according to our particular rule?

The answer is that one can. Though it has sometimes been thought that there is trouble even here, it is not at this point that the trouble arises. It is a special, and admittedly sophisticated production function, which is needed for this purpose (quite different from the production function with which we began); but it is a perfectly valid production function all the same.

Let us work it out in terms of our 'tractor' model (Chapter XII, above). Since there is no saving, $s = 0$ and $g = 0$. The quantity equations accordingly reduce to the simple forms

$$K = \alpha\xi, \qquad L = \beta\xi$$

(K, as before, is here the quantity of tractors—the quantity of capital in a physical sense). It is pK/π which is now to be taken as independent variable. Or (by the constant returns to scale, which are implied in the 'tractor' model) we may take the ratio of this 'capital' to labour—$pK/\pi L$. Now (using the price equations, which are independent of the growth rate) we must have, in equilibrium.

$$\frac{pK}{\pi L} = \left(\frac{p}{w}\right)\left(\frac{K}{L}\right)\Big/\left(\frac{\pi}{w}\right)$$

$$= \left(\frac{b}{1-ra}\right)\left(\frac{\alpha}{\beta}\right)\Big/\left(\beta + \frac{r\alpha b}{1-ra}\right) = \frac{\alpha b}{\beta}\left[\frac{1}{\beta + r(\alpha b - a\beta)}\right].$$

Putting $\alpha b / a \beta = m$ (as in Chapter XV), this reduces to

$$\frac{pK}{\pi L} = \frac{a}{\beta}\left[\frac{m}{1+(m-1)ra}\right]$$

an expression for the 'capital'-labour ratio in terms of technical coefficients *for a given technique.*

If technique is variable, as in the present case we must surely suppose, it is (as has been shown in Chapter XIII) highly probable that a will increase and β diminish, as r falls. As for the expression in the square bracket, it may move either way. Thus, though it is not certain that the required 'capital'-labour ratio will rise as r falls, it is highly probable that it will do so. We can draw out a curve that expresses values of $pK/\pi L$ that are consistent with equilibrium for different r; it is highly probable that it will be a downward-sloping curve. Thus if L is given, and pK/π is given, the equilibrium rate of profit will be determined from this curve. The higher is pK/π, the lower will be the rate of profit. And (of course) the lower the equilibrium rate of profit, the higher will be the rate of real wages (w/π).

After all that we have been through, it is clearly unnecessary to rework this argument for more general cases, as for that of 'many capital goods'. So long as we are solely concerned with the comparison of equilibrium positions, we can construct a production function, in which capital is measured by its value in terms of consumption goods, the marginal product of capital, in this sense, being the *rate* of profit. Such a production function must be sharply distinguished from the original production function, in which capital is measured in physical units, so that the marginal product of capital is rp/π (the net quasi-rent of a 'machine'). With *this* production function capital is pK/π, and its marginal product is equal to the rate of profit r.

Thus, once again, so long as we are only concerned with the comparison of equilibrium positions, the production function (or *a* production function) gets through How much use it is, when it has to be put into this sophisticated form, may indeed be questioned. Formally, however, it is valid.

4. Let us now turn to the period of adjustment—'1900 to 1909'. Production, as we have seen, will in general, over that period, be rising. But why is it rising? There is no change in (basic) technology,

and (as we are measuring it) no change in 'capital'. Even in the form $X = F(L, pK/\pi)$, the production function cannot hold.

Is there any way out? There are two ways out; let us look at them.

It will, in the first place, no doubt be objected that in looking at the basic technology, we are taking 'unchanged technology' in too restrictive a sense. Why should informational diffusion not itself be reckoned as a change in technology? Invention is not effective until the new knowledge has been spread, and its consequences have been worked out. Though we have pretended that our changes in technology are discontinuous, by admitting the gradualness of diffusion we have in fact allowed them to be continuous. In this other sense, during the period of adjustment, technology *is* changing. The production function is continually shifting; it is this which permits a rise in production even though labour and 'capital' are constant.

This may be part of the answer; but it cannot be the whole answer. For informational diffusion is only part of the process of adjustment; capital transmutation has also to be considered.

Suppose (a strong assumption, but we need strong assumptions to make our points) that informational diffusion is immediate. The immediate rise in production will then be greater than we have allowed; but it will still fall short of the whole increase that will be attained (in '1909') in the new equilibrium position. There will still be a rise in production (from 1900 to 1909) even though technology is unchanged—in the fullest sense—and labour and 'capital' are constant.

The only way in which we can maintain a production function relation in these conditions is by a further change in the way that we are to measure capital. Production is rising; so capital *must* be rising. Now 'capital', as we have said, is to be the same in 1909 as it was in 1899; if it is rising from 1900 to 1909, it must have dropped between 1899 and 1900. The change in technology must itself result in a *fall* in the capital stock, correctly measured.

This, I believe, is the answer; it is what we must say if we are to stick to a production function, through thick and thin.

What is the sense of it? There is being produced, in 1900, from the old capital, with the new technology, a particular output of consumption goods. By proceeding along the path that we have been supposing (reinvesting depreciation allowances *at historical cost*) it will be in train to produce an increasing output over the years that follow. Suppose that it did not want to produce an increasing output—that saving was to be zero *in this sense*—reinvestment would have to be less than we have been supposing. But if reinvestment was less, the output of consumption goods could have been (somewhat) higher. Zero saving, in this sense, will accordingly engender a path that starts higher (in 1900), but remains at the same level without rising, between 1900 and 1909. Along that path capital will be 'maintained intact', but the capital of the economy (in the value sense) will be lower in 1909 than it would have been along the other path. In this sense, therefore, our original path (with reinvestment at historical cost) was a path with positive saving.

Such a reinterpretation involves a considerable shift in ideas; but it is the only interpretation which enables us to go on making sense of a production function during a process of transmutation. Every technical improvement implies a loss of capital: *capital being measured in terms of the consumption that has to be forgone in order that the productive power that is embodied in the physical instrument should be replaced.* It is unnecessary (it should be noticed) to distinguish, for purposes of this definition, between improvements that affect the process of production of capital goods, and improvements that affect the efficiency of given capital goods in consumption-good production. Each works in the same way; in each case the improvement makes it possible to replace the productive power at a smaller sacrifice of consumption. The depreciation allowances (measured in consumption-good terms) that have to be set against gross output to reduce it to net are accordingly reduced.

Let us consider how we should proceed if we are to retell the story of our 'exercise' economy in the terms to which we have now come. From 1899 to 1900 there is a loss of 'capital' (pK/π); consumption is only a little increased, but there is an increase in net output (consumption plus net investment) because of the reduction in depreciation. This increase must itself be imputed (at least in the first place) to profits; there is therefore some presumption that the share of profits in total net output (calculated on the new plan) will rise. But it is not inevitable that it should rise; for the change in technology has a direct effect on the marginal products of both labour and capital—any sort of redistribution is *possible*.

Yet the fall in capital is itself a force tending to reduce the marginal product of labour—a force which may, or may not, be offset by the direct effect of the improvement, which may usually (though not necessarily) be expected to increase the marginal product of both 'factors'. The marginal productivity of 'capital' (now to be interpreted, it will be remembered, as the rate of profit) will almost necessarily rise, from the two effects together; for the 'reduction' in the capital stock will itself tend to raise the marginal productivity of capital, quite apart from what may happen as direct effect. This is in fact the clearest of the consequences that emerge. It is almost inevitable that the initial effect of the new technology will be to raise the rate of profit; but since that higher rate of profit is now to be applied to a smaller capital (pK/π), it does not follow at all inevitably that the share of profit—even the absolute share—will increase. It will probably increase, on our special assumptions (discontinuous innovation and instantaneous diffusion), and with the way of measuring profit to which we have come; but even so it will not necessarily increase.

I think it will be agreed that this makes sense. It would be more usual to say that the rate of profit on new investment is raised, while the profit that is earned on past investment may be lowered. On our present formulation it is the profit on new investment which is *the* rate of profit; it is the value of the previously invested capital that must be marked down, when (as will often be the case) it is unable to earn an equal rate of profit on its historical cost.

That is the position in '1900'. From 1900 to 1909, on the present interpretation, there is an increase in capital, with no change in technology. The familiar static production function properties will accordingly apply. As capital increases, relatively to labour, the marginal product of capital (the rate of profit) will fall, and the real wage of labour (the co-operating factor) will rise. The change in relative shares will depend upon the elasticity of substitution.

5. The point has come when we must attempt to go beyond our 'exercise'. The assumptions that we have been making may best be relaxed by steps.

(1) We have hitherto imposed the condition that the value of capital (pK/π) should be the same in the new equilibrium as in the old; and we have taken it that this value of capital is consistent with stationary equilibrium in each case. But this leaves it entirely

possible that the rate of profit may be different in '1909' from what it was in '1899'; at a higher rate of profit there may be positive saving, even with depreciation reckoned at historical cost. Accumulation of capital, reckoned in the way we have come to reckon it, may then have to go further than we have been supposing, before the rate of profit comes down to an equilibrium level. The effect on relative shares, in that further equilibrium, is a matter of the 'Harrod' definition of neutral invention; while in the equilibrium which we supposed in our exercise, it would be a matter of the 'Hicks' definition.[1]

This, of course, is merely an introduction. We must ease up our stationariness in this manner, before we go on to the next, more interesting, step, in which we abandon the assumption of a constant supply of labour.

(2) If labour supply is steadily increasing, the only equilibrium that is possible (if it is possible) will be a growth equilibrium of the kind that was studied in Part II of this book. If there was a growth equilibrium in 1899, the maintenance of that growth equilibrium in 1909 (with no change in technology) would have involved a growth in output, but no change in output per unit of labour. In order to reach this higher total output, positive saving would have been necessary (even with depreciation measured at historical cost). But this positive saving would only have enabled capital (on any definition of capital) to keep step with the supply of labour—so that the K/L ratio, or the $pK/\pi L$ ratio, would remain unchanged. Now (as we have seen) it is the $pK/\pi L$ ratio which is significant in the determination of the 'sophisticated' production function; and this ratio remains constant along the growth equilibrium path. There will still be a similar[2] relation between this ratio and the rate of profit, which can be interpreted as a relation between the 'capital'-labour ratio and the marginal product of 'capital'. All that has been said about the comparison of equilibria is, in consequence, substantially unaffected.

---

[1] See above, Chapter XV, pp. 180–2.
[2] When the relation between $pK/\pi L$ and r is worked out for a growth equilibrium, in which g is not zero, it will itself (in general) be affected by g, the general formula being

$$\frac{pK}{\pi L} = \frac{a}{\beta}\left(\frac{m}{1+(m-1)ar}\right)\left(\frac{1}{1+(m-1)ag}\right).$$

But if g is fixed, this makes no difference to the argument.

Nor is much difference made when we consider the passage to equilibrium. As a result of the invention, the economy is moved (ultimately) on to a higher equilibrium path; but even if there is a smooth movement to that equilibrium, there must be a transitional phase in which the growth rate of *output* is raised. If we use a definition of capital (and consequently of saving) according to which the rate of saving (or of capital accumulation) is unaffected by the invention, we shall be at a loss to explain, in production function terms, how it is possible for there to be a gradual movement into the new equilibrium—unless we are willing to attribute the whole of the 'lag' to slowness of informational diffusion, and that (as we have seen) cannot be exactly right. Here also, therefore, we have to fall back upon the same device as we have had to use previously; we must measure capital in such a way that the invention itself, by rendering existing capital inappropriate to the new technology, involves a loss of capital value. Depreciation will thus be written down, net output written up, and profits written up, at the moment when the invention occurs. There will be a concealed addition to savings during the process of transition; it will be to that concealed addition to savings that we shall attribute the (temporarily) higher growth rate.

(3) With further dropping of simplifications, formal analysis begins to fail us, and it is necessary to express ourselves in looser terms. When informational diffusion is admitted to be a continuous process, the capital revaluation becomes a continuous process; it is going on all the time, but it is still there. Once it is admitted that basic improvements are made continuously (or even frequently), the repeated attainment of an equilibrium (of some sort), which has been our analytical life-line, will have to be discarded. The main lessons which we have learned from our exercise can, however, be retained.

So long as we measure saving in terms of consumption goods given up, the capital that is accumulated by it must be valued in the same terms. Thus (whatever may be the case when one is making a static comparison) the only production function that can be used in a growth model is one which shows the product to be a function of capital that is measured (or valued) in this particular manner. Such a production function can be constructed, but it is an artificial construction, quite different from the technological relation between product and physical capital which the economists who first used the notion had (often at least) in mind. It may well be the case that it should not be thought of as a production function, expressing output as a function of labour and capital; it may be better to take it the other way round. If it is regarded as a capital function, showing the value of capital that is needed to produce, with given labour supply, a given output (which must of course be a feasible output), it makes better sense. If it is put in that way, it comes into line with other concepts (the capital-output ratio and its progeny) to which economists are more and more directing their attention.

If, however, we regard it as a production function, and endeavour to fit it to actual experience (as is done by the econometrists), we must somehow incorporate the loss of value, attendant upon technological improvement, which emerged so clearly in our exercise, and which will clearly persist, however well it may be hidden away, in actual data. For when we are working with actual time-sequences, we are not comparing equilibrium positions, for which the loss of value can be neglected. The economy that is being analysed is always in a state of transition, losing 'capital' by improvements, and offsetting that loss by accumulation. Much of the offsetting accumulation occurs quite passively, and remains unnoticed; but for a proper analysis it should be noticed, for it is always there. If we leave it out of account we inevitably attribute less of a rise in output to capital accumulation, and more to technical progress, than should be attributed—at least if one is using a production function technique. And so one concludes[1] that capital accumulation does not have much to do with economic progress. That, it has appeared from our present analysis, is very much a matter of the way one defines one's terms. There is much to be said for the approach which reckons the concealed accumulation as true accumulation, performed (indeed) by a wealthy economy very much in its sleep, by the reinvestment of its depreciation allowances on ever more productive terms. For it is, after all, the existence of the depreciation allowances which permits this accumulation to take place. It is very wrong to give the impression to a poor country, which is very far from equilibrium even on a past technology, that capital accumulation, in its case, is a matter of minor importance.

[1] Cf. R. Solow, 'Technical Change and the Aggregate Production Function' (*Review of Economics and Statistics*, 1957).

6. One further point before leaving the subject. I insisted, at the beginning of this chapter, that this whole production function approach belonged to Static method. That continues to hold, on every interpretation of the production function—however sophisticated is the form into which it is put. The 'loss of value on technological improvement', which is perhaps the oddest thing which has emerged from our investigations, is itself a consequence of their static character. The stationary equilibrium of '1899' (in our exercise) could only be stationary because its continuance was expected; the change in technology, that occurred in 1900, had not been expected; the 1899 values were constructed on the assumption (that turned out to be wrong) that it would not occur. The new (lower) values that were set (or should have been set) on the old capital goods in 1900 were based (in our story) on an expectation of permanence of the new technology. Without such an expectation of permanence no production function (of however sophisticated a sort) could have been constructed. There was thus a change in expectations (from one set of basically static expectations to another) in 1900; and such a change will naturally lead to a change in value. One might at first suppose that it need not be a fall in value; and it is indeed not necessary to suppose that for every sort of old capital good there would be a fall. It has, however, been shown that there can only be a gradual approach to a new (higher) equilibrium if there is (on the whole) a fall in value—a fall, that is, relatively to the level of consumption good prices.[1] It clearly makes sense if the relative unsuitability of the old equipment to the new technology leads to a fall in its value.

There I break off. To leave the discussion at this point, without drawing morals, or venturing upon policy prescriptions, is to leave it quite open-ended. But that is how I wish to leave it. The task on which we have been engaged is not closed at this point; it is far from being closed. It is only a part of a much larger enterprise, in which economists all over the world (one can now say, all over the world) are busily concerned. All I have tried to do is to draw

---

[1] The reader should perhaps be reminded of the device that was used in Chapter XIII to cover variability in the composition of the consumption bundle. By the use of this device the analysis of this chapter can be extended (to some extent) to admit the possibility of technical improvement taking the form of the introduction of new consumption goods. Even this can be brought within our concept of 'consumption in general'.

some of these threads together. Important advances, some along the lines that we have been exploring, some on other lines, are being made as I write; more are needed, and more will no doubt be forthcoming. I shall have fulfilled my intention if I have given some help towards their being made, not upon a united front (for that is too much to expect) but at least upon a connected front.

MATHEMATICAL APPENDIXES

THESE appendixes are arranged in the order of the chapters to which they refer; this is by no means an order of importance. Appendix A gives proofs of some properties that were used in the text of Chapter IX; but Chapter IX was itself no more than an example. The appendix does no more than illustrate ways in which such examples can be worked out. B and C (which belong together) are, on the other hand, quite central. Economists who are acquainted with matrix algebra will find that they are not to be overlooked. D and E are also concerned with important points; but these, it will be noticed, are relatively brief.

APPENDIX A

(REFERRING TO CHAPTER IX)

CHARACTERISTIC EQUATIONS OF STOCK ADJUSTMENT

1. THE purpose of the first part of this appendix is to give a more systematic analysis of the difference equation

$$E_{t+1}-E_t+\lambda E_{t-n} = 0 \quad (\lambda > 0)$$

on which the behaviour of a stock-holder, who adjusted according to the first principle that was examined, was found to depend.

The 'characteristic equation'[1] corresponding to this is

$$f(u) = u^{n+1}-u^n+\lambda = 0$$

which, if $n > 1$, is an equation of higher order than the second; but it is an equation the properties of which are not difficult to discover.

For real values of u, $f(u)$ can easily be graphed. Since

$$f'(u) = (n+1)u^n-nu^{n-1}$$
$$f''(u) = n(n+1)u^{n-1}-n(n-1)u^{n-2}$$

---

[1] 'Auxiliary equation', as I called it in my *Trade Cycle* (p. 77).

it is evident that $f(u)$ has a minimum at $u = n/(n+1)$, which I shall call γ, a stationary point of higher order at $u = 0$, and no other possible turning points. The possible real roots of $f(u) = 0$ are at once accounted for.

If $u = \gamma$ is a root of the equation, $\lambda = \gamma^n(1-\gamma) = n^n/(n+1)^{n+1}$. It is this we shall identify as λ_1. If $0 < \lambda < \lambda_1$, the equation has two roots that are real and positive; if $\lambda = \lambda_1$, these two roots become equal; if $\lambda > \lambda_1$, there can be no real positive roots. If u is real and negative, λ must be negative if n is odd, but λ is positive when n is even. Thus if n is even, there is one negative real root; otherwise the positive roots (if they exist) are the only real roots.

2. Consider the particular case in which $\lambda = \lambda_1$, so that

$$f(u) = u^{n+1} - u^n - (\gamma^{n+1} - \gamma^n) = 0.$$

If we put $u = \gamma w$, this reduces to

$$\gamma w^{n+1} - w^n + 1 - \gamma = 0,$$

or

$$n w^{n+1} - (n+1)w^n + 1 = 0.$$

This has two roots at $w = 1$ (or $u = \gamma$) as it should. If we take out *one* of them, the remainder are given by

$$n w^n - (w^{n-1} + w^{n-2} + \ldots + w + 1) = 0$$

which is clearly satisfied by $w = 1$, as it should be. It can be shown that all the other roots must have modulus less than 1.

For in the first place, there can be no root with modulus > 1. For by the 'triangle rule', that the modulus of a sum is not greater than the sum of moduli,

$$n|w|^n = |nw^n| = |w^{n-1} + w^{n-2} + \ldots + w + 1| <$$
$$< \text{or} = |w|^{n-1} + |w|^{n-2} + \ldots |w| + 1.$$

But this is impossible if $|w| > 1$, for there are n terms on the right-hand side, and each of these must then be $< |w|^n$.

It remains to prove that $w = 1$ is the only root with unit modulus. If $|w| = 1$, both w and $1/w$ must be roots. If $1/w$ is a root, then (multiplying by w^n)

$$n - (w + w^2 + \ldots + w^{n-1} + w^n) = 0.$$

So that if w is also a root,

$$n = w(1 + w + \ldots + w^{n-1}) = nw^{n+1}$$

so that $w^{n+1} = 1$. But if $w^{n+1} = 1$, and $w \neq 1$,

$$n(1-w) = w(1-w^n) = w-1$$

which is impossible, n being positive. So that $w = 1$ is the only root with unit modulus; all other roots (complex or negative) must have modulus < 1.

It follows that, apart from the double root at $u = \gamma$, the moduli of all roots of $u^{n+1} - u^n + \lambda_1 = 0$ must be $< \gamma$. The double root is the dominant root.

3. We now return to the general case. If $\lambda = 0$, the roots of $f(u) = 0$ are 1 and n zeros. As λ increases towards λ_1, the 'large' root diminishes towards γ, while one of the zeros will increase towards γ, through real values. If the number of remaining zeros is odd, one of them will take negative values, and the remainder will take complex values. If the number is even, all will take complex values.

It follows from what has just been proved that when $\lambda = \lambda_1$, all of these remaining roots are less (in modulus) than γ; that is to say, they are majorized by the real positive (double) root. At $\lambda = 0$, and clearly also when λ is small, the other roots are majorized by the larger positive root. It is almost obvious that this must happen over the whole stretch from $\lambda = 0$ to $\lambda = \lambda_1$. It can indeed be shown that the moduli of the complex roots (and of the negative root) must be less, over this whole stretch, than *either* of the two positive roots. For it has been shown that this is so at $\lambda = \lambda_1$; and if it were not to be so over the whole stretch, there must be at least one value of λ at which the modulus of one pair of complex roots becomes equal to one of the real roots—or, what comes to the same thing, to the modulus of one of the real roots. But this cannot occur.

For if u is a root of the equation, let $\bar{u}$ be its complex conjugate ($\bar{u} = u$ if u is real). Let v be another root and $\bar{v}$ its complex conjugate. Suppose that they have the same modulus. Then $u\bar{u} = v\bar{v} = M$ (say). u, $\bar{u}$ must be roots of $f(u) = 0$; so that

$$\lambda = u^n - u^{n+1}, \qquad \lambda = \bar{u}^n - \bar{u}^{n+1},$$

$$\lambda^2 = (u^n - u^{n+1})(\bar{u}^n - \bar{u}^{n+1}) = M^n\{1 + M - (u + \bar{u})\}.$$

Similarly, $\qquad\qquad \lambda^2 = M^n\{1 + M - (v + \bar{v})\}.$

So that $v + \bar{v} = u + \bar{u}$. But from this, together with $v\bar{v} = u\bar{u}$, it follows that either $v = u$, or $v = \bar{u}$. The two 'equi-modular' roots are either identical, or they are complex conjugates.

It is therefore impossible that the modulus of a pair of complex roots (or for that matter, of the negative root if it exists) should become equal to a real root. Since the positive roots majorize the other roots at $\lambda = \lambda_1$, they must do so over the whole stretch where they exist. Over .this stretch, between 0 and λ_1, it is the larger of the positive roots which.

will be the dominant root. And this (of course) is less than 1; though it will be usually not much less than 1.

4. In order to discover λ_2, we have now to do no more than to inquire into the values of λ which are such that there are roots of $f(u) = 0$ with modulus equal to 1. If -1 is to be a root, n must be even, so that $\lambda = 2$—a value too large to be of any interest. We may therefore confine attention to complex roots which, if unimodular, may be written

$$u = \cos z + i \sin z.$$

Substituting in $f(u) = 0$, and equating real and imaginary parts, we get

$$\lambda = \cos nz - \cos(n+1)z = 2\sin(n+\tfrac{1}{2})z\sin(\tfrac{1}{2})z,$$

$$0 = \sin(n+1)z - \sin nz = 2\cos(n+\tfrac{1}{2})z\sin(\tfrac{1}{2})z.$$

If $\sin(\tfrac{1}{2})z = 0$, λ would equal 0; this merely gives the real root $u = 1$ with which we are acquainted. Putting that on one side, we may take it that $\sin(\tfrac{1}{2})z \neq 0$; so that

$$\cos(n+\tfrac{1}{2})z = 0$$

whence $(2n+1)z = (2r+1)\pi$, for some value of r. And

$$\lambda = 2\sin(r+\tfrac{1}{2})\pi\sin\left(\frac{2r+1}{2n+1}\frac{\pi}{2}\right).$$

This formula, which gives the non-zero values of λ for which there is a root with $|u| = 1$, is periodic in r, as it should be. $\lambda(r+2n+1) = \lambda(r)$. Also $\lambda(2n-r) = \lambda(r)$. Thus the only values of r that need be considered are those that run from $r = 0$ to $r = n$.

For all these values the second element in the above formula for λ is positive; but the first equals $+1$ or -1 according as r is even or odd. Since $\lambda > 0$, r must be taken as even. Then, as r increases through these even values, λ will continually increase. The smallest value of λ which will give a pair of roots with unit modulus is thus identified as that for which $r = 0$. It is this (I maintain) which must be taken as λ_2. That is to say,

$$\lambda_2 = 2\sin\left(\frac{1}{2n+1}\frac{\pi}{2}\right).$$

It is readily shown that λ_2, as given by this formula, is greater than λ_1. For obviously $n\lambda_1 < 1$; and $n\lambda_2$ is an increasing function of n, which equals 1 when $n = 1$.

At $\lambda = \lambda_1$, the modulus of the largest root is γ (< 1). λ_2 ($> \lambda_1$) is the smallest (positive) value of λ for which the modulus of any root becomes equal to 1. It is not possible for a modulus to become > 1 (as λ increases) without passing through 1; and (as we have seen) this does not happen between λ_1 and λ_2. Thus λ_2 is identified as the 'second critical value'.

5. As n tends to infinity,[1]

$$n\lambda_1 = \left(1 - \frac{1}{n+1}\right)^{n+1} \quad \text{tends to } e^{-1}$$

$$n\lambda_2 = 2n\sin\left(\frac{1}{2n+1}\frac{\pi}{2}\right) \quad \text{tends to } \tfrac{1}{2}\pi.$$

The (fairly rapid) approximation to these limiting values is shown in the following table.

n	$n\lambda_1$	$n\lambda_2$
1	0·25	1·00
2	0·30	1·24
3	0·32	1·33
4	0·33	1·39
10	0·35	1·49
20	0·36	1·54
infinity	0·37	1·57

The ratio of λ_2 to λ_1, which begins at 4 when $n = 1$, rises very gently; even in the limit, when n is infinite, it is only 4·27.

6. I turn, finally, to the other difference equation

$$E_{t+1} - (1-\lambda)E_t - \lambda(E_{t-n+1} - E_{t-n}) = 0$$

which played a similar part in the special case of the 'enlarged Stock Adjustment Principle' that was considered in the text of Chapter IX. Here I can only offer a rather less exhaustive treatment.

The characteristic equation is

$$f(u) = u^{n+1} - (1-\lambda)u^n - \lambda u + \lambda = 0$$

[1] Since n is the ratio between the production period (n of our periods) and the decision period (one period) for n to become infinite is effectively the same thing as for the decision period to become zero. If decisions are taken continuously, our difference equation reduces to the 'mixed difference-differential equation' that was studied by Frisch and Holme in a well-known article (*Econometrica*, 1935). The critical values (e^{-1} and $\tfrac{1}{2}\pi$) are the same as those that they got for their form.

It may perhaps be claimed that the solution for discontinuous decisions is in some ways more interesting, and the mathematical analysis is no more complicated.

The second difference equation, that is studied in the second part of this Appendix, does not seem to be reducible to a differential equation in a corresponding way. This is confirmed, as we shall see, by the character of the solution which we shall find for it.

where λ, as before, is assumed to be positive. It is at once apparent that if $u = 1$, $f(u) = \lambda$; while if $u > 1$, $f(u) > \lambda$, so that there can be no real root > 1. When $u = 0$, $f(u)$ again $= \lambda$, while for $0 < u < 1$, $f(u) < \lambda$, so that it is possible (as in the other case) that there may be two real roots in this range. The possibility of negative roots here requires a more serious investigation.

For this purpose, let us write the characteristic equation in the *alternative form*

$$\frac{1}{u^n} + \frac{1}{1-u} - \frac{1}{\lambda} = 0$$

from which it is at once apparent that *if n is even*, $u = -1$ will be a root if $1/\lambda = 1 + \frac{1}{2}$, so that $\lambda = \frac{2}{3}$. There will be a negative root with modulus > 1, if $1/\lambda < 1 + \frac{1}{2}$, so that $\lambda > \frac{2}{3}$. Thus if n is even, and $\lambda > \frac{2}{3}$, there will be a negative root that will be explosive.

If n is odd, there can still be a negative root, but only for large values of λ. For if we put $u = -v$, and keep n odd, we get

$$-\frac{1}{v^n} + \frac{1}{1+v} - \frac{1}{\lambda} = 0$$

so that $(1/\lambda) < 1/(1+v)$ and $\lambda > 1 + v > 1$. Now if $\lambda > 1$, there is no question that the sequence must be explosive (whatever n), as is at once apparent from the original form of the characteristic equation. For we see from that form that the product of the roots is $-\lambda$, so that the product of the moduli of the roots is λ. It follows that if $\lambda > 1$, there must be some root with modulus > 1, and the same can readily be shown to be true if $\lambda = 1$ unless $n = 1$. λ must therefore be < 1 whatever $n(> 1)$, if there is to be any damping at all.

Let us return to the positive roots (if they exist). Values of λ which will give equal roots can be identified (as before) by eliminating u between $f(u) = 0$ and $f'(u) = 0$. It is quicker to differentiate the alternative form, which immediately gives

$$-nu^{-n-1} + (1-u)^{-2} = 0$$

or

$$u^{n+1} = n(1-u)^2.$$

Though this equation is not explicitly solvable, it is clear by inspection that it has one root, and only one root, between 0 and 1. The value of λ corresponding to this must be that at which the positive roots disappear. It seems safe to conclude that this must be λ_1, the 'first critical value'. It is indeed clear, without going further, that λ_1 cannot be greater than the figure that is to be found in this way.

For small values of n, the above equation can be solved (approximately) by trial and error. I get

n	1	2	3	9
λ_1	0·25	0·19	0·16	0·09

values which seem to justify the conclusion that is stated in the text.

We have still to consider the complex roots. As before, to find a complex root that is unimodular, we write $u = \cos z + i \sin z$. Substituting (again) in the alternative form of the characteristic equation

$$\cos nz - i \sin nz + \frac{1}{1 - \cos z - i \sin z} - \frac{1}{\lambda} = 0,$$

or

$$\cos nz - i \sin nz + \frac{1 - \cos z + i \sin z}{2(1 - \cos z)} - \frac{1}{\lambda} = 0.$$

Equating real and imaginary parts,

$$\cos nz + \tfrac{1}{2} = 1/\lambda, \qquad \sin nz = \tfrac{1}{2} \cot \tfrac{1}{2}z.$$

From the second of these equations we can (in principle) derive z, and then from the first we should be able to derive λ.

This proceeding can be carried through, to a sufficient degree of accuracy, in the following way.

Put $z = \pi - x/n$ so that the equations can be rewritten

$$1/\lambda = \tfrac{1}{2} + (-1)^n \cos x, \qquad \sin x = (-1)^{n+1} \tfrac{1}{2} \tan(x/2n).$$

$x = 0$ is clearly a solution of the second of these equations. If n is even it gives $1/\lambda = \tfrac{1}{2} + 1$, or $\lambda = \tfrac{2}{3}$; but if n is odd it gives $1/\lambda = \tfrac{1}{2} - 1$, or $\lambda = -2$, which is not a possible value.

We may thus henceforward suppose that n is odd, so that

$$1/\lambda = \tfrac{1}{2} - \cos x, \qquad \sin x = \tfrac{1}{2} \tan(x/2n)$$

and the solution at $x = 0$ is to be neglected.

If $n = 1$, $\sin x = \tfrac{1}{2} \tan \tfrac{1}{2}x$ gives $\cos x = -\tfrac{1}{2}$ and $\lambda = 1$. In fact, if $x < \tfrac{1}{2}\pi$, $\sin x > \tfrac{1}{2} \tan \tfrac{1}{2}x > \tfrac{1}{2} \tan (x/2n)$, when $n > 1$; so that, in general, there can be no value of x between 0 and $\tfrac{1}{2}\pi$. This suggests that it will again be more convenient to change the variable. Put $x = \pi - y$, and the equations become

$$1/\lambda = \tfrac{1}{2} + \cos y, \qquad \sin y = \tfrac{1}{2} \tan\left(\frac{\pi}{2n} - \frac{y}{2n}\right).$$

The second of these equations is satisfied for quite small values of y, which will give values of λ only a little in excess of $\tfrac{2}{3}$, so that these clearly are the critical values. By trial and error we have the following results:

n	y	$\tfrac{3}{2}\lambda$
3	15°	1·023
5	9°	1·008
7	6°	1·004
9	5°	1·002

so that, even among odd values of n, there is a very rapid convergence to the same value of $\frac{2}{3}$.

We may conclude that excepting for the case where $n = 1$, λ_2 may be taken to be equal to $\frac{2}{3}$ to quite a close approximation.

APPENDIX B

(REFERRING TO CHAPTER XIV)

MATRIX THEORY OF GROWTH EQUILIBRIUM

1. THOSE who are familiar with matrix notation will have noticed that our n capital-price equations could have been written in matrix form

$$p = p(rA+E)+wb$$

or

$$p(I-E-rA) = wb$$

where p is the vector of capital good prices, b is the vector of labour coefficients, and A and E are matrices of a's and e's respectively. The formal solution of this equation (assuming that the matrix on the left is non-singular) is

$$p = wb(I-E-rA)^{-1}.$$

The (single) consumption-price equation is similarly to be written

$$\pi = p(\epsilon+r\alpha)+w\beta$$

where α, ϵ are the vectors of α's and ϵ's, as previously written. Thus (putting $\pi = 1$) we have

$$\frac{1}{w} = \beta+b(I-E-rA)^{-1}(\epsilon+r\alpha)$$

as the general (scalar) equation of the wage curve, for the given technique.

2. In order to make further progress we must make use of the standard properties of *non-negative square matrices*, such as are proved in the article of that title by Debreu and Herstein,[1] through which this highly relevant mathematical apparatus was first made accessible to economists. Great as is my own indebtedness to that article, I have myself come to doubt whether their approach (with its dependence upon abstruse mathematical concepts, such as the fixed-point theorem) is in fact the method of attack which is best suited to our purpose. There is a much more elementary alternative, which seems to do all that is

---

[1] *Econometrica*, 1954.

needed.[1] It will not be necessary to write it out in full; a sketch may nevertheless be useful.

It is explained in most textbooks on matrices that if a matrix (such as E) has the property that E^m, when m is indefinitely increased, converges to zero (all of its elements tend to zero), it will be possible to expand $(I-E)^{-1}$ as a convergent series

$$(I-E)^{-1} = I+E+E^2+\dots.$$

This is rather obvious, in view of the rules of matrix multiplication, since, if m is any positive number

$$(I-E)(I+E+E^2+\dots+E^{m-1}) = I-E^m$$

so that the series expansion must hold, if $E^m \to 0$, as m increases. (This is a very general proposition, which holds universally, whatever the sign of the elements of E.)

If, however, E is a non-negative matrix (all of its elements non-negative) we can go further. For in that case (by the rules of matrix multiplication), every E^m (whatever m) is a non-negative matrix. And it is intuitively rather obvious (or can be tested by experiment) that a non-negative matrix will usually be such that repeated multiplication by itself either makes its elements get larger, or it makes them get smaller.[2] In the latter case, we do have $E^m \to 0$, for large m.

Suppose that u_0 is an *arbitrary* non-negative vector. Then, if E is a non-negative matrix, $u_m = u_0 E^m$ is a non-negative vector (for it is derived from u_0 by successive additions and multiplications without subtractions). The sequence

$$u_0, u_1, u_2, \dots, u_m$$

is a sequence of non-negative vectors, of which each is derived from its predecessor by the recurrence relation

$$u_{t+1} = u_t E$$

which is a set of simultaneous first-order difference equations, of which u_m is the general solution.

The method of solution of such simultaneous difference equations is exactly the same as that of a simple difference equation (of whatever order). We consider the possibility that $u_t = \lambda^t v$ (where λ is a scalar and v a fixed vector) could be a solution. Substituting in the recurrence relation, and dividing by λ^t, we get $(\lambda I-E)v = 0$, a matrix equation

---

[1] All that is needed in this appendix; in Appendix C (as will be seen when the time comes) we have to rely upon von Neumann's existence proof, which does depend upon the fixed-point theorem.

[2] There is an exception in the case of 'decomposable' matrices of which some elements get larger and some smaller; but that does not signify here.

independent of t. Written in full, it is a set of homogeneous linear equations in the n elements of v, which cannot be satisfied simultaneously unless the determinant of $(\lambda I - E)$ vanishes. Thus we get the characteristic equation of the matrix, which plays exactly the same part as the characteristic equation of difference equation theory.

Continuing the argument on precisely similar lines, we are bound to find (if the roots of the characteristic equation are distinct) that the general solution of the sequence is given by

$$u_m = \sum \lambda_r^m v_r$$

where the v_r are fixed vectors, and the sum is extended over the n roots (λ_r) of the characteristic equation. Again as in difference equation theory, the behaviour of u_m when m is large depends upon the character of the largest roots. Now (as we have seen) if E is a non-negative matrix, and u_0 is a non-negative vector, then u_m is a non-negative vector, whatever m. It follows at once that if there is a single root that is larger (in modulus) than any other, this largest root must be a positive root. For if λ_1 were a negative root that was larger in absolute value than any other, then (whatever v_1) the elements of $\lambda_1^m v_1$ would be changing sign as m changed from odd to even; they could not stay non-negative as they must do if E is non-negative. Similarly, if there was a pair of complex roots (conjugate to one another) which were in the same way dominant, each element in the dominating component of u_m would contain a cosine term, which would change sign in the same way over a longer cycle. Thus it is impossible that this largest root should not be a positive root (which must of course have a non-negative vector— its eigenvector (v_1) to go with it). If this dominant root is less than 1, all elements of u_m will tend to zero; and since this will be true whatever is the arbitrary non-negative u_0 from which we started, E^m must tend to zero.[1]

3. By this means we can get, sufficiently well, to the Debreu–Herstein theorem that a non-negative matrix must have a dominant root[2] that is real and positive. We shall not need to bother about the possibility

---

[1] If there is no *single* root that is dominant, there are complications. We need not attend to the case of repeated roots (two, or more, equal roots) which is of no particular importance in what follows. Something must, however, be said about the possibility that there is a negative root (or a pair of complex roots) equal in modulus to the (positive) dominant root—a case which will become important in Appendix C. Suppose, for instance, that $\lambda_2 = -\lambda_1$, λ_1 being positive, and greater than the modulus of any other root but λ_2. Then, for large m, u_m could tend to be proportional to $[(\lambda_1)^m + (-\lambda_1)^m]v_1$, which is alternatively positive and *zero*. Thus it remains non-negative; so this is a possibility which is not ruled out.

[2] At least *one* such root: see preceding footnote.

that the dominant root $= 1$. It will be sufficient to distinguish the two cases, where it is < 1 and > 1 respectively.

(i) If the dominant root < 1, $E^m \to 0$, and $(I-E)^{-1}$ is expressible as

$$I+E+E^2+...$$

which clearly is a non-negative matrix.

(ii) If the dominant root > 1, we still have

$$(I-E)(I+E+E^2+...+E^{m-1}) = (I-E^m)$$

for a finite m; so that

$$I+E+E^2+...+E^{m-1} = (I-E)^{-1}(I-E^m).$$

Multiply each side by an *arbitrary* non-negative vector u_0. The left-hand side is then a non-negative vector; and if $(I-E)^{-1}$ were non-negative, $u_0(I-E)^{-1}$ would be a non-negative vector, u_{00} (say). Then u_{00} is non-negative, and $u_{00}(I-E^m)$ is non-negative. But if the dominant root of E is > 1, then (as shown) $u_{00} E^m$ must tend towards $\lambda_1^m v_1$ as m becomes large. If $\lambda_1 > 1$, the elements of this must ultimately become greater than the corresponding elements in u_{00} (for both u_{00} and v_1 are fixed vectors). Thus it is impossible that $u_{00}(I-E^m)$ should be non-negative for large m. And so it is impossible for $(I-E)^{-1}$ to be a non-negative vector.

Thus if E is non-negative, with a dominant root less than 1, $(I-E)^{-1}$ is non-negative, and has the series expansion that has been given. If the dominant root > 1, $(I-E)^{-1}$ is not a non-negative matrix, and the series expansion is not valid. Whenever $(I-E)^{-1}$ is a non-negative matrix the series expansion is valid.

4. I return to the equation of the wage curve, as given in section 1 above.

The first condition for the feasibility of the technique that is expressed in the coefficients is that it should be practicable at $r = 0$; that is to say, the dominant root of E must be < 1. Put $(I-E)^{-1} = H$; then H is a non-negative matrix. We have

$$(I-E-rA)^{-1} = HH^{-1}(I-E-rA)^{-1} = H(I-rAH)^{-1}.$$

Now rAH is a non-negative matrix; so that if its dominant root is less than 1, $(I-E-rA)^{-1}$ is a non-negative matrix. Thus the condition for this is that r should be less than the reciprocal of the dominant root of AH—which is the *critical rate of return* that we have discussed in the text of Chapter XIV.

If these conditions are satisfied, $(I-rAH)^{-1}$ is expansible as a series, so that $(I-E-rA)^{-1}$ is expansible as

$$H+H(rAH)+H(rAH)^2+... = H+rH(AH)+r^2H(AH)^2+... .$$

So that, for the wage-equation, we have

$$\frac{1}{w} = \beta + b[H + rH(AH) + r^2H(AH)^2 + ...](\epsilon + r\alpha)$$

$$= h_0 + h_1 r + h_2 r^2 + ...$$

where the coefficients h_0, h_1, h_2,... are all non-negative *scalars*. It accordingly follows that $(1/w)$ increases with r; and indeed that all of the differential coefficients of $(1/w)$ by r are non-negative (it is indeed almost inevitable, when one considers their composition, that they should be positive). The fact that r is less than its critical value keeps the series *convergent*.

5. We thus have a proof that in the general case, the wage curve slopes downwards. But nothing follows, from what has here been found, about the curvature of the wage curve; it may bend either way. For if we write $h(r)$ for the above series, and primes for differentiation by r,

$$w = (1/h), \quad w' = -(1/h^2)h', \quad w'' = -(1/h^2)h'' + 2(1/h^3)h'^2.$$

Thus if $w'' > 0$ (the wage curve is inward-bending) we must have

$$2h'^2 > hh''.$$

Working this out, in terms of the coefficients,

$$(h_1 + 2h_2 r + 3h_3 r^2 + ...)^2 > (h_0 + h_1 r + h_2 r^2 + ...)(h_2 + 3h_3 r + ...)$$

whence

$$h_1^2 - h_0 h_2 + 3(h_1 h_2 - h_0 h_3)r + 3(h_2^2 + h_1 h_3 - 2h_0 h_4)r^2 + ... > 0.$$

Thus if the h-coefficients are in geometrical progression, the wage curve is linear (as is otherwise obvious). More interestingly, the larger is h_0 (relatively to the others), the more likely it is that the wage curve will be outward-bending. This, I think, is the proper generalization of the rule about m (the ratio of the coefficient-ratios) being $>$ or < 1, which looks so important when we are dealing with a one-capital-good model.

6. Nothing more remains to be done than to write down the corresponding equations on the quantity side, which have an obvious 'duality' with the price equations. In matrix form, the capital-quantity equations become

$$k = Ax + \alpha\xi$$

and the accumulation equations

$$gk = (I - E)x - \epsilon\xi$$

(k being the vector of capital stocks and x the vector of gross outputs). Substituting, as in the text,

$$(I - E - gA)x = (\epsilon + g\alpha)\xi$$

so that $\qquad (x/\xi) = (I-E-gA)^{-1}(\epsilon+g\alpha)$

and $\qquad (k/\xi) = \alpha+A(I-E-gA)^{-1}(\epsilon+g\alpha).$

If (as before) $(I-E)^{-1}$ is a non-negative matrix, and if g is less than its critical value (the same as that for r), we can use the series expansion, giving
$$(k/\xi) = c_0+c_1 g+c_2 g^2+\dots$$

where c_0, c_1, c_2,... (which have nothing to do with the capital–output ratio) are non-negative *vectors*, that depend on the technique.

In a similar way, from the single labour-equation, which in vector form is
$$L = bx+\beta\xi,$$
we get the *single* equation

$$(L/\xi) = \beta+b(I-E-gA)^{-1}(\epsilon+g\alpha)$$

which can be similarly expanded. But here it is to be noticed that this equation, as written in matrix form, is identically the same as the wage equation, save that (L/ξ) is written for $(1/w)$ and g for r. Accordingly, when it is expanded, the coefficients must be the same. Thus we have

$$(L/\xi) = h_0+h_1 g+h_2 g^2+\dots$$

the h's being the same as those we have met before.

This is a useful result which may easily be verified. If $g = r$, $gpK = rpK$; net investment = profits. Consumption out of profits = saving out of wages. Total wages (wL) = total consumption (ξ). So $(L/\xi) = (1/w)$, as it should do.

APPENDIX C

(REFERRING TO CHAPTER XVIII)

THE VON NEUMANN MODEL

1. No attempt will be made, in this appendix, to give a proper mathematical version of Turnpike theory. All that will be done is to add some notes on the structure of the theory, which may help to bring Chapter XVIII (and XIX) into relation with the work that has been done by the mathematicians. In this bridge-building (as well as in those chapters themselves) I have been greatly helped by Professor Morishima; this particular appendix is indeed to be regarded as a joint work by him and by myself.

2. We begin from the model that was used in Appendix B. There, with capital wastage expressed by e- (and ϵ-)coefficients, and with consumption and wages both positive, we had (in matrix form)

$$\text{price equations} \qquad p(I-E-rA) = wb,$$

$$\text{quantity equations} \qquad k = Ax+\alpha\xi,$$

$$\text{accumulation equations} \qquad gk = (I-E)x-\epsilon\xi.$$

When r and g have become equal to the critical rate of return, w and ξ both vanish; so the equations become

$$p(I-E-rA) = 0 \quad \text{or} \quad p(I-rAH) = 0$$

$$k = Ax$$

$$gk = (I-E)x$$

whence $\qquad (I-E-gA)x = 0 \quad \text{or} \quad (I-gHA)x = 0.$

p is thus the 'left-hand' eigenvector that is associated with the dominant root of AH; x is the 'right-hand' eigenvector that is associated with the dominant root of HA.[1] If the technique is feasible, H is non-negative; so that AH and HA are non-negative. It then follows (as was shown) that the dominant root[2] must be real and positive; and that it must have a non-negative eigenvector (either way) associated with it. If x is non-negative, k $(= Ax)$ is also non-negative. It is this k which gives the balanced composition of the capital stock, for the technique which is represented by A and E; it is this p which gives the equilibrium price-vector.

3. We can proceed at once from this to a 'circulating capital' model, in which all inputs are entirely used up within the period. Every d_{ij} is then equal to unity. $e_{ij} = d_{ij} a_{ij}$ (by definition); so that here we have $e_{ij} = a_{ij}$, or $E = A$. We can simply substitute and proceed as before; but it is more instructive to rewrite the equations

$$p[I-(1+r)A] = 0,$$

$$k = Ax,$$

$$gk = x-Ax.$$

Thus $x = (1+g)k$, and

$$[I-(1+g)A]k = 0.$$

Here then we find that $1/(1+g)$—or $1/(1+r)$—is the dominant root of the A-matrix (directly). p is the associated 'left-hand' and k is the associated 'right-hand' eigenvector.

[1] Subject to the qualification that was mentioned in the note on p. 318. It is this qualification which leads to the Morishima exception, to which we shall be coming.

[2] Note that the roots of these two matrices are the same.

The existence of the von Neumann path, the determinateness of the composition of the stock along it (Theorem I), and the existence (and determinateness) of the equilibrium price-vector, accordingly follow (in this 'circulating capital' case) from the already familiar properties of non-negative matrices. The rest of what is needed to establish Theorem II (in this case) has been, fairly well, provided in the text. As for Theorem III, it follows (in the same case) without difficulty from the same properties. For we must have, along any path that uses the top technique, and makes full utilization of all that is produced,

$$k_t = Ak_{t+1}.$$

Continuing *backwards* a large number of periods, from given k_T, this gives

$$k_{T-m} = A^m k_T$$

and we know, since A is a non-negative matrix, that this will approximate,[1] for large m, to

$$(1+g)^{-m}k$$

where k (which is of course indeterminate to the extent of a scalar multiplier) is the eigenvector that has just been identified. This is true for any k_T. It follows (as explained in the text) that it is not possible to proceed indefinitely, using the top technique with full utilization, excepting along the equilibrium path.

4. In von Neumann's own theory, all production is joint production; this makes things much harder. No more will be done here than to show what the mathematical difficulty is.

Once joint production is admitted, we can no longer write a_{ij} for the quantity of the ith good used in production of a unit of the jth (by a particular process); for a process (or *activity*) no longer results in the production of one good only. We can define the jth activity to be such that (when carried on at unit *intensity*) it absorbs a_{ij} of inputs and emits b_{ij} of outputs (one of each coefficient for each of the n goods, $i = 1, 2,..., n$). Every a and b will be non-negative, though (in economics) we will expect that in a particular process many will be zero.

Let y be a vector of *intensities*. We may then write for the input vector

$$k = Ay$$

and for the output vector (in equilibrium)

$$(1+g)k = By$$

so that in equilibrium

$$[B-(1+g)A]y = 0.$$

[1] Save in the Morishima case.

Similarly, on the price side, we would apparently have

$$p[B-(1+r)A] = 0.$$

But from these, by the methods we have hitherto used in our mathematics, we cannot get any further.

In order that these quantity equations and price equations should be solvable, in the same way as they were when there was one activity (or technique) for each output,[1] it will be necessary that the number of activities that are used should be the same as the number of commodities; for only so will the matrices A and B be square. This condition will be satisfied so long as the equilibrium point is in the interior (not on the boundary) of a facet of the production-possibility frontier. We will suppose that it is satisfied; though the other case can be dealt with by methods that we shall not examine.

Even under this condition, our equations, being equivalent to

$$[I-(1+g)B^{-1}A]y = 0$$
$$p[I-(1+r)AB^{-1}] = 0,$$

cannot be analysed by reference to the properties of non-negative matrices, since $B^{-1}A$ and AB^{-1} are not necessarily (or even probably) non-negative. It was nevertheless demonstrated by von Neumann that there are suitable conditions in which these matrices (with A and B non-negative) will have a positive root, with non-negative eigenvectors ('left-hand' and 'right-hand') associated with it.[2] This is the basic mathematical theorem (Theorem I in the joint-production case) which we have to skip. Everything else is (more or less) reducible into our relatively simple terms; but not this.

The 'no joint production' case is the special case (of this more general theory) where $B = I$; the von Neumann root is then the dominant root (with a modulus not less than that of any other). There should (mathematically) be another limiting case in which $A = I$, while B is any non-negative matrix; the von Neumann root will then (in the same sense) be the 'smallest' root. It is, however, not necessary that the von Neumann root should be at either extreme (in the general case); it may be in the middle. If the von Neumann root is the largest root, we must (by what has been already said) have 'simple backward-narrowing'; if it is the smallest root, we have 'simple forward-narrowing'; if it is in the middle, we have 'overlapping'.

[1] They may be solvable in other ways in other cases.

[2] It is not true that there will be such a root if A and B are any non-negative matrices; but it is true if they are such that, at any non-negative input prices, they will determine a 'proper' facet of the production-possibility frontier—one, that is, on which there is no output that is a free good at the corresponding output-prices. (On our diagram, Fig. 8, p. 219, AB and BC are 'proper' facets.)

5. These cases can be distinguished, as was shown (rather roughly) in the text[1] by a direct classification of feasible input- and output-proportions. A more rigorous presentation of the arguments that were there used would seem to be in place in this appendix.

Let Q be the set of feasible (top technique) output proportions, in a single period; let R be the corresponding set of input proportions. Let S be their intersection (or overlap). We may take it that S exists; for if it did not exist, there could be no balanced growth path with full utilization, and we are taking it that the existence of that path has already been established. Even so, in the general von Neumann case, there are the other three possibilities:

(i) $R \subset Q$. (All R are in Q, but not all Q are in R.) This is what happens under 'no joint production'; it is what we identified as the case of simple backward-narrowing—but postpone that for the moment. It is implied in this condition that $S = R$, $S \subset Q$; a reformulation which we shall find convenient.

(ii) The 'forward-narrowing' case in which $Q \subset R$, so that $S = Q$, $S \subset R$ in the same way.

(iii) The 'overlapping' case in which $S \subset Q$, $S \subset R$. (There is a fourth 'special' possibility, that $Q = R$, so that $S = Q = R$, to which we shall be returning later.)

At the next stage (as in the text) we take two consecutive single periods together. Let Q' be the set of feasible output proportions in the double period, R' the set of feasible input proportions, S' their intersection. They can be related to the foregoing by the following rules. R' is the set of (first period) input proportions which can produce an output in S. Accordingly

(*a*) if $S = Q$, the set R' which produces an output in S must coincide with the set R producing an output in Q. Thus if $S = Q$, $R' = R$;

(*b*) if $S \subset Q$, $R' \subset R$.

In the same way, Q' is the set of (second period) output proportions which can be produced from an input in S. Thus

(*c*) if $S = R$, $Q' = Q$;

(*d*) if $S \subset R$, $Q' \subset Q$.

Using these rules, we can classify the double period in terms of the single-period classification.

(i) If $R \subset Q$, then $S = R$, so that, by (*c*) $Q' = Q$,

and $\qquad\qquad\qquad S \subset Q$, so that, by (*b*) $R' \subset R$.

Thus $R' \subset R \subset Q = Q'$.

Continuing in the same way, by further lengthening (or redoubling) we get a backward-narrowing process

$$\ldots \subset R'' \subset R' \subset R \subset Q = Q' = Q'' = \ldots .$$

(ii) If $Q \subset R$, $S = Q$, so that, by (a) $R' = R$,

and $S \subset R$, so that, by (d) $Q' \subset Q$.

Thus $\ldots R'' = R' = R \supset Q \supset Q' \supset Q'' \supset \ldots$

a forward-narrowing process.

(iii) If $S \subset Q$, $S \subset R$, then, by (b) and (d),

$$R' \subset R, \ Q' \subset Q.$$

This gives no clear rule about Q' and R', save that (for the same reason as before) they must have a non-empty intersection. Here then we must start all over again. The same three cases will emerge (the fourth possibility being again neglected), of which the first (after all) will emerge as backward-narrowing, the second as forward-narrowing, and the third will repeat. Either, then, there is backward-narrowing, or forward-narrowing, at some stage or other; or it may happen that there is always an overlap, but a diminishing overlap, however far the lengthening is continued. If the overlap converges on the equilibrium path (more of this in a moment), it is only that path which is *both continually and ultimately viable*. This is in fact the case in which the von Neumann root is intermediate in modulus between the other roots.[1]

6. Before proceeding further (and clinching the preceding argument) let us pick up the possibility that $Q = R$—or $Q' = R'$, for the equality may occur at any stage of the doubling process. Once the equality arises, it must be preserved. For if $Q = R = S$, $R' = R$, by (a), and $Q' = Q$, by (c), so that $Q' = R'$. There is then no convergence to the equilibrium path, either backwards or forwards. Any input-proportions that are one-period feasible will produce outputs that are one-period feasible; these are again one-period feasible, as inputs; so the process can continue indefinitely, with the proportions remaining within the prescribed range. Similarly the other way. We have here an example of Morishima's exception; but it becomes evident, on closer examination, that it is by no means the only example.

For it is entirely possible (in a many-good model) that the backward-narrowing (or the forward-narrowing) process, though it continually

---

[1] In a two-good model, there are only two roots, so that 'perpetual overlapping' cannot occur.

reduced the range of feasible proportions *in some directions*, might leave it unreduced in others. Proportions (of inputs or of outputs) will be representable, in a two-good model, by a sequence[1] of points on a line. The range of feasible proportions will be shown by those points which lie upon a particular segment of the line. If that length continually diminishes (so that fewer and fewer points are left in), it must ultimately have nothing left in it but the one common point of all segments. But already, in a three-good model, the line-segment is replaced by an area on a plane; this might contract to a point (as before) but it need not do so. It might contract to a segment on a line, after which there was no further contraction. The narrowing process would then converge upon a set of proportions that was determinate in some directions, but not fully determinate in others. What would happen in this case is that there would be some proportions which (if taken as starting point) must converge, in one way or another, to the equilibrium path; but there would be others which (if they were taken as starting points) would not converge to the equilibrium path, but would fluctuate about it. With many goods, the opportunities for the emergence of special cases of this kind are naturally extensive. But they remain special cases, 'boundary' cases, which can only arise with particular values of the parameters; the point is that there are many ways in which they can arise.

7. In terms of characteristic roots, the Morishima cases are those in which there are other roots that have a modulus that is equal to the von Neumann root. The case of complete coincidence ($Q = R$) is that in which *all* the roots are of equal modulus. From *any* feasible initial position, which is not on the equilibrium path, there will then be a fluctuation about the equilibrium path, remaining viable (backwards and forwards). The latter cases (of convergence to a 'segment') are those in which there are some roots of equal modulus to the von Neumann root, and others of different moduli. Particular oscillatory paths may then occur, but it will not be possible to proceed on an oscillatory path from *any* initial position. If one writes out the solution of the sequence

$$k_t = A y_t = A B^{-1} k_{t+1}$$

in the regular form, valid even here so long as roots are not repeated,

$$k_t = \sum c_m \left(\lambda_m \right)^t v_m$$

(the v_m being associated eigenvectors, with their indeterminate multipliers arbitrarily fixed, and the c_m being scalar constants determined from the initial position), these conclusions may be readily verified.

[1] We assume that the number of proportion-combinations which are available to be chosen is finite.

8. It will be well to conclude by giving an example. A simple example must be confined to the two-goods case, in which the only possibilities that are open are (1) simple backward-narrowing, (2) simple forward-narrowing, and (3) a Morishima case on the boundary between the two. Such an example can be set out in the familiar terms of our original Growth Equilibrium model.

There are our two former 'industries': (1) a tractor-producing industry, using tractors to make tractors, and employing labour that is represented by the corn that is needed to pay its wages; (2) a corn-producing industry, using corn (in the same sense) as an input, with tractors as a co-operating factor. The corn is all used up in the single period; but the tractors that are used as inputs are only partly used up, some fraction of the tractor input being left over to appear as 'output' (in the von Neumann sense). The corn industry is accordingly reckoned to have two outputs (so that there is joint production); there is the corn that is its output in the natural sense, and there is also that part of the tractor input that is left over. The tractor industry has only one output, consisting partly of new tractors, partly of tractor input left over; between these we do not need to distinguish. Input and output coefficients for the two industries, in the sense just described, might then emerge as follows:

| | Tractor industry | | Corn industry | |
	Input	Output	Input	Output
Tractor	1	1·6	1	0·9
Corn	4	0	1	2

These are not at all unnatural-looking figures.

Let us put them on a diagram of the kind which we used on pp. 216–19 (Fig. 13). We have first to calculate the equilibrium prices, which result

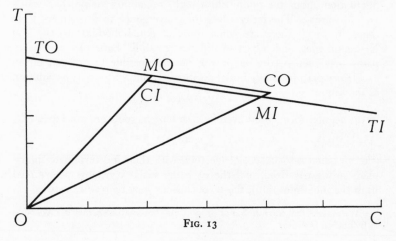

at once from the price equations

$$(p+4)(1+r) = 1 \cdot 6p$$

$$(p+1)(1+r) = 0 \cdot 9p+2$$

writing p (as in Chapter XII) for the price of the tractor in terms of corn. (The corn, as input, must of course be valued at the beginning of the period.) We get a quadratic for p, of which the positive root must of course be taken. So that $p = 51/7$ (very nearly), while r (incidentally) is approximately 3·3 per cent.

If the tractor industry is operated at intensity y_1, the value of its inputs will be $(p+4)y_1 = 79y_1/7$. If the corn industry is operated at intensity y_2, the value of its inputs would be $(p+1)y_2 = 58y_2/7$. Thus for a value of inputs $(79 \times 58)/7$ the tractor industry only could be operated at intensity 58; the corn industry only could be operated at intensity 79. This would give (approximately)

	Tractor industry		Corn industry	
	Input	Output	Input	Output
Tractor	58	93	79	71
Corn	232	0	79	158
	TI	TO	CI	CO

the figures that are plotted as *TI* (and so on) on the diagram.

TO is the outputs that can be got by using the tractor industry only; *CO* the outputs got by using the corn industry only; the 'top facet' of the output frontier (the range of outputs that can be got by using the *technique* in question—taken to be a top technique) is thus represented by the straight line *TO–CO*. The corresponding inputs are represented by *TI–CI*. It is at once obvious that it is only in the range *MO–CO* on the output frontier that there is an 'overlap'—proportions which can be top-technique output proportions *and* top-technique input proportions. But what corresponds to *MO* on the input range? It does not in general need to be the corresponding intersection, which I have marked as *MI*. If the corresponding point lay to the left of *MI*, the input range would be narrower than the output range (backward-narrowing); if it lay to the *right*, there would be forward-narrowing. But in fact, on the figures that we have been using, it is *MI* that is the corresponding point, as may readily be verified.

Suppose that the two industries are operated at intensities (y_1, y_2). Then the total corn-output is $2y_2$; total tractor output is $1 \cdot 6y_1 + 0 \cdot 9y_2$. If these are to have the same ratio as the input-ratio when only the corn industry is operated, we must have

$$\frac{1 \cdot 6y_1 + 0 \cdot 9y_2}{2y_2} = \frac{1}{1}$$

so that $y_1/y_2 = 11/16$. Meanwhile total corn-input is $4y_1+y_2$; total tractor-input is y_1+y_2; so that the ratio of tractor-input to corn-input is

$$\frac{y_1+y_2}{4y_1+y_2} = \frac{11+16}{44+16} = \frac{27}{60} = \frac{0\cdot9}{2}$$

which is the ratio of tractor-output to corn-output when only the corn industry is operated. So that, with these figures, MI is the corresponding point to MO.

It accordingly follows that if we start with any proportions that are between the rays that have been drawn on the diagram, we can go backward or forward, and the resulting proportions will still lie between the rays. Having done it once, we can do it again. There is no convergence (either way) to the equilibrium path; instead, there is an oscillation about it. That is the Morishima exception, in the only form that it can appear in a two-good model. Even here, it will be observed, it is a boundary condition, which only appears at particular values of the coefficients. It is important, as already appears in this case, not so much for its own sake, as because it assures us that forward-narrowing, as well as backward-narrowing, is a possibility that has to be taken seriously. More generally, the same would apply to 'overlapping'.

When this result is applied to the Turnpike problem, it confirms one in the belief[1] that while approximation to the top technique, for 'most of the way', is an important result, the consequential approximation to the von Neumann proportions, of inputs and of outputs, is a corollary that does not have to be taken at all so seriously.

APPENDIX D

(REFERRING TO CHAPTER XX)

THE TREND GROWTH RATE

1. THE comparison of consumption flows, with which we have been concerned in Chapter XX, makes no particular use of the 'single period'; it is therefore neater, in the corresponding mathematics, to work with continuous time. I shall accordingly proceed, in this appendix, to treat ξ, the consumption output, as a continuous function of time; and I shall discount at the instantaneous rate of interest, ρ. λ, the discount factor, is accordingly replaced by $e^{-\rho}$; and for the capital value (of an

---

[1] p. 233, above.

infinite stream) we have the regular formula

$$K = \int \xi e^{-\rho t}\, dt$$

the integral being taken from 0 to infinity, as always in this appendix, unless otherwise stated.

Our index P (the 'average period' of *Value and Capital*) which was defined as $(\lambda/K)(\partial K/\partial\lambda)$ in the text of Chapter XX, will accordingly emerge as $-(1/K)(\partial K/\partial\rho)$, which (when written in full) is

$$\frac{\int \xi e^{-\rho t} t\, dt}{\int \xi e^{-\rho t}\, dt}.$$

That this is some sort of a measure of the 'tilt' or growth-rate of the stream is rather obvious. In fact, if ξ has a constant growth rate γ, so that $\xi = X e^{\gamma t}$ (where X is constant), we have

$$K = \frac{X}{\rho - \gamma} \quad \text{and} \quad P = -\frac{\partial}{\partial\rho}(\log K) = \frac{1}{\rho - \gamma}$$

directly.[1] The measure of the growth rate which is defined by the use of our index is thus given by γ, where

$$\frac{1}{\rho - \gamma} = \frac{\int \xi e^{-\rho t} t\, dt}{\int \xi e^{-\rho t}\, dt} \tag{1}$$

(as was stated in *Value and Capital*, p. 188, n. 2).

2. Suppose that we were to try to fit to $\xi(t)$ a stream of constant growth rate, by the method of least squares. For the reasons that were stated in the text, it would only be sensible to do this (in the present context) by taking differences of *discounted* values. We might therefore try to minimize

$$\int (\xi e^{-\rho t} - X e^{\gamma t} e^{-\rho t})^2\, dt$$

where X and γ are parameters to be determined. (I assume that the discounting is sufficient to make this integral converge.) If we differentiate with respect to X, we have

$$0 = \int (\xi e^{-\rho t} - X e^{\gamma t} e^{-\rho t}) e^{\gamma t} e^{-\rho t}\, dt$$

---

[1] The $(1+\gamma)$ in the numerator, which appeared in the formula that was given in the text, drops out when we take continuous time.

and with respect to γ

$$0 = \int (\xi e^{-\rho t} - X e^{\gamma t} e^{-\rho t}) t e^{\gamma t} e^{-\rho t} \, dt$$

so that

$$X \int e^{2(\gamma-\rho)t} \, dt = \int \xi e^{(\gamma-2\rho)t} \, dt$$

and

$$X \int e^{2(\gamma-\rho)t} t \, dt = \int \xi e^{(\gamma-2\rho)t} t \, dt.$$

Now the integrals on the left, taken (as before) from 0 to infinity, are $1/2(\rho-\gamma)$ and $1/4(\rho-\gamma)^2$; so that

$$\frac{1}{2(\rho-\gamma)} = \frac{\int \xi e^{(\gamma-2\rho)t} t \, dt}{\int \xi e^{(\gamma-2\rho)t} \, dt}. \tag{2}$$

It is clear that this formula belongs to the same 'family' as (1). Since we may take it that $\rho > \gamma$, the chief difference between the two formulae is that (2) implies *heavier* discounting.

3. In practice, of course, no one would calculate a trend growth rate by the use of formula (2), which is most inconvenient to handle, owing to the presence of the unknown γ on both sides of the equation. A more practical method would be to take logs, and so to minimize

$$\int (\log \xi - \log X - \gamma t)^2 \, dt$$

(for if one is minimizing a difference of logarithms, the discount factor cancels out). If (as would always be the case with practical statistics), one is estimating the growth rate of a finite sequence there can be no question that this is a more sensible procedure. (It should, however, be noticed that it does not make sense when applied to an infinite sequence.) But there is no logical reason why we should have to calculate a growth rate in terms of *relative* discrepancies, which is what we do if we take logs. The method described in § 2 is at least as respectable as the logarithmic method. And the method described in § 1 may then be defended as a tolerable substitute for the second method—quite apart from its merits in economic theory.

APPENDIX E

(REFERRING TO CHAPTER XXI)

UTILITY AND SAVING

1. I BEGIN with a proof of the equivalence of the two concepts of *independence*. This is of course a matter which has nothing necessarily to do with intertemporal choice; we may accordingly adopt (for the moment) a simpler notation.

It is obvious that if we have a Cardinal Utility Function with separated utilities

$$u_1(x_1) + u_2(x_2) + ... + u_n(x_n)$$

the marginal rate of substitution between the jth and kth commodities, being equal to the ratio of their marginal utilities, will be independent of the amount of any other commodity than x_j and x_k. To prove the converse, assume a general utility function

$$u(x_1, x_2, ..., x_n)$$

with partial derivatives and cross-derivatives u_i, u_{ij}, ..., and suppose that $(\partial/\partial x_i)(u_j/u_k) = 0$, for all i, j, k that are different from one another. Expanding,

$$(u_{ij}/u_j) = (u_{ik}/u_k)$$

so that if we put $u_{ij} = \mu u_i u_j$, μ will be the same for every i and j that are different from one another. Differentiating with respect to x_k,

$$u_{ijk} = \mu_k u_i u_j + \mu u_{ik} u_j + \mu u_i u_{jk}$$
$$= \mu_k u_i u_j + 2\mu^2 u_i u_j u_k.$$

Similarly, differentiating u_{ik} with respect to x_j,

$$u_{ijk} = \mu_j u_i u_k + 2\mu^2 u_i u_j u_k$$

so that if none of the u_i vanish, we must have $(\mu_j/u_j) = (\mu_k/u_k)$ for every j and k that are different from one another. Thus, for a movement along an indifference surface, such that $du = 0$, we must have $d\mu = 0$. μ can only vary when u varies, so that μ is a function of u only.

Now if we adopt the ordinal viewpoint, and are willing to substitute for u any function $F(u)$ that increases with it, we shall have, for the (cross) second derivative of that function,

$$F_{ij} = F'.u_{ij} + F''.u_i u_j = u_i u_j(F'\mu + F'').$$

The bracketed expression is a function of u only; thus for some choice of F, it can be made to vanish. Thus, for *this* F, $F_{ij} = 0$, whenever i and j are different. Every F_i is a function of x_i only; the variables have been separated—for this particular utility-index.

2. Suppose we take this particular measure, which may now be written (as before)
$$u_1(x_1)+u_2(x_2)+...+u_n(x_n)$$

and impose the homogeneity rule upon it. The marginal utilities are thus to change in the same proportion when the x_i change in a uniform proportion. Thus
$$\frac{u_i'(\lambda x_i)}{u_i'(x_i)} = \frac{u_j'(\lambda x_j)}{u_j'(x_j)}$$

for any λ. Differentiating with respect to λ, and then setting $\lambda = 1$,
$$\frac{x_i u_i''(x_i)}{u_i'(x_i)} = \frac{x_j u_j''(x_j)}{u_j'(x_j)}.$$

The elasticities of the marginal utility curves must therefore be equal, for any x_i and x_j; they must therefore be constant. Integrating, we get the constant-elasticity form of the marginal utility curve,
$$u_i'(x_i) = q_i\, x_i^{-(1/\eta)}$$

where q_i is a constant, and η is the same for each commodity.

3. Passing now to the intertemporal problem, with the consumptions spread out in time, ξ_t replaces x_i, and for its marginal utility
$$U_t'(\xi_t) = q_t\, \xi_t^{-(1/\eta)}$$

as stated in the text. This is to be proportional to e^{-rt}, so that ξ_t is proportional to $q_t^{\eta} e^{\eta rt}$. For this to be a constant growth path, we must have q_t equal[1] to e^{-pt}, where p is a constant. Thus $\xi_t = Ce^{gt}$, where $g = \eta(r-p)$ and $C = \xi_0$.

To get the capital value (at time o) we must integrate the discounted value from o to infinity. Thus
$$K_0 = \int \xi_t e^{-rt}\, dt = C \int e^{-(r-g)t}\, dt = C/(r-g).$$

Thus $rK_0 = \xi_0 + gK_0$ (as we should expect); and s (the proportion of income saved) $= g/r$ (as it should do). But in order for this integration to have been possible, we must have had $g < r$. This implies that $(1-\eta)r + \eta p > 0$, which is only possible if $\eta < 1$, or if p is large enough to offset the excess.

4. We now assume that $\eta < 1$. The total utility of consumption at time t is the integral of the marginal utility from o to ξ_t. If $\eta < 1$,

---

[1] Strictly, we should say q_t is proportional to e^{-pt}; but it will do no harm to set them equal, since the 'unit' of utility is arbitrary.

the variable term in this integral is negative, so that we must introduce a positive constant to keep total utility positive. Thus

$$U_t(\xi_t) = \left[B - \frac{\eta}{1-\eta}\, \xi_t^{1-(1/\eta)}\right]e^{-pt}.$$

It follows from Stationariness that B must be the same for every t, so that B is identified as Ramsey's 'Bliss'.

At the optimal position, $\xi_t = Ce^{gt}$, so that

$$U_t(\xi_t) = \left[B - \frac{\eta}{1-\eta}\, C^{1-(1/\eta)}e^{g(1-(1/\eta))t}\right]e^{-pt}$$

$$= Be^{-pt} - \frac{\eta}{1-\eta}\, C^{1-(1/\eta)}e^{(g-r)t}.$$

The total expected utility is the integral of this from o to infinity. The negative term in the integral is clearly finite, so long as $r > g$, necessarily (therefore) if $\eta < 1$. But Be^{-pt} will only have a finite integral if $p > 0$.

If $p = 0$, it is necessary for the consistency of the theory that $\eta < 1$. But if $\eta < 1$, it is necessary for the consistency of the theory that $p > 0$. Thus (as Koopmans has, much more generally, shown) it is not possible to have a theory which incorporates a rate of time-preference unless we make it positive.

5. If (abandoning homogeneity) we take as the marginal utility function

$$U_t'(\xi_t) = (\xi_t - A)^{-1/\eta}e^{-pt}$$

we simply get
$$\xi_t = A + Ce^{gt}$$

where $g = \eta(r-p)$ as before, but C is now $\xi_0 - A$, the initial excess of consumption over subsistence. For the initial capital value, we integrate from o to infinity as before.

$$K_0 = \int \xi_t e^{-rt}\, dt = \int Ae^{-rt}\, dt + \int Ce^{-(r-g)t}\, dt$$

$$= \frac{A}{r} + \frac{C}{r-g} = \frac{A}{r} + \frac{\xi_0 - A}{r-g}.$$

For the capital value at time t, we similarly get

$$K_t = \frac{A}{r} + \frac{\xi_t - A}{r-g}$$

so that

$$rK_t = A + \left(\frac{r}{r-g}\right)(\xi_t - A)$$

$$= \xi_t + \left(\frac{g}{r-g}\right)(\xi_t - A).$$

It follows at once that

$$\frac{s_t}{1-s_t} = \left(\frac{g}{r-g}\right)\left(1-\frac{A}{\xi_t}\right)$$

as stated in the text.

INDEX